Ecology and Religion: Scientists Speak

An Open Letter to the Religious Community

The Earth is the birthplace of our species and, as far as we know, our only home, When our numbers were small and our technology feeble, we were powerless to influence the environment of our world. But today, suddenly, almost without anyone's noticing, our numbers have become immense and our technology has achieved vast, even awesome, powers. Intentionally or inadvertently, we are now able to make devastating changes in the global environment—an environment to which we and all other beings with which we share the Earth are meticulously and exquisitely adapted.

We are now threatened by self-inflicted, swiftly moving environmental alterations about whose long-term biological and ecological consequences we are still painfully ignorant: depletion of the protective ozone layer; a global warming unprecedented in the last 150 millennia; the obliteration of an acre of forest every second; the rapid-fire extinction of species; and the prospect of a global nuclear war which would put at risk most of the population of the Earth. There may well be other such dangers of which we are still unaware. Individually and cumulatively, they represent a trap being set for the human species, a trap we are setting for ourselves. However principled and lofty (or naive and shortsighted) the justifications may have been for the activities that brought forth these dangers, separately and taken together they now imperil our species and many others. We are close to committing—many would argue we are already committing—what in religious language is sometimes called "Crimes Against Creation."

By their very nature these assaults on the environment were not caused by any one political group or any one generation. Intrinsically, they are transnational, transgenerational and trans-ideological. So are all conceivable solutions. To escape these traps requires a perspective that embraces the peoples of the planet and all the generations yet to come.

Problems of such magnitude, and solutions demanding so broad a perspective, must be recognized from the outset as having a religious as well as a scientific dimension. Mindful of our common responsibility, we scientists—many of us long engaged in combating the environmental crisis—urgently appeal to the world religious community to commit, in word and deed, and as boldly as is required, to preserve the environment of the Earth.

Some of the short-term mitigations of these dangers—such as greater energy efficiency, rapid banning of chlorofluorocarbons or modest reductions in nuclear arsenals—are comparatively easy and at some level are already underway. But other, more far-reaching, long-term, and effective approaches will encounter widespread inertia, denial and resistance. In this category are conversion from fossil fuels to a nonpolluting energy economy, a continuing swift reversal of the nuclear arms race, and a voluntary halt to world population growth—without which many other approaches to preserve the environment will be nullified.

As with issues of peace, human rights and social justice, religious institutions can be a strong force here, too, in encouraging national and international initiatives in both the private and public sectors, and in the diverse worlds of commerce, education, culture and mass communications.

The environmental crisis requires radical changes not only in public policy, but also in individual behavior. The historical record makes clear that religious teaching, example and leadership are able to influence personal conduct and commitment powerfully.

As scientists, many of us have had profound experiences of awe and reverence before the universe. We understand that what is regarded as sacred is more likely to be treated with care and respect. Our planetary home should be so regarded. Efforts to safeguard and cherish the environment need to be infused with a vision of the sacred. At the same time, a much wider and deeper understanding of science and technology is needed. If we do not understand the problem, it is unlikely we will be able to fix it. Thus, there is a vital role for both religion and science.

We know that the well-being of our planetary environment is already a source of profound concern in your councils and congregations. We hope this appeal will encourage a spirit of common cause and joint action to help preserve the Earth.

January 1990

Carl Sagan
CORNELL UNIVERISTY
ITHACA, NEW YORK

Hans A. Bethe
CORNELL UNIVERSITY
ITHACA, NEW YORK

Elise Boulding
UNIVERSITY OF COLORADO
BOULDER, COLORADO

M.I. Budyko
STATE HYDROLOGICAL INSTITUTE
LENINGRAD, U.S.S.R.

S. Chandrasekhar
UNIVERSITY OF CHICAGO
CHICAGO, ILLINOIS

Paul J. Crutzen
MAX PLANCK INSTITUTE FOR CHEMISTRY
MAINZ, WEST GERMANY

Margaret B. Davis
UNIVERSITY OF MINNESOTA
MINNEAPOLIS, MINNESOTA

Freeman J. Dyson
INSTITUTE FOR ADVANCED STUDY
PRINCETON, NEW JERSEY

Richard L. Garwin
IBM CORPORATION
YORKTOWN HEIGHTS, NEW YORK

Gyorgi S. Golitsyn
ACADEMY OF SCIENCES OF THE U.S.S.R.
MOSCOW, U.S.S.R.

Stephen Jay Gould
HARVARD UNIVERSITY
CAMBRIDGE, MASSACHUSETTS

James E. Hansen
NASA GODDARD INSTITUTE FOR SPACE STUDIES
NEW YORK, NEW YORK

Mohammed Kassa
UNIVERSITY OF CAIRO
CAIRO, EGYPT

Henry W. Kendall
UNION OF CONCERNED SCIENTISTS
CAMBRIDGE, MASSACHUSETTS

Motoo Kimura
NATIONAL INSTITUE OF GENETICS
MISHIMA, JAPAN

Thomas Malone
ST. JOSEPH COLLEGE
WEST HARTFORD, CONNECTICUT

Lynn Margulis
UNIVERSITY OF MASSACHUSETTS
AMHERST, MASSACHUSETTS

Peter Raven
MISSOURI BOTANICAL GARDEN
ST. LOUIS MISSOURI

Roger Revelle
UNIVERSITY OF CALIFORNIA, SAN DIEGO
LA JOLLA, CALIFORNIA

Walter Orr Roberts
YORKTOWN HEIGHTS, NEW YORK
NATIONAL CENTER FOR ATMOSPHERIC REASEARCH
BOULDER, COLORADO

Abdus Salam
INTERNATIONAL CENTRE FOR THEORETICAL PHYSICS
TRIESTE, ITALY

Stephen H. Schneider
NATIONAL CENTER FOR ATMOSPHERIC RESEARCH
BOULDER, COLORADO

Nans Suess
UNIVERSITY OF CALIFORNIA, SAN DIEGO
LA JOLLA, CALIFORNIA

O.B. Toon
NASA AMES RESEARCH CENTER
NOFFETT FIELD, CALIFORNIA

Richard P. Turco
UNIVERSITY OF CALIFORNIA
LOS ANGELES, CALIFORNIA

Yevgeny P. Velikhov
ACADEMY OF SCIENCES OF THE U.S.S.R.
MOSCOW, U.S.S.R.

Carl Friedrich von Weizsacker
MAX PLANCK INSTITUE
STARNBERG, WEST GERMANY

Sir Frederick Warmer
ESSEX UNIVERSITY
COLCHESTER, UNITED KINGDOM

Victor F. Weisskopf
MASSACHUSETTS INSTITUTE OF TECHNOLOGY
CAMBRIDGE, MASSACHUSETTS

Jerome B. Wiesner
MASSACHUSETTS INSTITUTE OF TECHNOLOGY
CAMBRIDGE, MASSACHUSETTS

Robert R. Wilson
CORNELL UNIVERSITY
ITHACA, NEW YORK

Alexey V. Yablokov
ACADEMY OF SCIENCES OF THE U.S.S.R.
MOSCOW, U.S.S.R.

Affliations of signators for identification purposes only

Statement by Religious Leaders at the Summit on Environment

On a spring evening and the following day in New York City, we representatives of the religious community in the United States of America gathered to deliberate and plan action in response to the crisis of the Earth's environment.

Deep impulses brought us together. Almost daily, we note mounting evidence of environmental destruction and ever-increasing peril to life, whole species, whole ecosystems. Many people, and particularly the young, want to know where we stand and what we intend to do. And, finally, it is what God made and beheld as good that is under assault. The future of this gift so freely given is in our hands, and we must maintain it as we have received it. This is an inescapably religious challenge. We feel a profound and urgent call to respond with all we have, all we are and all we believe.

We chose to meet, these two days, in the company of people from diverse traditions and disciplines. No one perspective alone is equal to the crisis we face—spiritual and moral, economic and cultural, institutional and personal. For our part, we were grateful to strengthen a collaboration with distinguished scientists and to take stock of their testimony on problems besetting planetary ecology. As people of faith, we were also moved by the support for our work from distinguished public policy leaders.

What we heard left us more troubled than ever. Global warming, generated mainly by the burning of fossil fuels and deforestation, is widely predicted to increase temperatures worldwide, changing climate patterns, increasing drought in many areas, threatening agriculture, wildlife, the integrity of natural ecosystems and creating millions of environmental refugees. Depletion of the ozone shield, caused by human-made chemical agents such as chlorofluorocarbons, lets in deadly ultraviolet radiation for the Sun, with predicted consequences that include skin cancer, cataracts, damage to the human immune system, and destruction of the primary photosynthetic producers at the base of the food chain on which other life depends. Our expanding technological civilization is destroying an acre and a half of forest every second. The accelerating loss of species of plants, animals and microorganisms which threatens the irreversible loss of up to a fifth of the total number within the next 30 years, is not only morally reprehensible but is increasingly limiting the prospects for sustainable productivity. No effort, however heroic, to deal with these global conditions and the interrelated issues of social justice can succeed unless we address the increasing population of the Earth—especially the billion poorest people who have every right to expect a decent standard of living. So too, we must find ways to reduce the disproportionate consumption of natural resources by affluent industrial societies like our's.

Much would tempt w to deny or push aside this global environmental crisis and refuse even to consider the fundamental changes of human behavior required to address it. But we religious leaders accept a prophetic responsibility to make known the full dimension of this challenge, and what is required to address it, to the many millions we reach, teach and counsel.

We intend to be informed participants in discussion of these issues and to contribute our views on the moral and ethical imperative for developing national and international policy responses. But we declare here and now that steps must be taken toward: accelerated phaseout of ozone-depleting chemicals; much more efficient use of fossil fuels and the development of a non-fossil fuel economy; preservation of tropical forests and other measures to protect continued biological diversity; and concerted efforts to slow the dramatic and dangerous growth in world population through empowering both women and men, encouraging economic self-sufficiency, and making family education programs available to all who may consider them on a strictly voluntary basis.

We believe a consensus now exists, at the highest level of leadership across a significant spectrum of religious traditions, that the cause of environmental integrity and justice must occupy a position of utmost priority for people of faith. Response to this issue can and must cross traditional religious and political lines. It has the potential to unify and renew religious life.

We pledge to take the initiative in interpreting and communicating theological foundations for the stewardship of Creation in which we find the principles for environmental action. Here our seminaries have a critical role to play. So too, there is a call for moral transformation, as we recognize that the roots of environmental destruction lie in human pride, greed and selfishness, as well as the appeal of the short-term over the long-term.

We reaffirm here, in the strongest possible terms, the indivisibility of social justice and ecological integrity. An equitable international economic order is essential for preserving the global environment. Economic equity, racial justice, gender equality and environmental well-being are interconnected and all are essential to peace. To help ensure these, we pledge to mobilize public opinion and to appeal to elected officials and leaders in the private sector. In our congregations and corporate life, we will encourage and seek to exemplify habits of sound and sustainable householding—in land use, investment decisions, energy conservation, purchasing of products and waste disposal.

Commitments to these areas of action we pledged to one another solemnly and in a spirit of mutual accountability. We dare not let our resolve falter. We will continue to work together, add to our numbers, and deepen our collaboration with the worlds of science and government. We also agreed this day to the following initiatives:

1. We will widely distribute the declaration within the religious community and beyond. We have established a continuing mechanism to coordinate ongoing activities among us, working intimately program and staff resources in the religious world. We will reach out to other leaders across the broadest possible spectrum of religious life. We will help organize other such gatherings as ours within individual faith groups, in interfaith and interdisciplinary formats, and at international, national, and regional levels.

2. We religious leaders and members of the scientific community will call together a Washington D.C. convocations and meet with members of the Executive and Congressional branches to express our support for bold steps on behalf of environmental integrity and justice. There too we will consider ways to facilitate

legislative testimony by religious leaders and response to local environmental action alerts.

3. We will witness firsthand and call public attention to the effect of environmental degradation on vulnerable peoples and ecosystems.

4. We will call a meeting of seminary deans and faculty to review and initiate curriculum development and promote bibliographies emphasizing stewardship of Creation. We will seek ways to establish internships for seminarians in organizations working on the environment and for young scientists in the study of social ethics.

5. We will prepare educational materials for congregations, provide technical support for religious publishers already producing such material, and share sermonical and liturgical materials about ecology.

6. We will establish an instrument to help place stories on environment in faith group and denominational newsletters and help assure coverage of the religious community's environmental activities in the secular press.

7. We will urge compliance with the Valdez Principles and preach and promote corporate responsibility.

8. We will encourage establishment of one model environmentally sound and sustainable facility within each faith group and denomination. We will provide material for environmental audits and facilitate bulk purchasing of environmentally sound products.

It has taken the religion community, as others, much time and reflection to start to comprehend the full scale and nature of the crisis and even to glimpse what it will require of us. We must pray ceaselessly for wisdom, courage, and creativity. Most importantly, we are people of faith and hope. These qualities are what we may most uniquely have to offer to this effort. We pledge to the children of the world and, in the words of the Iroquois, "to the seventh generation," that we will take full measure of what this moment in history requires of us. In this challenge may lie the opportunity for people of faith to affirm and enact, at a scale such as never before, what it may means to be religious. And so we have begun, believing there can be no turning back.

June 3, 1991, New York City

Bishop Vinton R. Anderson
PRESIDENT, WORLD COUNCIL OF AMERICA

Rabbi Marc. D. Angel
PRESIDENT, RABBINICAL COUNCIL OF AMERICA

The Most Reverend Edmond L. Browning
GENERAL-SECRETARY, NAITONAL COUNCIL OF CHURCHES OF CHRIST

Reverend Joan Brown Campbell
GENERAL-SECRETARY, NATIONAL COUNCIL OF CHURCHES OF CHRIST

The Reverend Herbert W. Chilstrom
BISHOP, EVANGELICAL LUTHERAN CHURCH IN AMERICA

Father Drew Christiansen, S.J.
DIRECTOR, OFFICE OF INTERNATIONAL JUSTICE AND PEACE
UNITED STATES CATHOLIC CONFERENCE

Ms. Beverly Davison
PRESIDENT, AMERICAN BAPTIST CHURCHES

Reverend Dr. Milton B. Epthimiou
DIRECTOR OF CHURCH AND SOCIETY
GREEK ORTHODOX ARCHDIOCESE OF NORTH AND SOUTH AMERICA

Bishop William B. Friend
CHAIRMAN OF THE COMMITTEE FOR SCIENCE AND HUMAN VALUES
NATIONAL CONFERENCE OF CATHOLIC BISHOPS

Dr. Alfred Gottschalk
PRESIDENT, HEBREW UNION COLLEGE-JEWISH INSTITUTE OF RELIGION

Dr. Arthur Green
PRESIDENT, RECONSTRUCTIONIST RABBINICAL COLLEGE

His Eminence Archbishop Iakovos
PRIMATE, GREEK ARCHDIOCESE OF NORTH AND SOUTH AMERICA

The Very Reverend Leonid Kishkovshy
PRESIDENT, NAITONAL COUNCIL OF CHURCHES OF CHRIST

Chief Oren Lyons
CHIEF OF THE TURTLE CLAN OF THE ONONDAGA NATION

Dr. David McKenna
PRESIDENT, ASBURY THEOLOGICAL SEMINARY

The Very Reverend James Parks Morton
DEAN, CATHEDRAL OF ST. JOHN THE DIVINE

Dr. W. Franklyn Richardson
GENERAL SECRETARY, NATIONAL BAPTIST CONVENTION

Dr. Patricia J. Rumer
GENERAL DIRECTOR, CHURCH WOMEN UNITED

Dr. James R. Scales
PRESEDENT EMERITUS, WAKE FOREST UNIVERSITY

Dr. Ismar Schorsch
CHANCELLOR, JEWISH THEOLOGICAL SEMINARY

Dr. Robert Shuller
PASTOR, THE CRYSTAL CATHEDRAL

Dr. Robert Seiple
PRESIDENT, WORLD VISION U.S.A.

Bishop Melvin Talbert
SECRETARY OF THE COUNCIL OF BISHOPS
UNITED METHODIST CHURCH

Dr. Joy Valentine
FORMER EXECUTIVE DIRECTOR
CHRISTIAN LIFE COMMISSION
SOUTHERN BAPTIST CONVENTION

Affliations of signators for identification purposes only

A BRIEF HISTORY OF THE JOINT APPEAL

The Joint Appeal was established in December 1990 by heads of major faith groups and eminent scientists to facilitate collaboration for religious leaders seeking to put forward a scientifically-informed theological and moral response to the global environmental crisis.

This collaboration grew out of an "Open Letter to the Religious Community" sent by thirty-four internationally renowned scientists. Of the peril to planetary environment they wrote, "Problems of such magnitude and solutions demanding so broad a perspective must be recognized from the outset as having a religious as well as a scientific dimension." "Efforts to safeguard and cherish the environment need to be infused with a vision of the sacred."

Struck by the initiative, several hundred religious leaders of all major faiths from all five continents responded, "This invitation to collaboration marks a unique moment and opportunity in the relationship of science and religion. We are eager to explore as soon as possible concrete, specific forms of action."

In the months which immediately followed, the Joint Appeal reviewed the current state of activity among people of faith and encouraged commitment to a new level of environmental study and activity. The Summit on Environment, a two-day consultation in June, 1991, held at the American Museum .of Natural History and Cathedral of St John the Divine, consolidated formal agreement on priorities by senior leaders across a broad spectrum of religious life. A year-long effort is now underway during which major faith groups and denominations are initiating and strengthening individual programs. By late spring 1992, these will be sufficiently in place for religious leaders to bring to Washington evidence that they have finally and forcefully embraced an environmental agenda.

ABOUT THE DIALOGUE AND MISSION TO WASHINGTON

The Dialogue and Mission to Washington, a project of the Joint Appeal by Religion and Science for the Environment, is an initiative to strengthen and present to the Congress the American religious community's newly-energized commitment to environmental sustainability now being forged in unprecedented partnership with the American scientific community.

From May 10-12, 1992, fifty heads and senior leaders of major faith groups and thirty five Nobel Laureate and other scientists drawn from the American Association for the Advancement of Science and other national scientific associations will meet in Washington.

For an evening and a day, they will hear scientific updates on global environmental conditions and report on activities within their respective communities. In open dialogue conducted in the presence of Congressional leaders and the media, they will seek out common ground and vision in response to global environmental challenges. How can Religion and Science, so long estranged or at odds, jointly encourage new perspectives and values required to address root causes of the environmental crisis? On the third day they will report on these deliberations to the Congress in formal public hearings and private meetings. There will be no lobbying on specific pieces of legislation.

For the religious community, this will be the first such mission to Washington addressing environmental issues at so high a level of leadership across so broad a spectrum of faith groups.

The initiative, however, is not a single event but the continuation of an 18-month effort and an occasion to agree upon steps toward a still greater level of engagement.

Timing of this gathering is particularly opportune insofar as it will culminate a year of heightened activity by individual faith groups and denominations. Among the highlights thusfar are:

• November 1991 passage by Bishops of the U.S. Catholic Conference of their first pastoral statement on environment
• Establishment and finding by the Episcopal Church (USA) of its first program on environmental and sustainable development
• Strengthened initiatives from the United Methodist, Presbyterian, American Baptist, United Church of Christ, and Evangelical Lutheran churches
• Establishment of a National Council of Churches office on environmental justice
• A March '92 consultation organized by the Joint Appeal for over one hundred senior Jewish leaders to establish environmental program priorities
• April 1992 conference of World Vision USA marking the first engagement of environmental issues by so prominent an evangelical Christian body.

The goal of the May 1992 Washington meeting is to assure that the power and promise of this mobilization is understood in Washington and made more visible nationwide. A bipartisan committee of United Sates Senators has been established to guarantee that the religious community's perspectives and partnership with scientists will be heard.

Private meetings have already been scheduled with the Senate Majority and Minority Leaders and the Speaker and Majority and Minority Leaders of the House as well as chairs of appropriate committees. A special public hearing will be convened and conduced by members of the Senate Committees on: Commerce, Science and Transportation; Energy and Natural Resources; Environment and Public Works; Foreign Relations; and House Committees on: Energy and Commerce; and Foreign Affairs.

The recent entry of the American religious community into environmental study and action is a vital development. Few sectors of society are more effectively positioned to deepen the moral foundations of environmentalism and broaden its outreach into mainstream American life and values: Few sectors are better prepared and more committed to strengthen the link between issues of environment and concerns for economic and social Justice.

For this great and diverse constituency to embrace an issue of such magnitude is a daunting long-term undertaking. The effort has begun. But it needs occasions for mutual support, collective deliberation, and affirmation.

What's most important is to draw upon the power of this issue itself and the conviction that people of faith have a critical contribution to make.

Ecology and Religion: Scientists Speak

edited by

John E. Carroll and Keith Warner, OFM

Franciscan Press

Ecology and Religion: Scientists Speak
John E. Carroll and Keith Warner, OFM, editors

Franciscan Press
Quincy University
1800 College Avenue
Quincy, IL 62301
PH 217.228.5670
FAX 217.228.5672
http://www.quincy.edu/fpress

Book design and typesetting by Laurel Fitch, Chicago, IL.
Cover artwork by Brian M. Ballok

Printed in the United States of America
First Printing: May 1998
1   2   3   4   5   6   7   8   9   0

Library of Congress Cataloging-in-Publication Data
  Ecology and religion : scientists speak / edited by John E. Carroll and
  Keith Warner.
       p. cm.
    Includes bibliographical references.
    ISBN 0-8199-0986-6 (alk. paper)
    1. Human ecology—Religious aspects. 2. Religion and sci-
  ence. 3. Environmentalism—Religious aspects. I. Carroll, John
  E. (John Edward), 1944–   . II. Warner, Keith.
  GF80.E247 1998
  215--dc21   98-17882
                                                                CIP

Contents

PART TWO
RELIGIOUS ETHICS IN DIALOGUE WITH ENVIRONMENTAL ETHICS

PART THREE
THE RELIGIOUS EXPERIENCE IN AN ECOLOGICAL CONTEXT

Foreword

Wes Jackson

Man must and will have Some Religion
William Blake
Jerusalem, Plate 52

The "believer" may cite the reality of life as proof of the existence of God. For the "non-believer" life *can* be explained as "nothing but for it requires but little training. in physics or biochemistry to understand life in physical-chemical terms. This provided that one acknowledge the reality of emergent properties which show up at different levels all the way from atoms to ecosystems. One example of an emergent property would be the liquidity which results when the gases, oxygen and hydrogen, combine. Because emergent properties are common to both physical and biological systems their sudden ghost-like appearances don't impress those out to de-sanctify life. Blake anticipated this problem, though, when he said "if you can't see God in a grain of sand, you won't see God in Heaven."

So the existence of life is not a solid criterion, leaving us with the ultimate religious question—"why anything, why not nothing?". A colleague of mine put it recently, "if one can believe in the Big Bang, one might as well believe in God." We are left with the questions surrounding faith and how to order our lives in its presence or absence. Enough of that.

In a letter from Wendell Barry several years ago—if I remember correctly it followed a phone conversation in which we had been discussing all of this spiritual talk going on he wrote "I don't much like religious talk and I intend to avoid the subject as much as respect for it requires." But, Wendell went on to say, "since land is a gift, how to receive and use a gift involves religious questions." We have not been using the gift well. Before agriculture how to live on earth required little thought. But now we are a species out of context and by that I mean the sorts of contexts in which we spent our evolutionary history before the invention of agriculture. Both biologically and psychologically little stretch may have been necessary to garden but farming is another matter. Especially on sloping ground, we have had to learn how to protect the landscape and encode that knowledge into a language of behavior. Nature more or less provided this protection for free. Even so, we fail, and this failure to live sustainably or responsibly in our "out of context situation is a major part of what has been called the human condition.

This failure has its most serious consequences in agriculture. Acknowledging this failure and stuck with the need for a food supply coming from agriculture, The Land Institute has worked for nearly 20 years to explore, through experimentation, the possibilities of an agriculture more resilient to human folly in managing the sustenance from the earth. We began with the idea that we must depend less on human cleverness and more on nature's wisdom and in doing so we turned to nature's native prairie because there was a sustainable system. It featured material recycling and ran on sunlight. That prairie, like most ecosystems, featured both species diversity and perennial roots. We wanted to coax a prairie-like structure into producing edible grains and still adequately manage insects, pathogens and woods, all the while producing enough biologically-fixed nitrogen to support a bountiful yield. In such an agriculture, soil erosion would cease to be a major consequence of production since perennial roots will hold the soil. By honoring nature's arrangement, our research efforts point to the possibilities of a fundamentally different agriculture in the next century. And now for my point; a most frequently offered comment by someone who has recently learned of our work and the research necessary to bring this new agriculture on line is "we know how to farm well with the conventional crops if we just would." To which my question is, "why don't we?" Perhaps it is beyond our ethical stretch.

Here is the way I think about it. Imagine the agriculture I landscape divided up into a grid on which a farm family occupies each square of the grid, 160 acres say. Sometime or another, probably within a century but certainly within 500 years, someone will farm that land who, owing either to stupidity or wickedness or both will allow the ecological capital necessary for the current average level of crop production to be eroded. The restoration of that failing will require hundreds if not thousands of years unless the soils are very deep or fertility is brought in from elsewhere. By not acknowledging that humans are going to do irreversibly dumb things for a long time to come, primarily because of our "out of context existence, we are forced to ask a religious? Why should both the earth and future generations hurt because of the occasional farmer who commits such folly? Why not an agriculture more resilient to human folly.? I have been talking about agriculture only, but those are the kinds of questions those interested in ecology and religion are asking, the sort of questions featured in this volume.

The scientific-technological revolution has placed both oil and machinery at our disposal. A secular decision. Erode the land and reduce its natural fertility? Simply apply fossil fuel based nitrogen, phosphorus, and potassium and keep going. A secular decision. The *faith*, spoken or not, is in the inexhaustibility of the mine and well head *or* in human cleverness, not in the requirements of the creation. Given our repeated failures with this sort of faith are we not forced into dealing with ecology in the context of religious questions?

We are operating pretty much with the same predispositions of our paleolithic ancestors whose minds could more or less take without thought for the morrow. Nature provided. But once we appropriate parts of nature, problems mount. We suffer from the legacy of the gift of the original relationship for when we moved first into the agricultural era and later into the industrial era, the paleolithic mind more or less ignored that it was drawing on an extractive rather than a renewable economy.

But, there is more. The high energy epoch has allowed the erosion of essential traditional values we accumulated through the agricultural era on how to farm well, values gained mostly through the School of Hard Knocks during this eight to ten thousand years of "out of context" living.

Standing ahead of us in this volume is a treat of some solid thinking about our predicament and what to do. There are eighteen scientists here, sixteen of whom hold the Ph.D. in a scientific discipline. All have at least 20 years professional work behind them. In thinking about this list of people and their contributions, I am reminded of Aldo Leopold who said that "nothing so important as an ethic is ever written, rather it evolves in the mind of a thinking community." Here is a collection of modern thinking. Whether these writers have "seen God in a grain of sand" or in the sanctity of life, their search for meaning and understanding is of a high order. In a culture in which drugs seem to increasingly substitute for religion and instant gratification substitutes for culture these scientists plunge ahead, mostly because, I suspect, they know the stakes are high and that more philosophical spade work is needed on the old question regarding our proper relationship to nature.

If I had an essay in this volume I would build it around the mission statement of The Land Institute:

> When people, land, and community are as one, all three members prosper; when they relate not as members but as competing interests, all three are exploited.
> By consulting Nature as the source and measure of that membership, The Land Institute seeks to develop an agriculture that will save soil from being lost or poisoned

while promoting a community life at once prosperous and enduring. In that essay I would plug the idea of "oneness" or "wholeness" or "whole" or "Holy." I would talk about the emergent properties at the ecosystem level where people, land and community are one.

I would also talk about the importance of the "grain of sand" for it goes to the ultimate questions of "why anything, why not nothing." I would try to draw more attention to the non-living materials of the creation and the importance of those physicists and biochemists who have contemplated and experimented with life's origins. It is sobering to contemplate our beginnings on an entirely physical world where three phases merged: water, atmosphere and the earth's crust. As the ecologist J. Stan Rowe said, "That gave rise to us. We did not give rise to it." This non-living part of the world is not "nothing but." It is part of the "whole." It too is "Holy." Stan Rowe prefers ecosphere over biosphere, and so do I because it is more whole or holy.

Introduction

John E. Carroll
and
Keith Warner, OFM

The closing years of the twentieth century are witnessing a convergence of science and religion such as has not been witnessed in three or four centuries. This convergence includes an explicit overt effort to link ecology with theology, to connect ecological thought with spiritual thought, with religion (the latter broadly defined beyond the constraints of doctrine or institutions), to measure ecological values with spiritual values. The reasons put forth for this linkage (or, more accurately, this re-connection) at this particular time are numerous and include the idea that the connection is natural and that the artificial separation has run its course after nearly four centuries. A sense of human desperation in the magnitude, the complexity, and the possible cataclysmic nature of ecological challenge perceived to be on the horizon (or already here, depending on one's perspective) is also thought by some to be encouraging the linkage. Perhaps the most compelling reason for this re-connection, however, is the new perception we are developing toward the planet, toward the cosmos, and toward ourselves as a result of the new ecological and other scientific knowledge we are now gaining at a rapid rate through new technology. This new technology supports our new found ability to see our planet from afar, to understand better its place in the system and the exceedingly narrow range of conditions that that system maintains which happen to permit the existence of life as we know it. We cannot help but be moved, and indeed changed, by this new knowledge of ourselves and our universe, whether we wish to be or not. Interestingly, there is not a lot of difference between these new realities we are discovering in science and the twentieth century thinking about the meaning of connectedness, the meaning of ecology, the main tenets of ecological thought. Nor is there a lot of difference between these new discoveries and the main tenets of the world's religions, as these are most commonly interpreted and accepted. It is perhaps not surprising, therefore, that it is spiritually based people, religious people, who are rapidly taking upon themselves the development of lifestyles most compatible with not only their perception of the central tenets of their faith belief but also the most central ideas and principles of ecological thought, as singularly and dramatically demonstrated to us through the wide array of evolving and emerging twentieth century technology. Such technological evolution is giving them, and all of us, a taste of awe which can provide the foundation for living in adherence to both those central faith tenets and to ecological principle. And this situation vis-a-vis technology is, more than anything else, a celebration of technology rather than a critique of technology. It is a celebration of technology which is appropriate rather than inappropriate, that is, appropriate, in terms of scale and design, to the task at hand, rather than the much more common "overkill" type of large-scale and high energy-consumptive technology which is so much more common in our lives. It is the latter type which tends to control us rather than that which is controlled by us, and hence becomes the proper target of criticism by environmentalists who are sometimes perceived as anti-technology.

Such large-scale controlling technology has become very much of a "sacred cow" in our modern society, in our culture and way of life, and thus we are quick both to defend it and to take offense at any criticism made of it. Why? Because we perceive it to be good, to be desirable, to be necessary to our well-being and our future success. It has been, until recently, inherently a part of our perception of progress, of the way in which we perceive the "good life" or a high quality of life. Any critique of this perception of progress is, therefore, viewed as threatening, as inimical to the progress we so desperately hope to achieve. It may be a blind view but it is our culture's view, our society's view, as we perceive it. And that is important for perception is the foundation of all reason. There is no reason, scientific or otherwise, which is not fully underlain by human perception, assumption, attitude, bias.

In the area of politics and diplomacy, perception is reality, scientific "fact" notwithstanding. If, for example, people believe and perceive that there exists a certain environmental problem, then such a problem exists, regardless of what science has to say about it. If, on the other hand, people do not perceive (or do not wish to perceive) the existence of an environmental problem which science indicates exists, then, for all practical political purposes, such a problem does not exist. Perception thus becomes reality, scientific reason notwithstanding. Informed politicians and diplomats know this and act accordingly.

It is the values we choose to hold and the perception that stems from those values which both informs and directs our science, a science which is never and can never be purely objective. In fact, to be aware of this lack of scientific objectivity is to be scientific, for it can be proven scientifically that we cannot detach from any object which we are attempting to study, that we the observer cannot be separated from that which we observe. Thus, we know scientifically that we cannot be objective.

In knowing this, we must, if we are scientific as well as human, recognize the ascendent position of the value system to which we adhere. If we choose to think ecologically, to adhere to a value system based in and upon ecological principle, then that is the value system we get. If we choose otherwise, as we have done, in other words if we choose an anti-ecological value system, a non creation-nurturing value system, then that is what we get. If the principles of ecology represent a closer approximation of the reality upon which we're dependent, which seems to be the case, then any choice of a value system not synchronous with ecological realities will be costly to us as human parts of the creation, of the global ecosystem, of the cosmos. This is apparently what has happened.

As humans, we have the ability to reflect, to consider our circumstance, to have some idea of our situation in context. We also have the ability to choose. Both of these characteristics appear to be central to what it means to be human. More specifically, we have a choice to make as to how to live, as to what kind of a value system to live by. For guidance in this process, we turn to reason. But we also turn to various other people, institutions, inspired literature, and, hopefully, ourselves, our conscience, our "inner voice," our intuitive abilities. Of course, in the final analysis, we humbly surrender in recognition of powers far greater than we. But such surrender does not happen before a good deal of responsible decision-making, work and application throughout life.

One very important area of that decision-making, work and application, and one which is associated with all human traditions before very recent times is one which the great philosopher and spiritual guide the Mahatma Gandhi reminded us of in our own century: "swideshi."

Gandhi has indeed instructed us in "swideshi," the ancient concept celebrating the wisdom of depending upon one's immediate surroundings for the fulfillment of our most basic needs, food, clothing, habitat, and so forth, and moving out from there in ever-widening concentric circles to fulfill our proportionally less basic needs (but nevertheless needs) from perhaps more distant and varied sources. In so doing, most of our needs are fulfilled by people and places we actually know (or know more intimately), and so can have a greater sense of responsibility for and can control or influence to a much greater extent, not to mention being capable of moral judgement about. We thus leave very little to be provided from more distant places, supplied by people we cannot know or at least be minimally aware of, by labor conditions and ecological conditions we cannot be judges of, nor have a sense of responsibility for, moral or otherwise. This is not different from the Eight-fold Path to Right Livelihood given us by Gautama Buddha and practiced by sincere Buddhists. Nor does it differ from the Christian principle of subsidiarity, encapsulated in the guidance and teachings of Jesus Christ.

Nevertheless, today's news tells us of the significant expansion of market share of major American cereal companies in India after years of rejection by the Indian people of such outside influence and with many years of dependency on their own food supplies and food culture. This constitutes a clear reaction in India against "swideshi," and thus a further rejection of Gandhian philosophy and thought in that very nation which was the home of Mahatma Gandhi, the modern embodiment of much ancient religious thought, wisdom and enlightenment. This represents "further rejection" in that that nation made major decisions almost a half century ago to pursue the route of modern industrialization rather than the much more ecological path put forth by Gandhi, basic decisions made not long after Gandhi's death in 1948.

We have constructed for ourselves, whether in India or the United States, a modern industrial system much dependent on the complete reverse of "swideshi," on the reverse of all the world's central religious philosophies, and on the reverse of what is central to this book, namely of all interpretations of the principles of ecology. We have constructed a fundamentally linear (rather than ecologically circular) system, indeed, an anti-ecological system (i.e., a system which runs counter to the principles of ecology) of industrialization and global trade which enforces dependency of most modern peoples on a highly energy-intensive, wasteful, grossly inefficient system of long-distance movement of goods in ways which insure we cannot be accountable either in terms of ecology, human rights, exploitation of people or nature. At times we seek to judge on these questions, a truly hopeless task in the modern world of high consumption and constant acquisition. And our interpretation of science, our attitude toward science, toward technology, is designed in such a way as to support and, temporarily at least, to maintain this economic and political structure which holds for us so much threat of ultimate catastrophe, catastrophe for vulnerable people available for exploitation, catastrophe for our ecosystem upon which we are fully dependent, catastrophe for ourselves, for future generations yet unborn, the latter of whom will be deprived of their rights to a good life, deprived of the inheritance passed on to us by generations preceding our own.

Our attitudes toward science, therefore, are much more crucial to our broader life than we may at first realize, for how we view and receive science and what science tells us influences and even significantly controls the way we view and the way we do economics and politics and diplomacy. In other words, what we perceive in science, since we greatly accept science as fundamental reality, determines our perceptions of all the other systems in our lives, of how we are to live in the world, of how we are to manage our affairs.

This book is as much about people as it is about science. It is about people who are regarded by society as scientists, having the requisite education, training and professional experience. But, in addition to being fellow human beings living among and not separated from the rest of us, the contributors to this book have made significant faith commitments alongside their professional scientific commitments and are herein discussing their spirituality in the context of their science, their science in the context of their spirituality. Being true ecologists, they are well aware of the holism at work, of the inseparability, at least at the deeper level, of science and spirit, of science and spirituality, of science and religion.

The dialogue between religion and ecology has begun to move forward. Religious traditions and the ecological sciences have begun to influence each other in ways that were unimaginable two generations ago, but we have much further to go if they are to take full advantage of these interactions. The editors have gathered these writers together to broaden and deepen the dialogue through this book in the hope that the ecological sciences can become more effective at promoting environmental conservation and that religious movements can better serve their congregations by providing a framework of ethics and spirituality relevant to the ecological challenges they face.

Science seeks to articulate what is, and mature religious faith is rooted in the real world. The scientific community has begun articulating with an increasingly strong consensus that irresponsible human behavior is threatening the future of life on our planet. Because of our duty toward the natural world, an ethic which spans all the religious diversity represented in this book, religious leadership must be informed what the very real consequences of our actions are. Without good information, neither scientific, political nor religious leadership can be exercised.

The absence of a dialogue between religions and the ecological sciences has been appallingly obvious until recently, and this was part of the broader divisions between religion and the sciences. Two most notable historical examples of how religious leaders have failed to grasp the greater knowledge brought about by the scientific revolution are Galileo and Darwin. Galileo Galilei was treated scandalously at the hands of Pope Paul V and Catholic theologians of the seventeenth century, and the Darwinian revolution continues to be denied and disputed by some religious leaders even today. From one perspective, we can all appreciate the challenge religious thinking has faced by the radical reorientation of our worldview which science has provoked in society, and understand the resistance of religious leaders to this change. At the same time, adherents of all religions must acknowledge that we fail to love our neighbors and consider the needs of others when we deny or dismiss the grave threats to our planet's life support systems. Even in an age of secular values, most U.S. citizens claim to have a religious faith. Churches, synagogues and religious movements still hold a strong suasive power over the majority of North Americans, and as a whole, they have tragically failed to use that to influence human behavior toward the environment. We hope this book will challenge religious leaders to exercise leadership in this area. Religion is worse off for ignoring science because without it, religion can degenerate into irrelevancy.

The environmental crisis is a moral and ethical crisis because it emerges from human behavior. It is a religious crisis because most Americans still look to their religious traditions to form their moral thinking, and American religions, notably Christianity, have failed to provide their congregations with the ethical tools to construct a response. Christian Churches, for example, until recently have been perceived as unconcerned or irrelevant to the health of the environment. Through efforts such as the National Religious Partnership for the Environment, statements from the United Church of Christ on Environmental Justice, and pastoral letter of the Catholic bishops on the environment, this is beginning to change.

Just as American religious leadership has been challenged to greater maturity through this crisis, more has been expected of ecological scientists of late. Natural scientists in general and ecologists in particular have a special relationship with being "out in the field," but those studying the natural environment increasingly realize the responsibility they have to their greater society. Ecologists recognize that they must be the ones to educate society about the consequences of our collective environmental behavior. Ecological scientists do their work because they deeply care about some aspect of the natural world, and those contributing to this volume recognize that our society's behavior is deeply influenced by religious thinking. Ecological sciences are worse off for ignoring religion because without it, a most significant way of influencing human behavior toward the environment is lost.

The estrangement between religion and ecology has gone on too long, and the schism between them has hurt both sides and broader society. In the science departments of many Catholic universities, for example, religious themes are rarely brought to discussions. Fearful of having academic freedoms compromised, faculty split off religious values and Catholic moral teaching from the science they teach in the classroom, as though these have no relevance to any human activity involving science. Because religious leaders in the past have so often dismissed anything to do with the natural world as "worldly" and not "eternal," they have failed to recognize the ecological crises at the doorsteps of houses of worship. Society is worse off for this estrangement because both the spiritual and moral authority of religious traditions and the empirical knowledge of the environment are needed if we are to forge solutions to the environmental crises we face.

The antagonism or splitting between these two has at times taken place in our persons. For generations it has been unacceptable for scientists to speak of their religious faith or for religious leaders to speak of their belief in scientific theories. Religious and scientific dimensions of one's life were rigidly segmented. This kind of alienation has led to religious practice which is ignorant of the ecological limitations of life on our planet and scientific pursuits disconnected from social needs and ethical concerns. The scientific method has, at times, been used to overly-compartmentalize our approach to life, while religion has generally failed to approach its role in a sufficiently holistic way. The Latin root of the term "religion," *religio*, means to bind up, or re-bind, and this is a task which we now undertake. We seek a reconciliation between science and religion because they truly need each other. We hope this book can contribute to bridging this gap, making religious movements and scientific thinking more responsive to the environmental needs of our world.

It appears that the relationship between religion and science may at last be ready to move forward. Scientists concerned about the environment realize that they must reach out to religious groups even if they must put aside their philosophical differences with them, as Appeal for Joint Commitment in Science and Religion demonstrates. It has been said that the convergence of science and religion is one of the most significant social movements of this century. Like so many other public relationships, these two partners are brought together to dialogue by crisis. Like centuries-old opponents, ecological science and religion come to the table reluctantly, but both parties realize that they have a crucial role to play in addressing our massive environmental problems. It might be ironic, and a little bit sad, that it takes a common crisis to bring us together, but this is a theme consistent in human history. That there could be such a strong consensus on an interfaith level would have seemed hard to believe thirty years ago. As one contributor pointed out, photos taken from a moon-bound spacecraft twenty five years ago have shaped a global consciousness on an unimaginable scale. The vision of our fragile little blue planet spinning in space seems to have advanced an ecumenical consciousness more than any number of meetings between religious leaders.

The time has come for a clear contribution from environmental scientists, both from those with substantial academic credentials in science and from those resource managers and others who work daily in scientific areas, especially as applied to environmental science and natural resource conservation. This book is designed to give a venue for those working in the environmental sciences to speak about the interface between their religious faith and their scientific vocation. The contributors to this book are scientific men and women who have wrestled with the tension between these two aspects of their lives, and decided that they can be integrated, that they must be integrated so that the split may be overcome. In this book they critically re-appraise the vocation of the ecological scientist, the relationship between religious and environmental ethics, and the role the natural environment can play in forming a mature and relevant religious faith. We have solicited contributions which would express the diversity of the interface between the ecological sciences and religious traditions. The authors include experts in ecology, agricultural sciences, natural resource sciences, forest and marine conservation biology, entomology, environmental toxicology, forestry, and geography.

We have sought contributions from scientists of an ecumenical diversity of religious traditions: Protestant and Catholic Christianity, Judaism, Buddhism, and Baha'i. We sought to respond to the diversity of religious persons working in the ecological sciences. A majority of the contributors are from the Christian traditions, which is what we anticipate to be the majority of the audience for this book, but the perspectives of the Buddhist, Jewish and the Baha'i contributors may be the most thought provoking contributions in that they invite the audience to look on the relationship between their own faith and the ecological sciences. It proved impossible to locate a Muslim or Hindu ecologist who was willing to write about the religion-ecology interface. The diversity in the level of religious commitment among ecologists is mirrored in the contributors to this volume: some are ordained ministers and priests, others members of religious communities, but most are lay men and women.

We see the contributors to this volume having dual vocations, to the ecological sciences and a religious tradition; because of this they have a unique role to play. They serve as intermediaries between those most aware of our ecological crisis and those in faith communities who can encourage the incorporation of environmental concern into religious practice. They shuttle scientific information to religious communities which can help form more ecologically responsible behavior, and bringing authentically human values from their religious tradition to their work, which can help direct the ecological sciences toward a more holistic approach. Three clear themes about the interface between ecology and religion emerge from the essays in this book, which we believe give voice to the message of these unique ecological scientists: religious faith can inform and enrich the vocation of the environmental scientist, a dialogue between religious ethics and environmental ethics can help in the application of both, and the vocations of biologists and ecologists can call religious traditions to re-examine and renew their traditions, thus animating people of faith to live their lives in greater harmony with the earth.

The eighteen contributing scientists and practitioners of religion have dealt with the segmentation described here, but they have, through a diversity of experiences, decided that their dual vocations need to mutually inform each other. They are men and women who have conducted research in the ecological sciences, and some of them will be well known to the reader. Some may be professing their religious faith publicly for the first time, and to make oneself vulnerable in this way is intimidating. One contributor said he felt more anxious revealing his religious faith than his sexual history! Yet there is a hunger, or a longing, for reconciling the various parts of our lives that continues to ache.

We also commend the scientists in this volume because they recognized the enduring role that religion plays in the lives of human beings. Twenty or thirty years ago, it was fashionable to dismiss religious faith as irrelevant or superstitious, but like nature's cycles, popular thought has come full circle. Religion is probably still the most powerful influence on peoples' ethical formation in America. For those readers who might be atheists, the editors suggest that religion is a force to be reckoned with in this country. It continues to play a significant role in shaping the values, beliefs, and behavior. Realizing this, the contributors to this effort hope to inspire the reader to make the connections between science and religion.

These contributors are scientists in their own right. All but a few have received a Ph.D. in a science or natural resource conservation field, and those without one have significant field experience in research, public advocacy or education. These men and women have risen to the top of their fields, but they also know the limitations of science. The ecological sciences are critical to understanding the consequences of our behavior, but, by themselves, they seem inadequate to change the direction of our behavior. Partnered with the moral authority of churches, synagogues, and other religious organizations, the ecological sciences can make an impact on our society's environmental behavior.

Ecologists now have the opportunity to play a role in encouraging religious institutions to include the natural world in their consideration of ethical problems. It was the recognition of the role religions could play in addressing our planetary ecological crisis that led 34 prominent scientists (including Steven Jay Gould, Henry Kendall, and Carl Sagan) to organize and issue an "Open Letter to the Religious Community" in 1990 inviting cooperative efforts to preserve the environment. Six months later, an ecumenical gathering of religious leaders responded very favorably, with a series of eight points. Both the Open Letter and the response are printed as the frontispiece in this volume. This book is an effort to further the process of religion and ecology mutually informing each other for the benefit of the natural world. This Open Letter is an example of scientists, most of whom are not affiliated with any religious tradition, recognizing the role religion can play in averting greater environmental degradation. How much more authority in religious circles the contributors to this book have because they are men and women of faith!

The most significant response to this Open Letter has been the creation of the National Religious Partnership for the Environment. It consists of the United States Catholic Conference, the National Council of Churches, the Evangelical Environmental Network, and the Coalition on the Environment and Jewish Life. It has a consultative relationship with the Union of Concerned Scientists. The NRPE seeks to broaden exponentially the base of the mainstream commitment to integrate issues of social justice and environment, and urge behavioral change in the lives of congregations and individuals. The editors of this volume salute this effort and pray for its success.

Returning to the sources of our respective religious traditions emerges as a strong theme in this work, and we hope it is a message the reader takes to heart. A word or two about the Catholic Christian faith of the editors may prove helpful. Christianity has been often accused of being fundamentally and essentially anti-nature, and this criticism is based on the actions and articulated world-views of some Christians. Nature has been understood, in the eyes of some Christians, as material goods given to us human beings for us to do with as we wish; in this view, nature has no intrinsic worth. A more faithful exegesis of the Jewish and Christian scriptures reveals that there is no real justification for this viewpoint. There is considerable ambiguity and diversity of responses to the natural world in Biblical writings, as one would expect in a work with over 70 authors. The attitude of domination and exploitation toward nature seems to be much more rooted in the economic values of North American culture than in our religion's ancient scriptures. We believe that Christianity does share, in part, in the guilt of damaging nature, but the guilt does not lie in the origin of our religious tradition; rather the guilt lies in complicity. We Christians have failed to be counter-cultural. Some Christians have taken the attitude of domination and exploitation proffered by our capitalist culture and blessed with a few verses of two or three thousand year old scripture, stripped of their literary, anthropological and environmental context. To be true to the spirit of the founders of our faith we must critique and reject attitudes of domination, exploitation and greed. By embracing humility, service, and self-giving, we come much closer to what the early Christians had in mind, and it would seem that this returning to the roots of tradition is similar to the re-interpretation that those from other religious faiths are suggesting in this book. We hope to invite the reader to delve a little deeper in the attitudes in his or her own tradition.

There are three major sections to this book. The contributors to the first discuss how religious faith and religious values have supported and challenged their vocations to be ecological scientists, and how they have embraced the contradictions of being an environmental scientist with religious faith. The second section is about the dialogue that needs to occur between environmental and religious ethics. Science is about the investigation into what is, but most citizens in North America are not able to apprehend scientific lessons without help. With voices from the front lines of the environmental battles, like those who have contributed to this book, those with religious faith can help ecologists and religious leaders overcome their differences to encourage more environmentally and morally responsible behavior. The last section of this volume is a series of essays reflecting the ecological dimensions of religious experience. The authors examine their religious experiences, and those of others, in light of what they have learned about the ecology of the human-nature relationship. In most cases, the authors find some aspects of religious thought that are troublesome and should be downplayed while they have found other aspects of their tradition that seem to have taken on even greater meaning and compelling urgency. Our ecological problems are causing us to re-examine our values and beliefs; hopefully the more relevant and sustainable aspects of our religious traditions will be invigorated by this. We can now turn to the summaries of the three sections and their constitutive essays.

The first section of this book describes the perspective and experience of those who have a dual vocation: that of scientific ecologist and religious practitioner. The essayists demonstrate that they can be fully compatible, and indeed, mutually supportive. As mature religious men and women, they are not trapped in rigid myths, and as ecologists, they realize that the scientific method in and of itself cannot save. The authors of these essays describe how their dual vocations interact and what conclusions they draw about the ecological sciences as a result. To be an ecological scientist is more than conducting field research, establishing methodology, and verifying statistics. It also requires sustaining a motivation in their persons strong enough to see them through the long haul. It interacts with the values and ethics of society. Yet ecology, more than all the other sciences, is about relationship, about interconnection. These contributors have arrived through their scientific vocation at the deep spiritual insight: we are all related, and we are all substantially defined by our relationships. We cannot practice science "outside" the web of life with which we interact, and we dare not pretend that we can. As a result of their research and work these scientists have developed a relationship with specific people, organisms and places, whether the rural poor in Appalachia (Fritsch), or the frontier between Canada and the U.S. suffering pollution (Carroll). Interpreted through the lens of their faith commitment, their relationships with these specific people, places and organisms have led them to deeper reflection on what it means to be a scientist and a person of religious faith.

John Carroll's essay points out the very real limitations of science. Without the mooring of sound ethics values, science and scientists can reject or ignore other ways of gaining insight and knowledge. Carroll calls us to a stance of healthy skepticism toward science and technology.

We cannot possibly achieve a total objectivity, and Carroll demonstrates the price we pay for fooling ourselves into believing that we can. Both he and Gene Wilhelm remind us of the very sound ecological practices that developed in so-called "primitive" cultures who had nothing like Western science. We dismiss and ignore these more intuitive ways of relating to the Earth's web of life to our peril.

Stephanie Kaza provides a very personal account of the interaction between her Buddhist practice and scientific vocation. Her practice has profoundly formed her teaching of science and her advocacy on behalf of the natural world. From Buddhism she learned the value of careful attention and perception, and she has used and taught these skills in the classroom and the field. Attentiveness is essential to Buddhist practice, and it has strengthened her skills as a scientist. To encourage her students to develop skills of "full body attention," she believes a good teacher must take her students into the field and apprehend the complete context of a species' habitat. Her practice has led her to question the unquestioning faith in the scientific method by some members of the scientific community; as a Buddhist, her striving for nonduality conflicts with the near-religious quest for objectification with which some approach the scientific method. Kaza is moved to compassion when she witnesses suffering, and she asks how biological research which inflicts suffering can lead to good. The Buddhist belief in co-dependent arising is an invaluable contribution to our society's ecological debate, casting light on the efforts of many environmental advocates to promote an attitude of inter-dependence toward nature.

In *The Return to Natural Philosophy*, Edward O. Wilson writes of the need for dialogue between the religions and the natural sciences, and he proposes that a "natural philosophy" based on re-interpreting the role of natural law can be of great help in this. Science has been mistaken in its dismissal of religion, for as Wilson points out, religion's role is to codify and put into enduring, poetic form the highest moral values of a society. Since the advent of the scientific revolution, European and North American societies have struggled how to integrate these values with emerging scientific knowledge, but philosophers and theologians have not promoted natural law or natural philosophy which is thoroughly rooted in empirical knowledge. Only by returning to a natural philosophy, based in science but in dialogue with religion, can society hope for a true rapprochement between these two.

The ecological autobiography of Al Fritsch journals the evolution of a supremely practical ecologist. His life has taken him far from his Appalachian home, into the Jesuits, graduate degrees and political advocacy in the nation's capital, and he has now journeyed full circle back to a small community in rural Kentucky not unlike the one in which he was born. By returning to his mountain people, he brings a tremendous wealth of experience as a priest and public advocate, yet he spends the heart of his time in applied science. For Fritsch, ecology is not limited to study; he seeks to apply it in his life and the lives of his neighbors. In fact, Fritsch seems to embody the kind of scientist that Carroll calls for: rooted in human values and devoted to service of his fellow human beings. In his personal, poetic style, Fritsch describes his own journey toward self-understanding, a sojourn that has drawn heavily on his vocation to put ecological sciences in service of those in greatest need.

Their development as scientists and ecologists forms the basis for the reflections offered us by Mary Louise Dolan and Calvin De Witt. Dolan describes for us patterns in nature that give insight into the relationships which help define us. She uses the concept of "inscaping" to help model for us the profound ecological and spiritual nature of our relatedness. She believes that science gives us insight into how the world works, at least ecologically, and that it tells us that we are related. We choose whether or not we wish to live relatedly. To cut ourselves off or deny our relatedness will only perpetuate ecological destruction and spiritual alienation.

Calvin De Witt is both a minister in the Reformed tradition and a leading wetlands ecologist. In his own life he has been able to integrate these vocations, and in his essay he shares his suggestions for how to put these together. He believes that science is the best tool for acquiring information, but that religion and religious values have an essential role to play in determining a healthy praxis in regard to nature. He articulates what for him are guidelines for developing a belief system (in the Christian tradition) which will provide guidance for quality living on the earth. De Witt's insight into the need for praxis as well as good science and good ethics suggests a scientific version of what in theology is called a hermeneutical circle. This cyclical process is ideally suited to helping individuals and faith communities determine how to respond to situations of sin and injustice, but it can appropriately be applied here as well. It begins with a process of reflection on the reality in which one finds oneself. In the context being discussed here, it would be appropriate to review whatever ecological problem or situation confronts you. In response to this, a course of action, hopefully a collective one, can be taken. In the process of taking action, a dialectic occurs which will change the point of view of the actors, the reality they confront, and the relationships among all parties. The cycle continues as reflection needs to be begun again. Far from being a vicious cycle, the dynamic of this hermeneutical circle can give insight into behavior that is spiritually life-giving and ecologically responsible.

The second part of this volume addresses how both religious and environmental ethics benefit from entering into dialogue. The authors have special expertise and a distinctly helpful perspective in this because of their calling as ecologists and as religious persons. They have special expertise because as scientists devoted to caring for the earth, they have had to confront troubling moral questions about how the earth is harmed. They have reflected on these questions in their professional lives, and then deepened their reflection by evaluating our environmental behavior in light of the teaching from their respective religious traditions. Environmental ethics take on greater relevance for most people when they are situated in the context of a more encompassing ethic of life; they are more coherent and more likely to be acted on consistently if they are integrated with the heart as well as the head, and few things can effect this better than religious faith.

Susan Power Bratton's contribution, *Penning the Goring Bull*, gives a clear methodology for integrating religious and environmental ethics that offers us guidance for integrating environmental science and religious ethics. She addresses the differences between models of ethical thinking in the Judeo-Christian tradition. As she points out, those who look to the Hebrew Scriptures for ethical guidance are confronted with many different models from which to choose. Bratton demonstrates a process for selecting a Biblical ethical model to resolve conflict which is appropriate to our contemporary understanding of the behavior of environmental pollutants today. She makes clear that the Judeo-Christian tradition is puriform, and that Christians are able to choose from the models of ethical decision making most appropriate to our needs today. She demonstrates the pitfalls of operating out of an ethical decision making model that is not based on scientific reality. Bratton's experience as a biologist and scientist gives her the tools to be able to understand what actually happens when pollution migrates off-site, and she is able to respond to the ethical issues this raises more effectively as a result. Equally importantly, she is able to serve as an interpreter of the ethical problems which we face in the modern world for others in her Protestant tradition specifically and the Judeo-Christian tradition in general. Our contemporary environmental problems would have been inconceivable to those writing the Hebrew Scriptures, yet for religion to be relevant today, it must take them into account. Even though the scale and complexity of environmental issues are dizzying, they are rooted in human behavior; in their essence, environmental problems involve consequences of human actions. As Bratton demonstrates, religious values are still relevant for guiding human behavior.

The Baha'i faith, as William Gregg informs us, presents us with religious teachings that can help us overcome the terribly destructive split between the spirit and material worlds. He relates his personal journey into the Baha'i faith, and how its belief in the unity of truth lays a foundation for dialogue between the ecological sciences and Baha'i. This faith confirms the continuing evolution of the Earth, encourages a systematic approach to understanding its processes and advocates a unity among the human family as a means to overcoming the crises faced by our planet. Baha'is see no contradiction between embracing rigorous scientific pursuits and the necessary values of compassion, generosity and respect for diversity. This religion's belief in justice and eradicating poverty are two of the most critical ingredients necessary for more sustainable lifestyles. Gregg relates many encouraging stories of practitioners of his religion acting on behalf of the natural world, and it seems the high standards of Baha'i activism are a challenge to all people of faith. Their advocacy of the concept of "world citizenship" is most welcome in a social environment threatened by provincialism and NIMBYism.

Bob Patterson writes from the perspective of one who has labored for years to help provide a secure food supply for the poorest citizens of our planet. His eyes and ears have witnessed the tragic plight afflicting millions of poor farmers in the under-developed world who struggle to support their families on land that is continually exposed to logging, flooding, clearing, and inappropriate development. Patterson's Christian faith combined with his vocation as an agricultural scientist has led him to the conclusion that our behavior toward the land is an expression of our religious values, and that our current abuse of the soils, water and

air of our planet points toward a spiritual bankruptcy. Moved to compassion by seeing so many poor farmers struggle for dignity and self-
determination, Patterson has personally invested himself in the effort to
help secure access to food and food markets for them. Yet he returns to
the assertion that the greatest obstacles to hunger and famine are socio-
political, not biological; without a commitment to justice, our environmental problems cannot be solved, and his Christian faith calls him to
make justice and peace.

Carl Jordan provides a succinct history for some of the religious
and economic attitudes toward the environment in the United States. He
explains the social and religious reasons for the fusion of religious and
economic values on the American frontier, describing their appropriate-
ness to the world of the frontier. From this, a popular image of God in
the United States is still that of a free-market capitalist, concerned only
with personal ethics, the myth of progress, and control of nature. The
environmental situation in the United States has changed radically in the
past 150 years, but the Religious Right has failed to adapt their environmental ethics since the frontier days. Jordan suggests that both theology
and our economic models need to evolve in response to the changes in
society and our self-understanding. He advocates an understanding of
economics that moves away from the Laissez-faire stage of frontier economics, through regulatory and incentive stages to a co-operative form
of economics, based on ecology and sustainability. He laments an understanding of God which is ignorant of the crucial environmental issues
facing our society, an image of God which perpetuates the problems
rather than facing them in a mature way. He challenges us to consider a
God concerned with an ethical treatment of the environment.

A Buddhist perspective on environmental conflicts can point us
beyond the seeming inevitability of conflictual paradigms for making
decisions about environmental ethics. Joyce McCann investigates a specific sawmill closure in northern Arizona to understand the relationship
between the suffering of human beings and the suffering of the environment. She is troubled by the morality of a process which produced so
much suffering. By introducing relevant Buddhist values, she helps us
realize how Western European cultural and religious models seem to be
trapped in paradigms of conflict. This is clearly reflected in the struggles
between various bureaucratic agencies responsible for land stewardship
in the American West. She proposes several ideas which could serve as

the basis for alternative models: a non-conflictual approach would focus on the interdependency of human beings and nature and should be reflected in the behavior of our governmental agencies, and the use of freedom from suffering as a criterion in environmental decisions which impact the lives of human beings.

Science is a careful investigation into what is. As a Sister of Charity, Paula Gonzalez provides a compelling argument for basing our understanding of and behavior toward the natural world on a more complete scientific understanding of its origins, processes and inherent wisdom. Only by adopting a more humble stance, based on what is can we hope to live in a sustainable way on our planet.

The third section of this book is an attempt to situate the religious experience in an ecological context. The essays describe how our natural environments can inform our spiritualities and enrich our religious experiences. The contributors conclude that without developing a broader, more mature ecological consciousness in our religious traditions, there is little hope for changing the attitudes which have led to our environmental crises to begin with. All have been profoundly influenced by their own experiences in nature, and all have done serious theological reflection based on these experiences. Whether encountering a radically differing world view among primal peoples, a micro-universe among insects or a sea of life among Pacific Northwest forests or the Atlantic Ocean, the authors have taken from their experiences a realization that religious experiences that are not rooted in the reality of the natural world cannot be mature. The reader should not be surprised that environmental scientists reject an exclusively other-world locus for their faith; these contributors have learned to approach spiritual matters from ground up.

Gene Wilhelm's first introduction to an ecological theology came in the Arctic among the Inupiat people. His indigenous research assistant and local guide was disturbed by the ease and casualness with which the biologists killed and dissected their scientific subjects, and the questions he put to Wilhelm stayed with him. Because of his openness to hear the questions and implicit critique of this indigenous person, Wilhelm had the privilege to learn from him. He began to question many of the assumptions that went with the scientific world view. His research assistant's way of deeply relating to the non-human world is a perfect example of what John Carroll writes of when he suggests that there are "other ways of knowing" besides Western science. Wilhelm's journey into questioning the infallibility of the scientific method led him to doubt the utility of reductionism and the inevitability of hierarchy, which seem to have been the inevitable companions to the scientific world view as he was taught it. In an ironic twist, just as the "primal peoples" co-evolved with their environment, Wilhelm's spiritual journey and scientific journey mutually influenced each other. His emerging skepticism of hierarchy, reductionism and static world views in the scientific realm led him to conclude that similar problems are present in contemporary Christian consciousness. He attributes the failure by Christians to address ecological concerns to a disordered consciousness, one which fails to apprehend natural and spiritual reality. The questions posed by indigenous peoples should give pause to both scientific and religious thinkers. Wilhelm advocates a metanoia, a conversion or an integrated change of heart, soul and mind so as to re-direct us toward a harmonious relationship with nature.

Francis of Assisi was named the patron saint of ecology by the Catholic Church in 1980, so no volume about the relationship between religion and ecology would be complete without mentioning him. A Franciscan and entomologist, Jim Edmiston presents some biographical background of Francis' spirituality of nature, but he goes beyond this to develop some of the lesser-known aspects of the Franciscan intellectual tradition. This tradition can guide us today in our relationship with nature. Edmiston advocates several specific actions that can help remind us of our spiritual relatedness to all of creation, actions which any youth group or religious organization could do to raise awareness of how humans are dependent upon our environment for our well-being. Reflecting upon, deepening, and simply valuing this relationship is something that religious faith can help us with immeasurably.

Elliott Norse is one of the premier forest and marine ecologists in the U.S., and his contribution elaborates his reflections on the relationship between the genetic drive for procreation, the fear of death and annihilation and the need for rethinking our cultural and religious assumptions. As the only Jewish contributor, he discusses the genetic compulsion of the commandment from Genesis: "be fruitful and multiply" (the only Biblical commandment that has ever been fully observed, according to Calvin De Witt). Norse reflects on his own bittersweet experience of not passing on his own genetic material and the theological implications of his inevitable annihilation at death. He also points to the contradictions between, and the need to reconcile, his scientific vocation and his religious experience. The most striking contradiction he identifies is one which all the monotheistic religions (at the least) must confront: how can we believe in a creative, life-giving God while at the same time destroying the Earth, the life-support system granted us? If religions of all kinds are to mobilize and act to save our environment, as Norse advocates, they will have to address this contradiction. He has hope that a rapprochement between religion and science can save our planet.

Science-based ecological concern can contribute profoundly to a religious experience, as Robert Kent shows us. Like many with a scientific vocation, the religious and professional vocations seemed to be part of two different worlds, never intersecting. Through a series of fortunate events, he began to realize that he could not keep them separate, indeed, that he had the responsibility to speak of their relationship. He began to speak of ecological concerns and spirituality and at once like-minded people began to respond favorably, speaking of their own intuitive sense of interconnection. His testimony is that of a journey of integration.

The belief that Christianity is inherently anti-nature is taken on directly by Keith Warner, a Franciscan and geographer. He investigates what it means to have a sense of sacred space in wilderness. Landscape is an important yet ambiguous word, and the human experience in landscape, especially the spiritual experience in wilderness landscape, has generally been ignored. Warner's own experiences in wild landscape have been strong enough to motivate him to further study and he discovered that there is a significant minority tradition in Christianity which has valued wilderness landscape as an expression of God's creative love. Many and perhaps most of the most influential Christian mystics experienced God in a most powerful way in nature, and responded specifically to their experience in landscape. Only in the past few hundred years have we forgotten this relationship to natural landscape, and this ignorance impoverishes our collective religious experience today. He proposes that we develop affective, spiritual relationships with specific places to replace our lost sense of connection to the Earth.

Religion and ecology need each other to achieve their missions, if we understand their missions in a holistic sense. For example, "salvation" of humankind is a major concern in Christianity, but in recent centuries, this has been interpreted in an excessively spiritualized, extra-corporeal fashion, far removed from the Latin word "salvus," which includes the well-being of every aspect of a person's life. To achieve salvation, Christianity, indeed all religious traditions, must take into account the health and well-being of all life forms. Our common future requires it of us. Likewise, the ecological sciences cannot be content with simply acquiring and processing bits of data; the information that environmental sciences bring us must be presented in a way that helps us value the natural world. In the end, we will not save what we do not love, and we will not love what we do not understand. May we all grow in love and understanding of the natural world.

PART ONE

Religion
and the
Vocation of Science

Limitations of
"Western Science":
A Critique of
Failed Inclusivity

John E. Carroll, PhD

"The heart has its reasons, which reason knows nothing of" —Pascal

This book is about ecology and religion. Ecology is a science, usually lumped with the biological or life sciences (although in fact it is much broader). Thus, this book is about science and religion, and the contemporary convergence of the two. In some ways the practice of western science has become like unto a religion based on faith, and, although claiming to be based on reason and reason alone, fails in two ways: it fails at openness to other ways of knowing, ways which it knows little or nothing about and which it should be open to in its inquiry; and it fails to accept findings or reason which run counter to three centuries or so of scientific theory and practice. In the former, we cannot be certain that there are no other ways of knowing . Thus, it is unscientific to exclude the possibility. The perennial and always healthy if sometimes troublesome scientific question "why" has (and should have) no limits. It is unscientific to arbitrarily fix such limits. In the latter, we find the revelations of ecology, especially the first principle of connectedness, oneness of all, very hard to accept. It challenges all aspects of our value system and of our lives as we live them. We find other ecological principles, such as nature as guide, as teacher, as source of revelation, and the idea that there is no such place as "away," that everyplace is our backyard, equally difficult. We find the findings and implications of quantum theory, quantum mechanics, chaos theory, and the notion of an implicate order, all supported by scientific evidence, an equally hard pill to swallow, for we are all too aware of the implications of these findings to our value systems, to our assumptions about truth and reality, and to the way we live our lives. Thus, western science, as we are practicing it, has real limits, for there is a difference between western science as an ideal, which is wholistic and unitary, and the practice of western science as we know it, which is non-wholistic and fundamentally reductionistic in its nature.

"There is western science, and there are other ways of knowing.." These words of western-trained nuclear physicist Vandana Shiva of India are heresy in western science, for western science claims, and has always claimed, exclusivity as the only legitimate (i.e., scientific) way of knowing. Western science in practice tolerates no competition and claims a monopoly on truth, both that which is known and that which remains to be known. Interestingly, this claim of exclusiveness made by western science is itself fundamentally unscientific, by the standards of western science itself, for it closes down all inquiry which falls outside a rather narrow interpretation of its principle methodology, the scientific method. And, although western science is ultimately based on the intuitive and owes its nature and value to intuition, in practice if not in theory it places curbs on intuition when convenient to do so. Vandana Shiva's statement is heretical for one reason and that is its unacceptable (to western science) challenge of any exclusivity attributable to western science. The statement, which is especially significant in that it comes from the mind of a well trained and accomplished western scientist, does not challenge the validity of western science as a way of knowing; in fact, it is an acknowledgment of that validity. It is only in the domain of exclusivity that it runs amuck, for western science will brook no competition to the monopoly on knowing which it claims. This is an unscientific premise by virtue of the very definition of science in the modern western claim, due to its selectively closed access to open inquiry, to the ultimate scientific question, Why?

Additionally, science and its sister, technology, are viewed as "sacred cows" in our society, as untouchable and not to be questioned. This unscientific circumstance enhances the possibility for error for it separates science from its connectedness to us, from its humanity. In so doing it creates around it an aura of invulnerability, of having monopoly on truth, and thereby invites error, falsehood, and much too often, tragedy.

It is this kind of aura of invulnerability, of rightness, of presumptiousness, which led science, for example, to so vigorously deny the possibility of life within the earth itself, below the soil layer. This is perhaps why the recent startling announcement of the discovery of an enormous quantity of life within the earth, indeed more biota quantitatively than exists on the surface, a so-called lost world of ancient microbes evolving separately over millions of years from life on the surface, has been met with very little attention, in spite of both the startling nature of the discovery and the total contradiction it represents to conventional scientific wisdom.

Likewise, this same presumptuousness, this aura of invulnerability, has kept us wedded to the conventional notion of linearity as basic to physics and other areas of science. We take linearity for granted and yet, if ecology or chaos theory in mathematics or quantum physics have anything to tell us, they are telling us, that linearity does not exist, that it's an artificial way of viewing the world. As Michael Crichton's fictitious mathematician, Ian Malcolm, in the popular novel Jurassic Park says, "Real life isn't a series of interconnected events occurring one after another like beads strung on a necklace. Life is actually a series of encounters in which one event may change those to follow in a wholly unpredictable even devastating way. That is the deep truth about the structure of our universe. But, for some reason, we insist on behaving as if it were not true. "In other words," (is) sudden, radical irrational change built into the very fabric of existence"? We should know this. But our unscientific attitude toward science precludes our knowing this, permitting the fictitious tragedy of Crichton's *Jurassic Park* and many other not so fictitious tragedies in our world every day.

In practice what we define as western science is almost totally dependent upon and in service to non-scientifically-derived value systems, and is curbed and governed accordingly. Of course, as human beings part of a larger whole, part of nature, and subject to the influence of our genetic make-up, our life influences (including the nine months in the womb) and our surrounding environment, we cannot achieve total objectivity in any event. We cannot separate ourselves from that which we observe. We can only try. To the degree we assume pure objectivity, we create problems and invite trouble. Quite aside from that problem, however, is the realization that today, more than ever, our science, which is expensive to conduct, is subject to the influences of funding sources, be they government, defense industry, medical establishment, or university more beholden than it should be and less and less concerned about its own academic independence. It is said that an overwhelming percentage of American physicists, for example, are beholden for their basic support to defense industry and defense agencies of government, the so-called military/ industrial complex. Likewise, an increasing percentage of biologists are beholden to the profit directives of the growing biotechnology and genetic engineering industry. Independent scientists are few and far between. Can there be science without independent scientists? Can there be science in a climate which either blunts or discourages fully independent inquiry?

In a memorable scene in the motion picture "The Emerald Forest," a film about the destruction of the Amazonian rainforest by the construction of the giant Tucurui Dam, an indigenous Yanomami tribesman, looking out on the sea of forest destruction, asks "But how will the earth breathe?" This is a fundamental scientific question asked by a person whom most in our society would regard as the antithesis of science or of a scientific mind, a presumably superstitious aboriginal tribesman who speaks no western language, who is classified (by us) as illiterate, and who lives, behaves and dresses in non-Western ways which are outside of our comprehension. He is, conceivably, the last person we would think of as scientific, in the modern or western sense. And yet, how did he know that the planet would have trouble "breathing" if the forests are destroyed? Let us not be put off by the, by our standards, very unscientific format of the question posed, for this aboriginal tribal observer is on to truth. Has this person or his society applied what we call scientific method to arrive at the conclusion that the planet might have trouble "breathing" in this circumstance? Was he taught about the transpiration of plant life or about global oxygen balance or other questions of atmospheric chemistry?. Not very likely. The linkage has almost certainly been made through countless generations of his ancestry living in symbiosis with the planet and its ecosystems in this area, combined with deep intuitive and particularly observational powers which we have likely long since lost, given our generations of separation from nature and natural systems of which we are nevertheless a part. Let us not be too anxious to underestimate the powers and abilities of people we arrogantly call "primitive" or "uncivilized." Likewise, let us not be quick to demean the powers of observation which we have and which we can sharpen and refine, and the ability of deeper intuition which can come with sharpening of those powers.

Ecology has been called the "subversive science." And it is indeed! Ecology starts from the premise that all things are related to, are connected to, are interdependent with, ultimately are a part of all other things. This, indeed, is the very first and the most basic principle of ecology. All other modern western science, as conventionally practiced, operates on the assumption that this first and most basic principle of ecology is not true. Ecology, therefore, the science which studies the relationship of all things to all other things, subverts all conventional science in questioning the most basic principle in the rest of science, namely, that everything exists apart from, separate from, everything else. Cartesian, or Newtonian, or Baconian thought, the underlying philosophical premise of all conventional modern science, is inherently anti-ecological. Ecology can naught but subvert the others for its central and all its other premises lie opposite to and undermine the foundation of the others.

There are exceptions in that the Einsteinian and post-Einsteinian twentieth century discoveries in quantum theory and quantum mechanics in the field of physics and chaos theory in the field of mathematics appear to be in synchrony with ecological thought. But these two areas have yet to claim any dominance in their disciplines, albeit they are both growing in interest and in following. The popularized tenet of chaos theory in mathematics, known as the "butterfly effect," is a case in point, linking as it does ecological thought to mathematics. This is the phenomenon whereby a butterfly fluttering its wings in Peking, China, cannot help but cause an effect in New York City, fully on the other side of the planet. Ecology tells us we cannot do just one thing. Nor can the butterfly. No one would suggest that the butterfly's effect on the other side of the globe is in any way measurable, for it is not (at least at this time). How can we know, therefore, that this effect exists? We know it exists because we know that it cannot not exist. One thing leads to another, and another, and another, as in a set of dominoes falling against one another. Only in real life, which ecology tells us is circular, or at least non-linear, the falling dominoes do not end. What goes around comes around, in other words. And once again ecology undermines and subverts, for it argues, as does chaos theory, that reality is non-linear, while our functioning "scientific" world in practice argues that reality (and the world) is a linear sort of place with all happenings linear.

Quantum physics and quantum mechanics likewise support ecological thinking for their focus is on relationship, on the notion of relationship being reality, of relationship creating meaning. This is most akin to ecology's emphasis on context, that things exist only in context with, in relationship to, other things, and therefore context both defines things and creates meaning. Ecology carries this further in scientific terms in the functioning of "communities of life" (plant communities, animal communities, etc.) within "ecosystems," or, to put it another way, in the establishment and maintenance of "pattern," in a "fabric" or "web." All of these terms and the concepts that lie behind them are inherently ecological, an image of numerous strands being woven into a broader whole, a fabric, existing in relationship with one another, capable of developing and tightening but also capable of unraveling, of coming apart in a composite of interdependent events, events related to and dependent upon one another.

We appear to be returning to a view of reality dominant at an earlier time in our historical development and once again coming into its own, a reality of unity and connectedness, which has been directly contradicted in the "modern scientific era" and which is still contradicted by the established order, by the forces of power in the scientific establishment and in the society as a whole. This new/old view of reality to which we now return is spiritual as well as physical, which accepts and recognizes the existence of spirit, the existence of spirituality, the existence of religion, broadly defined. It is important, therefore, for us in modern times to now begin to understand the lack of a true dichotomy between science and religion, to recognize the false dichotomy which has prevailed for more than three centuries, and to look particularly at the application of the loss of that dichotomy to progress in our development and in our practice of ecological thought.

We face a problem of scientific fundamentalism which, as in technological fundamentalism, religious fundamentalism or any other kind of fundamentalism, causes blindness. It blinds us to the false assumptions to which we are too often wedded. It leads us to exclusivity when science, to be effective, must be characterized by its inclusivity, its willingness to include all possibilities to enfold all. Such scientific fundamentalism, such scientific exclusivity, which is far too pervasive in our practice of science, can only lead to the distortion and corruption of science, to a structural corruption which increasingly pervades our institutions, and scientific practice to adherence to dogma, all of which guarantee wrong answers, and tragedy, for us, for our ecosystem upon which we are dependent, and for future generations yet unborn.

We humans like to view the dinosaurs as a failed form of life. We think of those large reptiles of long ago as unintelligent pea-brained creatures who perhaps disappeared because they had not the sense, nor the mental or physical ability, to adapt to changing conditions. Not so.

They existed on earth for a far longer period of time than have humans and human-like creatures thus far. Compared to these great reptiles of long ago, we are as yet untested. We haven't been around long enough to take the test. If we fail and face the prospect of extinction ourselves, it may well be said that our great (and likely false) sense of superiority, our arrogance, our hubris, our pride, and the blindness associated with that, our unwillingness to yield to a truly scientific viewpoint, to be properly humble in the face of all, is that which did us in. May we become scientific, become open to all the possibilities, and not worship the false idol of reductionistic science.

Infinite Realms
of Observation:
Buddhist Perspectives
on
Teaching and Doing Science

Stephanie Kaza, PhD

When I began my studies at Oberlin College, I felt sure I would concentrate on the sciences. I had taken high school physics, chemistry, math, biology, and was fascinated by dissection; I thought I would become a surgeon. Yet after a year and a half exposure to a liberal arts curriculum, I went into traumatic paralysis trying to choose a major. I considered chemistry and math but also was intrigued by religion and psychology. Every week I flipflopped, suffering under the pressure to choose a single perspective. The crisis lasted an entire semester, establishing a dilemma which would haunt me through graduate school and on into professional life. Eventually I majored in biology, out of sheer love for the beauty and complexity of life forms.

In my first ecology course I was introduced to a relational view, epitomized by ecosystem studies. Seeing organisms in context seemed much more complete and satisfying than observing them as autonomous entities. By the 1970s, ecological problems were surfacing at a despair-inducing rate, and I found myself mesmerized, like many others, by the plight of marine mammals. I took on the messy tuna-dolphin controversy as my doctoral research and quickly realized neither biology nor ecology were enough to explain the situation. To analyze the dynamics of the controversy I also needed fisheries anthropology, marine mammal law, environmental ethics, and marine economics. Despite the urgings of my graduate committee to choose a single discipline focus, I turned to a systems approach of resource use analysis which synthesized many perspectives, each shedding light on the others.

But I was a little ahead of my time for most academic programs. So I shared my insights with others through science education, serving as education director for Point Reyes Bird Observatory and then the U.C. Berkeley Botanical Garden. In the meantime I had taken up the study and practice of Zen Buddhism. I learned to meditate, I studied Zen texts, and I lived for three years at Green Gulch Zen Center in northern California. I came to see how all thinking is conditioned by previous experience and values. Now even a systems approach to organisms and habitats was not enough. I needed to understand how powerfully human attitudes towards nature affect the shape of the landscape.

I took my curiosity to Starr King divinity school in Berkeley where I studied ethics and theology. My Buddhist perspective was accepted as compatible with the Unitarian-Univeralist curriculum, particularly since I was interested in spiritually-based social change. Here I gained considerable vocabulary in understanding human values and social systems. I sensed I was getting close to some of what underlies scientific process and decision-making. But where could I combine my love for ethics, religion, and ecology? To my great fortune, I was invited to explore these issues through my teaching and writing as a member of the faculty of the School of Natural Resources at the University of Vermont. In dialogue with colleagues and students I continue to ask serious questions about the roles of science and religion in shaping social values.

In this article, I reflect on four principles of Buddhist practice and philosophy, illustrating their relationship to science education and environmental policy. I draw on my own personal experience in a number of diverse settings, showing one person's exploration of the overlap between the worlds of science and religion. My primary science orientation has come to emphasize the fields of natural history, conservation biology, and restoration ecology. My primary religious orientation is Soto Zen Buddhism, a tradition in the Mahayana school developed by 13th century Japanese teacher Eihei Dogen and carried to me through Shunryu Suzuki Roshi and Kobun Chino Otogawa.

THE MIND OF ATTENTION

At the heart of good science training is cultivating a disciplined mind with astute capacities for observing the world outside the self. At the heart of Zen training is cultivating an attentive mind with astute capacities for self-observation (Aitken, 1984). The two naturally complement and support each other. In the scientific tradition, paying attention is central to understanding natural phenomena through careful observation. In the Buddhist tradition, paying attention is seen as a prerequisite for developing awareness of one's thoughts and actions. This, in turn, is necessary to break through the limited views of the self and perceive the nondual nature of the world. In both traditions, those who practice with rigor for a period of time become more capable of clear perceiving and also more humble about what they cannot perceive.

Field biology is based fundamentally on careful observation of the landscape, with particular attention to pattern. The experienced ornithologist, familiar with the birds in a particular region, can describe the cycles of breeding, migration, and mortality as well as the general distribution of species by habitat type. This knowledge is not based in written reports or books but rather in personal experience of a specific place with its specific birds. At Point Reyes Bird Observatory, where I served as education director, the scientific staff has been monitoring landbirds, shorebirds, and seabirds of central coastal California for 25 years. They have censused Bolinas Lagoon every month and know to the week when the western sandpipers will arrive and depart. They have banded all the wrentits and song sparrows in the coastal scrub and have tracked them from season to season. Every Christmas PRBO ornithologists and volunteer birdwatchers conduct a systematic bird count with other Audubon groups. Over the years they know more or less what birds to expect where—scaups and surf scoters at Drake's Bay, merlins and peregrine falcons at Bolinas Lagoon, ruby-crowned kinglets on Inverness Ridge (Evens, 1988). The cumulative on-the-ground knowledge of the over 150 bird species of the Point Reyes-West Marin area forms a basis for understanding the intricate patterns of these birds' lives. When counts are unusually low or rare species appear, these variations are noted against the backdrop of a broad picture.

A good field biologist pays attention at many different levels. To understand shorebird feeding patterns, one must be able to recognize individual species. To understand gull dominance hierarchies, one must be able to recognize individual birds. To understand life expectancies and causes of mortality, one must be able to monitor many individual birds of a species over their entire lives as well as track the health of the habitats they depend on. Further the biologist must be part of a community of attention that is observing the birds from various vantage points to put together composite pictures of their lives.

I believe in some ways, my mind was prepared for the rigors of Zen training by my experience as a naturalist in the field. I was taught to make careful notes of my observations in the Joseph Grinnell tradition and to scrutinize plant parts for field identification using Munz's *California Flora*. I trained myself to identify birds by their songs and trees by their silhouettes. I walked at night to develop sensory acuteness with my feet and ears. I cultivated a sense of place and pattern, first in the Santa Cruz hills and coast, and then in Marin County. The captivating joy of being with elegant columbines and silent owls quite easily and naturally taught me to pay attention. The reward was in the surprise of glimpsing the richness of the myriad lives all around me.

Zen training, however, is far more demanding than field biology. The realms of observation are infinite—from personal mental and physical habits to the nature of group dynamics, from family history to global consumption and production patterns. The point of mindfulness practice is to raise one's awareness of the *many* causative factors involved in any action and to develop the capacity to discriminate between them. Mindfulness is the heart of Buddhist meditation.

In the classic text, "Sutra on the Four Establishments of Mindfulness," the Buddha offers methods for cultivating mindfulness in four arenas: the body, the feelings, the mind, and the objects of mind (translation and commentary by Nhat Hanh, 1990). Each of these influences the way one perceives the natural world. To practice mindfulness of the body, one pays attention to the breath, the positions of the body, the actions of the body, the various body parts (one's stomach, liver, heart, etc.), and the eventual decomposition of the body as corpse. The last practice is a drill in impermanence, lest the observer assume a constancy in his or her perceptual faculties. Breath, posture, physical well-being all affect how alert one is to shape, pattern, and detail. Astute field observers, for example, develop a sixth sense for subtle cues in color or motion which can vary in accuracy depending on personal well-being or centeredness.

Mindfulness of feelings involves self-observation of pleasant, painful, and neutral feelings as they arrive and pass through the mind. These include feelings of discomfort or satisfaction with a physiological basis and feelings such as emotions and moods which may have a psychological basis. As in all mindfulness practice, the material for observation is endless. One practices identifying the feelings and sitting quietly and attentively as they arise, not shutting them out of the mind but learning to pay attention and not dwell on any particular mood as permanent. Almost all people, field biologists included, can recognize "gut level" feelings about different environments. One person may be terrified of the open spaces of the desert, another may be claustrophobic in the dark depths of a rainforest. The degree to which one is preoccupied with one's comfort or discomfort can distract from the capacity to observe the natural world with equanimity and full attention. Some of these feelings lie at the root of certain stereotypes which can prejudice people against the biological richness of a place. Because wetlands, for example, are squishy and unstable at low tide, walking with uncertain footing can be unpleasant; coping with muddy clothes may be a bother. Concern for one's own personal well-being can interfere with seeing a place for what it is.

Mindfulness of the mind and objects of mind are equally challenging practices. The Zen practicioner learns to recognize the Three Poisons—greed, hatred, and delusion—in their various manifestations as well as degrees of concentration, confusion, and habitual mental formations. One studies the five streams of form, feelings, perceptions, mental formations, and consciousness to see how the self is not permanent or autonomous but rather a temporary pattern in time and space (Nhat Hanh, 1990). It is in this realm of practice that one can observe how ideas and past experiences in nature shape how one perceives the natural world. Like a well trained scientist, the Buddhist student must go beyond oversimplified ideas to examine closely what actually exists. This is how John Muir challenged the reigning theories about the formation of Yosemite Valley by paying careful attention to boulder distribution, scree slopes, and hanging waterfalls. Against all criticism he suggested the evidence pointed to glacial carving and retreat.

In this time of environmental crisis and tremendous loss of biodiversity, many unexamined assumptions are driving human actions. Some cultural values are transmitted unconsciously from generation to generation—fear of snakes, hatred of wolves, eradication of weeds. Others such as those affiliated with consumerism take root very quickly in the media-saturated environment of today's world (Kanner and Gomes, 1995). I find now that my work lies more in developing social awareness of these hindrances than in carrying out biological field projects. I rely largely on my Zen training in mindfulness to illuminate values and attitudes behind environmental controversy or policy-making.

Looking back over twenty-five years of science and environmental education, I find that the main thing I have taught is how to pay attention. Whether it is paying attention to the plants themselves or to one's impact on the wilderness or one's prejudices towards certain landscapes—all of it is about looking closely and developing awareness. In many different circumstances I have seen people of all ages suddenly fall in love with a tree or bird, simply because they are paying attention and enjoying the fullness of that experience. I am convinced that this experience is at the heart of feeling concern for the well-being of a landscape or organism. When one perceives clearly, if even for a moment, the rich complexity and vitality of another being, one tastes the desire for its life to continue to unfold. This connection was obvious on whalewatching trips I led in Baja California. The crew would lower small motorboats into the lagoon and we would set off in search of sounding gray whales. The more curious females, sometimes with their calves, would approach and allow us to get quite close. Not infrequently the ardent whalewatchers could reach over the side and actually touch an impressive 50 foot giant! When they reboarded the ship raving about their encounters, it was as if they would never be the same again. I called this a "born again" nature conversion—the powerful remembering of what it is like to be completely attentive in the presence of another being (Kaza, 1983).

When I was education director at the U.C. Berkeley Botanical Garden, we used the practice of paying attention as a natural springboard for ethical response. We developed two programs based on conservation concerns—one on tropical forests, the other on California habitats. Both programs engaged participants in observing the features of plants native to each region. To illustrate the important role of pollinators in tropical ecosystems, we drew people's attention to flower shapes and insect foraging patterns. To demonstrate biogeographical distribution patterns, we pointed to the endemic natives of the California serpentine soils. Each program offered numerous opportunities to make direct contact with other life forms and to consider the threats facing these ecosystems. It was obvious to visitors that the chance of deeper engagement with the fascinating organisms would be much more limited in the future if habitat loss proceeded unchecked. We also participated in raising awareness about the role and presence of Strawberry Creek as a central feature of the Berkeley campus. Through an interpretive brochure, we traced the watercourse from the Garden to the Bay, showing how the creek had been altered and contained and where restoration efforts had slowed erosion and improved aquatic habitat. We wanted people to notice the creek and join in the effort to keep it vital and alive rather than forgotten and polluted.

Much of science today is taught through books, movies, or computers. All of these provide secondary interpretations, shaped by a team of editorial writers or photographers. From my Zen perspective, each of these are one or more steps removed from the commanding experience of paying attention directly to the organism or landscape and feeling the sensory impact of its presence. I personally take a strong stand on learning in the field and leaving the Discovery channel turned off. I am concerned that the heavy emphasis on text or screen-based learning builds cognitive skills but not necessarily perceptual skills (Bowers, 1995) . Movies too often convey a misleadingly condensed picture of a species or habitat. At the northern elephant seal breeding territory of Ano Nuevo State Reserve, I was astonished that visitors expected the behemoth seals to fight, mate, nurse, and squawk all in the half hour that they saw them. These are animals that sleep 20 hours a day if there is no disturbance. I finally realized that many people had seen nature specials on the elephant seals and were expecting their experience in nature to conform to the television!

Movies and computers both carry the disadvantage of absorbing one's attention visually by constant motion and change on the screen. They can perpetuate a kind of addiction to fast-paced peripheral change which is not at all characteristic of the natural world. Young people today are very prone to boredom because they are so used to highly distracting forms of entertainment and learning. They do not have much patience for the slow pace of the natural world. Observing a sleeping seal or a stalking heron takes time and a willingness to pay attention without the constant charge of adrenaline. Young people on extended field study programs can sometimes take several weeks to slow down enough to arrive and be able to actually see what is around them.

Paying attention directly with the body and mind offers a kind of intimacy that is not available through the screen or on paper. One tastes with one's own perceptual faculties the complex patterns of life as they have evolved over millions of years. Each direct encounter builds a richness of relationship that cannot be taken from the experiencer. As a Zen practitioner I have come to value this richness of relationship and intimacy as core to understanding my place in the world. I sometimes fear that science as a discipline removes people from the opportunity for relationship more often than it encourages it. I find I am drawn most to those fields of science which engage the full body-mind attention in relation to the natural world—field geology, field botany, conservation biology, restoration ecology. These seem to me to be the most supportive in cultivating what I understand to be the Buddhist approach to an attentive mind.

NO SEPARATE SELF

In Zen training the teachings and practices on the nature of the self challenge traditional western understandings in a radical way. European philosophy and Judeo-Christian ethical perspectives center on the notion of the individual as autonomous, impelled by will, and self-determined. Buddhist philosophy is built on the understanding and experience that the self is dependent on other phenomena and does *not* exist as an autonomous unit. The Buddha taught that an individual is nothing more than the five aggregates which comprise his or her temporary life shape: form, feelings, perceptions, thoughts, and consciousness. These accumulated patterns are like five dynamic streams passing through a point in time and space. Buddhist meditation instructions provide methods for observing these five streams and penetrating the delusion of a separate self. In this penetration, one tastes the profound nondualistic nature of reality. Temporarily freed of the delusion of an absolute self, one experiences the vast realm of causes and conditions that determine the many forms and events of the universe (Hongzhii, 1991). In this sense, one is not separate from the mountain, the waterfall, the bobcat. The experience of unity with the natural world generates a dramatic shift in orientation to the Other, whether in human or nonhuman form. No longer can it be seen as opposite, separate, or dualistically exclusive.

The Zen experience of nonduality challenges one of the most fundamental assumptions underlying western scientific method: that observer and observed exist independently and do not influence each other. It is in this context that I first began to question deeply some of the conclusions of manipulative studies of animals taken out of context. How could laboratory conditions ever duplicate the wild complexity of a natural habitat? How could Skinnerian behavior models fully explain an animal's response to food, light conditions, and other stimuli? The laboratory model assumes the animal's surroundings are more or less constant. In fact, every animal is responding continuously to changing conditions with a variety of adaptive behaviors. Some of these are easy to observe on a gross scale—Yosemite bears learning to climb food hanging ropes or peregrine falcons nesting under high rise building over-hangs. Other behaviors are inaccessible or only partially observable, since it is impossible to follow any organism in the wild through its entire life day and night.

The Zen perspective also led me to question how scientists could perform experiments on plants and animals which obviously caused suf-fering without acknowledging some concern for their subjects (Jordan, 1991). My high school biology students brought this to my attention rather forcefully during the standard frog dissection lab. For the first part of the lab, the students recorded their observations of behavioral patterns of the lively frogs hopping around in an aquarium. The next day they were to pithe the frogs and observe the internal anatomy, complete with beating heart and still reflexive muscles. Several students refused to pithe their frogs. In fact, they taunted me in the halls, calling me a "murderer"! They preferred their frogs alive rather than dead, and thought the frogs probably felt the same way. I ended up pithing a num-ber of frogs for those who were afraid they would bungle it. As for the outright rebels, I asked them to write statements of conscientious objec-tion to articulate their moral feelings. It was a turning point for me. My students convinced me that such death and cruelty were not necessary for their learning, and in fact, were detrimental to cultivating any sense of compassion, moral responsiblity, or oneness with these animals.

As my Zen training intensified, I came to see that no artifical barrier between self and other was tenable. This meant I could not kill a mos-quito, eat meat, cut firewood, or till soil without recognizing the full existence of other life forms as inseparable from my own. This did not mean I did not engage in these activities; it just meant I was no longer protected from my own suffering by the delusion of dualistic thinking. In part, this was responsible for my turning away from the "hardcore" aspects of manipulative biology. Field observation with minimal impact was acceptable, but more disturbance than that raised real questions. My religious training concerned itself with cultivating moral integrity based on nondualistic understanding of the self and other. How could I follow the prescribed methods of science if it meant going against my own moral integrity?

Some people who have had similar concerns have taken these to the animal rights movement, insisting on humane treatment of laborato-ry animals (Singer, 1990). While this has not been my path, I have been glad that the conversation has been raised and that universities now require more careful oversight of experiments involving live animals. For my part of the dialogue I have explored the conscious and unconscious barriers to nondualistic experience of the natural world that permeate everyday life in western culture. Among these are stereotyping, preferences, value judgments, and backgrounding (Kaza, 1995). My Zen training has been invaluable in its rigorous practices which illuminate inaccurate or delusional mental conditioning and holding to a self as separate and autonomous. Yet I am impressed that western social attitudes towards the natural world as alien other or objectified resource are so entrenched they are even present at western Buddhist retreat centers.

My primary work with the principle of "no separate self" is a collection of essays exploring "conversations" with trees (Kaza, 1993). In this writing I wanted to go beyond the usual barriers of difference to find some truthful meeting between person and tree. The work exposed many of the common mental habits which block nondualistic experience with the nonhuman world. While pattern recognition is helpful for spotting protected sites or food, stereotyping can distort or mislead. Though all blue oaks do have similar branching patterns and acorns, the distinct place, history, and context of each oak create quite different experiences between tree and person and for the tree itself. In the essays I wrote, a young Douglas fir forest gave me a sense of hope for the resilience of natural ecosystems; an old growth stand revealed the history of fear of forests as dangerous realms to be tamed and cleared. People also use stereotypes to lump species together, as in "the drooping majestic oak," thereby overlooking the ecological distinctions of distribution, genetic plasticity, and vulnerability to disease. In seeking out meritorious individuals for stories, I saw I wanted companions of stature to fit my own stereotyped images of the "big, old, and generous" tree.

Personal or cultural preference for certain trees or forests can also prevent full recognition of less preferred species. I found the rolling open bay-madrone woodlands of California to be much more alluring than the close-pressed thorny chaparral of the scrub oak. Often these preferences are based on the cultural value judgments of "good" or "bad." "Good" trees are those which provide slow-burning firewood, cool shade cover, or harvestable timber. "Bad" trees are harmful, messy or unpredictable, dropping leaves and limbs which clutter one's yard or damage one's home. Depending on one's perspective, a "good" tree can be seen as "bad" or "useless" and thereby justify the taking of its life. In Thailand, I was aghast to see beautiful slow-growing teak forests being cleared to plant foreign but fast-growing eucalyptus and pine as pre-ferred trees for the paper industry (Carrere and Lohmann, 1996).

For many people, trees are background scenery, a wash of green behind something else more important. The Other, in this case, then appears inessential or not worth noticing in any detail. This is demon-strated in the extreme in advertisements for cars which use the romantic image of a generic background forest to offset the shiny magnetism of a new expensive car. Hidden in the process of backgrounding is the denial of one's dependency on that very wash of green (Plumwood, 1993). In Maine the maintenance of such background scenery has been reduced to a narrow strip of trees along the wild and scenic rivers. Behind this is a moonscape of slash and broken soil, the paltry remains of a spruce for-est, now gobbled up for paper production (Lansky, 1992).

One extreme form of dualism which I feel has limited scientific analysis significantly is the emphasis on a reductionist approach. One organism or one chromosome is examined in great detail, generating explanations based primarily on the reduced part in isolation. This focus on the object independent of context conveys a dualistic split which does not reflect reality. Nuclear physicists have found this kind of isolation impossible, for nuclear particle behavior is strongly affected by the con-text of how particles are observed. Biologists who work with whole sys-tems gain greater insight into organisms as part of larger patterns (Capra, 1996). This analysis is certainly more complex, but from a Buddhist perspective it avoids the fundamental error of isolating one ele-ment from the rest as a separate existence.

In this area my Buddhist training has determined the kind of science I am willing to engage in. I can no longer handle plants and animals as inanimate objects entirely separate from my own existence. I far prefer to engage in scientific inquiry that is based on the assumption that we are all codependently existing and mutually affecting each other in many ways. This does not have to compromise the rigor of the investigation or analysis, but it does mean letting go of some of the habits of mind that perpetuate a human-centered perspective of the natural world.

THE LAW OF INTERDEPENDENCE

Ecology as a science has made its mark on the world by lifting up the central governing aspect of ecological systems: interdependence. Ecologists study biological relationships between flowers and pollinators, soils and trees, birds and food sources. Each small puzzle clue reveals a complex world in which organisms rely on each other in myriad ways. The nature of the relationships in total is what makes up a functioning ecosystem. Conservation biologists study what happens when relationships are damaged or destroyed within the system due to habitat loss, invasive species, or disturbance. Ecology has provided a rallying cry for environmentalists who intuitively sense that a systems approach is more inclusive and accurate in dealing with the natural world.

Buddhist philosophy likewise takes interdependence as its central tenet. A beautiful image of this comes from the Chinese Hua-Yen school of Buddhism (Cook, 1977). Imagine a fishnet shaped set of threads which stretch in all dimensions to the infinite corners of the world. At each crossing point in the net is a jewel with an infinite number of facets, each of which reflects all the other jewels in the web. This is Indra's Net, a metaphor for a universe in which all beings and events are interrelating and co-determining each other's existence. The core dynamic of the web is what flashes between the facets. It is the Buddhist student's task to understand the nature of these mutually causal relations from the particular perspective she holds in her position in the web. The Law of Interdependence is another way of stating that there is no separate self or independent existence, for each being and phenomena reflect all others.

The implications of interdependence for environmental work are profound. On the discouraging side one can imagine an infinite number of relationships, each endangered in some way by toxic wastes, urban sprawl, or ozone thinning. Ecological research has revealed important patterns of interdependence which are threatened by certain human activities. On the encouraging side, however, every action in the web counts. With conscious choice, people can become a positive, restorative force protecting seed stock or buffering creek erosion.

Buddhism has provided a philosophical grounding that perfectly complements and includes the ecological perspective of my science training. I no longer struggle with the Judeo-Christian biases of heaven vs.

earth or humans vs. nature. These oppositional categories never made intuitive sense to me and were not something I could find in my own personal experience with the natural world. Buddhism most explicitly includes *all* beings in the web of interdependence without claiming a hierarchical dominionistic role for human beings (Hunt-Badiner, 1990). This lines up with my understanding of evolution—that many beings evolved sophisticated relationships long before humans appeared, relationships that we were dependent on for our own evolution and existence. Doing science and practicing religion complement each other drawing on interdependence as the fundamental orientation to existence.

Buddhism, however, takes interdependence a step farther than ecology. This central law is also stated as co-dependent arising, or mutual causality, and part of this realm is the human mind. Thus human thoughts, habits, attitudes, values, and perceptions serve as agents in causing or influencing the behavior of other beings and events. For example, the perception of certain plants as "weeds" promotes the need for weed "killers" and thus an entire industry of chemical pesticides and the human health fallout from that. Or the perception that predators are "voracious" produces an aggressive campaign to eradicate wolves, coyotes, bobcats, and mountain lions in the west in the early twentieth century (Lopez, 1978).

My first glimpse of the usefulness of a Buddhist perspective in environmental problem analysis was in my doctoral research on the tuna-dolphin controversy (Kaza, 1979). I began with a thorough investigation of the biology of tuna schools and dolphin affiliations with these schools. This explained why it was effective for fishermen to throw large nets around dolphin groups to capture a tuna school. But it did not explain why the incidental killing of dolphins was so upsetting to the American public. For this I had to consider the aesthetic, kinesthetic, and emotional relationship between people and dolphins. To sort out the polarized finger-pointing between fishermen and environmentalists, I had to look at the role of stereotyping, the differences in short and long-term perspectives on ocean harvesting, and the economic and class distinctions between the two groups. It quickly became clear that the driving force behind the controversy was the conflict in values between the various parties.

Over time as I have studied one environmental problem after another, I realized that the tools of biology were inadequate to address the many complex factors of causality at work in each situation. For me, taking a Buddhist philosophical perspective had little to do with adding a religious overlay to what I could see. Rather, it meant bringing a commitment based in my spiritual practice, to look into every aspect of the problem and see what the primary determining causes were. Recently I evaluated the ethical tensions in the northern forest debate affecting the hardwood ecosystems of New York, Vermont, Maine, and the rest of New England (Kaza, 1994). Taking a neutral Indra's web perspective allowed me to look at the concerns of environmentalists and rural property owners, both caught in the rapidly advancing clearcutting machinery of corporate business.

This work introduced elements of class relations which I had not considered before. It became apparent that Indra's Web includes not only individual mental habits and values, but also underlying patterns of cultural relations with the environment. At about that time I became involved in helping students plan a student-taught course titled "Environmental Justice" which focused directly on these issues. The topics included discrimination in toxic waste dump siting, women's health issues and environmental hazards, people of color environmental groups, and prejudice in federal resource agencies. In another course I investigated patterns of domination which showed parallels between the treatment of women and the treatment of nature. Through the School of Natural Resources I helped with a new course on "Race and Culture in the Natural Resources," providing alternative perspectives to the traditional dominant views of the field. Engaging these perspectives offered a way to embrace a worldview based on interdependence.

What I see now is that cultural patterns of oppression play out through most realms of human endeavor, including science. Race, class, and gender bias can mutually reinforce each other in the justification for resource exploitation. For example, Perdue has many factory chicken farms in North Carolina where taxes and labor are inexpensive and environmental regulation lax. Most of the workers are lower class African-American women who stand all day in ice and blood and often become crippled with arthritis very early in their lives. Perdue makes a grand profit, but chickens and factory workers suffer.

I find my Buddhist orientation toward mutual causality best represented by the emerging fields of social anthropology or human ecology. I believe an interdisciplinary approach to environmental problems provides the strongest analysis and most astute insight into the various causes and conditions creating any particular situation. I have by now outgrown the limitations of any single discipline of science. It has become painfully clear to me that only a systems approach can account for the magnitude and entrenched nature of some of the most destructive patterns on the planet. In this I am completely aligned with my Buddhist training and I count it as an advantage (Macy, 1991).

THE PATH OF COMPASSION

Zen teachers speak of two pillars of practice which complement and guide each other. One is the path of wisdom, assisted by the realized spiritual being Manjusri who fiercely cuts through delusion in pursuit of truth. The other is the path of compassion, guided by Avalokitesvara, the bodhisattva or awakened being who hears the suffering of the world. In the Chinese tradition this realization of perfection is depicted in feminine form as Kuan Yin. Manjusri helps cultivate insight understanding based on experiential knowledge of the law of dependent co-arising. Avalokitesvara helps open the heart to respond to the pain and difficulties of all beings (Aitken, 1984).

In the world of science I find great encouragement for cutting through delusion in search of the truth. It is to me the most beautiful aspect about doing science. I admire the fire of passion burning in the eyes of those who are committed to this truth-seeking. Science teaches the art of asking questions and posing ideas that can be tested or investigated to see if they hold up to the test of on-the-ground data. I have always appreciated the collegiality among scientists in reviewing each other's work and offering critiques where appropriate. This sense of a community engaged in truth-seeking presents a powerful force for good in the larger society. However, as an idealist, I have been frustrated and disappointed by the degree to which competition and power relations have corrupted this fundamental truth-seeking in some aspects of science.

From my perspective as a Buddhist, what is missing from science training is the practice of compassion. The cultivation of compassion reinforces the insight of interdependence through a felt response to the plight of others. Compassion offers a direct experiential route to recognizing that the realities of birth, sickness, old age, and death will come to all beings. The Buddhist sense of compassion is distinct from a western notion of empathy or even pity. Literally, the roots of the word compassion mean "to suffer with." The path of compassion invites one to suffer with the existence of suffering—poverty, violence, epidemics, natural disasters—the list is endless (Eppsteiner, 1985).

Some Western critics of Buddhism find the recognition of suffering depressing or gloomy. In contrast to the Christian traditions which hold up the joy of the heavenly reward, Buddhism is much more realistic and grounded. The practice of compassion is itself a joyful antidote to suffering. The first teaching of the Buddha directly addressed the existence of suffering in the Four Noble Truths as a path to enlightenment (Habito, 1993). The first truth is that suffering exists. It is important to recognize here that the Buddha did not emphasize individual suffering, i.e. your suffering or my suffering, but just the existence of suffering in general. If one is caught in the particular pain of one's own suffering, it becomes yet another form of self-centeredness, preventing one from seeing the interdependent whole. Scientists, for example, suffer from grant rejections and the exhaustion of competitive striving, often taking their losses personally rather than as an indication of an overstretched system.

The second Noble Truth is that the cause of suffering lies in grasping or clinging to the delusion of a separate self. This delusion manifests itself in attachment to personal desires and preferences, in protective defenses that promote the individual ego, and in the denial of the existence of others upon whom one depends. The cultivation of compassion helps to mitigate against this natural human tendency to be absorbed in one's own small world.

The Third Noble Truth is that there can be liberation from suffering, that right in the midst of delusion, one can find the spaciousness of enlightenment. The Fourth Noble Truth offers the Eight-fold Path as a method to achieve enlightenment and thereby be free of suffering. One of the eight is Right Livelihood, or choosing a vocation which cultivates compassion. I see now that I have chosen a life of teaching because of my desire to cultivate compassion for myself and in my students. While it is true that some scientists make a point to speak out about the results of their research and engage public concern (Rachel Carson, Paul Ehrlich, Michael Soule, among others), many do not. There seems to be a vague assumption that anything to do with ethics or moral response is taught in other departments.

From a Buddhist perspective, this is not adequate. Doing scientific work without compassion too easily leads to objectification of research subjects, whether plants, animals, people, or landscapes. In some cases, experimental actions which induce suffering are rationalized as necessary. Witness the horrendous liberties taken in testing the first nuclear bombs. No warnings were given; no protective measures were taken for the nearby populace, and now the many resulting cases of leukemia and other cancers are coming to light. This, in my mind, is unconscious and unconscienable science, a not unexpected result of a training which omits compassion. Similar arguments are being advanced today on behalf of genetic engineering experiments. Release of genetically modified organisms is said to be necessary in order to advance to the next phase of production. In the haste for scientific and technological reward, very little attention is given to the possible suffering of other lives.

I find myself most at home in the field of Environmental Studies, where all the teaching—in economics, ethics, policy, and ecology—is motivated by a genuine concern for the well-being of the earth and its life forms. Compassion is a natural motivator for learning; our students want to know how to protect and sustain the life of beloved places. They want to understand the impacts on the southern countries of rapacious consumption in the North. They want to be engaged in campus ecology issues, to move institutional policy towards environmentally aware choices.

One of the most difficult things for young people and many others as well, is to accept the grief, rage, fear, and sorrow they experience in waking up to the state of the environment (Macy, 1983). In my own teaching I try to work with these states of mind as natural responses to the suffering of other beings. I do not want to protect students from their feelings, for I sense that this receptive place is where compassion arises. I want to offer practices that will help sustain students under the pressures of increasing environmental deterioration. I do not want them to drop out and give up because of an overwhelming sense of discouragement. They must function in a world in which many people in power are operating in almost total denial about the state of the environment. The practice of compassion keeps the heart open and willing to work with others.

I recently was asked to consult with the U.S. Forest Service on a project which promotes compassion in its own way. Staff of the south-west regional office were facing conflicts generated from native American spiritual use of the public forest lands. Rather than avoid the complex issues of multiple use, the Forest Service convened a gathering to investigate the role of spiritual and religious values in public lands management. Discussion ranged widely and many different points of view were represented. We were not aiming to solve specific conflicts, but to broaden the conversation beyond its previously limited resource-oriented base. I prepared research on the world's major religions and their attitudes and practices towards the natural world. Others developed commentary on sense of place, native American perspectives, types of research needed, and the role of federal management agencies. The gatherings, and the book which resulted (Driver et al, 1996), served to stimulate new depths of understanding in territory which is rife with moral dilemmas.

It has occurred to me that it would be illuminating to revise the standard scientific environmental impact statement format to describe a project in terms of the suffering it would cause. One could list the organisms and ecosystems that would suffer and how they would suffer in particular—death, disturbance, loss of reproductive faculties, population reduction, etc. One could then parallel this list with an analysis of the human parties that would suffer and what form their suffering would take. This could include economic impact but also psychological and spiritual impact. Suffering takes many forms but only a few of these are recorded on environmental impact statements. A more complete accounting would satisfy my Buddhist interest in considering compassion for all beings.

BRINGING SCIENCE TO THE TEMPLE

In reviewing my own journey through the two worlds of science and Buddhism, especially as they intersect in environmental studies, I have found more opportunities to explore the influence of Buddhism on science than vice versa. I carry a Buddhist perspective with me to the various realms of environmental policy and ethics I encounter and use this perspective to find ways to broaden the conversation. I prefer to translate this perspective into modes appropriate for each situation, what Buddhists would call using *upaya* or skillful means. I never introduce Buddhist concepts with an eye to converting or convincing anyone that these are the right or best approaches. But I take my commitment to the practice seriously and call upon it where it can be helpful. In this regard, I am one of a growing number of people practicing "socially-engaged Buddhism"—taking the practice off the meditation cushion and into the street to make some difference in the world (Kraft, 1994).

In contrast, it seems a greater challenge to me to bring a scientific perspective to the Buddhist community. My experience in this area is limited primarily to my home temple in northern California, Green Gulch Zen Center, where I lived for three years. In addition to the Zen practice area the center includes a 12 acre organic farm and flower garden. In the neighboring valley lies Muir Woods, the last remaining fragment of old growth redwoods close to San Francisco. Because the center is still young, less than 25 years old, it has been concerned primarily with establishing the meditation practice and hosting the community of interested practitioners. Stewardship for the land has rested primarily in the hands and minds of the head gardener and farm manager.

Since Buddhism takes a fundamentally nonviolent approach to other forms of life, the place has benefitted from a certain degree of benign neglect outside the intensively cared for farm and garden fields. Sparrows and finches have settled the brushy areas in great numbers and frogs have taken over the zendo pond. A pair of great horned owls have kept company in the valley for more than ten years, and red foxes and raccoons regularly patrol the large compost piles. The path of noninterference has allowed the land to recover from thirty years of cattle grazing and pesticide spraying on the hillsides to promote pasturage. To the extent that science has played a role in managing the Green Gulch lands, it has been in the development of beautiful organic agricultural soil. Through careful attention to cover crops, compost building, and soil amendments, the farm and garden staff have built a rich moist dark soil which supports squash, beets, potatoes, chard, kale, and ten kinds of lettuce.

Over the years there have been various efforts to take responsibility for managing the noncultivated areas of the valley. The most consistently successful work has been tree-planting: first to provide windbreaks and reduce soil erosion in the fields, then to begin to recover some of the forested areas which were depleted after the great San Francisco earthquake. Arbor Days have been conducted annually since 1975 with great enthusiasm but relatively little ecological guidance.

During my active years there we produced a set of recommendations for returning the valley to environmental health. These included removing non-native plants, establishing oak and redwood groves, opening the creek channel, and protecting bird nesting and watering spots. From a naturalist's perspective, it was easy to see how with a few gestures in the right places, Green Gulch would become a rich haven of biodiversity along the northern California coast.

But these things take time and commitment from more than one or two staff members. The most positive encouragement has come from staff at nearby Muir Woods who are promoting native plant propagation and restoration projects. Working together as good neighbors, the head gardener at Green Gulch and the head ranger at Muir Woods have helped each other move forward with habitat restoration. Beyond those at Green Gulch with a specific interest in environmental matters, however, the institution as a whole has not been very receptive to ecological advice nor committed to long-range planning in this arena.

I include this piece of the Buddhism-science dialogue in my life to show there is still plenty of opportunity for good work here. Though Buddhist philosophy and practice are most compatible with an ecological perspective, it is not necessarily true that all Buddhists are ecologically informed or committed. In fact, very few are. As in many communities or church groups, a few people will take the initiative to influence others to act in an ecologically responsible way. How many scientists bring the gift of their knowledge to their churches or temples? This process is still just beginning in the American Buddhist community, but I have great hopes that it will yet flower in the centers with direct responsibility for the land.

I believe that engaging in ecological restoration can generate personal and community spiritual restoration. The more opportunities we create for this, the more we can actually find practical and meaningful ways to live in nonviolent and conscious relationship with the land. This is my great motivation in exploring the relationship of science and Buddhism. The outcomes of such exploration may have very significant consequence for the health of human life and the land. It is my hope that the work we do together across these fields of endeavor will serve to relieve the suffering and promote the well-being of the world's myriad beings and places.

LITERATURE CITED

Aitken, Robert. 1984. *The Mind of Clover*. San Francisco: North Point Press.

Bowers, C. A. 1995. *Educating for an Ecologically Sustainable Culture*. Albany, NY: State University of New York Press.

Capra, Fritjof. 1996. *The Web of Life*. New York: Doubleday.

Carrere Ricardo and Larry Lohmann. 1996. *Pulping the South: Industrial Tree Plantations and the World Paper Economy*. London: Zed Books Ltd.

Cook, Francis H. 1977. *Hua-Yen Buddhism: the Jewel Net of Indra*. University Park, PA: Pennsylvania University Press.

Driver, B.L., Daniel Dustin, Tony Baltic, Gary Elsner, George Peterson, eds. 1996. *Nature and the Human Spirit: Toward an Expanded Land Management Ethics*. U.S. Forest Service: Venture Publishing.

Eppsteiner, Fred, ed. 1985. *The Path of Compassion: Contemporary Writings on Engaged Buddhism*, Berkeley: Parallax Press.

Evens, Jules G. 1988. *The Natural History of the Point Reyes Peninsula*. Point Reyes, CA: Point Reyes National Seashore Association.

Habito, Ruben. 1993. *Healing Breath: Zen Spirituality for a Wounded Earth*. Maryknoll, New York: Orbis Books.

Hongzhii, translated by Teigen Daniel Leighton with Yi Wu. 1991. *Cultivating the Empty Field*. San Francisco: North Point Press.

Hunt-Badiner, Alan, ed. 1990. *Dharma Gaia*, Berkeley: Parallax Press.

Jordan, William. 1991. "Pictures at a Scientific Exhibition" in *Divorce Among the Gulls*. New York: HarperCollins, pp 187–205.

Kanner, Allen D. and Mary E. Gomes. 1995. "The All-Consuming Self" in *Ecopsychology*, ed. Theodore Roszak, San Francisco: Sierra Club Books, pp 77–91.

Kaza, Stephanie. 1995. Mistaken Impressions of the Natural World, *Whole Terrain: Reflective Environmental Practice*, vol. 4:5–11.

_____. 1994. Ethical Tensions in the Northern Forests, in *The Future of the Northern Forest*, eds. Steven Trombulak and Christopher McGrory-Klyza, Hanover, New Hampshire: University Press of New England, pp 71–87.

_____. 1993. *The Attentive Heart: Conversations with Trees*. New York: Ballantine.

_____. 1983. Biophyllic Values in Cetacean Education. Working paper WA/SP/A2 for Whales Alive Conference, Boston, Massachusetts.

_____. 1979. Ph.D. A Systems Approach to Resource Management in Marine Mammals-Fisheries Conflicts.

Kraft, Kenneth. 1994. "The Greening of Buddhist Practice," *Cross Currents*, Spring 88–114.

Lansky, Mitch. 1992. *Beyond the Beauty Strip*. Gardiner, Maine: Tilbury House Publications.

Lopez, Barry Holstum. 1978. *Of Wolves and Men*. New York: Charles Scribner's Sons.

Macy, Joanna. 1991. *Mutual Causality in Buddhism and General Systems Theory*. Albany, NY: State University of New York Press.

_____. 1983. *Despair and Personal Power in the Nuclear Age*. Philadelphia: New Society Publishers.

Nhat Hanh, Thich. 1990. *Transformation and Healing: Sutra on the Four Establishments of Mindfulness*. Berkeley: Parallax Press.

Plumwood, Val. 1993. *Feminism and the Mastery of Nature*. New York: Routledge.

Singer, Peter. 1990. *Animal Liberation*. New York: Avon.

The Return to
Natural Philosophy

E.O. Wilson, PhD

I've chosen to speak today on the subject of natural religion. What I have in mind is a blend of scientific insight and personal conviction. I'll emphasize the word "personal." Albert Camus once said that all of a man's creative life consists of the recapture through the circuitous routes of art those two or three images in the presence of which his soul first opened.

In the end those wellsprings may dwindle, or they may be renewed by freshets from another source. But the integrity of mind depends on them; a body of work is to be judged by the coherence and the effectiveness by which they confront and make honest use of experience.

My truths, then, three in number, are the following: first, humanity is ultimately the product of biological evolution; second, the diversity of life is the cradle and greatest natural heritage of the human species; and, third, philosophy and religion make no sense without taking account of these first two images.

I spoke of coherence, which brings me directly to the subject of natural philosophy. I'm sure that the phrase "natural philosophy" can be taken many ways, and perhaps its scholarly examination is best left in the wise ministrations of scholars in 19th century intellectual history. But I'm reminded that the rosette of the United States National Academy of Sciences ... is the gold of science set on the purple of natural philosophy. I find something enchanting about that arrangement, something that touches the mystic chords of history while implying a richer future for science—and for philosophy.

Natural philosophy, as I understand it, encompassed in the early 19th century what we now call all of science, plus biblical criticism, but most importantly anything that touched on the natural world. Before the word "science" came into use in the mid-1800s there were chairs of natural philosophy in the universities. Then science split off as an intellectual activity, and the distinction was made, as Bertrand Russell later brutally put it, between science as that which we know and philosophy as that which we do not know. Religion, and ethics, and all the activities of consciousness and culture fell away, now outside scientific inquiry, thought to be untestable and far beyond the reach of intercoherence with the most successful enterprises of science.

But science has grown immensely; scientific knowledge doubles every ten to fifteen years. Science has come back to the examination of consciousness, culture, and even of ethics and religion. There is a growing sense that the two disparate cultures may yet remarry, in ways that transform both. What, then, does the future hold?

To start, I believe the time has come for a restoration of natural law to a central position in philosophy and moral reasoning. In 1986 I was one of four scientists invited by the Committee on Human Values of the Roman Catholic bishops of the United States to join them and a group of Catholic scholars to discuss this and other issues concerning the relation between science and religion. Like Freeman Dyson, a physicist, and Roger Sperry, a neurobiologist, who were also there, I represented a naturalistic, strongly humanistic view of the human condition.

The meeting was very congenial and covered most of the key subjects from birth control to free will—abortion was avoided, however—and I came away with a feeling that there is a convergence of interest on natural law, despite our very strong differences on the metaphysical foundation of moral precepts.

Natural law, as I understand its original version, is, first, that set of principles and guides to action that is universally grasped, second, innate in mankind, third, accepted by any rational person, and fourth, and here we run into the divergence of science and religion, either supernatural or transcendental in origin.

At the Cologne Cathedral in 1980, as I took note at the conference of bishops, John Paul II said that science has added "wings to the spirit of modern awareness." Yet that doesn't threaten the core of religious belief:

> "We have no fear, indeed we regard it as excluded that a branch of science or branch of knowledge, based on reason and proceeding methodically and securely, can arrive at knowledge that comes into conflict with the truth of faith. This can be the case only where the differentiation between the orders of knowledge is overlooked or denied."

That last sentence of His Holiness, reaffirming Augustine's two books of God, takes us to the heart of the real dialogue between religion and science. Although many theologians and lay philosophers like to deny it, I believe that traditional religious belief and scientific knowledge depict the universe in radically different ways, that at bedrock they are incompatible and mutually exclusive. The materialist (or "humanist," or "naturalistic") position can be put in a phrase: there is only one book, and it was written in a manner too strange and subtle to be foretold by the prophets and church fathers.

But there is another side to the story, one that makes the contrast in worldviews still more interesting. The materialist position presupposes no final answers. It is an undeniable fact that faith is in our bones, that religious belief is a part of human nature and seemingly vital to social existence. Take away one faith, and another rushes in to fill the void. Take away that, and some secular equivalent such as Marxism intrudes, complete with sacred texts and icons. Take away all these faiths and rely wholly on scepticism and personal inquiry—if you can—and the fabric of society would likely start to unravel. This phenomenon, so strange and subtle as to daunt materialist explanation, is in my opinion the most promising focus for a dialogue between theologians and scientists.

From the beginnings of Greek philosophy there has always been a great divide and thought about the meaning of life. Humanity is faced with a choice between two metaphysics, two differing views of how the world works from the top down and hence, the ultimate means for the selection of moral codes. The first view holds that morality is transcendental in origin and exists both within and apart from the human species. Moral precepts are like the theorems of mathematics. This doctrine has been refined within the Catholic church by the conception of natural law, which is the reading of the eternal law in God's mind: people reason out God's intent through a reflection of human nature, obedient to the principle that, as Aquinas expressed it, "Man has a natural inclination to know the truth about God and to live in society." The opposing view, the naturalistic view, is that morality is entirely a human phenomenon. In the modern, evolutionary version of this materialist philosophy, its precepts are not fixed in the stars but represent the upwelling of deep impulses that are encoded in our genes and find expression within the setting of particular cultures. They have nothing directly to do with divine guidance, at least not in the manner conceived by traditional religions.

I could well be wrong (and in any case I don't speak for all scientists), but I believe that the correct metaphysic is the materialist one. It works in the following way. Our profound impulses are rooted in a genetic heritage common to the entire species. They arose by evolution through natural selection over a period of tens or hundreds of thousands of years. These propensities provide survival for individuals and for the social groups on which personal survival depends. They're transmuted through rational process and the formation of culture into specific moral codes, which are integrated into religion and the sacralized memories of revolutions, conquests, and other historical events by which cultures secured their survival. Although variations in the final codes are inevitable, different societies share a great deal in their perception of right and wrong. By making the search for these similarities part of the scientific enterprise, and taking religious behavior very seriously as a key part of genetically evolved human nature, a tighter consensus of ethical behavior might be reached.

It will be useful to insert here a very brief account of evolution by natural selection. Genetic variation among individuals in a population of the same species, say a population of human beings, arises by mutations, which are random changes in the chemical composition and relative positions of genes. Of the thousands of mutations that typically occur throughout a population in each generation, all but a minute fraction are either neutral in effect or deleterious to some degree; they include, for example, the altered genes that cause hypercholesterolemia, hemophilia, and Tay-Sachs disease and the abnormally duplicated chromosomes responsible for Down's syndrome. When a new mutant (or a new combination of rare preexisting genes) happens to be superior to the ordinary, "normal" genes, they tend to spread through the population over a period of many generations and hence to become by definition the new genetic norm. If human beings were to move into a new environment that somehow gave hemophiliacs a survival and reproductive advantage over non-hemophiliacs, then in time hemophilia would predominate in the population and be regarded as the norm, and ordinary hemoglobin as the disease.

Two features of evolution by natural selection conspire to give it extraordinary creative potential. The first is the driving power of mutations. All populations are subject to a continuous rein of new genetic types that test the old. The second feature is the ability of natural selection to create immensely complicated new structures and physiological processes, including new patterns of behavior, with no blueprint and no force behind them other than the selection process itself. This is a key point missed by creationists and other critics of evolutionary theory, who often argue that the probability of assembling an eye or a hand (or life itself) by genetic mutations is infinitesimally small—in effect, impossible. But the following thought experiment shows that the opposite is true. Suppose that a new trait emerges if two new gene forms (mutations), which I'll call A and B, occur simultaneously. The chances of A occurring are one in a million, and the chances of B occurring are also one in a million. Then the chances of both A and B occurring simultaneously as mutants are one in a million million or one in a trillion, a near impossibility—as the critics intuited. However, natural selection short circuits this process in a dramatic fashion. If A has even a slight advantage by itself alone, it will become the dominant gene at its position. Now the chances of AB appearing is one in a million. In even moderately sized species of plants and animals (which often contain more than a million individuals) the change over to AB is a virtual certainty.

This very simple picture of evolution at the level of the gene has altered our conception of both the nature of life and man's place in nature. Before Darwin it was customary to use the great complexity of living organisms *per se* as proof of the existence of God. The most famous expositor of this "Argument from Design" was the Reverend William Paley, who in 1802 introduced the watchmaker analogy; the existence of a watch implies the existence of a watchmaker. In other words, great effects imply great causes. Common sense would seem to dictate the truth of this deduction, but common sense, as Einstein once noted, is only our accumulated experience up to the age of eighteen. Common sense tells us that one-ton satellites can't hang suspended above a point on the earth's surface, but they do.

So, given the combination of mutation and natural selection, the biological equivalent of watches can be created without a watchmaker. But did blind natural selection also lead to the human mind, including moral behavior and spirituality? That is the grandmother of questions in both biology and the humanities. Common sense would seem at first to dictate the answer to be no. But I and many other scientists, and especially evolutionary biologists, believe that the answer may be yes. Furthermore, it may be possible by this means to explain the very meaning of human life.

The key proposition based on evolutionary biology is the following: everything human, including the mind and culture, has a material basis and originated during the evolution of the human genetic constitution and its interaction with the environment. To say this much is not to deny the great creative power of culture, or to minimize the fate that most causes of human thought and behavior are still poorly understood. The important point is that modern biology can already account for many of the unique properties of our species. Research on that subject is accelerating, quickly, enough to lend plausibility to the proposition that more complex forms of social behavior, including religious belief and moral reasoning, will eventually be understood to their foundations.

A case in point useful for its simplicity and tractability is the avoidance of brother-sister incest. This is a phenomenon on which it may be possible to pivot a lot of analysis in natural law and ethics, if the factual basis holds up. In order to avoid misunderstanding, let me define incest as strong sexual bonding among close biological relatives that includes intercourse, of the kind generally associated with cohabitation and procreation, and excludes transient forms of adolescent experimentation. Incest taboos are very nearly universal as a cultural norm. The avoidance of brother-sister incest originates in what psychologists have called prepared learning. This means that people are innately prone to learn one alternative as opposed to another. They pick it up more readily, they enjoy it more, or both. The avoidance of sibling incest comes from the "potty rule" in mental development: individuals reared in close domestic proximity during the first six years of life (they share the same potty) are automatically inhibited from strong sexual attraction and bonding when they reach sexual maturity. The rule works even when the children reared together are biologically unrelated and later encouraged to marry and have children, as in the Israel kibbutzim and traditional minor marriages of prerevolutionary China. Those affected are usually quite unable to offer a rational explanation of why they have no attraction. Some unconscious process ticked over in the brain, and the urge, they explain, never came.

The inhibitory rule is an example not only of prepared learning but also of "proximate causation" as it is understood by evolutionary biologists. This means that learning is channeled in such a way as to create a response of importance to the survival or reproduction of the organism. Proximate causes are put into place by the assembly of genes through the process of natural selection. The ultimate causation, in other words the particular selection regime that enabled certain genes to predominate in the first place, is the well-documented effect of inbreeding depression. When mating occurs between brother and sister, father and daughter, or mother and son, the probability of matching debilitating genes in both homologous chromosomes of the offspring is greatly increased. The end result is a rise in spontaneous abortion, physical defects, and genetic disease. Hence genes prescribing a biological propensity to avoid incest will be favored over those that do not. Most animal and plant species display proximate devices of one kind of another, and it does indeed protect them from inbreeding depression. In some the response is rigidly determined. In others, especially the brighter mammals, it is based on prepared learning. Interestingly enough, the human proximate form of incest avoidance is nearly identical to that of the chimpanzee, the species to which we are most closely related genetically.

It is exquisitely human to semanticize innate tendencies. In many societies incest avoidance is underwritten by symbolically transmitted taboos, myths, and laws. These, not the emotions and programs of prepared learning, are the values we perceive by direct, casual observation. They are easily transmitted from one person to the next, and they are the behaviors most readily studied by scholars. But the phenomenon of greatest interest is the etiology of the moral behavior: that is, the chain of events leading from ultimate cause in natural selection to proximate cause in prepared learning to reification and legitimation in culture. Genes to brain to learning to choice to culture. If the terminal cultural form were somehow to be stripped away by a collective loss of memory, people would still avoid sibling incest. Given enough time, they would most likely invent religious and ethical rationalizations to justify their feelings about the wrongness of incest.

Crude genetic determinism has no part in this process. The existence of the three-step etiology in mental development, genes to learning rules to culture, in no way contradicts free will. Individual choice persists even when learning is strongly prepared by heredity. If some future society decides to encourage brother-sister incest, for whatever bizarre and unlikely reason, it now has the knowledge to do so efficiently. The possibility, however, is vanishingly remote, because the same knowledge tells us that incest avoidance is programmed as a powerful rule and protects families from genetic damage. We are likely to agree still more firmly than before that the avoidance is a part of human nature to be fostered. In short, and this is good news for scientist and theologian alike, incest avoidance is and will continue to be one of our common values. It is, if I may use the expression, part of natural law.

It will immediately occur to you that incest avoidance might be no more than a special case in the evolution of social behavior. A vast difference you're saying to yourself, separates this relatively simple phenomenon from economic cycles, religious rites, and presidential elections. Might such particularities fall within a wholly different domain of explanation and require a different metaethic? Perhaps, but I don't think so.

But to come quickly to the point that most troubles critics of evolutionary ethics, and indeed the whole of scientific materialism, it doesn't follow that the genetic programs of cognition and prepared learning are automatically beneficial even in a crude Darwinian sense. Behaviors such as xenophobia and territorial expansion may have been very adaptive in the earlier, formative stages of human evolutionary history, but they are destructive now even for those who practice them. Although the cultural "ought" is more tightly linked to the genetic "is" than philosophers have traditionally conceded, the two do not automatically translate one into the other. A workable moral code can be obtained not just by understanding the foundations of human nature, but by the wise choice of those constraints needed to keep us alive and free in a rapidly changing cultural environment that renders some of our propensities maladaptive.

Let me illustrate this approach to moral reasoning by taking an example that has proved especially troublesome to the Roman Catholic church. In *Humanae Vitae*, Paul VI used the best interpretation concerning Human nature available to him to proscribe artificial birth control and to protect the family. He said, in effect, that you should not prevent conception when having sex because that is what sex is for, and as such reflects the will of God: he said, "To use this divine gift destroying, even if only partially, its meaning and its purpose is to contradict the nature both of man and of woman and of their most intimate relationship, and therefore, it is to contradict also the plan of God and his will." In other words, Paul VI used an argument from natural law.

I believe that there is a way out of the impasse that this strict argument from natural law has created. All that we have learned of human biology in recent years suggests that the perception of human nature expressed by Paul VI was incomplete. A second major function of sexual intercourse, one evolved over vast periods of time, is the bonding of couples in a manner that enhances the long-term care of children. Only a minute fraction of sexual acts can result in conception, but virtually all can tighten the conjugal bond. Many circumstances can be imagined, and in fact exist, in which family planning by artificial birth control leads to an improvement of the bonding function while promoting the rearing of healthy, secure children.

If this more recent and better substantiated view of human sexuality is accepted, a revision of *Humanae Vitae* could easily be written that accomplishes the main purpose of Paul VI and the modern Church, permits artificial birth control, and in fact serves as a model of the utilization of scientific findings by religious thinkers.

I'm now going to present a radical suggestion: the choice among the foundations of moral reasoning is not likely to remain arbitrary. Metaethics can be tested empirically. One system of ethics and hence one kind of religion is not as good as another. Not only are some less workable, they are in the profoundest sense less human. The corollary is that people can be educated readily only to a narrow range of ethical precepts. This leaves a choice between evolutionary ethics and transcendentalism. The idea of a genetic origin of moral codes can be further tested by a continuance of biological studies of complex human behavior, including religious thought itself. To the extent that the sensory system and nervous system appear to have evolved by natural selection or some other purely natural process, the evolutionary interpretation will be supported. To the extent that they do not appear to have evolved in a manner congenial to modern evolutionary biology, or to the extent that complex human behavior cannot be linked to a physical basis in the sensory and nervous systems, the evolutionary explanation will have to be abandoned and a transcendental explanation sought.

Which position, scientific materialism or religious transcendentalism, proves correct will eventually make a very great difference in how humanity views itself and plans its future. But for the years immediately ahead, this distinction makes little difference if the following overriding fact is realized. Human nature is at the very least far more a product of self-contained evolution than ordinarily conceded by philosophers and theologians. On the other hand, religious thought is far richer and more subtle than present-day science can explain, and too important to abandon. Meanwhile the areas of common concern are vast, and the two enterprises can converge in most of the areas of practical moral reasoning at the same time that their practitioners disagree about the ultimate causes of human nature. They can, in fact, reach a partial consensus on the meaning of natural law. They can play together on the broad fields of culture this side of transcendence.

What then, is the best relation between religion and science toward which we might aim? I would say, an uneasy but fruitful alliance. The role of religion is to codify and put into enduring, poetic form the highest moral values of a society consistent with empirical knowledge, and to lead in moral reasoning. The role of science is to test every conclusion about human nature remorselessly and to search for the bedrock of ethics—by which I mean the material basis of natural law.
Science faces in religion its most interesting challenge, while religion will find in science the necessary tools to retain moral leadership in the modern age.

I'm going to close by exiting through the arena of my greatest passion of all, and one that can and should be one of those intermediate common grounds of moral reasoning between science and religion just noted. I speak of the second image with which I opened this lecture, the stewardship of the living environment.

Those who care about the long-term welfare of the human body and spirit will be wise to turn more of their attention to the ongoing process of species extinction. The accelerating destruction of tropical forests alone, which is proceeding at the rate of about 140,000 square kilometers a year equal to the state of Florida-is eliminating biological diversity wholesale. Conservatively estimated, the present destruction continued during the next several decades will result in the loss of over one-quarter of the species of plants and animals on Earth. The reason is that although tropical forests cover only six percent of the land surface, they contain more than half the species of the world. Other major habitats, including coral reefs, are declining as well. The average life span of a species and its evolutionary descendants in the geological past has been one to ten million years. This means that during an average human lifetime humanity will eliminate a large part of a heritage older than the human species. In a word, we are destroying the Creation. The decline occurring right now is the greatest since the age of dinosaurs 66 million years ago. The potential value of these doomed species is incalculable, as sources of pharmaceuticals, new agricultural crops, petroleum substitutes, nitrogen fixers, recreation, aesthetic pleasure, and surely most important of all, that deep and uniquely human spiritual strength that comes from witnessing the Earth as it was before the coming of man. Fewer than ten percent of the species of organisms even have a scientific name. They are going, like the dead of Grey's elegy, leaving their nature unsung, their genius unused.

In conclusion, science and religion, more precisely contemporary scientists and religious thinkers, may not easily arrive at a single metaphysical understanding of how the world works. But they can find a common middle ground in addressing the malign qualities of human nature and of the consequent long-term threats to human welfare. Environmental consciousness, leading to a careful stewardship of the living world, is an immediately urgent testing ground of that basic proposition.

From remarks presented in the 1991-92 Dudleian Lecture at Harvard University. Published with permission.

Science, Ethics and Praxis:
Getting it All Together

Calvin De Witt, PhD

It was late evening and some students approached me with a question. They had heard my lecture earlier that day at the symposium on *God, the Environment, and the Good Life* at the University of New Hampshire. "How do you as a scientist, a student of the Scriptures, and someone directly involved in town politics, put it all together?" We moved to a table, talking. I reached for a napkin on which I sketched a triangle.

SCIENCE AND ETHICS

Since my youth I have kept my science and theology together. The main reason was that, in the Reformed Tradition, I had not only learned that study of science and theology was respectable and legitimate, but also that science and our religious faith were compatible. Science was esteemed, as were the arts, politics, and the trades. Also esteemed was our "rule of faith and practice" —the Bible—and the theological research and scholarship that enriched our understanding of Scripture. Integrity was the mark of both the Creation and the Word, and also of the relation between them, the reason being that both shared the same Author—the Author who was persistently just and perpetually consistent.

In my youth I learned that there is great concordance between the world of nature and the Bible—the two great books enjoyed by my culture. How the natural world works (studied by science) was in accord with what is right (studied by theology and illuminated by the Bible). And so for these students, I wrote "Science" at one corner of my triangle, and "Ethics" at another. Parenthetically, under "Science" I added the explanatory question, "(How does the world work?)," and under "Ethics," "(What is right?)."

As a child I developed a deep interest in reptiles—an interest that continued through my teens and on into my graduate studies. And it was from experience gained while researching the physiology and behavior of reptiles on the desert of southern California that the label I would now write for the third point of the triangle began to emerge. I was doing my work for my doctorate in zoology at The University of Michigan which brought me to the desert in search of my subject, the Desert Iguana. It was on the desert that I learned something about our species that previously had not struck me: we have immense capacity for taking action on things and in areas we know next to nothing about. Uninformed by science and ethics, or even eschewing scientific and ethical knowledge, we can and do act upon the world in ways that have great consequence, and often do so not only in ignorance, but also in cultured ignorance.

I had selected a site for study of the environmental physiology of Desert Iguanas on the alluvial fan at the mouth of Deep Canyon—a dry river delta—several miles to the east of Palm Springs. Once in a century or so, this canyon would discharge floodwaters from torrential rains in the San Jacinto Mountains, spouting them onto this delta which fanned the waters out to the desert beyond. However, almost always it was as we observed it then: a quiet, dry, gently sloping plain, overlooking the desert below. Its infrequent deluges were mutely announced by an Indian village whose remains rested high and off to one edge out of flood's reach—a proclamation of the wisdom of an earlier people. Water's arid absence here did not diminish the ominous reality displayed in this sloping plain. Had a torrential rain dumped onto the mountains above, we might have been swept off our study site by its floodwaters.

As my wife and I studied how the Desert Iguana survived on this hot dry delta, we were startled one day by jobbers who parked their tank truck near us, sprinkled water on the desert for a few days, laid down a concrete slab on the wet soil, and built a house on it. It was one of many buildings that would be placed on this plain. House would be added to house, and lot to lot, until the city of Palm Desert would cover most of the sloping delta. At some point during the next few decades my study site would become the approach lane to a drive-in bank and, unfortunately the abundant population of Desert Iguanas there would be reduced to a single example, housed in the local zoo.

Below my study site toward Palm Springs, a second surpise of similar nature came when men and machines arrived and leveled some shifting sand dunes. The areas they flattened were sprinkled from tank trucks, followed by a similar slab-laying and house-building sequence. The flattened dunes had been subdivided by lines scribed on a plat map and were transformed into a housing "development" that was acclaimed by a leading national magazine. Driving my car through drifting sand on paved streets I had come upon a brand new ranch-style house, cracked in the middle with one end hanging downward into a wind-scoured hole. At a nearby residence a neighbor complained that Riverside County did not send plow trucks frequently enough to keep streets clear of drifting sand. People settling there acted as though they did not know where they had chosen to live. Their subdivision stood in blowing winds and the shifting dunes of the open desert. In their air-conditioned oblivion they did not know where they lived.

Human knowledge about how the world works (science), and about what is right (ethics), had little effect on what people did there in the desert. The dune levelers had transformed dirt-cheap land into high-priced lots. Human settlers to whom they sold knew nothing of shifting dunes or alluvial fans. Neither did their interior quarters of house and cars permit them to know the desert's searing heat. The "developed" landscape stood in mute testimony to cultured ignorance of these home bodies. Living there, they did not know where they lived. Desert residents, they knew nothing of the science and ethics of desert life. Their praxis was divorced from desert knowledge and wisdom.

THE SCIENCE-ETHICS-PRAXIS TRIAD

On the third corner of the napkin I wrote "Praxis," adding beneath it the parenthetical question, "(What then must we do?)." Now completed, the triangle's corners were occupied by "Science," "Ethics," and "Praxis." This triad would provide the framework for addressing the students' question.

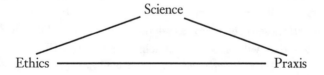

Today, as I write, I am not in the desert of southern California nor in the beech-maple forest of New Hampshire, but on a glacial drumlin in Waubesa Wetlands—a large marsh 4 miles south of Madison, Wisconsin. Here we have our home, and here I study creatures whose watery habitats I and my neighbors have worked to save. While my lizard study site now is covered by a city where people live alone in the land—absent the desert creatures—my wetland study site remains occupied by all kinds of native wetland creatures. Surrounding it is my Town of Dunn, whose land stewardship plan helps people understand, serve, and keep this and other wetland ecosystems. The town stewardship plan encourages restoration of the landscape, protects agricultural lands, and strives to transmit an intergenerational heritage of homes and habitats for the animals, plants, and people that live here. We live largely in accord.

While house-building on slabs poured onto desert sands alerted me to the question of praxis, it mainly was service to my wetland and my town that brought the third point to that napkin. As organizer and steward of the Waubesa Wetlands Scientific and Agricultural Preserve, and as Supervisor and later as Chair of the Town of Dunn, I came to realize that science and ethics do no earthly good unless put into practice. I also came to realize there what I had learned on the desert: praxis uninformed by science and ethics usually creates more problems than are solved.

The science-ethics-praxis triad depicts a way of thinking, with each of its three points illuminating and illuminated by the other two. It represents a way of life in which accomplishment is sought in the company of scientific and ethical knowledge. It pictures a sustained and dynamic interaction among science, ethics and praxis as requisite for integrity in individual lives, in community, and in the wider world. While partly achievable at each corner of the triad, integrity is not fully achievable apart from the dynamic interaction of all three. Pursuit of integrity through this dynamic interaction enables development of a worldview that degrades neither us nor the world—a worldview that can achieve and sustain quality in land and life.

But *will* these three operate in dynamic interaction? Will they interact in ways that will preserve and achieve integrity of human life and environment? That all depends upon what we know and understand and know about ourselves and the world (science), what we believe we should do (ethics), and what we in fact do and how we respond to our successes and failures (praxis). Beyond this, it also depends upon our will. Will we, if given the opportunity, strive for a quality world?[1] If so, what enables or motivates us to do so? What would make us strive relentlessly for integrity in land and in life?

TAKING ACTIONS ON THINGS FOR WHICH THERE IS NO THEORY

While having operated in ways consonant with this science-ethics-praxis triad for decades, I had not articulated it until that meeting around a table in New Hampshire. Having acted upon it for decades, it was only then I became aware of how to represent what I had been doing. Thus, this experience not only provided a framework, but also taught me that I had been engaged for a long time in something I have not previously articulated—something for which I did not have a framework or theory.

Operating without a framework or theory was something about which I became even more aware following a lecture I gave to the Land Resources class at Au Sable Institute on the Town of Dunn in 1995. I had told the class how when, as Town Chair, I and my fellow citizens had developed and implemented a land stewardship plan, and how after a couple of decades of work our town was granted the *Renew America* Award for growth management in 1995. Earlier that summer at Au Sable I had presented a series of ethical principles in my opening stewardship address based on research into biblical texts. I had presented these principles as basic for developing a responsible caring for the land and its life.

And now, following my lecture on the Town of Dunn, I was being asked by the Land Resources class, "How were you able to implement these obviously biblical principles in the public square—in your Town of Dunn?" I was surprised by my answer, and so was my audience. I told them that when I held town office, I had not yet articulated these principles. They had not occurred to me and I had not sought to discover them. I explained that it was only after concluding my terms of political office in Dunn that I spelled out these principles, not before. In exploring my surprising answer, I also observed that what we did in the Town of Dunn, however, nevertheless was fully consistent with the principles that I had not then articulated.

As I answered the questions from this class, I recalled the comment made to me by a pastor friend a few years earlier, "Cal, you are doing things for which we do not yet have a theory." He had told me then what I was better coming to realize now. I had been operating more out of who I was rather than from any systematized body of knowledge. Of course, this again raises the question of how we can act upon something we have not articulated.

A MATRIX OF TELLING STORIES AND SINGING SONGS

The answer lies largely, but not exclusively, in storytelling and songsinging. It is as much the story telling and song singing, as it is analytical scientist, that provides the explanation. My youth was immersed in story-telling and song-singing, but not merely this. The stories we were told and the songs we sung were all tied together to form a system of remarkable consistency and integrity. Nearly every story and song was consistent with every other. All had their interconnections with other stories and songs. Story-telling and song-singing, with cross-referencing integrity, formed a major part of the matrix from which my work developed then and continues to do even now. Theory and framework, when they come, frequently follow praxis, not the other way around.

Beyond these stories and songs was their exposition. It was exposition by my elders, and it took two forms: word and deed. Accompanying the stories and songs were expository sermons—scholarly analyses in which the content and meaning of these songs and stories were unpacked, elaborated, analyzed, explained. For me there were 1000 of these from ages 6 to 16, all delivered with deliberate consistency and integrity. Stories and songs there were but explained and elaborated in every scholarly way. Beyond oral exposition was exposition in deed: the expository lives of people had developed and grown from the matrix to publish in land and life. These people themselves became living stories and songs: lives to be told and work to be sung. They lived their lives as psalms.

Stories, songs, and their exposition in word and deed—these, interactively and with consistent mutual integrity, formed the matrix from which we grew our lives. It was from this matrix that praxis emerged for me. Beginning in the confined world of my childhood home, it gradually extended outward to neighborhood children and families, customers on my newspaper route, activities at church and school, and the work of learning and teaching in the university. From there, the matrix fed and nourished my praxis in the Town of Dunn and into the wider world.

How can one practice things for which one does not yet have a theory? From a consistent and integrated matrix of stories and songs and their scholarly and practical exposition.

Of course, in discovering this, I have come to wonder as a scientist,

"What is the nature of this system of stories and songs? What is the nature of their scholarly and practical exposition?" In attempting to answer these questions, I come to a difficulty that is particularly troublesome. How I describe, in our time, what I believe, without being misunderstood or thought to be freakish? Shouldn't we simply leave matters of belief undiscussed in our pluralistic society? Should I take the risks associated with describing something of the matrix from which I have developed?

THE PROBLEM WITH RELIGION, BIRTHPLACES, AND BIRTHDAYS

My colleague at the University of Wisconsin-Madison, Raymond Kessel, has helped me here very much, unbeknown to him. He is a geneticist, and also counsellor in human genetics. In a seminar we presented together some years back, he told the audience that understanding genetics helps greatly to reduce and remove prejudice among people. Explaining what he meant, he told us that knowing how a person's genetic blueprint was responsible for their form, the shape of their ears, the color of their skin, and so forth, that one would understand much of how people look and act and through this also discover that it is no one's fault that they looked ugly or beautiful, were tall or short, yellow or black. None of us is able to select our parents parents or our genetics. And so we find it possible not to blame people for their looks and form, but can appreciate and respect them for what they are.

His observation is important to us here because our cultural inheritance is in many ways similar to our genetic inheritance. As for our genetics, who and where our parents were when we were born, whether they were rich or poor, Buddhist or Hindu, bond or free. Each of us comes with a genetic and cultural heritage we ourselves have not selected. Each of us enters the stream of life when and where we enter it and each of us stands at a different point in this stream, having entered at a different time and place through no decision of our own. So none of us need be ashamed of where we entered. Thus it is not our doing that the family into which we are born is religious or irreligious, Islamic or Christian. Respecting this fact helps very much in our listening and learning. We learn from this why people can not be like we are. It enables us to develop understanding rather than prejudice.

It is with these considerations that I open the topic of religion. We know that the word, "religion," has come into disfavor in many quarters with good reason. We associate it today with murderous cults, bigotry, brutal warfare, oppression, and doctrinaire imposition. "If that is religion," we say, "we will have nothing to do with it." But, nevertheless, we might well have been brought up within a religious family and through them have gained a religious heritage. Rather than immediately judging those whose upbringing has been different from our own, we can, given our understanding of the nature of genetic and cultural heritage, move to understand what we see, and the people of various faith and nonfaith we meet. In the process we will come to wonder about the very word itelf, the word, "religion."

RELIGION AND TIES THAT BIND

Etymologically, this word means something quite different than what is implied by the troubling associations that circumstances have compelled us to attach to it. Apparently derived from the Latin, *religio*, it has to do with tying things together. A religion is a system whose components are tied together to form some kind of consistent integral whole. Religions, of course, may differ significantly one from another in kind and in quality. This Huston Smith recognizes in his scholarly comparative study of religions. A low quality religion, for example, might degrade both its adherents and the world in which they live. An example is one that might exterminate their own members in the name of their religion. Yet a child born into such a religion must still be appreciated. By contrast, a high quality religion is a system of thought and action in which everything is held together in some kind of consistency and integrity for the purpose of helping people live rightly in the world. And a child born into such a situation also must be appreciated. As people grow up and mature they may shift from low to high quality, or vice versa, for various reasons. But no matter, each kind and quality of religion affects how one lives in the world. None must be discounted.

Religion is not something irrelevant to human life—no matter what its label or whether it even is given the label, "religion." More than being relevant, physicist Max Planck would say that it is necessary. In his 1937 essay on religion and science he writes, "People need science in order to know; religion in order to act." He explains that in everyday life "our decisions, made by our will, cannot afford to wait until we gain complete knowledge or become omniscient." Instead, "We need a basis for acting in the world." As we "...stand in the stream of life, surrounded by a multitude of demands and needs" he reminds us that we often must "make quick decisions or immediately implement certain plans."

Secular philosopher Max Oelschlaeger supports Planck's assertion when he writes: "I think of religion... as being more important in the effort to conserve life on earth than all the politicians and experts put together... My conjecture is this: *There are no solutions for the systemic causes of ecocrisis, at least in democratic societies, apart from religious narrative.*"[2]

Now it may be true that some among us would prefer not to identify our system of beliefs as "religion," but that does not diminish the claim that it is our system of beliefs that enable us to act. No matter what name we apply to it, not many would deny the need for "a system of thought and action in which everything is held together in some kind of consistency and integrity for the purpose of helping people live rightly in the world." And this of course will soon bring us back to one such system—the one that was my own cultural inheritance. But before it does, we must enter briefly the world of paradigms.

PARADIGMS AS EXAMPLES

It was immediately following an oral examination of a graduate student that I found another way to get at the interesting idea of acting on things before one has a theory. The candidate had been asked to define the word, "paradigm." His answer raised additional questions that drove me to pick up my copy of Thomas Kuhn's *Structure of Scientific Revolutions* when I returned home, and there to find the author responding, in the second edition, to the criticism that he had used the word, "paradigm" in the first edition 22 different ways. While not agreeing with all 22, Kuhn nevertheless affirmed that he had used the word in several different ways. There was the definition that sees it as a kind of mindset out of which a culture operates—the definition we use when talking about "paradigm shifts." But there also is the definition in which "paradigm" is seen as "an example"—an example from which theory can be developed—an example for which there might yet be no theory.

My immediate response to this finding, in December and January,

1995–1996 was to begin writing a book on *The Dunn Paradigm*. In it I told a number of stories based upon my experience in Town office. Following each, I mined each for their lessons and principles. But now I can take this further. I now feel enabled to investigate the matrix within which my life is rooted and has developed as a paradigm—as an example from which principles can be identified and theory be constructed.

My attempt to distil and systematize the principles out of which I believe I operate may of course be counterproductive in the sense that those who do not take seriously the belief system from which I have been operating might cast off the principles I will articulate. But before doing so, the wise reader will recognize not only that every one of us operates out of some kind of matrix—identified or not—and that the stories and songs from which these principles are distilled are themselves likely to be far more universal than a particular tradition. If such stories and songs are derived from the common quest of all human beings to discover how the world works, what is right and what must be done, then principles expressed in the words of one belief system cannot simply be put aside because of their mode of presentation. Underlying the matrices there likely are truths greater than the forms available for their expression.

A MATRIX OF STORIES, SONGS, AND EXPOSITION

The matrix of story, song, and exposition with which I entered the stream of life was one that respected science heartily, yet did not hold up science as arbiter of absolute truth. It promulgated a system of ethics, yet continously reformed this system as knowledge from the Word and the world increased and was clarified.[3] It sought to bring goodness and integrity to human life, yet did not pursue happiness or other possible by-products of goodness and integrity for their own sakes. It sought wholeness and care for Creation, yet was not afraid to take from Creation what was needed to sustain life and achieve contentment.

In time, I found this matrix of story, song, and exposition consistent with what is socially and ecologically necessary to live rightly on earth. Moreover, I also found that it contained the resources necessary for developing new insights for unanticipated conditions in the world and human society. I also learned that much of this is consistent with Judaic and Islamic belief systems and other monotheistic traditions that respect the biblical heritage. That is all to the good of course and even to be expected, since religions should in many ways be consistent with the way the world works.

What then is the nature of this system of stories and songs? In my tradition, it is a system whose primary source of stories and songs is the Bible, comprised of the Hebrew Bible (or Old Testament) and the New Testament. It is a compilation of 66 books the set of which has been broadly identified as authoritative over the centuries. One of these is the book of Psalms—a collection of 150 songs to be sung—a song book that sometimes is published separately as a "Psalter" translated from the good Hebrew poetry in which it has been written into good poetry in English and hundreds of other languages, and accompanied by music. Being models of biblical concreteness and exemplary poetry, the Psalms usually are accompanied by other songs from across the ages, that "in spirit, form, and content" are positive expressions of "Scripturally religious thought and feeling" and represent "the full range of the revelation of God."[4] Most of the other 65 books are story books that report historical events in the life of the early Jewish people and during the early years of Christianity, through which an understanding of what is necessary for living rightly in society and the wider Creation are conveyed. Besides stories the collection includes the wisdom literature, of which the Book of Proverbs is perhaps best known, a set of New Testament letters to new Christian churches, and at the start of the collection, the five books of Moses—the Torah, or Law—that put forth in story form God's expectations for the early Hebrew people and their successors.

The scholarly exposition of these stories and songs, and of the other books, is a highly disciplined matter, conducted by highly educated scholars who are governed by the discipline of hermeneutics—rigorous methods of interpretation befitting a collection of books that most biblical scholars treat as holy and inspired by God.[5] The practical exposition of these stories and songs in my youth came from the lives of the people around me, many of which were exemplary in putting into practice upgrading the poor, visiting the sick, rehabilitating prostitutes, singing in prisons, doing honest work, and tending the land.[6]

DERIVATIVES FROM THE MATRIX

What comprises the matrix of stories, songs, and their expositions with which I entered the stream of life? What principles can be derived from it? How does it motivate people to strive for a quality world? In exploring these questions, we can use this matrix as a paradigm—in the sense of its being an example—and work to derive from it some general teachings and principles. In so doing, I run the risk of misidentifying what these principles are. Nevertheless, here are the principles I believe can be derived from the matrix.

Authorship and Integrity of the Cosmos.—There is but a single just and loving Author of all-that-is, including temporality and chance, who creates all creatures good and declares all creatures good.[7] This means that (1) all things are consistent, justly ordered, and have integrity, whether apparent or not. This is captured by Einstein, for example, in his exclamation, "Raffiniert ist der Herrgott, aber boshaft ist er nicht!"[8] This also means that (2) the just and discoverable consistency within the world makes science possible, including description of principles and laws.

The Creation and all the Creatures Belong to their Creator.—Neither the Creation, nor any of its creatures belong to human beings, but to their Creator, who cares for all of it. The earth is the Lord's and everything in it; the sea belongs to God together with all the creatures it contains.[9] Thus, (3) the things of the land and things of the sea are held in trust and must be treated with respect and cared for. Beyond the other creatures, we also belong to God, who cares for us and thus, (4) we need not be anxious about our lives or sustenance.

Intrinsic Worth of the Creatures.—The divine authorship of all things means that (5) creation and all its constituents have intrinsic worth apart from their utility or perceived pleasantness, and thus the whole Creation and every creature must be respected.[10] God loves the world and cares for it,[11] and imaging God, (6) we must love the world and take care of it. This also means that (7) while we may make responsible use of the fruits of Creation we may not destroy its fruitfulness. Thus, (8) the prerogative of destruction and extinction lies only with the Creator, not with people.[12] And, (9) while we may employ creatures in responsible ways, we must not press them relentlessly;[13] (10) we must assure repeated opportunity for the creatures of earth to enjoy their rest and Creation's blessings.

Human Beings as Part of Creation.—Because we also are creatures, (11) we human beings do not stand apart from "environment" but are part and parcel of the whole.[14] The whole is sometimes identified as the Creation. The integrity of the whole Creation must be upheld and cherished, not just some favorite "parts." Furthermore, (12) as the rest of Creation serves us so should we serve the rest of Creation.[15] Con-service and con-servation is the rule.

Human Beings as Imagers of God.—Yet, (13) as con-servants, human beings have a special honor not shared with any other creature, of imaging God's love to the world.[16] It is a special honor with special responsibility. God is love; and we should image God's love. Imaging the Creator's love and care for the creatures prevents us from abusing them, compels us to have concern for the biosphere, and brings us to protect and conserve it. Thus, (14) human beings are called to be earth keepers.[17] Earthkeeping is an important way of imaging God's love for the world.

Penalty for Eschewing our Reflection of God's Love.—While expected to image God's love for the world out of love and gratitude to God, (15) people who despise God's laws and destroy the earth, themselves will be destroyed.[18] Yet (16) people who believingly practice God's love for the world will have everlasting life.[19]

Creation is a Powerful Teacher.—The just and discoverable consistency of Creation is rooted in God's order and thus (17) for those who study the works of Creation, Creation is a powerful teacher. Thus, (18) having been created justly and rightly by God, the Creation is in many ways normative, and its normativity can inform its observers not only how the world works, but also how the world ought to work.[20] For example, the Creation teaches in many ways that biological death is basic to life, contrary to what one might surmise if they separated themselves from observing natural ecosystems function.

Mindless Selection Should be Constrained in Mindful Society.— Darwinian principles may operate creatively and thoughtlessly in the biotic world. However, (19) when thoughtless Darwinian principles are found to operate in the thoughtful world of human beings, they must be constrained and even countered in order to assure sustainability of human society and the Creation.[21] Thus, (20) fitness of human culture comes not from seeking the supremacy of the individual, race, nationality, sex, or economic status but from service to Creation and human community. Self-interest is always secondary to seeking God's rule. Therefore (21) whatever benefits accrue to one's self come as by-products of seeking the integrity of the whole Creation.[22]

Contentment Rather than Maximization is a Worthy Goal.—Given God's ownership of all things, and human responsibility to God, (22) the aim of human beings and human societies should be contentment, not the maximization of things, or pleasure, or accomplishments.[23] Thus, (23) whatever things we hold in trust, whatever joy we experience, and whatever accomplishments we achieve should come as by-products of our loving and self-giving service. Contentment is worth far more than money, possessions, wealth, or fame—to us and to the rest of Creation.

Truth Must Always be Sought.—In whatever human beings do or say, in whatever they learn and teach about the world and how things ought to be, and in whatever actions they take in the world, (24) human beings must consistently be truthful and seek the truth, never misrepresenting the world nor what is happening within and to the world.[24] Thus, (25) when there is danger people must sound the alarm;[25] when there is no danger they must not be alarmist. When there is need for prophets they should prophesy; (26) when corrective actions result from the warning of prophets, the prophets should rejoice and not grumble.[26] Moreover, (27) when there is need to know people should seek to find out. And, (28) when there is confusion people should seek to clarify. Thus, (29) truth must be defended and consistently be sought.

The Whole Creation Praises its Creator.—Finally, (30) the whole Creation gives testimony to God's divinity and everlasting power.[27] Thus, (31) in our life and work we should help others share in receiving Creation's testimony and (32) we should assure that the testimony of the creatures and of Creation to their Creator is not diminished or extinguished.

STRIVING FOR A QUALITY WORLD

Early on we asked, "If given the opportunity, would we strive for a quality world? If so, what is it that would enable or motivate us to engage and persist in such seeking? What would make us strive relentlessly for integrity in land and in life? The answer to this basic question is implicit in my "derivatives from the matrix" set forth above. Yes, we would strive for a quality world if, among other things we believed that we should be about imaging God's love for the world in our life and work. Our motivation would come from pursuing and restoring the integrity in response to its Author, whose integrity we wish to image with our own. We would strive for this integrity out of gratitude to the Author and Finisher of our own worthfulness. We would do so in order to return to our Creator the worth-ship that flows from our God-given worthfulness. Striving for a quality world would for us be a kind of grateful worship.

GETTING IT ALL TOGETHER

"How do you as a scientist, a student of the Scriptures, and someone directly involved in town politics, put it all together?" the students had asked me. With a triangle sketched on a napkin, with the words "Science," "Ethics," and "Praxis" written on its corners, I explained how I kept science, ethics, and praxis in dynamic interaction. Action flowed from combining scientific and ethical knowledge. With this sketch I had begun an heuristic exercise that did not end that evening but would continue to what I would articulate here: my own development grows from a matrix of story telling and song singing that, together with their expository proclamation in word and deed, provided the basis for action— action that could be taken even when there was yet no framework or theory. Thus my science does not operate on its own, but in tandem with what I have described here as quality Religion, defined as a system of thought and action in which everything is held together in some kind of consistency and integrity for the purpose of helping people live rightly in the world. High quality religion, so defined, is not only relevant, but necessary for living rightly on earth. Quality *religio* is needed for "getting it all together."

NOTES

1. I am reminded here of what a colleague of mine recently said: "I sure am glad I was not a friend of Jesus Christ. I have no doubt he was a very good person, who did everything as it should be done. And that is just my problem. If I were his friend I just could not have the fun I am having now.

2. Oelschlaeger, p. 5.

3. A phrase I learned in my youth that expresses this is *Ecclesia reformata semper refermandum est* — "the reformed church is ever reforming."

4. Statement of Principle for Music in the Church, In: *Psalter Hymnal*. Grand Rapids, Michigan: Board of Publications of the Christian Reformed Church, 1976, p. v.

5. An illustration of the level of scholarship involved here is my discovery only in his recent obituary that the pastor of my youth had his Doctorate of Theology from the Free University of Amsterdam. As a youth I had never known this, but his expository sermons, with their rich reference to Hebrew and Greek texts (as well as to Dutch) said as much.

6. See for example the article on Neerlandia ****

7. Genesis 1; Apostles' Creed; Nicene Creed; Athanasian Creed; Belgic Confession, Article II.

8. "Subtle is the Lord, but malicious is he not." For further insight on this, see the frontispiece in the book by Abraham Pais, *'Subtle is the Lord' The Science and Life of Albert Einstein* (Oxford: Oxford University Press).

9. Psalm 24:1; Contemporary Testimony.

10. Cf. Job 38–40; Psalm 104.

11. John 3:16; Psalm 104.

12. Cf. Job 40:19.

13. Cf. Exodus 20:10; Deuteronomy 5:14.

14. Genesis 2:7.

15. Genesis 2:15.

16. Genesis 1:27.

17. Genesis 2:15.

18. Revelation 11:18.

19. John 3:16.

20. Gordon Spykman, *Reformational Theology: A New Paradigm for Doing Dogmatics*.

21. Cf. Matthew 6:33.

22. The word sometimes used for the wholeness and integrity that should be sought is "the Kingdom of God," and has its expression, for example, in Matthew 6:33.

23. I Timothy 6:6–21.

24. Proverbs 14:5; John 8:31ff.

25. Ezekiel 33:1–6.

26. Jonah 3–4.

27. Psalm 19:1; Acts 14:17; Romans 1:20.

Touching the Earth

Al Fritsch, SJ

Ecology is more than a scientific discipline; it is a tale of my personal journey to a deeper connection with our Earth. Allow me to take you through a personal narrative that includes not only my public interest career, but also my agrarian roots, liturgical upbringing, scientific education, Ignatian training within the Society of Jesus, and the work with the poor of Appalachia. What is presented here, as though through the seasons of one's life, is how this touching of the Earth has culminated in a special religious experience in the Holy Land and at Calvary's rock. It is my hope that this testimony may allow all to appreciate and better understand their own journey.

At times in our lives many of us strive to uncover the hidden foundations of our faith. This task is more difficult for those of us who regard part of our religious ministry to be saving and urging others to help save the Earth. Those who are also scientists generally have a strong rational propensity for staying in touch with the Earth, which involves planning, design, hypotheses, experimentation, and conclusions. The more academically inclined believers bolster their findings with references to others they regard as authorities, or help legitimate their own personal scientific-religious experiences. But what about scientists who are not academically inclined? Can our active experience give legitimacy to our witness?

In late 1970 after the euphoria of the first Earth Day begins to wear thin, Mike Jacobson, Jim Sullivan, and I establish the Center for Science in the Public Interest. We have been working with Ralph Nader's Center for the Study of Responsive Law, and both organizations still flourish in Washington, D.C. In seven years my portion of the operation would become Appalachia—Science in the Public Interest. Up until this writing I have been a person with a single career—if public interest is such. For myself as a Jesuit priest, this is a contemporary example of the intersection of religion, science, and environment. My creative juices flow more easily away from the expectations and restrictions of larger established institutions. Freed from the need to publish in learned journals, to follow tenure tracks, and to deal with university politics, or to try to make a buck for some industry, we chart our own course in independent public interest organizations. No syllabus dictates what we work on or the form of advocacy, writing, talks, research, or consulting. No day has a dull moment, for each is uniquely different from the day before.

Working in the public interest puts the life of a scientist in a wholly different context. Its advocates are generally more liberal than conservative, more decentralist than centralist, more in touch with people than ideas, more prone to get angry than to pass over offenses, more oriented to social ecology than deep ecology, more vocal than quiet, more practical than theoretical, more inclined to believe in a radical reform of the system than for minor adjustment of capitalism, more evolutionist than creationist, more vegetarian than red meat eaters, and more willing to stand apart from such controversies as the choice of plastics-versus-paper—rather, they prefer to use neither. But the definition is incomplete. Unfortunately, those prone to defining people by such sets of numbers as salaries, golf scores, value of their cars, or the poshness of neighborhoods have little patience with public interest types. So be it.

As advocates for the well-being of our whole communities, public interest folks seek the opposite of special interest people. Likewise, they try to distance themselves from compromising environmentalists who pay lip service to ecological concerns while protecting their own acquired affluence and privilege. Working with political insiders is hardly public interest, even with public figures in the public limelight. A more radical stance is called for. The public interest challenges the current economic system's limitations and is convinced that the struggle is over a fundamentally new political and social order. In this new order where major divisions between the wealthy and poor would be eliminated, all would have a healthy and wholesome quality of life, and the Earth's bounty would be shared by all. Furthermore, believers profess that such goals spring from the uncompromising conviction in the dignity of every human being before God. On the other hand, ecological crisis is fostered through disrespect for other people and the Earth itself.

In the first year after the initiation of the NAFTA treaty, Mexico went from a land of three to two dozen billionaires—and some have called this progress. That land, like much of the world, and even parts of our country, contains a few "haves" and many "have-nots." How, in such times as these, can we take meaningful steps to break down the barriers that separate people into such classes? Why not keep in touch with our traditions, where we discover democratic principles, cooperative endeavors with the poor as equals, dislike for despots and elitists, the reality of racial justice, and a can-do homesteader mentality? Don't we find within that religious tradition a fundamental option for and with the poor? Aren't these a vast and ever-growing multitude who, in a divine and humorous way, are to lead in saving our wounded Earth? Doesn't Good News become a glad tidings for the poor: everyone has something to contribute, all are leaven and all are part of the rising dough.

Are we at a time of massive cultural decline exemplified by ecological crisis, or is there a New Age coming with changing attitudes about our relationship with our Earth? I am uncertain, but I find more lessons in history than in New Age philosophy. I prefer to lean toward a traditional approach and will show why on a phenomenological journey through my selected life experiences—my personal historic pilgrimage told in the present tense. In this case I happen to pass by Calvary. I find that the power of God draws me to a goal I have not articulated, that is, Calvary where my Savior died. Through such imagery my life becomes remote preparation, actual journey, attaining a goal and the return. This wayfaring consists in touching Earth from childhood to older age, albeit in different ways. Youthful play yields to the drudgery of educational preparation, the arduous movement through hostile conflicts and struggles, the spiritual goal, and a priceless treasure worth sharing with others.

LATE WINTER: WANTING TO TRAVEL

After the winter rains comes the mud puddle—a fitting beginning in dealing with our Earth. Mud beckons our restless hands to create from a natural plastic substance a new form, a shape, a figure as we role play our Creator-God. Why so fidgety except that we are made, as Robert Coles describes, even from infancy for travel. We are restless wanderers, exploring, and getting ourselves dirty in the act. But in some ways the movements of earliest years are the most carefree, the times we take the largest risks and gamble the highest stakes. For here we discover revelation, natural phenomena, getting our bearing (the *here*), and learning what it means to be sustainable.

Revelation

My birthplace rests on the headwaters of Limestone Creek, nearly at the highest point of Mason County, Kentucky. From here it flows four miles to the Ohio River. Here the early Transylvanian explorers Simon Kenton and Daniel Boone discovered the canebrakes that would be America's first Washington, created in 1775 after a young fellow Virginian was victorious over the British in New England. In late winter and early spring Limestone Creek flows rather strongly and makes young boys' dream of the power of the flowing water, movement, wandering.

One day several of us decide to dam the creek and make a temporary lake, totally ignoring our lack of engineering experience and having little more to work with than mud, rocks and sticks. Our small earthworks temporarily holds, and the water starts backing up rapidly. Our ever-industrious uncle on the next farm calls over, "what on earth are you doing?" In desperation for a meaningful answer I gingerly grab a large wiggling copper-colored crawdad in the drained portion of the creek and raise it up for him to see. Uncle Pete is satisfied that we are out to capture, eat, or dissect these creatures. I do not have the courage to say we are just playing in mud.

Natural Phenomena

The hydrologic cycles become virtually attached to us. Farm youth have to learn the foibles of the seasons—playing probabilities with livelihoods at stake. Gamblers ensnared in the natural cycles of life. Birth and death, spring and fall, sowing and harvest. On the farm we live and breathe life's cycles watching calves being born and sometimes needing to assist, sowing tobacco plant beds, jobbing (planting) corn, picking strawberries and blackberries and elderberries, making hay bales and struggling to get them in the barn on time. All such tasks allow us to be perceptive enough to know when it will rain or not, depending less on official weather reports than the feel of breeze, humidity, time of year, and temperature. All my life I prefer to go outdoors and touch the weather and know what it is going to be like today.

And what is land without water? During dry times, Kentucky clay soil can crack so deep that I have sometimes had a nightmare of getting swallowed up in a dry weather fissure. Yes, our family works together, but we pray together for the gentle clod-soaking types of rain. Nor do we neglect to sprinkle the thirsty fields with Easter Water, all the while begging the good Lord for plentiful and properly delivered rain for an abundant harvest in autumn.

Getting a Bearing

Except for milking cows, working on Sunday is a no-no. However, that cow-milking monastic regularity overwhelms my carefree youth. The transition from milking by hand to electric devices doesn't make more free time, only more cows. However, the milker's free-time is most deeply appreciated, even if it is to get away and scale the limestone ledges. In Mason County these rolling hills are encrusted with fossilized ocean life six hundred miles and a half million years from the nearest sea. It is fun watching excited visitors gather chunks and overload their vehicles. However, their unusual behavior makes permanent dwellers look more closely and find these ancient rocks crawling with fossilized and pulsating life. The microcosm unfolds before the patient observer. Insects crawl and buzz about, a thousand-legged, a small spider, a sweat bee, a yellow jacket. I can actually see smaller creatures and discover the true pilgrims—those little black ants in single file crossing back and forth over the boulder from hill to harvest. Macrocosm is a mirror of microcosm, or is it the inverse? And somehow this rocky place becomes so embedded in our brain that it situates forever our *here*, our home. And now it is milking time again.

Sustainability

The farm barely withstands the Great Depression, having survived more by the grace of the local bank and the knowledge that my folks are very hard working. Under advice from our County agent, Mr Collins, we undertake the latest techniques, rotating crops, adding our crushed limestone to the fields, returning agricultural wastes and manures. We strive to become a premier place; the weeds cut, fences mended, barns in good repair and orderly. Every tool has its place in farming, and my Dad's direction is instrumental in converting eroded land into good pasture by good liming and filling in washed areas with dams and sod to slow water flow. We truly practice touching the soil. Row crop fields become wheat and rye croplands the second year, hay the third, pasture the fourth and then start over. These crops furnish feed for cattle, chickens, hogs and horses—the food and power of the farm. Homesteaders and livestock alike sustaining each other. We learn the other's rhythms, knowing when to slow or rest. Strangely animals make life more human, slowing the pace, something the relentless gas-powered tractor replacements of a later economy could never do. With the coming of gasoline-powered machines, fuel (feed) is no longer grown, but bought from oil companies demanding pay in cash, translated into more crops, more farmland, more tractors, more hours of work.

SPRINGTIME: PREPARATION FOR THE JOURNEY

In youthful years, Earth takes on a role of stepmother and hand-maid. The observational skills and vivid memory of early years become preparation for later journeys. During this grand creative stage I take my first fumbling steps, followed by scampering, skipping, jumping, climbing, and spreading out arms as though to sprout wings and fly. Reality blazes forth like the morning sun, and the jewel-colored gems of fresh dew evaporate more quickly in springtime. Divinely touched we hit the road in an orange school bus. The warming sun enhances and photosynthesizes youthful zest and exuberance, but that creeping bus brings on a sense of realism. My world expands beyond the farm and our mothering hills. Mud puddles dry and turn to dust. Textbooks invite a new kind of restlessness. But our minds open and we learn about strange animals in distant lands, people different from us, large bodies of water, and mountains far taller than our Kentucky Knobs.

Restlessness

It is wartime and the spill-over comes to Kentucky. Old ways are dying and winds of change bring ration stamps, propaganda movies, col-lected milkweed pods and recycling scrap for the war effort; relatives off to war—blue, silver, and gold stars in windows—screaming headlines that beckoned grade schoolers to read, e.g., Tobruk, Sicily, D-Day, Normandy, the Bulge, V-E Day, an unmentionable bomb, and V-J Day.

We jostle and try to keep occupied on the bare bluff overlooking Limestone Ball Park now turned prison-of-war encampment. We are youthful spectators coming to watch soccer played by German twenty-year-olds in the cramped quarters of their compound. They come from lands where our relatives and neighbors are fighting, and yet we can't help but admire them in their happiness to be an ocean away from war. Our hands-short farmers also like their free labor and enthusiasm. As might be expected, even our recess games are war games. Then one day Sister Victoria lets us go outside and wave goodbye, when the prisoner convoy leaves town. Peace is coming.

Conservation

Post-war pace quickens more and a consumer culture presents us with television, new appliances, farm implements, faster cars with tail fins, quarter-a-gallon gas with no ration stamps, and plastics. Waste materials is a new category. It is early high school years; we are introduced to the Kentucky Conservation Corps and its summer camps of fishing, proper shooting and other skills. My classmates' longest trip to date is a 200-mile bus ride to Dale Hollow Lake, a portion of the TVA system with its dammed lakes and its miles of shore. Here scores of fellow Kentucky youth struggle to reach beyond county and school loyalty and try to respect nature for what is in all its rugged beauty on the Tennessee border. In this out-of-the-way place (before the newly formed lakes have been discovered by the tourist crowd), we are taught that small fish are returned, a gun needs to be handled properly, and there is a season for everything under heaven. Conservation enters our vocabulary as a good word indelibly printed on our youthful minds by sacrificing Corps leaders.

Science for its own sake

The fragile and complex Earth beckons us to understand, respond, and to prod more deeply. The sciences are fascinating—geology, botany, zoology, chemistry, physics. My chemistry set gives way to high school and college courses, and then graduate studies. The door opens to a deeper and more systematic look into atoms and molecules and the excitement of burrowing into matter. The discipline differs from looking out to the yonder distant stars at the first origins of the universe and the Big Bang. Though astronomy seems at times more alluring, humble chemistry is simply more down-to-Earth. Suddenly "plastics" sprout dollar signs and add to the appeal of 1950s chemistry. Dupont calls it "better things for better living through chemistry." As budding chemists, we eagerly strive to handle (analyze or synthesize) chemicals with reverence and care, using the finesse of a bulldozer operator moving tons of earth by the touch of a finger. We hear that successful chemists possess the magic touch and more; they are masters of evolution itself and beyond, but where to, a few of us ask. Shouldn't science be for the benefit of all, not the learned elite?

Composition of Place

Questions give way to a calling and thus my detour in scientific education as I enter the Society of Jesus. At Milford in 1956, precisely when Soviet tanks suppress the distant Hungarian Uprising, fifty of us undergo our first Thirty Day Retreat in the Spiritual Exercises of St. Ignatius. Follow the Lord's call. Thus we try in our own unique ways to prepare ourselves to go out to all the world and tell the Good News. But first we have to listen. The Spiritual Exercises focus on the biblical-based personal journey through life as well as meditations on Jesus' journeys in life to death and beyond.

Following the retreat comes several years of experiments geared to helping us to discern and to toughen our spiritual fiber; one is even called a pilgrimage, for St. Ignatius often calls himself the "pilgrim." During this early spiritual training our thoughts move back to 1522 and Ignatius making his elementary novitiate in a cave at Manresa. In this fitting down-to-earth place, he finds God and a rather flexible prayer life obtained patiently through trial and error and God's good grace. He prepares and undertakes his pilgrimage to the Holy Land to follow in Jesus' footsteps. In the waning hours of this brief experience, he must return to the Mount of the Ascension chapel to determine whether Jesus' left or right foot is imprinted on the stone. It is the need to know detail for composing his sacred *here*. Jesuit commentator Michael Buckley says it is typically Ignatius to present a progressive descent into matter. You can find the same sort of movement in the Incarnation—Jesus, the Christ, becoming one with us.

Summer: Pilgrimage with Commoners

It takes time for me to get started—30 years of training and education to be exact. But finally the day arrives on a hot, humid June day in 1970, when I journey to the nation's capital and stay temporarily at a small community of fellow Jesuits at Jennifer Street in Northwest Washington, DC. Priesthood allows me to enter peripherally into parish life and perform services for room, board and small stipend. Restlessness over so many years now gives way to a public interest career. With time I attempt to define public interest, to find the place of eco-justice in the total schema of things, to justify the citizen's duty to speak out even when not asked, and to respond to restlessness by knowing the critical time to act.

Public Interest is a political, economic and social sort of package all wrapped in one. The methods of science are all the same, but the emphasis is on acting in such a way that the work becomes responsive to the needs of others, whether the poor, the consumer, the whistle-blowing professional, or the-rank-and-file citizens. Advocate Ralph Nader's leadership has been utterly pervasive in the public interest movement and his creative insight, enormous energy, and constant enthusiasm is the extra energy that has jump-started public interest science. His sense of fair play and justice, disregard for financial gain, and rock solid credibility has endured the years. He has constantly called for unbiased research, accurate and meaningful presentation, and strong indignation at what has happened to others through greed and misdeed. I, for one, do not have the stamina, fortitude and single-mindedness to come close to equaling his drive and effectiveness, and yet a number of us have attempted in our own way to follow his example—breathlessly trying to keep up.

Eco-Justice

In 1972 I go to Europe for the United Nations Conference on the Environment in Stockholm. This first-of-a-kind meeting sets the global stage for seeing the planet as one major problem area with many sub-issues. Here thinking globally and ecologically is championed by one of our Center's advisors: internationally known scientist, Rene Dubos. In later years, I would modify his adage "Think globally, act locally" to a less catchy "Think and act locally so as to think and act globally with others." Earth Day had only occurred two years before and now Americans are sharing their issues and concerns with people from many other lands. We realize that individuals can't solve all problems in isolation; we need information, tools, resources and assistance from others. Environment becomes a public interest issue that transcends corporate, political, local, regional, national, racial, ethnic, or even academic interests; it encompasses the planet.

In the Stockholm non-governmental organization (NGO) meeting a rather hefty and vocal Kenyan woman rushes to the stage where a panel of notable all white males are preparing to speak, wedges herself among the participants, and says she represents the ninety percent of the world unrepresented here. Much of the virtually all white audience appears horrified at such an intrusion, and a minority of us clap and enjoy her testimony. It leaves a vivid memory and division. Though of this white male caste I now become quite sensitive about the whiteness, maleness, and privileged affluence of this environmental movement.

Authority

The mid-1970s are a dizzy array of talks, conferences, programs, publications, and hearings. Reviewing the daybooks of this period gives me a headache. The Nixon and Ford years are filled with countless programs in and beyond DC, including the first series of waste management conferences funded by the new U.S. Environmental Protection Agency. Our Technical Information Project holds meetings in fourteen cities from Anchorage to Miami. But even amid the whirl of travel (about 50,000 miles a year by auto and plane) there's still time to reflect and ponder such reoccurring questions as "Who speaks in the public interest?" Critics say they recognize and affirm the authority resting in democratic electoral process, but they find public interest people flaunting that process through self-appointment.

I pride myself on being democratic and so the criticism stings. It forces me back into my religious and prophetic tradition for answers. Certainly some of the prophets are most reluctant to confront opponents. Does not Jesus on his final entry into Jerusalem through direct talks and especially his driving money-changers from the Temple precipitate the same question? On whose authority do you speak or act?

His indignation surges up over a special interest crowd turning his Father's house (which is a place of prayer for ALL the people) into the special preserve of a commercial elite. That outburst is countered by the establishment's anger and plotting. He answers with an authority solidly rooted in his whole person obedient to the prompting of the Spirit. This key passage is found in all four gospels and is pivotal in the manner in which he is opposed by contemporary secular powers; his actions give us a rationale and inspiration for speaking with what one harassed medical doctor I had met in Texas calls "the authority of my baptismal water."

Critical Time

My first public interest activities in the 1970s deal specifically with chemicals in the environment: lead in gasoline, mercury in fish, pesticides in water, tobacco additives. Some have been wins and some losses or postponements. The time is a forever *now*, but a multitude of issues press in from all sides and call for a priority-setting procedure granting limited resources. All the while my native Kentucky is wounded by surface mining of coal—and one must always go home when there's trouble. Our little victories like exposing the dangers of aerosol sprays do not refrain the restlessness to move nearer the old homestead. Washington, D.C. is a nice place to write *99 Ways to a Simple Lifestyle*, but a poor place to put it into practice, for DC has a super-fast pace, is urban, and is surrounded by three of the five richest counties in America. My restlessness becomes a series of pushes and pulls and the gnawing fear that I am losing touch with my roots.

By early 1977 Appalachia—Science in the Public Interest is born in south central Kentucky. The three ingredients we look for in a location is impoverishment of the people, perceived needs that public interest science can address, and access to travel. We know the counties are some of the poorest, we have sent a team to survey public interest science needs, and we choose a place adjacent to an exit of Interstate-75. By the following year we have purchased a good site for a demonstration center and a staff is funded through an infusion of money from the National Science Foundation's "Science for Citizens" program.

The Carter years are expansive, optimistic. We participate in setting up solar groups at the state (Kentucky Solar Coalition), regional

(Southeast Connections) and national level (Solar Lobby). In a short time renewable energy will triumph. Then comes the dry Reagan years (1981-88) and survival for our Center depends on a diversity of funding sources (good ecology), consulting, grants, volunteers and sales of our "Simple Lifestyle Calendar." With time we develop a complete solar demonstration House, other low-cost buildings, an appropriate technology library, nature trail, certified organic gardens, and examples of various types of appropriate technology. The latter is a people-centered approach that includes small-scale, people friendly, low resource use, and environmentally benign methods for growing food, storing and purifying water, composting human and other wastes, obtaining fuel, and securing building materials.

AUTUMN: REACHING OUT AND TOUCHING CALVARY

The hills involve shadows, darkness and light. Living simply does not make us immune from meanness and strife where poverty abounds. The year 1987 is a low mark when our land trust manager is killed, one of our houses destroyed by arson, petty theft and trashed conditions abound, and countless other episodes now forgotten. Appalachian life is never easy, and then when we look out we see shadows turn to light—the turning of the leaves, wildflowers, radiance of the sun on the fruitful garden, animals wild and tame, joy and appreciation of visitors and guests, and acts of kindnesses at the most unexpected time.

The Poor

Our public interest work has been directed primarily among lower income Appalachians. Much appropriate technology starts with lower-income people, who are isolated and limited in communicating and sharing ideas. For them "appropriate" is not what is to be appropriated from elite by poor folks, but what is suitable among those who are making do with what they have. Communicating ideas, however, is not enough for new concerns; questions always arise. How can one have a good cistern for storing drinking water, if the rainwater itself is polluted or the catchment surface is corroded by acid rain? Should non-native or exotic species be planted in an artificial wetlands to purify domestic gray water? Which native materials offer the best and lowest priced insulation for homes?

We discover that the often lacking quality of Appalachian self-respect can be enhanced by actively sharing and acting as a conduit for sharing technologies among people beyond the region itself. Thus I do not hesitate to travel first to all parts of North America, then to Europe and on to Peru, Puerto Rico, Dominican Republic, Haiti, India, and finally Israel.

Approaching the Rock

A most memorable experience involves a trip to the Holy Land in 1992 through my sponsorship by Professor Sydney Blair of the Loyola University Medical School. This information-sharing tour is among the two dozen facilities of the Society for the Protection of Nature in Israel, the largest environmental organization in the Middle East that includes Jews, Christians and Moslems. Our delegation from 27 countries travels extensively from Eliat in the south to Mount Hermon in the north. Since the specific program is a secular ecological one and I have arrived just when it commences, I have virtually no time to see the religious sites. However, when making a stopover at Jerusalem a Greek Cypriot in our party offers to conduct me on an early morning pre-departure visit to the Church of the Holy Sepulchre. We rise very early and walk hurriedly to the Old City of Jerusalem. The Church of the Holy Sepulchre is open and an early Mass taking place at the Empty Tomb. After the Liturgy I hasten breathlessly up the steep steps to the spot where Jesus died—Calvary. My unworthiness nearly overwhelms me. Before me is the hole into which pilgrims put their hands to touch the rock on which Jesus died. I pause and hesitantly put my hand in. The rock is hard and cool. Suddenly at this instant a great calming experience comes over me.

The Feelings

This *is* my home, my holy place. But this "my" is not possessive as such, but one of affinity with others—for Jews and Arabs and everyone who call it home. And are the limits on Calvary or beyond and how far beyond? Is this not a sharing in the very thoughts of Jesus on Calvary? As the lamentations of Good Friday proclaim in anguish and deep hurt "What have you done to me?" Jesus' suffering and death is for his land

and his people, and this extends beyond the place and country to an entire Earth. Is not the rejection he experiences extended to the damage done to Earth and people in our day? Sacred blood making holy the place, the land, the Earth, and making meaningful blood shed by innocent victims in all times and places, a tragic-bound commons, a community of redemptive work extending in space and time to include our public interest work.

Deepening Understanding

The impact of touching Calvary in this breathless moment while racing against a clock does not vanish during the rest of this whirlwind trip. What seems lacking is any form of sentimentality, even little awareness of person as such, but a deeper consciousness that Jesus is present in the movement to save and heal our wounded Earth. In fact, what he has said and done in the Temple needs to be said and done now in our age by each of us, if we only have the same courage and strength. Suddenly an ecological, technical, scientific and partly political trip is turned without any pre-planning into a retreat experience. It is intriguing how the unexpected and unwished has somehow become a goal, for I had never foreseen going to the Holy Land as a pilgrim.

Ground Zero

Saving the Earth is part of our survival instincts, but it becomes all the more worthwhile because sacred blood has been spilled on Calvary and nowhere else. Earth and people are inseparably redeemed and tied together in the mysterious events of salvation history, in which our God has participated in a direct and unique manner. For us believers, Calvary becomes the ground and central point from which all direction begins and the point to which all attention turns; it is a believer's ground zero. From here Earth healing takes on a renewed form.

The day after the experience our party hikes down into a valley path about a dozen miles northwest of Jerusalem, which leads through a wilderness to a small river flowing down from the metropolitan area to the Mediterranean Sea. The rushing torrent proclaims by its smell that what was once rustic, scenic, and even perhaps pristine, has become the virtually unprocessed open sewage system of greater Jerusalem. The growing courage of the Calvary experience brings out my indignation at the debriefing session that evening. "The prophet Jeremiah would turn over in his grave, if he saw this. *Our* land needs a treatment plant." Collective responsibility goes beyond our native land.

THE RETURN: THE COMING OF WINTER

Being ordained without a pastoral charge I have a rare opportunity to substitute or do "supply" work at Liturgies when regular pastors are away or ill. It has occurred about two thousand times and involves the challenge of delivering homilies to a mix of people with wide ranges of age and learning. The religious experience of celebration, the connection to the Divine, and the sharing, meets the more immediate cares and concerns of these people in the pew. Spreading the "Good News" of our common faith, goals and aspirations is often tested by the bad news filling the media and my work-week concerns. In reality we have to balance bad news with good news to actualize God's power within us.

A note of caution

If we lose sight of our ongoing journey and cease to touch the Earth, we may waiver in enthusiasm and faith. Failing to touch the Earth could weaken our resolve and faith. Too many of our fellow travelers have grown foot weary and reach in joggers' language the "wall." They doubt whether they can go on. They seek out cultures of death and powerless denial, negation, and excuse. It is up to believers to show how to touch and be energized by this Earth and the creating hand of God. We are "humus" and into this we shall return. We need not look up and out for a then and there, but down to the *here* and *now*. To touch the Earth with respect is empowering; to neglect it leaves us bewildered and lost.

The touched rock becomes a touched Earth. It comes at the autumn of life, at the pilgrimage climax even unbeknown to me. In my springtime and summer I have learned from the natural revelations of our farm world, my local bioregion with its plants and animals, the geological formations, and the way to predict the weather. Later that revelation expands in studying science texts and learning from teachers. I stoop to fathom the *here* with its proper bearing; I strain to know the *now* of critical importance by being willing to risk the trite and make hay while the sun shines. But the last of the triad to attain is the *we*. This quest for the *we* involves overcoming the "me," accepting my limitations and inability to do meaningful things alone, and acknowledging the need to be cooperative. Alone I can do little to save our Earth; together we can heal this wounded Earth. A shared community of believers with a common religious experience calls out *we*.

On this final return trip the *we* remembers together its past, and that is Liturgy celebration. We recall our plans, our hopes, our goals. We help each other when we stumble; we remind ourselves that we live in a throwaway society that will trash the old in a wink, deny the goodness of all creation, and regard our creative role in creating waste. We ought to conserve our precious resources, even our past treasures. To save our Earth requires the fullest use of our religious and scientific gifts—and that needs be preached in the pulpit and practiced in the laboratory of our Earth. We can do it with God's help.

Patterns of Relationship

Mary Louise Dolan, CSJ

"This ambush, this silence,
 Where shadow can change into flame,..."
 —Theodore Roethke. "The Longing"[1]

I am a scientist. I am a religious person. I would like to explore some relationships between religion and science, particularly the science of ecology. My thesis is that both religion and ecology are concerned with relationships. My basic assumption is that there is some "order" in the universe. My basic methodology involves using patterns to gain insight.

Patterns of relationship seem to pervade the Universe. Ecology is the science of relationships, defined as "the totality or pattern of relations between organisms and their environment"[2] Religion is "the quest for the values of the ideal life, involving three phases: the ideal, the practices for attaining the values of the ideal, and the theology or world view relating the quest to the environing universe"[3] Religion and ecology are both about relationship.

I would like to first look at how I came to my view of religion and ecology. I have long been intrigued by beauty and mystery. So it is not surprising that I became a biologist, one who studies *bios logos*, the word of life. After being rather broadly trained as an undergraduate, I studied cellular biology and spent much of my professional life trying to understand and teach about cells. These activities have had a major impact upon my "world view."

As a scientist, one is trained to speak within the limits of what the data will allow. So one learns to confine one's dogmatic statements to precise areas of experience and, even then, await the results of the next experiment. One learns to make distinctions, to generate hypotheses, to experiment, and to formulate models which can be tested. This approach tends to become a habit of mind.

Doing science is hard work. It requires long hours, and struggle, and a willingness to let everything that has been known be challenged by the data. Scientific understanding, like one's models of God or self, involves ongoing process. In this sense, science and religion have something in common. Both delve into the unknown. Both involve willingness to let the data revise understanding. Both, in my experience, lead to surprises, and both reveal, and are motivated by, a delight in the beautiful.

Given this basic approach, it is not surprising that when I recently became involved with ecospirituality, I found myself using what I already understood to find points of entry into what I did not know. I kept asking myself "How in the world did a cellular biologist get mixed up in spirituality (bad enough in itself) but in spirituality which related to ecology (even worse because it was not my scientific discipline)? Although the answer to that question is still unclear, I'm beginning to think that the question is unimportant. The fact is, I *am* involved in ecospirituality, and the important questions now follow from that fact, not precede it.

What I have found along the way, however, has been surprising. I have found that what I knew about science, and more specifically what I knew about cells, has helped me to understand a great deal about both ecology and spirituality. (By spirituality I mean applied religion.) In terms of ecology, this does not mean that I consider myself to be an ecologist; I am still practically as ignorant of ecology's discipline content as before. I do, however, think that knowing about cells has given me what could be called an "ecological" outlook. Another way to say this is that although I do not know specific discipline facts about ecology, cells have taught me what could be called ecological principles. And these principles, amazingly enough, hold true in the area of spirituality also.

My point in describing this personal history is that pattern and relationship are important, and I would like to explore the relationship between religion and ecology in this context.

INSCAPING

I have long been intrigued by the idea of "inscaping." It is a term Gerard Manley Hopkins used to describe "that 'individually-distinctive' form (made up of various sense-data) which constitutes the rich and revealing 'one-ness' of the natural object"[4]. To me, the term means a "stacking" of realities, somewhat like boxes within boxes. My idea is that if something can be learned about one reality or box, some things can be inferred about other realities or boxes. My reference point for this idea comes from biology. Cells make up tissues, which make up organs, which make up organisms which operate and constitute ecosystems. Although there are certainly important differences on the various levels, there are similarities in the ways operations work. There are, for example, similarities in the ways cells and organisms relate to their environments. It is possible, then, to look at one level of reality , for example, cells, for insight into understanding other levels, for example, organisms.

When I began learning about ecospirituality, I encountered the fact that most of the connections between science and religion were being made by physicists. So I read works linking physics and religion. I found a relationship between my notion of inscaping and David Bohm's concept of wholeness and the implicate order[5]. Bohm, a theoretical physicist, used holograms as his basic consideration. Holograms make a photographic record of the interference pattern of light waves coming off an object and "each part contains information about the whole object"[6]. This notion of order, which he calls the implicate order, allows one to say that "everything is enfolded into everything"[7]. Bohm also believed that "what should be said is that wholeness is what is real, ...all our different ways of thinking are to be considered as different ways of looking at the one reality, each with some domain in which it is clear and adequate...."[8]

The concept of implicate order illuminated my notion of inscaping and, in fact, expanded it into the realm of physics. Bohm's ideas about wholeness dealt with science. But it seemed to me that more than science was involved. My study of ecospirituality was revealing similar statements about wholeness. Thomas Berry, for example, quotes Aquinas as saying that the Universe *together* participates in the goodness of God and that the *whole* represents God more fully than any individual does[9].

Patterns of relationship and the primacy of wholeness seemed to characterize both scientific disciplines and ecospirituality.

RELATIONSHIP IN SCIENCE

Wholeness and relationship pervade the natural world. We know that complex interrelationships of parts can constitute new levels of being. The intimacy and variety of these relationships are being revealed by contemporary science. What we as individuals and as a species need to appropriate, however, is the *meaning* of our connectedness to the rest of the material world. Science can tell us *that* we are related; it is we who choose to *live* relatedly. Not doing so counters, at the very least, our very biology.

Patterns of relationships extend throughout the natural world. Atoms, molecules, cells, organisms, social groups, and ecosystems are constituted by, and constitute, levels of organization. The most fundamental level of being is that studied by quantum physics. Experimental findings in this discipline have completely changed our conceptions of "reality," and of science. Quantum theory "has come to see the universe as an interconnected web of physical and mental relations whose parts are only defined through their connections to the whole."[10] Energy and matter are equivalent, related by the speed of light. Photons of light act as waves and particles. Bell's theorem states that any two particles that originated from a single source (such as two electrons formed from a collision of energies) would later behave as if they maintained some kind of on-going, non-local connection unaffected by time or distance. The theorem "implies, at a quantum level, that the physical world is an inseparable whole."[11]

By their interactions subatomic particles constitute protons and neutrons. Protons, neutrons and electrons interact to constitute atoms, and atoms interactively constitute molecules.

Complex organizations of molecules constitute cells, the basic living unit on the planet. Cells are in turn like micro-ecosystems. They contain numerous organelles, structures such as cell membranes, ribosomes, and mitochondria. Each of these organelles is in turn made up of complex arrangements of proteins and lipids. Each organelle is distinct; each is related to the others. Two cellular examples of this are (1) DNA and (2) cell membranes.

I will briefly describe these two examples because they illustrate relatedness. They show how one level of cellular being is enfolded within others. These examples are matter for inscaping, for implicating. The events I will describe occur *within* cells[12], but they correspond to phenomena which also occur *among* cells, *among* organs in an organism, and *among* organisms in an ecosystem. The principles these cellular examples illustrate are ecological principles.

My first cellular example, DNA, is the molecule which encodes a cell's life activities. It is made of a series of molecular building blocks which specify instructions for making the proteins which carry out life's functions. DNA is the chemical pattern, or blueprint, for life. It is passed from generation to generation and maintains constancy in a species. It also remains flexible enough, through change or mutation, to provide for variety and evolution. DNA, in one sense, controls all cellular activities. It contains instructions for all that a cell can be or do and is very important in itself. In another sense, however, DNA is completely dependent upon its surroundings for its being and functioning. It is made, and repaired, and replicated by other molecules (proteins) which were in turn made using instructions from DNA. It functions by responding to protein or hormone signals from its environment. DNA functions in response to its environment and its responsive functioning in turn alters its environment. It is a molecule which functions in relationship to the whole cell, in fact to the cell in environment. It is constituted by relationships among many atoms, exists as itself, and functions in relationship.

Cell membranes, my second cellular example, are complex, fluid arrangements of lipids and proteins. They are more complex than DNA in that they are constituted by several kinds of molecules. Cell membranes have the dual, seemingly contradictory, functions of separating the cell from its environment and connecting it to its environment. They mark off the cell as entity and connect all that goes on inside the cell to all that occurs outside it. Put another way, they constitute the cell as separate and constitute it as social.

Much work is currently being done on understanding how cell membranes mediate external and internal cellular events. Some ways involve the passage of materials through the membranes; some involve internalizing or externalizing materials using membrane vesicles, some involve direct physical contact between membrane proteins or lipids and molecules inside or outside the cell. The specific pathways vary, but the connectedness is intimate on a molecular level, and extensive. The membrane is a whole, but, like DNA, it is a whole that is also totally implicated. (Do some "implicating" now—how about skin on a body, or organisms in a group?).

Multicellular organisms, plants and animals, are even more complex levels of being. In multicellular beings, part of a cell's environment is other cells. Interactions among cells are extremely important for devel-

oping organisms and for maintaining adult organisms. Information on
these topics form the subject matter of many science courses. My point
is that the interactions among cells represent yet another level of relatedness, another "box" in the stack. To give just one example which
caught my attention, a recent article described experiments studying the
interactions among developing muscle cells in an amphibian embryo.
The authors describe the interaction and say that "We call this interaction [among the same kind of cells] a community effect, which we define
as an interaction among many nearby progenitor cells, as a result of
which these cells activate tissue-specific genes and differentiate coordi-
nately as a uniform population."[13] If you would change nouns such as
"cells" and "tissue-specific genes" to appropriate alternate terms, the
sentence could be describing the formation of cells, or social groups, or
ecosystems. (Try it!)

Cells and tissues, then, represent another level of "inscaping." They
in turn generate another level of being, a complex multicellular organism such as a human who functions using many organ systems. Our various systems, digestive, circulatory, skeletal and others, are made of separate organs, each composed of interacting tissues in turn made up of
interacting, responsive cells. The organs co-operate to sustain a person's
life.

Patterned relatedness certainly operates on physical and biological
levels. The relationships are both horizontal, such as between atoms or
between cells, and also vertical, such as between atoms and molecules or
between cells and tissues. Details being elucidated by scientific experiments increasingly show that "separateness" exists only in "relationship."

How does the science relating to cellular and organismic biology
apply to ecology? Here is how a fairly recent Ecology text is organized[14].
Part One, The Individual and the Environment, deals with the individual
organism and its physical environment and resources. Part Two studies
populations, one kind or species of organism. Part Three, Social
Interactions, deals with behavioral interactions among individuals in the
same population. Part Four examines Population Interactions, or how
different species interact among each other. Part Five, Organization of
Communities, considers the cumulative effects of interactions among
many species. Part Six, Distribution of Communities, discusses the distri-
butions of communities in space and time. Part Seven, Ecosystems, sum-

marizes all the interactions of species within a community with each other and with their physical environments. It seems to me that these levels of organization extend and enlarge the levels of organization already described for atoms and cells and organisms. The world and its processes are all of a piece. As David Bohm says "the whole universe is actively enfolded to some degree in each of the parts....The more fundamental truth is the truth of internal relatedness, because it is true of the more fundamental order, which I call the implicate order, because in this order the whole and hence all the other parts are enfolded in each part....Vice versa, however, the idea of implicate order means that we are enfolded in the world-not only in other people, but in nature as a whole....Indeed, it can be said that, as we are not complete without the world which is enfolded in us, so the world is not complete without us who are enfolded in it."[15]

MIND AND RELATIONSHIP

I would next like to briefly consider how "mind" might relate to what has already been said. Although clearly outside my area of professional expertise, mind serves as an appropriate bridge between what is traditionally viewed as the content of science, the "physical" world, and the content of religion, the "spiritual" world.

Several ideas relative to mind and inscaping seem pertinant. One fascinating notion is James Hillman's idea of the psyche. He calls it "psychological polytheism." He says that "The psyche is not only multiple, it is a communion of many persons, each with specific needs, fears, longings, styles, and language...."[16] "We are imagining the psyche's basic structure to be an inscape of personified images."[17] This certainly is an intriguing idea about the psyche; it is consistent with the ways atoms, and cells, and ecosystems are constituted. It implies that the whole, the psyche, is constituted by interaction of parts such as, in my case, my science-psyche, my spiritual-psyche and so forth.

Another idea relates to the mind-body relationship, one of those zones of interaction which challenge neat categories. David Ray Griffin says that "the mind-body relation is not a great exception in the scheme of things but paradigmatic for a type of relation pervading nature....The human person is...a nested hierarchy of experiences, with lesser experiences inside of more inclusive ones. The relation between the mind and

the brain cells is repeated by the relation between each cell and its constituents...."[18]

Multiple vertical and horizontal relationships may be involved in
generating mind. Patterned relationships, documented precisely with
"hard data" for quantum physics, cell biology, and ecology, may also
characterize mind. There is no doubt that body influences mind. Some
studies examining the relationships between psychic states and the
immune and endocrine systems provide evidence that mind also affects
body. Could a pattern of patterns be emerging?

RELIGION AND RELATIONSHIP

Having made a case that science demonstrates that relationship is
ingrained within the Universe and that patterning also abounds, I would
like to explore religion and relationship.

First of all, the very word religion means to tie back together. This
implies that religion is about reestablishing connection. In this regard, I
rather like William Irwin Thompson's remark that "One needs only to
reconnect (re-ligio) what is broken. If the way of life is not broken away
from the tree of life, then one does not need a religion to reconnect it."[19]
Perhaps religion is more properly concerned with extending and articulating the relationships between matter and spirit than with re-connect-
ing them.

Secondly, religion and science are related within the lives and experience of religious scientists (and scientific religious?). The minds and
actions of these persons relate these two areas. Perhaps this relates to
James Hillman's psychological polytheism, but both scientific and religious ways of seeing and being certainly cohere in many humans. The
relationships are most likely as varied as the persons involved, but in
each case there *is* a kind of relationship.

Thirdly, religions have always addressed at core the relationships
between the world and the Divine. Views about the nature of God, the
nature of the world, and the nature of the connections between them
have certainly varied through spacetime. One can argue, in fact, that
opinions on these questions have been a major source of separation
among humans. Isn't it ironic that what claims to reconnect actually separates? I would argue that this separation is also illusory, a separation in
belief only. It is impossible to be really separated, physically or spiritual-

ly, from each other. As Thomas Berry says "We may think we are separated, we may feel separated, but it is impossible to *be* separated."[20]

Fourthly, I would like to postulate that the content of religion, and perhaps God, might ultimately be the most complete level of wholeness and the most profound expression of relatedness. Might not Bohm's "everything is enfolded into everything" be another way of addressing the imminent/transcendent Beingness of God, totally present and totally Other? This, of course, cannot be proven using the methodological approach or techniques of science. But as a scientist, I do like order and continuity, even in this age of chaos! I choose to believe that order and continuity are possible. In fact, I would rather believe this than believe that there is an inconsistency between how God is and how the rest of the Universe is. I would rather believe a theology that is consistent with scientific findings than trust theologians whose conclusions contradict science. And since we are in the realm of discussing a Being who by definition is Ultimate Mystery, we are here in the realm of belief, and belief involves choice.

Religious belief boils down to belief. Belief is based on personal experience and also flows out of the experience of others. There is here also a relationship. It is the faith and experience of others which save me and my belief from the illusion of separateness. So that although I have to be true to my experience and belief, I cannot do this in isolation. I am influenced by and must also attend to the experience and belief of others.

There are several theologians who express views which seem consistent with the idea of an inscaped God. Sallie McFague postulates that viewing the Universe as God's body is an "attractive, powerful" metaphor[21]. "To think," she says, "of the entire evolutionary process, with all the billions of galaxies of stars and planets from the beginning of time, some fifteen billion years ago, as the 'body' of God, the visible 'sacrament' as it were of the invisible God, is a model of profound immanence and overwhelming transcendence. God is immanent in all the processes or reality, expressing the divine intentions and purposes through those processes, and at the same time God, as the agent of the process, is transcendent over it though as its internal source, power, and goal rather than as an external controller."[22] This view would seem to be consistent with the traditional Christian belief that "in God we live and move and have our being"[23]. We are enfolded in God.

John F. Haught also seems to be talking about inscaping when he suggests that "The religious adventure may now be situated within a more comprehensive cosmic epic."[24] What an interesting reversal of the usual way of looking at matters! He says that "More and more explicitly the sciences are representing the cosmos itself as a story, or perhaps even better, as an adventure. Adventure, according to Whitehead's definition, is the aim toward novel forms of order, or toward increasingly wider beauty. Viewed over the long haul, the Universe appears to be an adventure toward increasingly intense versions of ordered novelty, toward a surpassing and always elusive beauty. Thus, in a certain sense, we can now envisage the entire cosmos, *not just religion* [my emphasis] as a pilgrimage....The cosmos is not a static point of departure for the religious journey; it is itself a journeying."[25]

The consequences of imaging God and the Universe this way are massively extensive and eminantly practical. Considering them is beyond the scope of this essay, has been done by others, and is most appropriately left to *your* imagination. Suffice it to say that science and religion can both agree that we are intimately related to earth and cosmos. We are totally implicated in them. And as a religious scientist, I believe that we and the entire cosmos are totally implicated in God. "Everything in nature is enfolded eternally into God's own compassionate experience. This way of thinking about the world should make a difference ecologically. For everything that happens in the world happens also to God. God is our ultimate environment."[26]

As a scientist and as religious person, I am reminded of a statement of Wendell Berry which tells the gift of both scientist and religious person. As Berry walks the land, he notes that "The presence of the creation here makes this a holy place, and it is as a pilgrim that I have come. It is the creation that has attracted me, its perfect interfusion of life and design. I have made myself its follower and its apprentice....It is the privilege and the labor of the apprentice of creation to come with his imagination into the unimaginable, and with his speech into the unspeakable."[27]

REFERENCES

1.   Theodore Roethke. "The Longing" in The Collected Poems. New York:

Anchor Press/Doubleday, 1975, p 182.

2. Webster's 7th New Collegiate Dictionary. G and C Merriam Co., Springfield,MA, 1963, p 262.

3. The American College Dictionary. New York: Random House, 1955, p 1024-5.

4. W.H Gardner, in Poems and Prose of Gerard Manley Hopkins. Baltimore: Penguin Books, 1953, p xx.

5. David Bohm. Wholeness and The Implicate Order. New York: Ark Paperbacks, 1980.

6. Ibid., p 177.

7. Ibid.

8. Ibid., p 8.

9. Thomas Berry. Reinventing the Human. Video from Friends of Creation Spirituality, PO Box 19216, Oakland, CA 94619.

10. Fritjof Capra. The Tao of Physics. Boston: Shambala, 1991, p 142.

11. Robert Gilman. The Next Great Turning. In Context #34, Winter 1993, p 12.

12. See, for example, James Darnell, Harvey Lodish and David Baltimore. Molecular Cell Biology, Second Edition. New York: W H Freeman and Co., 1990, Chapters 7-14, 19, 23.

13. J B Gurdon, E Tiller, J Roberts and K Kato. "A Community Effect in Muscle Development." Current Biology 3(1):1, 1993.

14. Paul R Ehrlich and Jonathan Roughgarden. The Science of Ecology. New York: Macmillan Publishing Co., 1987.

15. David Bohm. "Postmodern Science in a Postmodern World" in David Ray Griffin (ed). The Reenchantment of Science. Albany, New York: SUNY Press, 1988, pp 66-67.

16. Thomas Moore, in Thomas Moore (ed). A Blue Fire: Selected Writings of James Hillman. NY: HarperPerennial, 1989, p 37.

17. James Hillman, op. cit., p 48.

18. David Ray Griffin, in D R Griffin (ed). The Reenchantment of Science. Albany, New York: SUNY Press, 1988, pp 157-8.

19. William Irwin Thompson in David Spangler and William Irwin Thompson. Reimagination of the World. Santa Fe: Bear and Co., 1991, p 111.

20. Thomas Berry. Lecture given at Spiritearth, Weston MA on May 8, 1993.

21. Sallie McFague. "An Earthly Theological Agenda." In Carol J. Adams, Ecofeminism and the Sacred. New York: Continuum, 1993, p 95.

22. Ibid.

23. Acts 17:28.

24. John F Haught. "Religion and the Origins of the Environmental Crises" in Michael Barnes (ed). An Ecology of the Spirit. New York: University Press of America, 1994, p 39.

25. Ibid.

26. John F Haught. "Good News For The Entire Universe, Not Just Us Humans." Praying #61, July-August 1994, p 12.

27. Wendell Berry. "A Walk Down Camp Branch." Wild Earth 4(2): 70, Summer, 1994.

PART TWO

Religious Ethics in Dialogue with Environmental Ethics

Penning the Goring Bull: Evaluting Five Potential Christian Ethical Responses to Environmental Pollution

Susan Power Bratton

Although there have been numerous books and articles published in the field of religious environmental ethics, most discussion in Christian environmental ethics remains very general. The concept that Christians should be good "stewards" of natural resources, for example, legitimizes Christian participation in the secular sphere of resources management, but does not define or limit the types of environmental (or economic) actions appropriate for Christians. A substantial portion of the more sophisticated Christian ecotheological literature deals primarily with cosmological issues, which may be helpful in raising Christian awareness of the importance of human relationship to the environment, but often provides little direct guidance concerning personal responses to specific environmental problems. The purpose of this paper is to investigate three actual cases of conflict in the area of pollution regulation and management and to evaluate the usefulness of five Christian ethical models, including personal purity, simplicity, stewardship, rights for natural objects, and neighborliness, in resolving the pollution problems.

THE POLLUTION CASES

Case 1: Indoor air pollution in research and teaching laboratories. During the last decade, I have worked at two academic institutions, one state-run, the other church-related, that have had problems with indoor air quality. At one site, an ecological research laboratory, the early reports of health impacts were primarily from laboratory technicians with repeated sinus and bronchial infections. As recognition of the problem developed, or perhaps as it worsened due to changes in management of the air circulation system, secretaries, custodians, faculty and students reported symptoms ranging from rashes, to headaches, to fatigue. (See Sherman 1988, Goodish 1990, Scott 1990, and Samet &Spencer 1991 for information on the health effects of chemical exposures and of indoor air pollution.) The on-site administrators were quite conscientious about forwarding the complaints to the health and safety division, who had neither the equipment to analyze the pollution sources nor the expertise to eliminate them. The senior faculty members (primarily male, and generally not working in the building all day) were either indifferent, since they weren't noticing any health effects themselves, or were actually antagonistic, accusing the secretaries and technicians of psychological problems. Ultimately, a custodian, a black woman who could ill afford the extra medical bills generated by building-induced respiratory problems, fainted during a pollution event. That afternoon, a technician measured the levels of the several chemicals in the air in the hallway, near the location where the custodian had collapsed. None of the compounds detected exceeded the U.S. federal standards, but formaldehyde and ethyl benzene were between 40 and 60% of the allowable concentrations (Hathaway, Proctor, Hughes & Fishman, 1991), and toluene was well above trace levels.

The second setting where I encountered the indoor air question was the science building of a church-related college. Several people had reported building related health difficulties, including headaches, nausea, fatigue, eye irritation, temporary loss of motor coordination, loss of memory and rashes. Testing by professional consultants indicated elevated levels of carbon dioxide, but the firm made no attempt to evaluate presence of volatile organic compounds. An undergraduate class organized an (unofficial) air test one afternoon and found that the indoor air had three times more carbon dioxide than outside air, a high (but legal) level of formaldehyde, a trace of benzene, and 1200 parts per million of ethanol, which did exceed the U.S. standards of 1000 parts per million. Although some of the faculty were willing to file health reports when they were experiencing sudden onset of symptoms potentially induced by poor building air quality, other faculty considered the complaints invented or psychological, and tried to discredit any student attempts to check fume hoods or determine patterns of air flow.

The two institutions in question should have been among the most "ethical" in the United States, at least in resolving problems with environmental pollution, but neither seemed able to respond effectively. Both these sites had some common components in their indoor air problems: laboratory effluent was probably a factor; the management of the air circulation systems probably did not provide adequate air flow or renewal; many of the victims were women or lower social status employees, such as custodians, technicians and secretaries, who stayed in the same enclosed air space all day; many senior staff, including scientists (or particularly scientists), did not take the problems seriously or actually opposed taking any action to alleviate them; both institutions were probably operating within legal standards much of the time; violations were unintentional; and the health impacts and injuries were the result of one's own or someone else's work related activities.

Case 2: Release of agricultural effluents into ground water and into the Chesapeake Bay by Christian farmers. A second case is that of the continuing degradation of water quality in the Chesapeake Bay, USA, caused by a combination of industrial effluents; automobile produced nitrogen compounds; sediment from building sites; urban and suburban runoff containing petroleum compounds, pesticides and fertilizers; effluent from sewage plants; toxins from marine anti-fouling paints; leachate from coal mines; and agricultural runoff, including eroded top soil, fertilizers and pesticides. High levels of nutrients reaching the Chesapeake Bay result in blooms of periophyton, which in turn shade and kill the grass beds. Poor water quality in the Chesapeake Bay has exacerbated a decline in the oyster and other fisheries, which probably began with overharvest, but now threatens the income of local watermen. (Horton, 1991) Although, they are hardly responsible for the total magnitude of the environmental disaster, the practices of farmers in the Susquehanna River drainage are an important component of the increased loads of nutrients reaching the Bay itself. Among these agriculturalists are many Amish of Swiss or German Anabaptist origin, who are very conscientious about their care for the land and have always made heavy use of manure and other fertilizers. Ironically, due to the Amish community's concern that farm size be limited—to discourage pride and encourage humility and equitable integration into the Amish community (Gelassenheit)—Amish farmers have intensified their agricultural practices in order to make an adequate living off their small (by contemporary standards) holdings. In 1978, Amish farms in Lancaster County, PA, averaged 84 acres, and generally ranged from 30 to 120 acres in size. Additional land is now available only at very high prices, at least partially because of competition with suburban housing development and with corporate farmers. (Kraybill 1989, Hostetler 1980, Horst 1988) Many Amish have increased the size of their dairy herds, and have removed hedge-rows and even woodlots to put more acreage into production. Where the latter has been done along streams, it eliminates vegetation that would reduce the amount of sediment and nutrients reaching the water. This case is similar to case I in that the origin of the pollution is work or economic activity, and that the livelihood or health of other humans is being threatened, although the impacts are unintentional. Unlike Case 1, however, there is a large natural ecosystem involved, and those producing the pollution often do not personally know those likely to be affected by it.

Case 3: The release of hazardous pollutants by manufacturing firms in the U.S. and in Mexico. A third case is the prevalence of cancer or birth defects near certain industrial complexes. In Brownsville, Texas, for example, there has been a high incidence of anencephaly, lack of brain development in fetuses. Some suspect hazardous chemicals produced by the *maquiladoras*, U.S. owned industries just across the Rio Grande River in Mexico, may be to blame. The plants *are* releasing a number of potentially hazardous organic compounds into the air and into the Rio Grande River. Researchers are presently attempting to correlate the pollutants to clusters of birth defects. This case is similar to the Case I in that it involves personal injury as the result of the economic activities of another party. It is also similar to Case 1, in that the victims are primarily working class people who may have limited access to national or international legal systems. This case differs from the first two, however, because the releases of hazardous materials may be intentional, and there is little doubt some of the firms involved moved operations to Mexico at least partially to avoid U.S. laws and regulations.

CHRISTIAN PURITY ETHICS

The first question to ask, especially in investigating the first two cases is: why are the existing dominant ethical models or the social values or virtues emphasized by the Christian groups involved ineffective in regulating the sources of environmental pollution? The Evangelical Christian college discourages use of personal pollutants, by banning tobacco and alcoholic beverages, and the Amish are committed to simple life-style as a central community value, yet these emphases have not produced social responses that have resolved the pollution problems. Since Christianity has long been a major contributor to western cultural values, perhaps these cases can provide some clues as to why techno-industrial society often lacks both Christian and "cultural" ethics that really deal with pollution in a concrete way. The first logical step, therefore, is to investigate an apparent disparity in the indoor air case—why would some Christians perceive of release of cigarette smoke as deeply morally wrong—enough so that it is formally forbidden—and not perceive of release of formaldehyde from a laboratory as problematic? Why, in the Christian college case, didn't the ban on the toxins, alcohol and tobacco, extend to their indoor air analogs?

Why prohibit drinking ethanol, while allowing the students to breath it?

In locating the source of this discrepancy, the first thing to recognize is that in Evangelical Christian circles, alcohol and tobacco are considered personal pollutants, and any Christian prohibition on their use is an example of a *purity ethic*. This is much like the Old Testament laws that made purity a central issue for both individuals and the nation of Israel. A person must be pure—free from unclean foods and substances—to remain within the social group or to enter the temple and participate in worship. For Jews, uncleanness arises from such diverse sources as eating unclean animals (pigs, birds that feed on carrion, etc.), contact with bodily discharges, and contact with corpses. The Jewish people, similarly, can be contaminated by idolatry. The uncleanness is not just physical, it is also spiritual—a state that remains with the individual until a proper, group sanctioned ritual is performed to remove the "dirt." The unclean is thus the opposite of the "holy," which always remains pure. The discovery of an unclean substance inside, not just a Jewish religious sanctuary, but in some contexts within a home or (in Biblical narrative) a military camp, would result in immediate remedial action.(Levine 1989, Rose 1992, Gammie 1989, Patrick 1985, Birch 1991)

In some Christian circles, alcohol and tobacco are more than toxins that may eventually harm you. They are associated with undesirable behavior of other types (partying, dancing, sexual immorality), and complete abstention (or nearly so) may be a condition of membership in a Christian social group, such as a local church, a denomination or a school. Personal use of alcohol or tobacco is considered spiritually as well as physically contaminating. During the 19th and early 20th century, when ax-bearing Christian women called for the demise of "demon rum," they were fighting a source of spiritual degradation as well as a source of social evils. As Douglas (1966) has shown, purity ethics are often used to define a social group and its membership, and for ancient Israel, dietary laws "would have been like signs which at every turn inspired meditation on the oneness, purity and completeness of God."

The release of formaldehyde as the by-product of laboratory operations has no association with traditional "sinful" behaviors, and hopefully it is not being purposefully consumed by an individual. Since contemporary Christian purity ethics are primarily based on personal possession or consumption, we have conceptual difficulty extending them to cases where someone else is remotely injured by a poisonous compound. The ancient Israelites, in contrast, did treat substances themselves as sources of defilement that could contaminate other objects, such as a seat, or clothing, or the temple.

The contemporary disassociation of impurity from place has interesting implications for the ethics of manufacturing potentially harmful substances. In the United States, religious ethics concerning the possession and use of alcohol and tobacco have historically only weakly covered production and sales. Mennonite and Baptist farmers who do not smoke tobacco may grow it as a cash crop, and many Christians who do not drink alcoholic beverages, work in or patronize establishments that sell them. In the U.S., agriculture is considered a very worthy occupation, and is often idealized (e.g., Thomas Jefferson and his nation peopled by small farmers) by the Protestant work ethic. Since the sale of a high value cash crop, such as tobacco, may make the difference between paying the taxes and interest on the farm and losing the property, U.S. Christians are very unwilling to hold the farmer responsible for the production of a potentially toxic crop. In techno-industrial society, if involvement in sales of an "impure" substance is necessary to the individual's livelihood, we tend to divorce it from the question of consumption and the associated behaviors.

Committed environmentalists utilize a form of purity ethic when they only buy "green" products, restrict grocery shopping to "natural" foods, or completely avoid pesticides. It would be very difficult to get contemporary western society to believe, however, that if someone disposed of something improperly, the dirt would stay on them even when the substance was remote from them, and they would thereby be spiritually or ritually contaminated. A purity ethic, therefore, is unlikely to gain wide acceptance as a solution to environmental pollution. Since current Christian purity ethics are very strongly based on sexual behavior and personal consumption, their transfer to higher levels of social organization such as corporate municipalities, and nations (and among Christian denominations) is unlikely. A key limitation environmentally is contemporary Christian unwillingness to extend purity ethics, even in areas of established concern, such as alcohol consumption, to most business establishments and types of employment. I also suspect that the long standing Christian emphasis on converting the user rather than on regulating the producer (the temperance movement not withstanding) is one of the reasons Christians are often unwilling to consider industrial production of toxins as a moral issue of Christian interest.

SIMPLICITY

Perhaps more of a surprise than the narrow spectrum of purity ethics is the apparent failure of Amish simplicity to curtail water pollution. The difficulty, in non-technical language, is that religious simplicity and cow manure are perfectly compatible, while cow manure and the Chesapeake Bay are not. One product of Amish efforts to preserve community and simplicity—small farm size—may actually have encouraged greater concentrations of pollutants.

The failure of simplicity to limit water pollution is rooted in the way simplicity itself is socially defined and expressed, and in the competing or conflicting values generated by the Amish work and land care ethic. Through Christian history the practice of simplicity has been extremely culturally relative. Monasticism, for example, has often forwarded intense asceticism, which indeed leads to almost no possessions (sometimes not even clothes), and little food consumption due to repeated fasting. Some monastic groups, however, have allowed the monastery, as an institution, to become rich or to hold large acreages of agricultural land, even if individual monks remain poor. The Amish are, by the standards of strict desert monasticism, very middle-class, since they own their own land and feed their families well. They wear plain clothes, however, and avoid personal possessions that would make the individual stand out from the group. The Old Order Amish disparage automobiles because they lead to pride and to the dispersion of the Amish community, not because they produce pollutants. The Amish concept of Gelassenheit is not intended to cope with water pollution per se. This situation, in fact, suggests that taking a Christian value, such as simplicity, and presenting it as an environmental ethic without completing adapting it to actual environmental problems is very likely to be only coincidentally effective. For industro-technical Christians giving up enough to make a real difference can be inhibited by the social matrix in which they live.

VALUES CONFLICTS

In looking at competing values between the Amish work and land management ethic and pollution control, it can be easily demonstrated that this difficulty applies to Cases 1 and 3 as well. Both the Amish farmer and the university scientist find part of their self-identity in their work and in the valuations of their peers. Cultivating fields, raising dairy cattle, running laboratory experiments and teaching chemistry to under- graduates are not, in themselves, evil actions. Optimization of produc- tion is good, from an Amish perspective, as is making enough profit, not just to keep shoes on the horses, but to buy a farm for a second son who might not inherit one otherwise. The well managed farm helps to preserve the Amish family, and the family is, to the Amish, the most important element in the Christian community.

In the indoor air case, the fact that the self esteem of scientists is strongly tied to their technical and professional knowledge and produc- tivity, may explain why so many of the scientists involved tried to dis- miss the pollution reports. The tendency of scientists to disbelieve that their activities might be physically harming someone else, isn't always an expression of scientific expertise, although it is often portrayed as such. It can also be a psychological way of removing a potential conflict through denial. The scientist is doing something very important for an entire culture, that places a high value on scientific achievement, so how could he or she, at the same time, be doing something wrong? Those of us residing in western industrial settings also find much of our self defini- tion in our schedules and temporal commitments. In neither of the insti- tutions having difficulties with indoor air, did it ever occur to anyone to simply shut down the laboratories for a couple of weeks and see if the air quality improved, or to stop all scientific progress for a few days and completely map the air flow in the buildings.

Values conflicts have probably delayed investigation of the *maquiladoras*. The Centers for Disease Control, when investigating the high rate of fetal deformity, initially ignored potential environmental causes, and had to be politically convinced they might need to track industrial effluents. Worries about economic recession may have made the U.S. government reticent to further regulate industry. Protection of infants is certainly a key social value in industrotechnological culture, and industrial progress also is. We usually deal with infant nurture on the family level, however, while "the economy" is a national or corporate issue, and thus often takes precedence.

LINKING THE INDIVIDUAL AND THE COMMUNITY

Having investigated two ethical models that are given high priority by actual Christian groups, but have not been adequate to resolve the three pollution cases, the next step is to determine what characteristics an effective ethical model would have. First, the ethical model must have a basis that overrides the values conflicts. It must be able to modify or curtail the traditional Protestant work ethic, which holds (on however weak a Biblical foundation) that making your fortune and being economically productive honors God. This suggests there should be a strong Biblical rationale for the ethical model and it should be tied to widely accepted Christian values. The model must both adapt to and confront existing social and cultural patterns.

Second, unlike the purity ethic discussed above, the ethical model must be viable at several different levels of social organization. It has to influence the behavior of both individuals and of communities, so it must integrate individual and group behavior and standards. Contemporary Christianity often falls ethically flat on its face, when it has to make transitions from the individual level, to the family level, to the corporate level, to the national level. This is at least partially because Christians (and philosophical environmental ethicists) are using different ethical standards for these different levels of social organization. Some differentiation, is, of course, necessary, but all too often, one level is largely exempt from the standards of another. In the case of simplicity, for example, most Christians can imagine pursuing simplicity as a personal goal within the framework of a religious group with a common viewpoint, but the entire U.S. and Europe suddenly seizing upon simplicity, or better yet, asceticism, as a major cultural value, seems less likely than a comet hitting the planet. Simplicity, as a virtue, does not transfer easily among levels of social organization. Christian groups that have maintained simplicity as a central value over long periods of time have partially isolated themselves from the surrounding culture, including other Christian communities.

Third, the ethical model must make the problems and conflicts and their sources identifiable. Grandiose models that do not identify the components of an environmental conflict are almost invariably ineffective.

Fourth, the ethical model must be compatible with other areas of Christian ethics. They should, for example, meet Christian criteria for forwarding social justice, and not conflict with other values within the Christian community. In the Amish case, simplicity may not be solving the environmental problem, but an ethical model that disparaged simplicity would be unacceptable because it would undermine key Amish community values.

Fifth, the model must provide relatively clear guidance to individuals and groups concerning the extent and form of their responsibilities. A problem with the purity ethic (as practiced today) is that it provides no standards for community response to producers of toxins.

Sixth, an effective ethical model must identify wrong or improper actions and attitudes as clearly as possible, while clarifying appropriate individual and community responses to violations of the ethic. Contemporary environmental ethics rarely addresses the question of appropriate penalties, yet some form of penalty or social sanction may be necessary to maintaining community relationships.

RIGHTS FOR NATURE AND STEWARDSHIP

In the three cases presented above, the common ethical dilemma is not specifically environmental, but is rather that the work or employment related activities of one group are damaging the health or livelihood of another. The second critical ethical concern, in Case I and 3, is that those most likely to be injured (women, minorities, and lower-salaried employees) are those least likely to be able to defend themselves administratively, legally, or through seeking other employment. A second critical ethical concern in Case 2 is the slow destruction of a large estuarine ecosystem, which supports a diversity of non-human life.

In Case 1, *a natural rights* approach recently justified in Christian theological terms by Nash (1991) is a poor fit, because natural objects or ecosystems are not being damaged. Although it is applicable in the second case, it does not socially tie the interests of the Amish to those of the watermen. The concept of *Christian stewardship* is a possibility for both cases, because the conflicts clearly concern resource management. Stewardship also traverses the social hierarchy more easily than simplicity does. Individual Christians may steward their homes, jobs and finances, and we can easily conceptualize a national government serving as a steward of rivers or forests.

In the cases investigated here, however, stewardship has several weaknesses. First, Christians see stewardship primarily as wise use. "Wise" use is, at best, difficult to evaluate—why should my uses be any less wise than yours? Second, the "Protestant ethic" tends to equate wise use with profit, steady economic growth, and prosperity (what one might term "anthropogenic providence"). Although we can say dumping hazardous waste in the Rio Grande isn't wise use of our resources, it makes it sound as if the company just executed poor business judgment, and might, at most, lose some money. Actually the company may have threatened the lives and health of children living miles away. Carefully composed discourses on Christian environmental stewardship, such as Wilkenson (1991), openly discourage viewing the creation as "natural resources," and encourage viewing the creation as "environment." Yet the vocabulary of stewardship itself remains problematic. "Good stewardship" is difficult to define as a virtue, because it is relative to both the ecosystem in question and the type of human interaction intended.

Another difficulty with the stewardship is its associations within Christian ethics as a whole. Pastors do discuss stewardship in sermons, but they almost always expound either on management of personal finances or on donations to the church. The usual assumption is that God has provided riches for Christians which they now have an obligation to manage as God wishes. This avoids at least two major ethical issues: first, were the financial or material resources obtained in an appropriate manner, and second, how one manages something that is not financial. Occasionally a pastor will discuss stewardship of time, but the sermon will almost invariably center on competition between work and recreational time and family and church centered activities (the pastor will emphasize the family and the church). Stewardship *within* the economic sphere is rarely a pulpit issue. Better farm productivity, or producing more scientific research superficially appear to be good stewardship of land and of intellectual talents. Although authors such as Hall (1990) present very temperate models of the Christian steward, in actual practice, one of the greatest failures of Christian stewardship ethics is that they imply good morals will be correlated with high, long term productivity, while asking few questions about acceptable costs.

NEIGHBORLINESS

A possible solution, in all three pollution cases, is a religious ethic based on *property and personal boundaries*. This might initially seem limited to individuals and families, thus lacking the desirable social linkages. It might also superficially appear to have less Biblical support than a purity ethic. The Hebrew scriptures (Old Testament), however, has numerous passages concerning the responsibilities of individuals to their neighbors in terms of preventing property damage and personal injury. Today we tend to ignore some of these, because most of us no longer own straying donkeys, but they might be generally termed the *laws of neighborliness*, and they are based on a few simple principles that are still quite applicable.

First, members of a holy community are responsible for the impacts of their businesses and households on the property of others. In Exodus 22:17, if a fire breaks out and bums grain, the one who started the fire must make restitution. In Exodus 21:33, if a man digs a pit and a neighbor's animal falls into it, the owner of the pit (an obvious hazard) must pay the neighbor but may keep the dead animal. In Exodus 22:5, if a family let their livestock stray and graze in someone else's field, they must compensate the damaged owner from their own fields.

Second, if a member of a community knows something he or she owns is dangerous, he or she is personally liable for the damage it does if he or she did not contain it properly. In Exodus, 21:28–32, for example, if a bull gores someone, and the owner knew the bull "had a habit of goring" and did not keep it penned, the owner is to be stoned along with the bull. (The owner could ransom his or her way out of this, but the bull could not.) The bull of Exodus is the cultural equivalent of some of the solvents used in research and industry—we know they can be deadly so it is the responsibility of the owner (or user) to keep them penned. Like bulls, pollutants are most dangerous when they are roaming uncontrolled around the countryside—and like bulls, some are much more dangerous than others.

Thirdly, we should not do anything that physically harms our neighbor or our neighbor's family. The Bible discusses this not only in terms of actual injuries, accidental or otherwise, (see, for example,

Exodus 22), but also declares, following a passage on slander, "Do not do anything that endangers your neighbor's life. I am the Lord" (NIV, Lev. 19:16)[1] The Law thus forbade threatening or risky actions, as well as providing standards for compensation once damage had occurred. This component of the model is very important because the purpose of the Protestant work ethic is presumably care of the family. Neighborliness provides a clear limitation to the work ethic—you can not support your family at the expense of someone else's. Neighborliness is also very compatible with Amish concepts of simplicity and of Christian community.

In the Misnah and the Talmud, Jewish rabbis extended the concepts found in the book of Exodus to include a wide range of property damage and human injury cases, among them consideration of environmental pollutants. The rabbis, for example, held that even if a damaging agent was moved or carried by natural forces, the person "who set an object in motion" was responsible for the damages it caused (Tainari, 1987). Jewish interpretation of Biblical precedents not only holds self injury to be wrong and to be avoided to the extent possible, but also enjoins against any sort of wasteful destruction, including that of one's own property. This latter prohibition, known as *ba'al tashhit*, is based on Deuteronomy 20:19-20, which states that one may not needlessly cut the enemy's fruit trees during a siege. (Tameri 1987, Novak 1992, Shomrei Adamah 1993) Rabbinical decisions concerning boundary maintenance between neighbors mediated strongly against activities inflicting personal injury on others. In addition, "disturbing tranquillity, infringing on the airspace, or obstructing the view of a neighbor were also seen as inflicting damage." Tainari (1987) concludes that: "Halakhic sources insist on the removal of dangerous industries or firms, whether the danger envisaged is physical (when health is affected), or aesthetic (when, e.g., the scenery is impaired)." Historically, polluting businesses, such as threshing floors, tanneries and kilns were not to be placed in Jewish villages, and exceptions were made only in politically dire situations, such as the restrictive ghettos, where the Jewish population had absolutely no other choice.

CONTEMPORARY DIFFICULTIES

Although the Hebrew scriptures makes individual responsibility clear, it was not written in a time when large corporations, with layer after layer of managers and experts, ran farms and businesses.

Historically, if someone's goats got into your orchard, finding the owner was probably quite easy, especially if you still had the goats. Rabbinical writers, for example, ruled the person whose fields were damaged by trespass grazing was permitted to slaughter a goat in the ritually correct manner, after warning the owner three times. The owner then had to retrieve the carcass (Tamari 1987). In our contemporary circumstances, collecting barrels full of toxic waste or contaminated groundwater only leads to further economic or health losses for the injured party. Further, if the offender is corporate, "an ownee, who is responsible, may be difficult to identify.

We must therefore make a conscious effort to adapt neighborliness to our more tangled social structures. Developing Christian language that identifies the individual's responsibilities within large, contemporary organizations, such as government agencies or corporations, is, in fact, critical to viable Christian ethics in general. For example, the owners or the salaried representatives of the owners (in a corporate case with many stock holders) would be responsible for maintaining and forwarding the internal regulations and organization within a business that ensure the health and property rights of others. Like the owner of the bull, they might beg lack of knowledge on the first offense, because they truly may not know what their employees (or industrial processes) have been doing. After a problem has been identified, however, the owners are morally responsible for regulating the activities of their business. If they know something they are selling is a potential pollutant or potentially hazardous, they have a responsibility to warn the buyer. This also works on an individual or family basis. If I buy or use something, such as batteries containing heavy metal or anti-freeze containing formaldehyde, that can potentially pollute the environment, the responsibility to manage the materials safely and to dispose of them properly (hopefully through recycling) is mine. In the indoor air cases, scientists would be responsible for reducing and containing their effluents, although if air circulation systems were inadequate, the scientists would be responsible to report the problem to the deans or trustees, who control the budgets, and have the authority to provide a safe resolution for everyone involved. Note here, that unlike the Exodus cases, responsibility must be shared, and thus has to be defined in terms of the individual's actual sphere of control.

A common contemporary corporate argument for not penning the bull is that an adequate fence is too expensive. What if the laboratories can not be operated without producing pollution or what if the institutions can not afford to fix the problems? Tamari (1987) cites rabbinical decisions where potentially damaging professional activities were permitted because those involved had no other way to earn a living. In general, however, rabbinic opinion has been that operations causing harm to the public or to the community should, if possible, be moved or terminated. Since, in all three cases cited here, it is technically possible to greatly reduce or eliminate effluents utilizing available technology or better management practices, neighborliness requires the responsible parties to attempt to reduce both health impacts and economic injury to the fullest extent possible.

In using the concept of neighborliness to determine Christian ethical responses in these pollution cases, we need to recognize that an individual's or community's call to neighborliness operates on three levels. First, for human communities to function properly, individuals must help to maintain day to day "boundaries." The laws of neighborliness in Exodus establish a basic standard for group safety, and are the minimum necessary to maintain community peace in an agricultural environment. The first level of neighborliness, therefore, is just ordinary, thoughtful management of business activities, and a conscientious attempt to protect the interests of others, and prevent personal injury and property damage. A farmer would have restrained her bull in any case. The Torah just informs her that she should do it in a way that reduces risk to other members of the community. A second level of neighborliness, is found in the parable of the good Samaritan, where a person with no relationship to the injured man takes responsibility for damage done to him by others—the robbers who left him by the roadside. This implies that neighborliness incorporates healing or repairing damage which the responsible member of the community did not personally cause. We might note that Christian interest in environmental healing often skips phase one of neighborliness—establishing community responsibility for boundaries. It is silly to attempt healing the injured, however, if my bull is still standing on my neighbor's chest. First, we have to pen the bull, then we can attempt to remediate the damages. Finally, there is perhaps one level of neighborliness above the good Samaritan, and that is the person who is willing to risk life or livelihood for the sake of others. The good Samaritan spent time and perhaps some money. If a person risks losing his or her life or livelihood to protect others from environmental injury, such as the "whistleblower" who reports a violation at risk of his position, this person is the ultimate "good neighbor."

CIVIL LAW OR CHRISTIAN VALUES?

Now what happens if people are suffering injury from pollution, while the polluting activities of a firm or an individual (or a nation) are not violating current laws? In the case of indoor air pollution, both sites were probably within the law much of the time, yet people were still becoming ill. In some cases a pollutant release by a single laboratory or company may not, by itself, be harmful, but when many companies are legally releasing industrial by-products into rivers like the Rio Grande, the total pollutant concentration or repeated exposures may be hazardous to human health. If pollutants are producing personal injury, I propose that for Christians the call to neighborliness supersedes the legal mandates. If, for example, my bull doesn't gore people, but he steps on their feet or slams his rear end into vegetable carts, this is not literally "goring" under the Old Testament law, nor will it usually result in a fatality. I might, the first time it happens, suspect it was an accident, but after five broken toes and several ruined sandals, it would be a fair conclusion the bull is either exceptionally clumsy or he is doing this on purpose. This is not a case within the letter of the law, but if we read the sense of Exodus, we would conclude we should keep him penned, since we know he has a problem and can injure others.

One of the problems presented by utilizing an Old Testament ethic is that in ancient Hebrew society, the community responded to violations of religious law by imposing social sanctions on the offender. Today, religious communities have little ability to enforce moral codes, other than via exclusion of the unrepentant. One of the problems in all three of the cases presented here is that the individuals responsible for the pollution have little fear of suffering any personal loss should they injure someone else. The ethic of neighborliness should encourage the support of the community for the development of appropriate social sanctions, enforced through civil law, that encourage individual responsibility. I will suggest that these sanctions should not be solely corporate fines, but demands for social reparation that require erring individuals to confront the damage they have done to others. A possible strategy might be requiring those who have released hazardous materials to personally help clean up a spill or a hazardous waste site by participating in public service environmental projects. This could also be exercised by the Christian community encouraging "environmental repentance" or "environmental penance," which would consist of activities aimed at raising the awareness of an individual who had injured someone else via pollution.

Environmental crime is so common place in our industrial-technological society, that we might ask, how can we enforce social sanctions without arresting almost everyone? Our first need is *to* target those lapses of community interest that are doing the most damage and, second, to target those that are helping to maintain selfish or detrimental attitudes. The book of Exodus provides another clue when it states: "if, the bull has had the habit of goring and the owner has been warned but has not kept it penned up and it killed a man or woman, the bull must be stoned and the owner also must be put to death." One of the central issues here is the knowledge of the owner, particularly the person who knows the bull is dangerous and does nothing to contain him. In the pollution cases "sins of knowledge" would include attempts to suppress reports of on-the-job pollution problems, releases of toxics at night or at times when they will probably not be monitored, secret disposal of hazardous waste, falsifying data on effluents, and suppressing information concerning risk of accidents or possible health effects of exposures. The captain of a supertanker or a nuclear plant, for example, should be held socially responsible for immediately notifying people or businesses that might suffer from an accident, since the community needs to know when a bull is on the rampage and heading towards town. If one holds that "sins of knowledge" undermine neighborliness, the transfer of a manufacturing operation from the U.S. to Mexico is a highly immoral act if one of the purposes of this transfer is avoidance of U.S. environmental laws that protect either workers or people who live near the plants, and the company's management are knowingly willing to risk injury to others.

The use of religious ethics to provide guidance in pollution cases does not preclude dialog with other sources of ethical thought. The neighborliness and stewardship models of environmental response could easily, for example, enter into dialog with Sagoff (1988) over the question of the rights of the individual versus duties to the community. Sagoff's discussion of "imperfect duties" is relevant to the question of the degree to which neighborliness should be expected or expressed. Sagoff (1988) is also wrestling with the question of reasonable application of legal sanctions, and whether the morally optimal can be reasonably socially attained in pollution regulation.

OTHER MODELS

A last issue to be covered is the relationship of neighborliness to other ethical models. First, there is no reason more than one ethical model can not be applied in a specific case. In the three cases presented here, this is perfectly appropriate. Case 1 and Case 3 fall into the categories of social and economic oppression of minorities, discrimination against women and unfair treatment of employees. They are therefore violations of Biblical mandates to pursue justice for the poor and afflicted, to treat other people fairly in terms of business transactions and wages, and to forward God's righteousness within the human community. (Bullard 1990) Case 2 includes the damage or loss of a large natural ecosystem. One could, therefore, invoke a natural rights argument. The stewardship model would also be appropriate here, and would imply that in using the Chesapeake Bay for food, transportation, recreation, and disposal of waste, we have a responsibility not to degrade its fertility or its biotic diversity, both divinely created properties of the Bay. (Nash 1991, Bratton 1993) These models must be developed to the point, however, of imposing definite behavioral or economic limits, or they will not provide enough guidance to be helpful.

One of the failings of Christian environmental ethics is that, in actual practice, Christians do not give environmental issues a very high priority. This problem has several roots, including the Christian tendency to be most concerned about matters that seem beyond the reach of civil law, such as sexuality, while leaving other issues, including the regulation of business, to the government. An excessive emphasis on personal purity can, in fact, inhibit development of ethical responses to a wide variety of community problems. The Hebrew and Christian scriptures devote a great deal of discussion to business and economic activities, because these are capable of both causing and relieving human suffering. Identifying pollution as a source of unnecessary human mortality and injury, and as a source of unnecessary damage to other people's property and to the creation, should rank it with similar ethical problems, such as drunken driving, that present substantial risk to others. Dealing with pollution, first and foremost, as a source of unnecessary injury and destruction, should also clarify its role in unraveling the fabric of human communities. The only reason we are willing to let our contemporary bull roam through schools, factories and suburbs is because we can not see or hear him coming. This, however, makes the bull even more dangerous than a bull we can see, and places a greater responsibility on all of us to keep the bull penned.

NOTES

1. All Biblical quotations are from the New International version.
2. In evaluating the impact of potential sanctions in industrial or institutional pollution cases, we might find a corporate executive much more concerned about being publicly embarrassed or of losing business time doing public service as restitution for a violation, even for just a couple of weeks, than he would of paying a $200,000 fine, which is really a corporate and not a personal expense. A small financial deficit is usually borne by the stockholders, not by upper level management whose salaries will not be affected. If a corporate manager needs to be convinced hazardous pollutants are a community concern, a short stint wearing a genuinely ugly orange jump suit and dragging 55 gallon drums of chemical goo from an illegal dump to a truck is appropriate restitution and spiritually educational. This "toxics camp" strategy of sanctions is only one of several possibilities, but from a social and Christian ethical perspective it has several advantages. First, our prisons are overcrowded and very expensive to run. The average jury would hesitate to send anyone who is functioning at all productively in society to an adult correctional institution, which does anything but correct. The cost of "toxics camp" could be paid by the offending corporation, and it requires no security other than a default jail sentence if the "toxics trainee" does not cooperate. Further, there is nothing like wading waist deep through a dump site to make the negative side of pollution clear. Someone remanded to "toxics camp" would not have to go immediately, since they probably aren't a danger to society while watching television and playing racquetball back in an upper middle class suburb. Toxics camp could be assembled and run by a technical contractor when enough violators had been convicted (e.g. twice a year, during prime summer golf weather and the height of winter ski season would be best). The toxics camp strategy is versatile enough to provide the "oil spill experience" for those who most need it.

REFERENCES

Birch, B.C. 1991. *Let Justice Roll Down: The Old Testament, Ethics and Christian Life*. Louisville, KY: Westminster/ John Knox.

Bratton, S.P. 1993. *Christianity, Wilderness and Wildlife: The Original Desert Solitaire*. Scranton, PA: University of Scranton Press.

Bullard, R.D. 1990. *Dumping in Dixie: Race, Class and Environmental Quality*. Boulder, CO: Westview Press.

Douglas, M. 1966. *Puilty and Danger. An Analysis of the Concepts of Pollution and Taboo*. London: Routledge.

Gammie, J.G. 1989. *Holiness in Israel*. Minneapolis, MN: Fortress Press.

Goodish, T. 1990. *Indoor Air Pollution Control*. Chelsea, MI.: Lewis Publishers.

Hall, J.D. 1990. *The Steward: A Biblical Symbol Come of Age*. Grand Rapids, MI: William B. Eerdmans.

Hathaway, G., Proctor, N., Hughes, J., & Fishman, M. 1991. *Proctor and Hughes' Chemical Hazards of the Workplace*. New York, NY: Van Nostrand Reinhold.

Horst, M. 1988. *Amish Perspectives*. York, PA: York Graphic Services.

Horton,T. 1991. *Turning the Tide, Saving the Chesapeake Bay*. Washington, DC: Island Press.

Hostetler, J.A. 1980. *Amish* Society.Baltimore, MD: Johns Hopkins University Press.

Kraybill, D.B. 1989.The *Riddle of Amish Culture*. Baltimore, MD: Johns Hopkins University Press.

Levine, B.A. 1989. *The JPS Torah Commentary: Leviticus*. Philadelphia, PA: The Jewish Publication Society.

Nash, J.A. 1991. *Loving Nature: Ecological Integrity and Christian Responsibility* Nashville, TN: Abingdon Press.

Novak, D. 1992. *Jewish Social Ethics*. New York, NY: Oxford University Press.

Rose, A. 1992, *Judaism and Ecology*. London: Cassell.

Patrick,D. 1985. *Old Testament Law*. Atlanta, GA: John Knox.

Sagoff, M. 1988. *The Economy of the Earth: Philosophy, Law and the Environment*. Cambridge: Cambridge University Press.

Samet, J., & Spencer,J.D., eds. 1991. *Indoor Air Pollution: A Health Perspective*. Baltimore: Johns Hopkins University Press.

Scott, R. 1990. *Chemical Hazards in the Workplace*. Chelsea, MI.: Lewis Publishers.

Sherman, J. *1988.Chemical Exposure and Disease*. New York, NY: Van Nostrand Reinhold.

Shomrei Adamah. 1993. *Judaism and Ecology*. New York, NY: HADASSAH, The Women's Zionist Organization of America.

Tarnari, M. 1987. *"With All Your Possessions ": Jewish Ethics and Economic Life*. New York, NY: The Free Press.

Wilkenson, L.ed. 1991. *Earthkeeping in the Nineties: Stewardship of Creation.* Grand Rapids, MI: William B. Eeerdmans.

The Bahai Faith

and

Biospheric Sustainability

William Gregg[1]

INTRODUCTION

Increasingly, our troubled world appears to be in the throes of a modern spiritual crisis. Despite unprecedented advances in science and technology, achieving a peaceful and sustainable global society often seems an impossible dream as evidence of ecological, economic, and social instability mount on every side. While people often turn to religion in times óf personal crisis, the role of religion in solving global problems remains to be fully realized. Many unfortunately see religion as ineffective in the global arena, irrelevant to scientific inquiry, and even as a contributor to conflict and instability. In this paper, I endeavor to present a religious point of view which is inclusive, in harmony with science, and relevant to finding effective solutions to complex problems.

I first heard of the Baha'i Faith in 1970. I was completing field work at a research station in southeastern Pennsylvania for my doctoral dissertation at Duke University. This station attracted students and researchers from many institutions to study the process of vegetation change on abandoned fields. In addition to their own research, visitors assisted with the station's long-term research, which involved intensive surveys of small vegetation plots.

That summer, Peter, a visiting graduate student from Colorado, joined my survey team. Of the many things we discussed that first day on the ground under the blazing sun, I learned that Peter had never been to Pennsylvania, nor did he know anyone in the area. Back at the lab, I was surprised to overhear him enthusiastically accepting an invitation to a picnic the next weekend from people who appeared to be long-time friends. When I hazarded mention of my perplexity, Peter told me that he was a member of the Baha'i Faith, and that these friends whom he had never met before were members of the local Baha'i community.

Having never heard of the Baha'i Faith, my curiosity prompted me to probe a little further. Peter readily shared the interesting principles of this independent world religion articulated by its Prophet-Founder, Baha-u-llah (1817–1892), whose Arabic name, incidentally, means "Glory

137

of God." We began a summer-long discussion of religion, ethics, and social and environmental issues. As a scientist, I was intellectually drawn, in particular, to the Baha'i principle that science and religion must agree.

As a youth, I attended a private school affiliated with the Protestant Episcopal Church. The school's curriculum included daily chapel services and formal instruction in sacred studies beginning in the sixth grade. In studying the history of the Christian Church, I was struck by the frequent conflicts between the ecclesiastical and the scientific communities. My religious background predisposed me to believe in the religion of my family and culture. However, all my education affirmed the validity of the scientific method, and caused me to question the moral authority of the Church in denying the value of science in shedding light on such mysteries as creation and evolution.

I was immediately attracted to the Baha'i view that truth is one (i.e., all knowledge is borne of God); therefore, the pathways of science and religion must converge. The pursuit of knowledge requires the combined application of the intellect and the spirit. Religion enables the believer to discover and appreciate supernatural realities. With the tools of science, the trained mind can unlock knowledge of the material universe through empirical study of God's handiwork. Thus the scientist can confirm through the intellect that which the person of faith learns through the metaphoric language of the Prophets of God. If their conclusions do not agree, Baha'is believe that either the scientific or the religious thinking is flawed.

The following statements of 'Abdu'l-Baha (1844–1921), son of Baha'u'llah, from a talk in 1911 to the Theosophical Society in Paris articulate the Baha'i viewpoint. ('Abdu'l-Baha, whose name translates to Servant of the Glory, was designated in Baha'u'llah's will as the sole authoritative interpreter of his teachings.)

"Religion and science are the two wings upon which man's intelligence can soar into the heights, with which the human soul can progress. Should a man try to fly with the wing of religion alone he would quickly fall into the quagmire of superstition, whilst on the other hand, with the wing of science alone he would also make no progress, but fall into the despairing slough of materialism."[2]

"When religion, shorn of its superstitions, traditions, and unintelligent dogmas, shows its conformity with science, then will there be a great unifying, cleansing force in the world which will sweep before it all wars, disagreements, discords and struggles—and then will mankind be united in the power of the Love of God."³

The vast diversity of religions and sects present different and often contradictory theologies. The Baha'i view is that religious understanding, like science, unfolds progressively. Through the ages, God has revealed Himself to humankind through Prophets (or Manifestations) who have influenced the course of human civilizations in the East and the West. We know many of their names—Abraham, Moses, Krishna, Zoroaster, Buddha, Christ, Mohammed, and Baha'u'llah. Others are known in legend or are lost to history. From the Baha'i perspective, since all religions have emanated from one Source, they are all pathways to spiritual truth. Religion is one. This continuity is readily apparent in the remarkable universality of their moral teachings.

"All the Manifestations of God and His Prophets have taught the same truths and given the same spiritual law. They all teach one code of morality. There is no division in the truth. The Sun has sent forth many rays to illumine human intelligence, the light is always the same."⁴

However, Baha'is believe that each Manifestation also has left temporal teachings appropriate to the stage and condition of contemporary human societies. Teachings on such practices as marriage, burial, sanitation, diet, modes of punishment, and forms of worship have varied greatly. Baha'is appreciate the historic basis for these practices (even though some may be inconsistent with modern science), while acknowledging the timelessness of religion on a metaphysical plane.

Logically, religion should be dynamic and responsive to the changing condition of human society. If the teachings and practices of religious institutions appear anachronistic, there is a danger that religion itself may appear to be irrelevant.

Baha'is believe that each Manifestation of God initiates a new prophetic cycle. Each prophetic cycle brings a reawakening of religious inspiration that unlocks human potentialities and opens new possibilities for the advancement of civilization. To Baha'is, with Baha'u'llah's appearance in the last century, a new age has dawned that will culminate ultimately in world peace.

Over the years, my spiritual journey that began in 1970 led me to explore the profound dimensions of this Faith. I was encouraged in this journey by another especially compelling principle: the independent investigation of truth. In other words, the search for religious truth is regarded as a personal quest for knowledge of God. Each seeker must follow his or her own path. In the words of Baha'u'llah: "Where is the man of insight who will behold the Words of God with his own eyes and rid himself of the opinions and notions of the peoples of the earth?" — Baha'u'llah.[5] Through my search, I gradually came to believe the principles and teachings of Baha'u'llah to be a practical prescription for harmony between nature and humankind. The more I learned, the more compelling was my desire to be a part of the Baha'i world community. In 1979, my wife and I publicly declared our affiliation with this new religion that we had admired for so long.

BAHA'I TEACHINGS RELATING TO BIOSPHERIC SUSTAINABILITY

Man's Relationship with Nature

Nature as a Reflection of the Attributes of God. Baha'is believe that Nature is a pathway to the knowledge of God. Symbols and metaphors of Nature abound in the Baha'i sacred writings. Baha'u'llah's writings make frequent reference to Nature as the handiwork of God and the visible evidence the attributes of God:

> "Nature is God's Will and is its expression in and through the contingent world. It is a dispensation of Providence ordained by the Ordainer, the All-Wise."

"No thing have I perceived, except that I perceived God within it, God before it, or God after it."[7]

In a well known passage, Baha'u'llah reveals:

> "...whatever I behold I readily discover that it maketh Thee known unto me, and it remindeth me of Thy signs, and of Thy tokens, and of Thy testimonies. By Thy glory! Every time I lift up mine eyes unto Thy heaven, I call to mind Thy highness and Thy loftiness, and Thine incomparable glory and greatness; and every time I turn my gaze to Thine earth, I am made to recognize the evidences of Thy power and the tokens of Thy bounty. And when I behold the sea, I find it speaketh to me of Thy majesty, and of the potency of Thy might, and of Thy sovereignty and Thy grandeur. And at whatever time I contemplate the mountains, I am led to discover the

ensigns of Thy victory and the standards of Thy omnipo-
tence."[8]

It is clear, however, that although the evidences of God are manifest in
Nature, the Essence of God remains beyond human understanding.

"He is, and hath ever been, veiled in the ancient eternity of His
Essence, and will remain in His Reality everlastingly hidden from the
sight of men."[9]

Respect and humility before Creation.

Baha'i teachings underscore the deep respect and humility that must
characterize the relationship of man to Creation. Baha'u'llah instructs
humanity to regard the earth with the utmost humility and gratitude:

> "Every man of discernment, while walking upon the
> earth, feeleth indeed abashed, inasmuch as he is fully
> aware that the thing which is the source of his prosperity,
> his wealth, his might, his exaltation, his advancement and
> power is, as ordained by God, the very earth which is
> trodden beneath the feet of all men. There can be no
> doubt that whoever is cognizant of this truth is cleansed
> and sanctified from all pride, arrogance and vainglory."[10]

Individual Baha'is recite daily a prayer which attests to each believer's powerlessness and poverty before the might and wealth of the
Creator, which are readily recognized through the natural world.[11]

The Unique Station of Man.

The Baha'i Faith teaches that, physically, man is a part of Nature
and embodies the characteristics of all the lower kingdoms of existence:
the cohesion of elements from the mineral kingdom, the power of
growth that further characterizes the vegetable kingdom; and the additional power of sense perception which has evolved in the animal kingdom. However, man occupies a higher station by virtue of the additional
faculty of spiritual awareness and the superpower of intellect. Baha'is
believe these capacities are an "eternal blessing and divine bestowal—the
supreme gift of God to Man" that enables humans to discover the
secrets of the material Creation and to contemplate underlying spiritual

realities. "All the powers and attributes of man are human and hereditary in origin—outcomes of nature's processes—except the intellect,
which is supernatural."[12]   Where a storm of controversy rages between
creationists and evolutionists, Baha'is believe that the corporal form of
man has evolved through many stages, but that the particular attributes
of consciousness and spiritual awareness were always latent throughout
human evolution. This view provides a conceptual framework for reconciling scientifically based understanding of biological evolution with
religious perspective on the unique station of man.

"Throughout this progression there has been a transference of
type, a conservation of species or kind. Realizing this we may acknowledge the fact that at one time man was an inmate of the sea, at another
period an invertebrate, then a vertebrate and finally a human being
standing erect. Though we admit these changes, we cannot say man is
an animal. In each one of these stages are signs and evidences of his
human existence and destination."[13]

> "The animal is...a captive of the world of nature and
> not in touch with that which lies within and beyond
> nature; it is...unconscious of the world of God and inca-
> pable of deviating from the law of nature. It is different
> with man. Man...is capable of discovering the mysteries
> of the universe. All the industries inventions and facilities
> surrounding our daily life were at one time hidden secrets
> of nature, but the reality of man penetrated them and
> made them subject to his purposes. According to nature's
> laws they should have remained latent and hidden; but
> man, having transcended those laws, discovered these
> mysteries and brought them out of the plane of the invisi-
> ble into the realm of the known and visible."[14]

Man alone has the capability and the responsibility to investigate
and contemplate the wonders of the universe:

> "Reflect upon the inner realities of the Universe, the
> secret wisdoms involved, the enigmas, the inter-relation-
> ships, the rules that govern all."[15]

Through the power of intellect, God enables humanity to understand the laws of nature and, through this understanding and spiritual

awareness, to wisely marshall the forces and resources of Nature for sustainable human development.

"The path toward sustainable development can only be built upon the deep comprehension of humanity's spiritual reality—a reality that lies at the very essence of human beings. It is our spiritual nature that is the source of human qualities that engender unity and harmony, that lead to insight and understanding, and that make possible collaborative undertakings. Such qualities—compassion, forbearance, trustworthiness, courage, humility, cooperation, and willingness to sacrifice for the common good—form the invisible yet essential foundations of human society."[16]

To Baha'is, the unique station of man requires that education be universal and compulsory. Education in a spiritual context is absolutely prerequisite to the development of a sustainable human civilization.

> "Knowledge is as wings to man's life, and a ladder for his ascent. Its acquisition is incumbent upon everyone." — Baha'u'llah.[17]
>
> "If a child be trained from his infancy, he will, through the loving care of the Holy Gardener, drink in the crystal waters of the spirit and of knowledge, like a young tree amid the rilling brooks.... Therefore must the mentor be a doctor as well: that is, he must, in instructing the child, remedy its faults; must give him learning, and at the same time rear him to have a spiritual nature.... Teach them to dedicate their lives to matters of great import, and inspire them to undertake studies that will benefit mankind."[18]

Principle of Interconnectedness

Baha'i teachings encourage holistic thinking, an ecological perspective, interdisciplinary approaches, and ethical behavior—all based on principles of interconnectedness and reciprocity. Indeed, to Bahai's, the very concept of a sustainable global society requires universal recognition of these principles.

"(C)o-operation and reciprocity are essential properties which are inherent in the unified system of the world of existence, and without which the entire creation would be reduced to nothingness."[19]

"For every part of the universe is connected with every other part by ties that are very powerful and admit of no imbalance, nor any slackening whatever. In the physical realm of creation, all things are eaters and eaten: the plant drinketh in the mineral, the animal doth crop and swallow down the plant, man doth feed upon the animal, and the mineral devoureth the body of man. Physical bodies are transferred past one barrier after another, from one life to another, and all things are subject to transformation and change, save only the essence of existence itself."[20]

Baha'i writings explicitly confirm the continuing evolution of the earth, and its myriad components, in accordance with universal laws:

"... it is evident that this terrestrial globe, having once found existence, grew and developed in the matrix of the universe, and came forth in different forms and conditions, until gradually it attained its present perfection, and became adorned with innumerable beings, and appeared as a finished organization."[21]

Baha'i teachings also encourage a systems approach in understanding the processes of change:

"[The] temple of the world...[has been] fashioned after the image and likeness of the human body.... By this is meant that even as the human body in this world, which is outwardly composed of different limbs and organs, is in reality a closely integrated, coherent entity, similarly the structure of the physical world is like unto a single being whose limbs and members are inseparably linked together.

Were one to observe with an eye that discovereth the realities of all things, it would become clear that the greatest relationship that bindeth the world of being together lieth in the range of created things themselves, and that co-operation, mutual aid and reciprocity are essential characteristics in the unified body of the world of being, inasmuch as all created things are closely related together and each is influenced by the other or deriveth benefit therefrom, either directly or indirectly."[22]

Baha'is believe that achieving planetary sustainability must be based on understanding the relationship between the spiritual and material planes of human existence:

"We cannot segregate the human heart from the environment outside us and say that once one of these is reformed everything will be improved. Man is organic with the world. His inner life moulds the environment and is itself also deeply affected by it. The one acts upon the other and every abiding change in the life of man is the result of these mutual reactions."[23]

Baha'i writings explicitly foretell the dire consequences of failure to cultivate the linkage between spiritual values and use of the earth's resources:

"...ye walk on My earth complacent and self-satisfied, heedless that My earth is weary of you and everything within it shunneth you..."[24]

"...until material achievements, physical accomplishments and human virtues are reinforced by spiritual perfections, luminous qualities and characteristics of mercy, no fruit or result shall issue therefrom, nor will the happiness of the world of humanity...be attained. For although, on the one hand, material achievements and the development of the physical world produce prosperity...on the other hand dangers, severe calamities and violent afflictions are imminent."[25]

The Oneness of Humanity

The establishment of a harmonious equilibrium in human relationships is prerequisite to achieving planetary sustainability. The failure of human beings to regard each other as members of one universal family—to apply the Golden Rule to the whole human race—is an important factor in the deterioration of the global environment.

Poverty is universally acknowledged as a major cause of environmental degradation. Poverty is symptomatic of a pervasive spiritual apathy by those who have access to the earth's wealth toward those who do not. The technological means to combat this condition exist. It is technologically feasible to provide decent housing, adequate nourishment, clean drinking water and sanitation as the birth right of every member of the human family. It is medically possible to eradicate parasitic and childhood diseases afflicting large segments of humanity. It is possible to give all peoples the means to avoid unwanted pregnancies. It is possible to provide every child access to education and the means to earn a livelihood.

However, Baha'is believe that only a revitalization of the human spirit can reverse the paralysis of will that affects the efforts of governments and institutions in positions to achieve equitable distribution of resources and sharing in the benefits of technology. The widespread sharing of information, technologies, and resources will take place only when the positive spiritual values of love, compassion, generosity, fairness, responsibility and respect for others replace narrow self interest, apathy, and prejudice.

Baha'i writings place particular emphasis on the abolition of all forms of prejudice. Prejudice based on nation, religion, race, sex, economic status, or ethnicity is antithetical to the unity of humankind, and to the achievement of world peace upon which sustainable development depends.[26]

> "All prejudices, whether of religion, race, politics or nation, must be renounced, for these prejudices have caused the world's sickness. It is a grave malady which, unless arrested, is capable of causing the destruction of the whole human race."[27]

When the legacy of hatred and mistrust erupts into war, the environmental effects can be devastating—witness the massive defoliation of the tropical forests during the Viet Nam war; the environmental destruction associated with the migrations of millions of refugees from conflicts in central Africa, the massive slaughter of wildlife during the Angolan civil war, and the contamination of the atmosphere, land and sea from the burning of Kuwaiti oil fields by Iraq during the Gulf War. While the end of the Cold War has perhaps lessened the ultimate biospheric threat of nuclear winter, clandestine access to nuclear materials may soon enable fanatically prejudiced individuals and groups to threaten millions of people with the environmental desolation of nuclear destruction.

To Baha'is, the operating principle and the overarching goal for humanity's collective life on the earth—indeed, it's veritable salvation—is the oneness of humankind.

> "Since We have created you all from one same sub-

stance, it is incumbent on you to be even as one soul, to walk with the same feet, eat with the same mouth and dwell in the same land, that from your inmost being, by your deeds and actions, the signs of oneness and the essence of detachment may be made manifest."[28]

"...regard ye not one another as strangers. Ye are the fruits of one tree, and the leaves of one branch."[29]

"The oneness of humanity ... speaks to the longing of people everywhere for a world infused with such a spirit of community, fellowship and compassion that human misery and degradation, violence and oppression will become intolerable and eventually unthinkable."[30] The principle of the oneness of humankind encompasses a profound respect for humanity's diversity, which parallels the importance attached to biological diversity in the following passage:

"...diversity is the essence of perfection and the cause of the appearance of the bestowals of the Most Glorious Lord....Consider the flowers of a garden: though differing in kind, colour, form and shape, yet, inasmuch as they are refreshed by the waters of one spring, revived by the breath of one wind, invigorated by the rays of one sun, this diversity increaseth their charm, and addeth unto their beauty. Thus when that unifying force, the penetrating influence of the Word of God, taketh effect, the difference of customs, manners, habits, ideas, opinions and dispositions embellisheth the world of humanity. This diversity, this difference is like the naturally created dissimilarity and variety of limbs and organs of the human body, for each one contributeth to the beauty, efficiency, and perfection of the whole."[31]

Baha'is believe that acceptance of this principle is leading to sweeping changes in human relationships and institutions, which have accelerated following the end of the Cold War. An important aspect of this process is the willingness to cede certain prerogatives of national sovereignty to provide for the collective well-being of the human family.

"The well-being of mankind, its peace and security, are unattainable unless and until its unity is firmly established."[32]

"The oneness of mankind...implies an organic change

in the structure of present-day society, a change such as
the world has not yet experienced....It calls for no less
than the reconstruction and the demilitarization of the
whole civilized world—a world organically unified in all
the essential aspects of its life, its political machinery, its
spiritual aspiration, its trade and finance, its script and language, and yet infinite in the diversity of the national
characteristics of its federated units."[33]

The growing public acceptance of the principle of the oneness of
the human family is contributing to a global ethic of biospheric sustainability. In the last few years, this emerging ethic has spawned numerous
international treaties to address planetary issues such as climate change,
biodiversity, desertification, deforestation, marine pollution, nuclear pro-
liferation and stratospheric ozone depletion.

In 1993, the Baha'i International Community suggested that the term
"world citizenship" be adopted to encompass those principles, values,
attitudes and behaviors that the world's peoples collectively must
embrace to achieve a sustainable civilization. World citizenship fosters
legitimate loyalties to one's nation and cultural heritage, but also encompasses a wider loyalty based on love of the human family as a whole. In
this context, Baha'is anticipate that arbitrary political boundaries will
become progressively less important in implementing solutions to
regional and planetary problems.

In the words of Baha'u'llah': "It is not for him to pride himself who
loveth his own country, but rather for him who loveth the whole
world. The earth is but one country, and mankind its citizens"[34]

III. BAHA'I CONTRIBUTIONS TOWARD A
SUSTAINABLE BIOSPHERE

The Baha'i Faith is an activist religion. Work in the service of
humankind is regarded as worship.

"The essence of faith is fewness of words and abundance
of deeds...."[35]

Increasingly, such Baha'i deeds have focused on community development and environmental conservation. Providing the framework for
the necessary consultation, planning, and decision making at all levels, in

accordance with Baha'i principles, is the Baha'i administrative order.

The blueprint for the Baha'i administrative order was set forth by Baha'u'llah and His son, 'Abdu'l-Baha. Baha'is believe their existing institutions constitute the embryonic framework for the future development of a spiritually based world civilization. The administrative order operates on three levels: local, national, and global.

The local spiritual assembly is elected annually. Each Baha'i community has jurisdiction over local affairs. Each year, Baha'is elect representatives to a national convention, which elects the members of the national spiritual assembly (NSA).[36] The members of the NSAs meet every five years at an international convention held at the World Centre of the Baha'i Faith on Mount Carmel in Israel.

Each of the administrative bodies consists of nine members, who have collective (but no individual) authority. Baha'i elections are based on spiritual reflection; nominating, campaigning, and partisanship have no place. Each voter prayerfully strives to identify men and women possessing outstanding spiritual and intellectual capacities. Consequently, there are no vested interests, and the elected bodies are free to pursue the best course of action based on scientific inquiry and spiritual principle.

Grassroots Activities.

Grassroots social and economic development projects provide practical opportunities to demonstrate the integration of scientific knowledge, culturally appropriate technologies and spiritual principle. The aim is to uplift and help local communities to become self sufficient and self reliant. Although improvement of material well being is a tangible short-term benefit, far more important is the development of a long-term learning process that encourages community self-esteem, flexibility, resourcefulness, and cohesion.[37]

Momen cites five elements necessary in the local planning and development process.[38] The first is *universal participation*. The greater the participation of community members the greater the probability of achieving the broad agreement and unity conducive to success. The whole community should be involved, including women as well as people of minority ethnic and religious backgrounds.

To foster a climate conducive to universal participation, the second element is *consultation*. To Baha'is, free and open consultation is an essential process for fostering unity through consensus. The goal is to arrive at the very best ideas by eliciting input from all the members of the community in an atmosphere that encourages courtesy, humility, detachment, patience, moderation, responsibility and fairness. The process of consultation stands in contrast to traditions in which decisions are made by a few community members or by individuals outside the community altogether.

The third is *development of local institutions* to provide a framework for consultation and community participation. The goal is to create bodies that are representative of the community's economic and cultural diversity. Elected Baha'i assemblies provide models of genuinely democratic government that can implement projects "of the people, by the people, and for the people."

The fourth is *education*. Broadly conceived, education includes acquisition of intellectual understanding and practical skills. as well as participation in a learning process that enables individuals and communities to learn about themselves and their surroundings, to integrate their accumulated knowledge with that of other peoples, and to apply this knowledge for their spiritual and material well-being.

The fifth element is *moral and spiritual development*. Secular projects are rife with examples in which the benefits of development have been dissipated through selfishness, greed, and corruption, resulting in strife and disharmony. Baha'is believe that material progress must go hand in hand with development of spiritual values. In this context, moral and ethical teachings are seen as prerequisites for achieving the general good and maintaining harmony, and an integral part of the process of community development.

Early Baha'i development projects focused mostly on education.[39] Following World War II, Baha'i communities began to establish schools for children in developing countries who lacked any access to education. The schools provide both elementary and moral education and are open to all children, regardless of sex, class, race, ethnic origin or religion. Many include literacy training for adults. Between 1946 and 1986, the number of these schools increased from 4 to 598.[40] Curricula frequently include service projects for local communities.

By the mid-1980s, Baha'i schools and training centers with specific missions in rural development were operational in India, Bolivia, Haiti, Papua New Guinea, Zambia, and elsewhere. These institutions emphasized development of skills in agriculture, carpentry, nutrition, health and hygiene, use of alternative energy sources, and other fields needed to help empower local communities in achieving self-reliance. Many projects have aimed specifically at improving the status of women, and restoring cultural identity and pride of native peoples who have suffered cultural impoverishment resulting from centuries of domination by European societies. The first Baha'i radio station, operated largely by indigenous people in the Andean region of Ecuador, was established in 1980. The station fosters cultural pride through development of native dance, music and folklore, and promotes agricultural and other economic activities that take into account local traditions, capabilities, and priorities. Similar stations have since become operational in Bolivia, Chile, Liberia, Panama, and Peru, and in South Carolina in the United States.

Because of the rapid expansion of Baha'i Faith as a world religion during the past few decades, Baha'i communities often include individuals from many economic, racial, ethnic, and religious groups in which prejudices are often long-standing. Increasingly, the communities are gaining valuable practical experience in achieving unity in diversity and in working effectively on projects for the common good.

In 1983, the Universal House of Justice sent a message to the Baha'i International Community (BIC) encouraging systematic application of Baha'i teachings to societal problems, and established an Office of Social and Economic Development to help foster and coordinate these activities. Within four years, there were nearly 1500 projects underway, most of them small scale. Many of these projects focused explicitly on environmental problems. For example, a Baha'i school in Haiti sponsored the distribution of more than 100,000 trees between 1985 and 1987—and now distributes 120,000 trees annually—to reforest degraded lands in the Western Hemisphere's most impoverished country. Today, Baha'i communities are involved in a prodigious variety of environmental activities including the following[41] :

- symposia, summer schools, camps, youth conferences and other forums on environmental issues;
- development of environmental education curricula and programs;
- development of media (such as a bimonthly newspaper, "Ecology and World Unity," published by the Baha'i Community of Argentina);

• recycling, beautification and environmental remediation projects (such as the "Clean and Beautiful Swaziland" campaign, which received UNEP's prestigious Global 500 Award);
• organic farming and fish farming projects;
• reforestation efforts (including the Hawaiian Baha'i community's "Breath of Life" project to replant native trees);
• contests, exhibitions, and festivals to promote conservation, environmental protection and celebration of diversity through the creative arts; and
• advocacy projects to implement Agenda 21, the global action plan for sustainable development adopted by the 1992 Earth Summit (e.g., the campaigns of Baha'i communities in several European countries to promote world citizenship in schools).

Baha'i scholarship has begun to focus on application of Baha'i teachings to environmental issues, and several significant contributions have been published during the past few years.[42]

In 1986, at the invitation of the World Wide Fund for Nature, leaders of major world religions met in Assisi, Italy, to explore ways to achieve greater harmony between Nature and Faith. This unprecedented gathering expanded the dialogue among religious leaders, and between religious communities and nongovernmental organizations concerned with conservation and sustainable development.

Following the events at Assisi, the Baha'i International Community became the sixth member of the World Wildlife Fund's Network for Conservation and Religion and published a statement on nature and the environment. The statement stressed that resolution of environmental problems requires a transnational approach and a new political order based on "economic justice, equality between the races, equal rights for women and men, and universal education," as well as recognition of the role of the world's religious teachings in inspiring efforts to build a new ecological ethic.[43] The Statement concludes that "the major threats to our world environment ... are manifestations of a world-encompassing sickness of the human spirit ... mastered by an overemphasis on material things and a self-centeredness that inhibits our ability to work together as a global community."

The Universal House of Justice subsequently published a compilation of Baha'i teachings on conservation which called upon Baha'i communities to integrate environmental conservation activities into community life.[44] An Office of the Environment was established at the BIC office in New York to help link community-based initiatives with international expertise and major global initiatives.[45] The structure has enabled the BIC to develop working relationships with many United Nations agencies and regional commissions, and to participate actively in international forums on conservation and development. One such forum was the 1992 United Nations Conference on Environment and Development (UNCED).

Baha'i activities at UNCED focused on fostering the principle of the oneness of humanity as the key to achieving biospheric sustainability. Baha'is participated in both the intergovernmental conference as well as the '92 Global Forum—a parallel and unprecedented gathering of 27,000 representatives from about 11,000 nongovernmental organizations (NGOs) from at least 171 countries. A Baha'i pre-Summit statement emphasizing the oneness of humanity received broad support from other religious groups and was selected for presentation at UNCED's plenary session on behalf of religious organizations generally.[46] More than 140 Baha'is participated in the Forum. The Baha'i community coordinated a symposium on values and institutions for a sustainable world civilization; published a collection of art work and essays on environmental protection and peace by children from around the world (the book, entitled "Tomorrow Belongs To The Children," was distributed to all heads of state in 1993); and hosted the Forum's evening music and cultural programs celebrating the world's cultural diversity.

A lasting contribution to UNCED from the Baha'is was a 15-foot-tall, hourglass-shaped "Peace Monument," symbolizing the fact that time is running out for humanity unless unity in the Summit's spirit of global cooperation be achieved (Figure 2). To dedicate the sculpture, containers of soil from 42 countries were passed hand-to-hand along a line of children in national costumes and deposited in the monument. Soils from additional countries are being added each year.

Since the Earth Summit, the Baha'i International Community has prepared subsequent statements on humanity's relationship with the planet for the United Nations Commission on Sustainable Development,[47] the World Summit for Social Development,[48] and the Summit on the Alliance between Religions and Conservation World.[49]

In view of the relatively small number of Baha'is and the modest financial resources available, the contributions of the Baha'i community to biospheric sustainability during the past decade have been exceptional. These contributions reflect the relevance of Baha'i teachings to complex environmental problems and the rapid maturation of Baha'i institutions.

A PERSONAL NOTE

I received my doctoral degree in ecology from Duke University in 1971. In the aftermath of the initial Earth Day celebrations in 1970 and 1971, public environmental concern was at its zenith. The Federal Government had recently enacted numerous laws that established the national interest in protecting air and water, rivers, wetlands and the coastal zone, wilderness, and endangered species. The National Environmental Policy Act (NEPA) of 1969—perhaps the most significant environmental legislation in the nation's history—required full public disclosure of the environmental impacts of any Federal action significantly affecting the quality of the human environment. NEPA created an enormous demand for ecologists and environmental specialists to help agencies meet their responsibilities. Jobs were plentiful, and agencies actively recruited recent graduates from the few universities that had environmental science programs. I landed a position with the National Park Service as an in-house consultant on park planning teams. Not long afterward, I was asked to set up an interdisciplinary group of specialists to prepare NEPA analyses on park plans.

For the next several years, I worked with planning teams in most of the nation's biogeographical provinces and in several foreign countries. In area after area, human activities outside park boundaries seemed to be affecting park ecosystems more than activities within the parks themselves. All my experience reinforced the view (1) that Nature does not recognize artificial human boundaries, (2) that protected areas are parts of larger increasingly human-dominated ecosystems, and (3) that most protected areas will have a bleak future unless local people share an understanding of the changes taking place in their region and a desire to manage their activities in ways that sustain their ecological heritage. Understandably, most parks were reluctant to use their limited budgets on research and demonstration activities involving areas outside park boundaries.

In 1974, I assumed responsibilities for overseeing NPS compliance with environmental laws and administrative requirements. About this time, I first heard of the intergovernmental Man and the Biosphere Program (MAB), which was being developed under the auspices of the United Nations Educational, Scientific, and Cultural Organization (UNESCO). The purpose of MAB, then as now, is to foster the knowledge, skills, and ethical behavior required for harmonious relationships between human activities and the environment. An important MAB goal is to establish a World Network of Biosphere Reserves to serve as bench marks for assessing trends in essentially natural ecosystems and experimental laboratories for demonstrating environmentally compatible (we now say "sustainable") human uses. I followed closely the federal government's early efforts to designate the first biosphere reserves in the United States. These areas included important ecological research reserves and many of our finest national parks, such as Yellowstone, Everglades, Sequoia, and Great Smoky Mountains.

In the mid-1970s, UNESCO began to clarify the vision of biosphere reserves.[30] Biosphere reserves would be internationally designated on the basis of nominations from countries participating in MAB. They would link protected areas with the surrounding ecosystems and human communities. They would encourage regional cooperation to discover practical solutions to complex problems of conservation and resource management. They would encourage the pooling of intellectual, technological and financial resources. With the active participation of local people, they would become showcases for creative approaches to conservation and human use of the ecosystems. By providing a permanent consultative framework for sharing data and experience, biosphere reserves would foster cooperation necessary to help solve regional and global problems. Designation of these "landscapes for learning" by the international community would serve to galvanize support for local efforts to implement the biosphere reserve concept. At the time, I was impressed by how integrative this concept was and how complementary with the teachings of the Baha'i Faith. In 1980, when the job of coordinating the National Park Service's participation in MAB unexpectedly became available, I enthusiastically applied and was selected.

For 15 years, I have witnessed the parallel emergence from obscurity of both the Baha'i Faith and the World Network of Biosphere Reserves. On the one hand, the Baha'i International Community is now involved in numerous projects that foster community development, based on contemporary science and technology balanced with spiritual principle and respect for traditional knowledge. On the other hand, the World Network now comprises 324 areas in 82 countries. In order to help solve complex problems of conservation and development, the Network is encouraging unprecedented communication between natural and social scientists, and among scientists, decision-makers and local people.[51] A UNESCO conference involving 114 nations recently endorsed a global action plan for biosphere reserves,[52] and a growing number of nations have approved their own action plans.[53]

In reviewing the biosphere reserve concept, J. Ronald Engel, Professor of Social Ethics at the Meadville/Lombard Theological School (an affiliate of the University of Chicago) sees in biosphere reserves an ethic of human community (based on spiritual principle) emerging alongside the ethic of resource management (based on science and technology) that characterizes most contemporary protected areas.[54] Engel has also suggested that, in the longer term, biosphere reserves may become the sacred spaces of a future world civilization—in effect, celebrations of the "reorientation of contemporary society to the natural world"—and that the world network, when complete, "will represent in microcosm as perfect a model of the biosphere conceived as a cooperative organic whole as it is possible to achieve ... and a nearly perfect model of a sustainable global culture."[55] It has given me great professional satisfaction to promote projects so consistent with my personal beliefs.

To be able to serve as a witness to the stirrings of concord—i.e., religious teachings confirming science, man in harmony with man, and human needs in balance with Nature—is to look optimistically toward the next millenium.

"The Lord of all mankind hath fashioned this human realm to be a Garden of Eden, an earthly paradise. If, as it must, it findeth the way to harmony and peace, to love and mutual trust, it will become a true abode of bliss, a place of manifold blessings and unending delights. Therein shall be revealed the excellence of humankind, therein shall the rays of the Sun of Truth shine forth on every hand."[56]

REFERENCES CITED

1. 'Abdu'l-Baha. *Paris Talks: Addresses Given by Abdu'l-Baha in Paris in 1911–1912.* 11th ed. London: Baha'i Publishing Trust, 1971.
2. 'Abdu'l-Baha. *The Promulgation of Universal Peace: Talks Delivered by Abdu'l-Baha During his Visit to the United States and Canada in 1912.* 2nd ed. Wilmette, IL: Baha'i Publishing Trust, 1981.
3. 'Abdu'l-Baha. *Some Answered Questions.* Wilmette, IL: Baha'i Publishing Trust, 1981.
4. 'Abdu'l-Baha. *Selections from the Writings of Abdu'l-Baha.* Chatham, England: W. and J. McKay, 1978.
5. 'Abdu'l-Baha. "Tablet from Persian." Cited in Research Department of the Universal House of Justice, "Conservation of the Earth's Resources." Haifa, Israel: Baha'i World Center, 1989.
6. 'Abdu'l-Baha. Previously untranslated tablet cited in Baha'i International Community, "The Baha'i Faith and the Summit on the Alliance between Religions and Conservation." New York: Baha'i International Community-Office of the Environment, 1995. 3.
7. Baha'i International Community. "The Baha'i Faith and the Summit on the Alliance between Religions and Conservation." New York: Baha'i International Community-Office of the Environment, 1995.
8. Baha'i International Community. "The Prosperity of Humankind." Haifa, Israel: Baha'i International Community-Office of Public Information, 1995.
9. Baha'i International Community. "Sustainable Development and the Human Spirit." New York: Baha'i International Community, 1995.
10. Baha'i International Community. "A Global Strtegy and Action Plan for Sustainable Development." NY: Baha'i International Community, 1994.
11. Baha'i International Community. *World Citizenship: A Global Ethic for Sustainable Development.* NY: Baha'i International Community, 1994.
12. Baha'i International Community. *A Baha'i Declaration on Nature.* NY: Baha'i International Community, 1987.
13. Baha'i World Center. *The Baha'i World, 1993–1994: An International Record.* Haifa, Israel: Baha'i World Center, n.d.
14. Baha'i World Center. *The Baha'i World, 1992–1993: An International Record.* Haifa, Israel: Baha'i World Center, n.d.
15. Baha'u'llah. *Epistle to the Son of the Wolf.* Wilmette, IL: Baha'i Publishing Trust, 1976.
16. Baha'u'llah. *Gleanings from the Writings of Baha'u'llah.* 2nd rev. ed. Wilmette, IL: Baha'i Publishing Trust, 1976.
17. Baha'u'llah. *Hidden Words of Baha'u'llah.* Wilmette, IL: Baha'i Publishing Trust, n.d.
18. Baha'u'llah. *Prayers and Meditations of Baha'u'llah.* Wilmette, IL: Baha'i Publishing Trust, 1974.

19.   Baha'u'llah. *Tablets of Baha'u'llah Revealed after the Kitab-i-Aqdas*. Chatham, England: W. and J. McKay, 1982.

20.   Bell, Richard W. "Environmental Care: The Baha'i Experience." In Bell, R. W., *The Environment: Our Common Heritage*. Australia: Association for Baha'i Studies, 1994.

21.   Dahl, Arthur L. *Unless and Until: A Baha'i Focus on the Environment*. London: Baha'i Publishing Trust, 1990.

22.   Effendi, Shoghi. *The World Order of Baha'u'llah: Selected Letters*. Wilmette, IL: Baha'i Publishing Trust, 1974.

23.   Secretary of Shoghi Effendi. Letter of February 17, 1993. Cited in "The Baha'i Faith and the Summit on the Alliance between Religions and Conservation." NY: Baha'i International Community, 1995. 4.

24.   Engel, J. Ronald. "The Symbolic and Ethical Dimensions of the Biosphere Reserve Concept." In Gregg, W. P., S. L. Krugman and J. D. Wood, Jr., ed. *Proceedings of the Symposium on Biosphere Reserves, September 14–17, 1987*. Atlanta, GA: U. S. Department of the Interior-National Park Service, 1989. 21–32.

25.   Engel, J. Ronald. "Renewing the Bond of Mankind and Nature: Biosphere Reserves as Sacred Space." *Orion* 4(3): 1985. 52–59.

26.   Momen, Moojan. *Baha'i Focus on Development*. London: Baha'i Publishing Trust, 1988.

27.   *Unity and Consultation: Foundations of Sustainable Development*. Wilmette, IL: National Spiritual Assembly of the Baha'is of the United States.

28.   United Nations Educational, Scientific, and Cultural Organization. *Program on Man and the Biosphere: Seville Action Plan*. Paris: UNESCO, forthcoming.

29.   United Nations Educational, Scientific, and Cultural Organization. *Report of the Task Force on Criteria for Choice and Establishment of Biosphere Reserves*. MAB Report Series No. 22. Paris: UNESCO, 1974.

30.   United Nations Educational, Scientific, and Cultural Organization and the United Nations Environment Program. *Conservation, Science and Society: Contributions to the First International Biosphere Reserve Congress, Minsk, Byelorussia, U.S.S.R., 26 September–2 October, 1983*. 2 vols. Paris: UNESCO, 1984.

31.   United States Man and the Biosphere Program, Biosphere Reserve Directorate. *Strategic Plan for the U. S. Biosphere Reserve Program*. Washington, DC: Department of State, 1994.

32.   Research Department of the Universal House of Justice. *Conservation of the Earth's Resources*. Haifa, Israel: Baha'i World Center, 1989.

33.   The Universal House of Justice. *The Promise of World Peace: A Statement by the Universal House of Justice*. Southhampton, England: Camelot Press, 1985.

34.   van den Hoonard, W. C. "A Pattern of Development: An Historical Study

of Baha'i Communities in International Development." Baha'i International News Service No. 157 (August 1986). 15.

35. White, Robert A. *Spiritual Foundations for an Ecologically Sustainable Society*. Ottawa: Association for Baha'i Studies, 1989.

A Call for Just

and

Sustainable Human
Development

Robert Patterson

The enslaving poverty which has a firm grip on so many of God's people is the product of a host of interrelated forces—including unjust social structures, exploitation of the defenseless, lack of adequate natural resources, absence of technological understanding, and rapid expansion of populations. This condition of enslaving poverty and hunger is perhaps the most tragic condition of our time, and yet this intolerable condition can be overcome if God's people have the will to act.

The thesis of this essay is that just and sustainable human development represent keys to eliminating the slavery of poverty. Obstacles to development which I am identifying as an intolerable violation of God's creation include maldistribution and unsustainability, flagrant disregard of human dignity, solidarity, and equity, and rejection of current understanding of the importance of ecological integrity as a precondition for enhancing food availability. Why do these obstacles exist? To be very frank, individual and corporate greed lies at the heart of the matter.

This essay emphasizes the need to care more fully for the land and all ecosystems as givers and sustainers of food for all, and ultimately for human well-being. Partnerships among those truly dedicated to a just society out of a strong sense of concern and humility, and committed to action, represent mankind's only hope for a global future.

Imagine that your child left for school this morning feeling a growing hunger in the belly, weakened by the need for medical care that is unavailable, clothed so shabbily that self-esteem is lacking, and destined to return to your home later today having learned little, if anything, that will prepare the child adequately for the challenges and opportunities of the rapidly approaching twenty-first century. Sadly, at least half a billion parents experienced that anguish this morning. For reasons sometimes difficult to understand, these families simply lack the resources to obtain the basic food and medical care needed to sustain minimum activity and normal development of their offspring. An estimated 10,000 of these children—God's children also, perhaps we should remind ourselves—will die of either hunger or, more likely, hunger-related causes before you finish reading this essay. Such is the fate of innocent children, and the despair of parents in many parts of God's world, a world of incredible contrasts regarding food availability, and painfully, a world where continuing, and in some cases worsening, injustices driven by greed and callousness appear to prevent each of us from becoming more human.

Our humanity and God's gifts to His earth are united in a singular passage of scripture (Matthew 25:37) which confronts me each time I place myself in the presence of hungry children: "When did we see you hungry, and feed you?" Our response to date to this compelling passage of scripture is deeply troubling for a number of reasons, the most compelling of which is that the hunger God's children will experience this night as they attempt to sleep is completely avoidable. All the basic resources required to sustain a level of food production equal to the needs of the inhabitants of our planet are present in abundant quantity. Unfortunately for hungry and well-fed alike, our inability to distinguish between our needs and wants, and then to act on that understanding, has created inequities in food availability of most distressing proportions. Even more troubling is the fact that in certain parts of virtually every continent, the economic distance between well-fed and under-fed is widening rather than narrowing.

Caring, sharing, and justice—three simple but powerful and defining words—express the depth of our compassion and love for our neighbors who of necessity follow quite a different path from that we can readily comprehend. Our Christian faith journey is guided by certain "pillars," or beliefs, which define our vision for a just society, and which frame our approach to acting out our faith. For example, we believe hunger is a tragedy resulting from mankind's greed, discrimination, and naivete about the delicate yet resilient ecosystem which produces our food. We also believe that the driving force for changing the human condition lies within each of us, and especially those of us representing wealth and power. I believe a key to reducing poverty and hunger lies in listening to poor people, and in helping them acquire ownership of the existing resources which are the key to their achieving self-determination. I also believe it is intolerable that decisions are being made which determine the fate of hungry children without their parents being full and equal partners with those representing wealth.

I believe that chronic hunger and poverty represent continuing threats to our keeping faith with the Scriptures. A firm commitment to the teachings of the Holy Scriptures should reflect both the moral and ethical standards inherent in those teachings. I also believe that global poverty and hunger, if addressed in accordance with the Judeo-Christian tradition, can and will be eliminated, and the well-being of hungry people elevated to such a degree that they can more fully achieve their God-given potential on earth. The essential point of this essay is that for all God's people to have a future with hope, all children must receive proper nourishment, and this will happen only if humankind responds positively to the call in this collection of essays for a renewal of concern, humility, hope, and action.

One of the most unsettling realities of the present age is the enormous disparity in food availability both within and between countries. The technological miracle which has allowed a small part of humankind to be exceedingly well fed, sheltered, and clothed is occurring at heavy cost. Part of the cost is that the affluence enjoyed by some prevents that segment of society from being able to comprehend fully the degree and basis of human suffering. The far greater cost, however, is borne by those who cannot know food security so long as such a resource-depleting standard of living is embraced. Northern Ireland's Nobel Peace Prize winner Mairead Maquire sharpened the focus on this issue during an August, 1995 Peacemaking Jubilee with the assertion that "Human life is sacred—God gives it and we have no right to take it away." Human life can be erased just as surely by withholding or mismanaging food production and distribution as with bullets.

The whole point is that these children exist today. Their bodies—their blood and brains—will not wait until tomorrow for the protein, vitamins, and minerals which must be had today. Nothing which is done later in their lives, after more conferences and workshops have framed more "blueprints for responsible development," can compensate for inadequate nutrition today. Cognitive potential, and the motivation and capacity for doing work, have a physiological and biochemical basis, and if the child's nutritional needs of today are compromised, then the God-given potential of all the tomorrows is lost. Why is our political and economic will to launch incredibly expensive satellites, military programs, shopping centers, and sports arenas so much stronger than is our desire to put a decent plate on the table of our neighbor's hungry child? In truth, today affluent nations have the means to put a nutritional plate on the table of each hungry child on the planet, if those nations want to.

I believe that the fundamental barriers to ensuring food adequacy for the world's hungry are far more political than biological. But I also believe with equal conviction that the environmental consequences of actions affluent peoples are taking to preserve and enhance their standard of living are doing grave damage to the ability of poverty-stricken nations to increase their food-producing capacity to levels which could diminish their poverty.

Quite disturbing moral and ethical questions arise about the harm being done to soil, water, air, and associated ecosystems as use of a broad spectrum of technologies to increase yield throughout the Americas, Europe, Africa, and Asia is intensified. Especially troubling is that biological and engineering achievements which have so greatly increased the ability to convert natural and synthetic resources to useful plant and animal products also have enhanced greatly the capacity to degrade, and even destroy, the very environment upon which the survival of humankind depends.

A compelling question thus arises from these concerns: "How can food be ensured for all while simultaneously being faithful to the Judeo-Christian tradition of respecting all of God's creation?" The Holy Scriptures teach us to respect the basic goodness of the earth, and the ecological soundness entailed in God's gift of good soil, water, and air to all. The challenge is to act with conviction, and in a spirit of faithfulness, on the insights gained from probing the natural world, and above all else, to treat these resources most respectfully as they are managed to strengthen food availability to the hungry.

The capacity for altering natural ecological systems is rapidly becoming truly remarkable. For example, advances in genetic engineering technologies have greatly enhanced ability to control virtually all aspects of food-producing and harvesting systems. Command of fossil fuel and pesticide delivery systems permits alteration of the physical and biological environments in which food is produced in both impressive and disturbing ways. For example, since the end of World War II the highly technical field crop-producing enterprise has experienced a continuously declining yield of energy per unit of energy invested (both fossil fuels and human energy considered), even though grain yields have increased during this time frame. The most efficient rice-producing system, for example, continues to be the one practiced in southeast Asia, in which the primary investment is human energy, rather than the fossil fuel-intensive system practiced in the U.S.. The same observation is made for virtually all of the handful of crops which literally stand between humankind and starvation (wheat, rice, corn, grain, sorghum, soybeans, peanuts, peas, dry beans, sugar cane, sugar beet, cassava, and banana).

Incidentally, if the true cost of processing is considered, the U.S. sugar beet enterprise actually yields less energy than is required to grow the crop! The U.S. food-producing system continues to be predicated on a seemingly endless supply of fossil fuel energy. Each additional pound of nitrogen fertilizer adds much less to U.S. corn or wheat grain yields than to the yield of grain crops in India. Yet it is the Indian farmer who must decide, in the absence of any synthetic nitrogen fertilizer, whether to commit his limited supply of cattle manure for fuel for cooking or for fertilizer for the crop. Fossil fuel energy supplies are not unlimited, and presumably neither is the patience of the hungry, although it seems so at times.

All too often the true cost of utilizing a particular food production enterprise is not considered adequately. For example, when farming sloping Columbia River Basin watershed land, thus allowing soil particles and chemicals (both pesticides and fertilizer) to move down slopes and into streams which supply water to the Columbia River, great damage is done to the ecosystem which sustains the salmon, the "staff of life" of many Pacific Northwest Indian tribes. The Yakima, one such group which has depended on the salmon to provide protein for their children's well-being for centuries, has an interesting comment about the desire for high wheat yields: "To plow the land is akin to cutting the mother's breast." Just how important is the well-being of Native American children in comparison to the desire to produce grain for an expanding export market?

A related question has to do with the morality of shipping excess crop to chronically hungry countries desperate to stabilize their own food production. Consider the plight of the Zairian (now Democratic Republic of Congo) rice producer when he cannot sell his harvest because a shipment of Arkansas rice (with no insect parts and sand particles) has just arrived at his village market. Or the Polish potato farmer who cannot compete with U.S. potatoes which have suddenly arrived at his local market. Or the eastern Germany wheat farmer who traditionally sells to the Russian market, but can't now because U.S. wheat has just arrived in Russia obtained with U.S.-provided certificates of purchase. Or the Nicaraguan poultry farmer who has just observed U.S.-shipped frozen poultry arrive in his country and destroy his already meager marketing opportunity. Or the Nicaraguan grain sorghum producer who had hoped to sell his crop to the poultry farmer for livestock feed until the shipment of grain from a well-intentioned U.S. development group arrived in the country. Or the Honduran fisherman whose estuary has been totally destroyed because chemicals added to shrimp farming holding ponds (whose water is pumped to and fro by engines manufactured in the U.S. and given to the Honduran government by the U.S. Agency for International Development) have killed the fish upon which he and his family depend for their survival. Or the Puerto Rican farmer who remembers when he could sell all the rice he grew on his farm, but today knows that every grain of rice eaten in Puerto Rico was grown in the U.S.. Or the Mexican grain farmer, who sees cattle ranchers in his valley today purchase corn from midwestern U.S. farms rather than from him because their supply is more reliable (and he is standing less than one hundred miles from the center of origin of corn!). Or the Chinese cotton grower who sees his marketing opportunities evaporate as U.S. cotton begins to dominate the market in his district.

All these scenarios I have personally observed, and as the son of a farmer I assure you that the pain in the hearts of each of these farmers was real as they described their bitterness at losing marketing opportunity. *Access to market*—the three most important words to any farmer, and especially to farmers struggling to survive in poverty-stricken areas, where cash for purchase of their produce is in short supply. No farmer will produce beyond the subsistence level unless someone is willing to give him something he and his family need for their excess of production. When by our well-intentioned but extremely naive approach to development we create disincentives to produce at the local level we exacerbate rather than relieve chronic hunger.

The turn-of-the-century naturalist John Muir observed "...when I tug at a single thing in nature I find it attached to the rest of the world." Muir's vision, which led to the protection and preservation of exceedingly valuable ecosystems in the western U.S., represents the philosophy which must be practiced today if a reasonable level of food production is to be sustained. A crucial part of any sensible strategy for sustaining an adequate food supply for our planet involves *nurturing, repairing,* and *sharing* the soil, water, and air which have made our earth so productive to date.

The indiscriminate and senseless contamination and waste of precious natural resources, especially the fragile wetlands and woodlands which are so vital to preservation of wildlife biodiversity, which in turn are so important to primary food production, truly compromises the ability to feed children yet to be born everywhere in the world. For example, thirst for wood products is slaked by adding many square miles of pulpwood plantations in areas which, if disturbed, simply will not support viable numbers of flora and fauna along seacoasts. Draining wetlands to grow a pulpwood tree dilutes the estuarine waters downstream to such an extent that shellfish may not reproduce, and the estuary itself ultimately fails to serve as adequate habitat for wildlife. Global food production frankly is impossible to sustain at an acceptable level in the absence of functioning wildlife habitats. For these habitats to be functional and thus sustainable they need to be properly buffered, which requires large border areas—areas into which intrusions are being made at an alarming rate.

In large measure we are victims of our own success. Progress in crop and livestock germplasm enhancement research has led to increased plant and animal tolerance to all kinds of environmental stresses. Enhanced yields from environmentally invasive resources (such as pesticides) have placed some exceedingly sensitive ecosystems in great jeopardy. As we approach what the agronomist refers to as the "yield plateau" (the point where a crop appears not to respond yieldwise to additional inputs) we tend to try novel approaches to boost yield, whose longer-term ecological consequences are seriously open to question. For example, the use of genetically-engineered crop seed which is tolerant to an herbicide of choice for a particular weed situation in that crop could lead to even more serious pest problems in a few years, thus "requiring" the use of pesticides which are yet to be formulated, and which could be even more invasive.

Fortunately, genetic variability appears to exist for virtually every kind of stress in the crop environment which reduces yield and quality of crops. The creativity and resourcefulness of plant and animal breeders and geneticists represent perhaps the best opportunity to decrease reliance on technologies which are potentially quite environmentally invasive. But the genetic resources breeders and geneticists need to enhance food germplasm in an environmentally secure manner most often are located in remote areas of the world which presently are suffering horribly from over-cutting (mahogany to build our furniture and sailing ships) over-burning (land clearing to provide pasture for livestock as a source of our prime rib), mining (we do not have enough gold and silver), and dam construction (more electricity is needed from non-fossil-fuel sources). Heavy metal pollution of waterways needed by indigenous peoples for drinking, cooking, and bathing leads to brain damage. These minerals are felt to be needed to sustain affluent lifestyles. How ironic it is that most of the areas being degraded by these activities—areas which contain life-giving plant and animal genes for benefit of all, are populated by the poorest and hungriest people (Amazonas, hill country of Haiti and Honduras, Kasai of Zaire, the Nile valley, tributaries to the Volta River-Dam complex, as examples)—people who stand to suffer the most as these rich sources of genetic biodiversity continue to be degraded.

Mankind's passion for altering God's good earth, water, and air to whatever extent is required to elevate a standard of living seems to have no limits. The time has come for concerned Christians to look most carefully at the consequences of scientific approaches to food security *through the lens of our faith tradition.* We well remember the tradition of faithfulness to the land as described in both Old and New Testaments. I also recall fondly the emphasis placed on farming "for good of the land" as practiced by the farmers in the community of my youth. They "put back" at least as much as they "took from." I also recall the emphasis on taking what was needed, whether it was gathering in the field or at the old fishing pond. The farmers in my community would never have considered cutting more trees than they would transplant as seedlings (for their children's children). There was a genuine belief that *all* of us do literally borrow from our children, and their children. They knew that their basic needs were met by the land, and that they had an obligation to respect the soil and associated ecosystems as life-giving and life-sustaining. One did not borrow without repaying, whether a tool, a debt, or God's natural resources.

Mankind seems to have lost the feeling for being connected to the land. There are both spiritual and physical consequences to our being disrespectful to the life-sustaining earth. There is a very special dignity associated with managing food-producing resources respectfully. I am referring to the quiet satisfaction and confidence which can help us to sleep comfortably at night, and to look in the eyes of our children the next morning, knowing that we have been faithful to them as well as to God. Standing in the middle of a cornfield near Saybrook, Illinois a few years ago, I heard the world-champion corn producer Mr. Herman Warsaw remark as he was digging into the soil surrounding the roots of what was to become yet another record corn crop, "I try to do right by my soil, knowing that if I have done that, good yields will follow." His remark was reminiscent of comments made by other older-generation farmers who also displayed a quiet kind of patience and dignity, coupled with the desire for a stable ecosystem as well as a high yield. Achieving yield stability, a prerequisite for food sustainability, involves giving back to the land—crop residues for improved windbreaks, and native plant species along drainage ditches, on hillsides, and at field edges to nurture the precious wildlife species so crucial to yield stability. Above all else, an absolute minimum of dependence on non-target-specific (or, general purpose) pesticides is required if we are to restore dignity and justice to the land of our fathers and grandchildren.

Sound stewardship of the land must be the basic goal which dominates in the current struggle between ecology and economy. The dilemmas truly are severe in hungry parts of the globe. When people are displaced as a result of human conflict, the consequences can be devastating for all concerned. For example, when Zairians (now the Democratic Republic of Congo) from the Shaba region are forced to return to their tribal (Baluba) homeland in the Kasai, their relatives welcome them back with open hearts, knowing that these additional mouths to feed will put severe strain on the land, reducing the duration of the fallow, and thus crop yields, even more. The shorter the fallow period, the poorer the soil (less organic residues returned to the land), and the less productive the soil becomes. How the U.S. and other governments can endorse a military dictatorship which causes such a tragic human migration defies rational thought. Kasai children are desperate for protein to prevent kwashiorkor, the protein-deficiency disease (a Ghanian word literally meaning "taken from the mother's milk"). Military regimes supported by the U.S. and others governments literally take mothers from their children, and put them in the fields and market places for even longer hours, denying the next generation the precious nurturing and nutrition so desperately needed.

While populations have increased greatly (and greatest) in the hungriest parts of the world, the carrying capacity of the land has rarely been exceeded, except in the cases of enforced migrations. The real problem in many cases is that the agricultural priority has been forced (by actions from outside the local village) in the direction of cash crops for export, leading to the ever-greater marginalization of subsistence farmers. Such a pressure on the village to produce charcoal (from the few remaining trees) and palm oil (instead of vegetable crops), for example, creates a strong dependence on outside commercial interests, which always dictate price, and frequently the manner in which local resources are used.

Desperate villagers, having witnessed the loss, or degradation, of their farmland, may agree to work with the waves of gold and silver seekers who are invading remote areas in Brazil, Indonesia, the Phillippines, and Zimbabwe, and participate in mining activities which silt and poison their rivers and lakes, not realizing the horrendous trade-off they are making—a little cash *vs.* birth defects and neurological problems caused by the exceedingly toxic mercury used to capture gold from sediment, for example. The environmental damage is catastrophic, and renders unusable for food production land that is desperately needed if they are to overcome the condition of chronic hunger in their villages.

Direct food aid should be restricted to acute needs, and never given when the hunger situation is chronic. To avoid paternalism, and all that entails, development initiatives must be in the form of *equivalent partnership*. This means listening , trusting, and believing that all are ecologically interdependent upon one another. All must believe that the use of a toxic material for food production in another part of the world would never be advocated if its use "at home" would not be accepted. Sustainable food production, or development in its various forms, is about the collective survival of all, not just the "first-world" neighborhood. A very wise Australian Aborigine woman once told a development worker "...If you have come to help me you can go home again. But if you see my struggle as part of your own survival then perhaps we can work together." She understood so well the truth of our global interconnectedness.

I sincerely believe a return to the land stewardship practiced by earlier generations is essential if our planet is to sustain an adequate supply of food for all. Needs and wants must be reevaluated, and a strong desire to restore the land to a more fully food-sustaining condition must become a priority. There is evidence that such a mood is in the wind. I find most encouraging the fact that present day farmers and agricultural scientists in Europe are revisiting the philosophy of the noted German medical doctor-turned-agricultural researcher, Dr. A.D. Thaer. Prior to Thaer's time, European farmers practiced a simple three-crop rotational sequence which served their needs reasonably well. But as the population of European countries grew, this system became increasingly inadequate to meet the people's food needs. Almost 200 years ago Dr. Thaer advocated the use of a seven-crop rotation, including soil-building crops interspersed with the food crops, to restore the health of the soil "for the long run," as he phrased it. This system, a very sustainable system wherever it has been utilized on the planet, was emphasized in Europe until the Second World War, at which time it was abandoned in favor of highly mechanized, intensive, chemically-dependent farming. The result has been land that is decreasingly productive, and waterways which are not drinkable, fishable, or swimmable. Today European scientists are encouraging farmers to return to the Thaer system, which relies on crop and livestock residues, rather than on resource-depleting and hazardous chemicals, because their research has demonstrated that it may be sustainable.

I once had a Malaysian graduate student working with me on a soybean irrigation project at my university. One hot, dry August day when Bakar Tambi and I were carrying irrigation pipe (it was during Ramadan, and I was trying to respect Bakar's deep faith in his Moslem religion and refrain from drinking water also), he asked me "How many feet of irrigation pipe could you get from one Phantom jet?" Somewhat irritated, I told Bakar that "I have no idea. But why?" The reply was, "I was just thinking, if your country had sent aluminum to southeast Asia in the form of irrigation pipe instead of jets, you would never have needed to send your soldiers to Vietnam." Bakar was an older student at the time, and had worked in agricultural extension in northeast Malaysia prior to receiving permission from his government to come to the U.S. for additional education. He knew the value of irrigation in southeast Asia. Clearly I was the one becoming educated, and learning about values that day.

God's covenant is with "you and your offspring *forever*" (Gen. 13:15). To me *forever* means that I must dedicate my thinking along lines which lead to restoration of the only earth we have, the one which God has entrusted to us. So much solid research data from long-term crop production trials underscores the value of good soil stewardship, and the productive potential of the land if we "give back" in proportion to what we "take from." To feed God's people properly, the gap between our faith and environmental sciences must be narrowed, and perhaps even eliminated. Consumption and production based on genuine need, rather than want, will enable all of us—producers, consumers, and scientists—to be morally disciplined to our respective professional callings, and above all else, more comfortable in our Judeo-Christian faith journey.

Just and sustainable human development as humankind approaches the 21st century frankly involves a call for a renewal of concern, humility, hope, and action. Poverty and hunger cannot be understood or resolved apart from efforts to alleviate ecological degradation, overpopulation, and excessive consumption by relatively affluent societies. Poverty and hunger are significant causes as well as effects of ecological degradation. Overpopulation jeopardizes both human development and ecological integrity by increasing stress on scarce resources and upsetting environmental balances. Overconsumption by a few deprive many of scarce resources needed for development, and contributes to global ecological decline. Equity among nations, therefore, is as much an issue of ecological ethics as social ethics. In the same manner, population stability promotes both social justice and ecological responsibility.

Acute and chronic poverty and hunger, rapid population growth, and environmental decline are tightly interconnected, and closely related to overconsumption. These are moral as well as technical issues. The massive global hunger and poverty confronting humankind today because these issues have not been properly addressed is unacceptable, because this condition is unjust and contrary to God's will. Mankind's desire to make responsible human development a matter of justice and a priority of Christian faithfulness must be the continual prayer of all who truly seek to do His will.

Is God a
Free-Market Capitalist?

Freedom, Economics
and Religion in the Development
of the American Frontier

Carl F. Jordan

THE AMERICAN FRONTIER

When the early European settlers arrived on the shores of North America, they found an expanse of resources available for exploitation. Forests, game, minerals, and prairies for farmland could be had by those brave enough to eliminate the Indians, and enterprising enough to build an infrastructure that could capture the resources. From the 17th century when early colonists arrived on the East coast, through the 18th century when pioneers moved across the Appalachians, to the 19th century when the West beyond the Mississippi was won, North American settlers found an opportunity to transform an untamed land into a civilization, and they did so expeditiously.

However, it was not just the abundance of resources waiting to be tapped that enabled the conquering of the American Frontier. There were other factors that facilitated the transformation. After the American Revolution, there was a democratic government which not only allowed, but encouraged personal freedom and responsibility. There was an economic system which rewarded entrepreneurial initiative in capturing and distributing resources. And there was a religion which gave the settlers a moral right to take the resources and use them for their own benefit.

The combination of rich resources, personal freedom, free-market capitalism, and Christianity was a powerful one. It allowed rapid and efficient exploitation of the abundant resources of America, unfettered by bureaucratic rules and regulations, and encouraged by a government which promoted such exploitation.

OPPORTUNITY AND FREEDOM

The quest for individual opportunity was a paramount factor in the migration of many European settlers to North America. The Puritans came to America because they rejected the elitist social privilege of Europe. They had a fundamental belief that rewards should be based on hard work and initiative and not on where one happened to be born in society. The Puritan's ability to make do with what they had gave rise to the North American frontier ethic that stressed rugged individualism and glorified the independent pioneers who could make it on their own in a hostile wilderness. An American ideal of independence was "I can do it myself. I don't need nor want the government interfering in my business." The country was for the people who occupied the land, not for a government or king.

Personal freedom also was important in the development of North America because pioneers could do what they felt was important to conquer the wild frontier and turn it into a hospitable environment that supplied them with physical goods to satisfy material wants. For the most part, settlers were uninhibited by an economic and political system that restricted their actions. The land and its resources was there for the taking, and there was more than enough land and resources for the settlers that arrived. Personal freedom was an important ingredient in the democratic system that evolved in North America, in which the main function of government was to serve the people in their quest to express and fulfill themselves.

CAPITALIST ECONOMY

The frontier is a place where there are more resources than can be efficiently utilized by the people occupying the land. The main problem in settling a frontier is to put those resources to work and allocate the benefits among the citizenry. Laissez-faire capitalism is ideally suited to this situation. If there is one thing that free-market economics does well it is to efficiently allocate resources where such resources are unlimited. For this reason, free-market capitalism has often been called "frontier economics."

On the North American frontier, free market capitalism ensured that resources were rapidly exploited and expeditiously used for the benefit of the people who did the work and took the chances. The benefits of development quickly returned to those who did the work of development. There was a direct feedback loop which encouraged hard work and responsibility. That feedback was profit, the "invisible hand" that ensured rapid feedback between producers and consumers.

Another part of the capitalistic system that enabled rapid exploitation was that of saving and putting aside for the future. This included not only saving money, but also investing it in a way that could bring greater future rewards—building a bigger barn, buying more cattle, or investing in new farm machinery—and getting more control over the land.

CHRISTIANITY

Religious leaders of the North American frontier taught that Man's theological duty was to subdue the wilderness. They preached that nature was created for the benefit of Man. It was Man's duty to tame the wild, and transform it for his benefit. Wild places were worse than useless. They were an embodiment of some evil. Trees were weeds, wild animals unclean and expendable. Cleared land was not only a physical need but a moral need. Pioneers were simply carrying out the scripture of Genesis which said "fill the earth and subdue it."

These views are understandable in the context of development. As the frontier opened, there were relatively few people, and the forces of nature were a threat to their continued existence. It was important for human survival that nature be conquered. Therefore, the command to subdue the wilderness was a key component of the world's best known guide to survival, the Christian Bible.

It was convenient to interpret the Bible's exhortation that man should multiply and have dominion over the earth as meaning that man should use nature to the greatest extent possible in achieving these ends. This human-centered interpretation of the Christian Bible worked well on the American frontier.

In North America, Christianity was more than a religion. It was a philosophy. It was an ethic that governed all aspects of the society. To be a good Christian, one had to work hard, show initiative, and be thrifty. Christianity was important in the conquering of the frontier.

PROGRESS AND DEVELOPMENT

Personal freedom, free market capitalism, and Christianity interacted in the United States to produce the world's most rapid and phenomenal example of "progress and development." Progress means increasing control over nature, increasing the exploitation of nature, increasing the accumulation of material goods by humans, and increasing the amount of landscape dominated by human-made structures. The idea of progress assumes that the benefits of the process called progress should go to people. Humankind is at the center of the religion called progress.

Progress and development transformed North America from a land rich in resources and few in people and with none of the amenities desired by the European colonizers, to a land much poorer in resources, with many people living in a style of luxury undreamed of by their ancestors. Progress was the "American Way."

THE CLOSING OF THE FRONTIER

In the second half of the 19th century, the North American frontier began to close. The transcontinental railroad was completed. The Indians were pacified or killed. The West became civilized. Territories became states. Most significantly, all land was "owned," either privately or by the state or federal government. No longer was there free open land available for homesteading or for building a ranch or for cutting timber.

Nevertheless, frontier mentality still was the basic attitude of North Americans. Although there were big cities in the East, there was still the romantic image of the West, where a Man was still free and could be master of his own destiny. The notion was glorified in movies, songs, art, and books. Even today, many Americans act as though their country were still a frontier. Public lands are treated as though they belonged to those who exploit them. Cattle are grazed, timber is clear cut, and off-road vehicles tear open new paths.

THE POST-FRONTIER ECONOMY

The free market system does one thing very well. It solves the problem of allocating goods and services by providing necessary information and incentive. It is an ideal system for the frontier, where the objective is to transform unlimited natural resources into objects of private ownership. However once the frontier is closed, the free market is less than ideal.

Once commonly held resources such as timber in national forests and clean air and water are no longer infinite and become limiting, the free market is unable to adequately solve the problem of sustaining the supply of these resources. The free market assumes unlimited resources and/or unlimited substitutability. However, this assumption ignores the fact that ultimately a closed system such as the earth sets limits or boundaries as to what can be done by way of achieving that utility. As a result, these resources are undervalued, or in cases such as clean air, given almost no value at all.

The market and its present accounting system are failing to adequately serve humanity because the market price for most natural resources, including a pollution-free environment, does not reflect their utilitarian value. Their value in use is not reflected in their value in exchange. The price that is paid for them is not indicative of their value for satisfying physical or psychological needs or human desires.

To deal with the problem of essential resources that have little or no market value, the government has instituted regulations which protect, to a certain extent, these resources from over-use. The Clean Water Act is an example, in that it prohibits disposal of hazardous wastes into waterways. Certain utilitarian values of nature such as clean air are so important that a monetary value must be attributed to these resources in order to protect them. The costs of not having clean air are the medical costs associated with people suffering from conditions caused by air pollution. To calculate these costs, the doctor and hospital bills for all problems related to air pollution such as asthma could be tallied, as well as the costs of the employer to cover the employee's sick time.

A well recognized utilitarian value of nature is the prevention of siltation of reservoirs by intact forests. The value of a forest in protecting a watershed can be attributed by calculating the costs associated with dredging a reservoir where the protective forest has been destroyed. If the cost of dredging the reservoir is greater than the market price for the timber in the forest, it makes economic sense to ensure that the trees are left in place. For this reason, many states have regulations prohibiting the cutting of trees along stream banks. But because watershed protection, clean air and clean water are public goods, they are value-less in a free-market system, and therefore, like anything that has value but is not guarded, they disappear. They can be conserved only if their value is attributed outside the marketplace.

Although the value of some nonmarket resources can be attributed, there are others for which it is impossible even to impute a value. These resources are said to have intangible values. Enjoyment of a hike through the wilderness, or the sighting of a whale or an eagle are examples. Some intangible values, such as maintaining the global carbon dioxide balance, can be approximated by estimating the cost to society of a rising sea level, but such estimates are so rough and would take place so far in the economic future that they have little meaning. Other intangible values such as the value of a native culture may not have an attributable value at all. Such values can be preserved only if it is considered ethical to do so.

THE NEED FOR ALTERNATIVES

Free market capitalism works well on the frontier. However, the frontier is now closed and to sustain society in the coming century, we must modify an economic system which is based on the assumption that resources (including sinks for pollution) are inexhaustible, are produced free by nature, or can be substituted for by something else. Because we are becoming more crowded, we need rules to regulate who does what, when something that someone does affects someone else negatively.

COMMUNISM

Communism arose in reaction to the insensitivity of free market Capitalism to the needs and desires of working class people. Capitalism exploited terribly the poor who had no way to win a fair share of the profits gained through their sweat and toil. Theoretically, Communism was the ideal answer to the plight of the worker—give the ownership and thereby the profits to all the workers who contribute to the creation of wealth. It urged the abolishment of the Capitalistic free market system which benefits only those who are rich to begin with, and who get richer through exploitation of the poor. In the same way that Communism seemed to offer a remedy to exploitation of labor, Communism also may seem to offer a remedy to exploitation of resources. In a Communistic system, attributable and intangible values could be simply assigned, thereby incorporating the true value of resources into the economic system.

As we all know, Communism failed on national and international levels. However, the "Communist empire" failed, not because it was Communistic, but, to a large degree, because it was not. A Communist system is a system owned by and regulated by its members, that is, all its citizens. Russia and its satellites really were not Communistic. Ordinary citizens could not and did not participate in governance. The Communist empire failed because The system was a hypocrisy. It was a dictatorship, or a series of dictatorships. It was not the economic system which failed, but rather the political system. The countries were run for the benefit of the dictators, not for the citizens.

However, just because the experiments in Communism have failed on a national scale, does not mean that there have been no successful communes. There are a number of successful communes, even within the United States. The lobster fishery along the coast of Maine is a good example. Lobstermen carefully control access to the resource, and ensure that it is not depleted. An important difference between successful Communistic systems such as the lobster fishery and the national failures of Communism is in their size. Successful communes are almost always on a small scale, where everyone personally knows everyone else, and all members are more or less economically equal (a classless society). Social pressure is a factor which prohibits a clique from seizing absolute power. Decisions are made with the intent of benefitting all the members of the society.

EVOLUTION OF CAPITALISM

Because the frontier is closed does not mean that further improvement of the lives of citizens is not possible within an economic system that is still basically capitalistic. It is just that improvement must be done in a different way—through cooperation that improves the quality of resources rather than through competition for exploitation of resources that are becoming scarce. Quantitative growth, in the sense of more automobiles, more airplanes and more expensive houses is not the only alternative. We can develop qualitatively. We can change and improve our lives in other ways. There are a series of steps in which an unregulated free market society can change into one that recognizes the finiteness of resources while at the same time allowing for continuing qualitative development.

Colby (1990) has recognized and defined four separate stages:

1. FRONTIER ECONOMICS (LAISSEZ-FAIRE STAGE).

In frontier economics, technologies are developed with the purpose of increasing the power of the socioeconomic system to increase production by extracting resources from the environment, as well as to dampen the negative impacts of nature's variability on economic activities. Central to the frontier economics paradigm is the belief that environmental damage can easily be repaired where necessary, and that infinite technological progress founded in human ingenuity, together with economic growth will provide affordable ways to mitigate environmental problems.

2. ENVIRONMENTAL PROTECTION (REGULATORY STAGE)

The environmental protection stage begins with the suspicion that environmental problems are perhaps a little more serious than originally assumed. The principal strategy is to legalize the environment as an economic externality, in a modest variation of the frontier economics mode of development. The environmental protection perspective is defensive or remedial in practice, concerned mainly with ameliorating the effects of human activities. The approach focuses mostly on controlling damage and on repairing and setting limits to harmful human activities, but it is not concerned with finding ways to improve development and ecological resilience. Government agencies are created and are responsible for setting these limits. Environmental impact statements or assessments are institutionalized in many industrial countries as a rational means of assisting in weighing the costs and benefits of economic development before they are started. Areas of common property are set aside as state property for preservation or conservation. National parks and wilderness reserves also are created. Resource depletion and ecosystem services are generally not perceived in policy making as serious limiting factors for economic development. The interaction between human activity and nature in the environmental protection paradigm is still seen as a question of development versus environment.

3. RESOURCE MANAGEMENT (INCENTIVE STAGE).

The resource management stage marks the beginning of a recognition that nature is critical in supplying not only goods, but also critical services to the economy, and that cooperation with nature is essential. The basic idea is to incorporate all types of capital and resources such as forests and fisheries as well as traditional human, infrastructural, and monetary resources into calculations of national accounts, productivity, and policies for development and investment planning. The objective is to take greater account of the interdependence and multiple values of various resources, and management of global commons resources. Not only stocks of physical resources but also ecosystem services need to be considered as resources and capital that should be maintained, as well as used more effectively, by the use of new technology. The stabilization of population levels and reductions in per capita consumption through increased efficiency in the industrial nations are viewed as essential to achieving sustainability. It is understood that the scale of human activity is now so large that it affects the life-supporting environment, and that these impacts have a feedback effect on the quantity and quality of human life. Basic ecological principles are essential for management to maintain the stability of the life-supporting environment.

4. ECODEVELOPMENT (COOPERATION STAGE)

The essential step that will prevent humans from ultimately destroying the habitabilty of the planet is the recognition that they are part of the planet's system of stocks and flows of material and energy, and are not some remote controller, immune from the effects of their desires and decisions. Whatever humans do ultimately comes back to affect them one way or the other.

Ecodevelopment more explicitly sets out to restructure the relationship between society and nature by reorganizing human activities so as to be synergetic with ecosystem process and functions. In this stage, humans move from economizing ecology to ecologizing the economy, and realize that great economic and social benefits can be obtained from fully integrated ecological economic approaches to environmental problems.

The ecodevelopment approach recognizes the need to manage for adaptability, resilience, and uncertainty, and for coping with the occurrence of nonlinear phenomena and ecological surprises. Rather than asking how can we create and then how can we remedy, ecodevelopment attempts to provide a positive, interdependent vision for both human and ecosystem development. This approach emphasizes that planning and management ought to be embedded in the total environment of the system under consideration, including all the actors concerned, which means that global system awareness must be coupled with local responsibility for action.

The term development, rather than meaning only growth, management or protection connotes an explicit reorientation and upgrading of the level of integration of social, ecological, and economic concerns in designing for sustainability. This perspective emphasizes a shift from a system in which the polluter pays to a system in which pollution prevention pays, and also stresses the need to move from throughput-based physical growth to qualitative improvement. Such development not only implies becoming more efficient in the use of resources and ecosystem services, but it also emphasizes the need for improvement in terms of synergies gained from designing agricultural and industrial process in order to mimic and use ecosystem processes in an explicit manner.

THE STUMBLING BLOCK

Some environmental problems during recent decades have been dealt with through regulation, indicating a transition of the economy to the beginning of the regulatory phase. However, for the most part, capitalism is still stuck in phase one, the complete Laissez-faire stage. And instead of encouraging the evolution toward the incentive stage of environmental amelioration, the country is beginning to take a step backward. The mood of the 104th Republican-dominated Congress has been to retreat on such issues as clean water and protection of species diversity. There is much political pressure from the conservative right to repeal part or all of such regulatory protection laws as the Clean Water Act and the Endangered Species Act.

Why this retreat? Why is there such resistance to leave behind the old ways when it is clear that they are doing such damage?

Because of the close, historical association in the U.S. of personal freedom, economic opportunity under free market capitalism, and conservative Christianity, it is assumed by the Religious Right that the three are inextricably linked together in a single, all-encompassing philosophy. That philosophy demands that any deviation from uninhibited exploitation of a nation's resources under laissez-faire capitalism is an anathema to God. The Religious Right, with their fundamental belief in the infallibility of completely unregulated free-market capitalism, would have us believe that God is a free-market capitalist. Unfettered utilization of resources is assumed in the philosophy of the extreme right to be a religious duty. To them, religion means the blatant right to extinguish a species if it is in the way of a proposed shopping mall. But there is no logical reason that a particular economic system and Christianity, or any other religion for that matter, must be tied together under one umbrella philosophy. An economic system encompasses one set of assumptions or beliefs, a religious system another.

Conservative Christians certainly have a right to bring their religious values into the public square. The question is not whether religious faith should make a political contribution. But if religious values are to influence the public arena, the spokespersons ought to make clear the scope of religion and the scope of economics, and not muddle the two in the effort to intimidate on religious grounds those opposed to a conservative economic agenda. But this has not been their tactic. Since the 1980's the powerful influence of the Religious Right has been an important factor in making our political debate even more divisive, polarized and less sensitive to ecological issues by proclaiming that they, and only they have the moral right to speak for God.

There is ample evidence in the Bible itself that the assumption the Earth was created solely for the economic use of Man is false, and that God is concerned with more than accumulation of material goods by human beings. In the story of the flood, God makes a covenant, not just with Noah and his family, but also with the non-human creation: "Behold I establish my covenant with you and your descendents after you, and with every living creature that is with you, the birds, the cattle, and every beast of the earth" (Genesis 9: 9-10). Knowing that they all give joy to their creator, Christians should treasure and protect every species.

Environmental responsibility is at the heart of our Biblical traditions. Extermination is a sin, and the best test of a nation's righteousness is not its gross national product and military firepower, but how it treats the world that it inhabits. God mandates in Genesis 1:28, that Man have dominion over the fish of the sea, and over the fowl of the air, and over every living thing that moveth upon the earth. The word "dominion" has been interpreted by the religious right to mean exploitation. But a meaning that is more fitting with the spirit of the Bible is stewardship, an interpretation that God cares about *all* the creatures that He created.

American Capitalism is not evolving quickly enough out of the frontier stage, let alone into the Incentive Stage and Cooperation Stage. There are a number of reasons, but here I am going to focus on one: Christianity as the predominant religion during the period when the frontier was conquered, and the interpertation of the Christian Bible's exhortation to use the resources of the earth to multiply has resulted in a conviction among some that Christianity is an integral part of a philosophy that (demands) free market economics and at the same time is divinely blessed.

In the 1950s, communism was a bogey-man to be feared and persecuted. The witch hunts of Senator McCarthy in the early 1950s was a symptom of the paranoia in America in the face of other styles of government which had arisen in Russia and Eastern Europe. To question the desirability of progress (free market exploitation of resources) was "anti-American."

To question the desirability of the American way, in the years after World War II, was tantamount to being a communist sympathizer. "Godless Communists" was an epithet of choice to describe those who question America's exploitative frontier vision of progress.

Although the threat of warfare with Russia and eastern Europe has disappeared, the conservative right wing politicians have not disappeared. They have re-surfaced as "The Wise Use Movement," and/or the Religious Right. It is no longer the advocates for labor who are being portrayed as threats to God-fearing Americans and to family values. Rather it is the environmental advocates who are pictured as the enemy to traditional American values. Those who support rules and laws that would prevent exploitation of America's commons (its air, water, forests, rangeland, and fisheries) by a priviledged few are branded as "McGovernicks," in referral to the unsuccessful 1972 presidential candidate George McGovern who advocated a liberal agenda for this country.

Despite the lack of logic of the argument that a Christian God is necessarily associated with a free market capitalistic system, the conservative Christian minority insists on making the association. Any attempt, they say, to curtail the supposed rights of property owners to do as they please on their land is regarded as communistic. And because communism is associated with godlessness, those who oppose unregulated free-market capitalists are branded as anti-god or un-Christian.

The so-called religious right, the very conservative Christians, are firm believers in laissez-faire capitalism. In the minds of some, the basic philosophy that markets should be unrestrained by government regulation has been melded with fundamentalist faith and become part of their religious doctrine. Christianity is perceived by many as being synonymous with uninhibited pursuit of narrow self-interest.

Because on the frontier, survival depends on conquering nature, and free market capitalism was important in conquering the frontier, God was considered to be a free market capitalist, and Christianity was crucial in the moral justification of the conquest. It was convenient to have a free market capitalist as a God.

WHAT CAN BE DONE

Once the frontier is conquered, survival depends upon living in harmony with nature. How can an interpertation of God be changed to incorporate a more benign attitude toward nature?

Let us consider the nature of God. Primitive peoples usually worship pantheistic gods. They do not understand thunder and lightning, fire, and wild animals, rivers and rains, yet they know that these things strongly influence their lives, for good and for bad. They certainly don't consider themselves above nature. They fear nature, and so they worship it.

Modern science has led us to understand nature. We no longer are afraid of it. We believe that we can control it. Our lives have certainly become better in the short run, because of our ability to control it. As Man began to understand nature, and to control it for his own benefit, he no longer feared nature, and thus no longer feared a natural God.

Because God (with a human face) obviously was more powerful than nature and rules over nature, this obscured the man/nature unity, and led Man to believe that he had the right to use and change nature as he pleased. This worked all right on a frontier situation, where man's survival depended on conquering nature.

What needs to be done to get Man to once again respect nature is to dissociate God and Christianity from the economic system which was so effective in conquering the frontier—the Free Market System.

The first chapter in the Old Testament of the Christian Bible contains the verses that have split humanity into those that would put Man above nature and thus give him the right to exploit nature, and those that view Man as part of nature and give Man the responsibility of preserving nature.

GENESIS: AN ASSUMPTION

The frontiersmen have interpreted the word *dominion* to mean ownership, in the sense that the fish of the sea and the other creatures of nature have been placed on earth merely for the convenience of human beings for use in their efforts to multiply. Creatures, including resources, are seen as having no other purpose or value than to serve humankind.

The other camp interprets *dominion* to mean stewardship. They interpret the Bible as saying that human beings have responsibility for preserving the well-being of all living creatures, ensuring that they not perish from the face of the earth. Creatures, including resources, have an intrinsic value that exists apart from any use they might have for people.

As we evolve from a society that depends upon conquering nature for survival to a society that depends on interacting sustainably with nature, the vision of a God, whether Christian, Muslim, Buddhist, or whatever, it is most important to understand the changing nature of God. On the frontier, God is a free-market capitalist. But when the frontier is conquered, there is room for another interpretation of God. God is an advocate of an economic system that puts value on commonly owned resources. God is a protector of those resources.

Earlier peoples had natural gods. It is unlikely however, that Man will again take up worshipping jaguars. But what we can try to do is to disassociate god with the free market system. Let us reform the economic system, and do so independently of any religious implications.

Let us examine the most important assumption of the free market economic system: that money is an indicator of wealth.

In fact, it is not. Money is a device which permits efficient allocation of privately held goods. True wealth includes much more than cars, television sets, or other manufactured goods that can be privately manufactured and owned. Wealth includes clean air, clean water, and natural surroundings that relieve rather than cause stress.

The saying that "money is the root of all evil" is more true today than ever. Money itself is not the evil. It is the blind pursuit of money in the belief that it will bring wealth that causes the problem. While it may bring material wealth, it does not bring spiritual wealth, and often is negatively associated with it. Witness the state of the royal family in England.

Given that money is an entirely inadequate measure of wealth, and that the failure of money to value commonly held goods such as clean air, clean water, tropical forests and biodiversity, is there any type of currency which could do better?

The money cycle fails to adequately value many resources, because the money cycle is a system deeply embedded within another system, the flow of energy through the biosphere. (Fig. 1) The flow of energy drives the money cycle, not vice versa, and the flow and storage of energy includes all the world's resources, not just those that are privately owned or manufactured.

There has been a growing appreciation for the need of an alternative to classical economics. The fundamental assumptions of economics distort the world view of those who participate in it. Mainstream economics is based on the belief that money drives resource production, and this in turn drives the world. That limited perspective has resulted in the wastage of resources, and their conversion into pollution, because resources and pollution assimilation are not valued by mainstream economics.

An alternative view is provided by "Ecological Economics." Ecological economics holds that the money cycle is merely a spin off of resource movement through the biosphere. Because of its focus on resources, their use and ultimate disposal instead of upon money, it is better able to appraise what Man is really doing to his environment, when he decides to clear cut a forest, dispose of carbon into the atmosphere, etc.

If we can change our economic system from the paradigm that money controls resources and man controls money, to the paradigm that resource flow controls man, and that money merely facilitates the transaction, then we may begin to move toward a philosophy that man has the need to consider more carefully what is happening to resources.

Neo-classical economics is based on faith, and the tenets of that belief have become part of religious dogma of many groups. Since the belief in traditional economics lies in faith, not in scientific facts, it can't be argued in a scientifically rational manner. One accepts it as a matter of faith or belief, in the same way one accepts religion as a belief.

Economics is not a science, but a religion. It worked well in the past, but it holds little promise for the future. We must re-interpret Man's relationship with nature. For man's resource systems to be sustainable, they must work with nature over the long term. They cannot continue to be exploited in the short term, as they are driven to be by capitalist competition.

How or why do people change religions? Because the old religion no longer holds out hope for meeting problems that the individual faces. Some environmentally conscious people have abandoned Christianity and taken up Oriental religions, which have the view that Man is not above nature, but rather is part of nature. It is unlikely however, that the majority of North Americans will become Buddhists in time to save the environment. However, it might be easier to convince many Americans to modify somewhat their view of how the economy works, from the view that money drives resources, to the view that resources drive money.

There is no evidence that God is a free-market capitalist. The religious faith in completely free-market capitalism must be abandoned, just as are other religions when they no longer are relevant. The next step in the cycle of religious evolution is to put man back into nature, and to have natural gods. Except this time, we will not worship jaguars and thunder. Rather we will worship (believe in) an economic system which views natural resources, not money, as the basis for human health and welfare.

OTHER ASSUMPTIONS

But let us examine some of the assumptions of mainstream economics that are held as a matter of faith by those in the capitalistic system.

Some basic assumptions of capitalist economics are:

People act in their own self-interest
People act "rationally" (go along with what everyone does)
More is better
Scarcity can be solved by substitution
Pollution is an externality
The economy must continue to grow

These are not facts: these are assumptions—beliefs. They are accepted because they seem to work fairly well on the micro-scale and in the short term. They do not work well on the macro-scale over time periods greater than one economic horizon—one to two decades.

There has been a growing appreciation for the need of an alternative to classical economics. The fundamental assumptions of economics distort the world view of those who participate in it. Mainstream economics is based on the belief that money drives resource production, and this in turn drives the world. That limited perspective has resulted in the wastage of resources, and their conversion into pollution, because resources and pollution assimilation are not valued by mainstream economics.

The fact that Russia and its satellites banned religion also has little to do with the failure of the system. Many citizens remained deeply religious throughout the dictatorships. In contrast, many Americans are athiests or agnostics, and have no problem in reconciling their lack of belief in a God with their belief in a participatory democratic republic.

The predominant religion of a country has nothing to do with its economic system, and the economic system is not necessarily tied to a political system. A Muslim society can be capitalistic and a dictatorship. A Buddhist society can be communistic and democratic. A Christian society can have a dictatorship. An ingredient that contributed to the success of the U.S. is a truly participatory democracy. It is the power of the voters to send messages to their representatives, and to vote them out of office if they fail to respond that provides the feedback which has allowed the American system to work. There is no theoretical reason why a communal system could not be embraced by a democratically elected, participatory government, even though it has never happened on the scale of a country. (see chart below.)

CONCLUSION

An admirable quality of The United States of America is the ability of its diverse peoples to live peacefully together and tolerate and respect each others views, despite disagreements between views. But the strategy of the religious right is to condemn those with whom they do not agree. The Christian Coalition and its conservative Republican allies are using the environment as a wedge issue. Christians who don't agree with the Coalition's "voter guides" find their faith suspect by the

MARKET	NON-MARKET	
	ATTRIBUTABLE OR ASSIGNABLE VALUES	INTANGIBLE OR NON-ASSIGNABLE VALUES
Lumber - logs, plywood, veneer	Maintenance of global air quality - removal of particulate and gaseous material	Maintenance of global carbon balance
Fiber - paper, fodder, clothing and shelter		Maintenance of atmospheric stability
Fuel - firewood, methanol	Maintenance of tropical water quality - erosion control, flood control, regional water quality	Habitat for native people
Chemicals - oils, resins, esters, phenols		
	Recreation - hunting, tourism, filming, aesthetics	Intrinsic worth of species, culture, and ecosystems
Pharmaceuticals - quinine, nicotine, caffeine, alkaloids	Genetic stocks 1. new food plants and animals	Natural laboratory for evolution and natural selection
Exotic flora and fauna - house plants, pets	2. new chemicals 3. potential biological control agents	Maintenance of diversity - back-up systems for ecosystem services and global life support system
Research plants and animals	4. new germ plasm to reinvigorate food or fiber stocks (diease control or yield improvement)	Cycling of essential nutrients
		Absorption and breakdown of pollutants
	Fixation of solar energy to support production systems	

Table 1. Some market and non-market values of goods and services of tropical moist forests (from Farnworth *et al.* 1983).

Religious Right. This effort to portray as immoral and un-godly anyone who disagrees with their agenda is in itself immoral.

The tactic of attacking on religious grounds anyone who opposes an economic agenda is the method of witch hunters. Religion is used to intimidate those who don't intellectually conform. It is an expression of intolerance. And like any intolerance, it is a threat to Democracy. The threat of the religious right is based on the fallacious assumption of a moral link between a religious belief and an economic system. But economics is one sphere of human activity, religion another. There is no link. God is not a free-market Capitalist.

LITERATURE CITED

Colby, M.E. 1990. Environmental Management in Development: The Evolution of Paradigms. World Bank Discussion Paper 80. The World Bank, Washington, D.C. cited in Folke, C. and T. Kaberger. 1991. Recent trends in linking the natural environment and the economy. pp 273-300 *in* Folke, C. and T. Kaberger (eds). 1991. Linking the Natural Environment and the Economy: Essays from the Eco-Eco Group. Kluwer Academic Publishers, Dordrecht.

Suffering on the Arizona Strip:
A Buddhist Critique of
Conflictual Paradigms

Joyce McCann

ACKNOWLEDGEMENTS

I would like to thank Carol Robb of the San Francisco Theological Seminary, Barry Stenger of the Graduate Theological Union, and Keith Warner OFM for helpful comments and discussion. I am also most grateful to the many individuals who provided documents and interviews for this project. Thanks are especially due to Karen Alvey, Brian Avery, Sharon Galbraith, Roger Holland, Tod Hull, Andy Lindquist, Anita MacFarlane, Jim Matson, Rick Miller, Scott Nannenga, and Peggy Palmer.

Joyce McCann

INTRODUCTION

In February of 1995 a small sawmill in northern Arizona closed as a result of challenges to the U.S. Forest Service over timber management practices on the North Kaibab. The closure of the sawmill resulted in the dislocation of over 200 workers, which has caused great suffering to the workers, their families, and the nearby dependent rural communities. The process which led up to the mill closure has also left a residue of bad feelings and mistrust that will negatively impact the ability of the community, government agencies, and environmental groups to work together in the future. Together with related issues, such as wilderness preservation, many in the community even see this as part of a broader assault on the very survival of rural culture.

Regardless of the rightmindedness of wildlife and forest preservation, I am concerned about the morality of a process that has produced so much human suffering. It is clear, not only from the details of this small example, but from many similar examples throughout the world, that environmental decision making processes, as currently practiced, are often a tangle of largely unresolved conflicts, resulting in little positive outcome either for the environment or for human stakeholders.

In this paper I explore aspects of three environmental ethics theories that address decision making in cases such as the North Kaibab example, where both human and environmental interests are at stake: (1) The Kantian philosophical approach of Paul W. Taylor in *Respect for Nature: A Theory of Environmental Ethics* (Taylor, 1986); (2) the Christian multi-disciplinary approach of James A. Nash in *Loving Nature: Ecological Integrity and Christian Responsibility* (Nash, 1991); and (3) the largely Buddhist-inspired philosophy of Jay B. McDaniel in *Of God and Pelicans: A Theology of Reverence for Life* (McDaniel, 1989).

Taylor, Nash, and McDaniel are among the few environmental ethicists who have approached the issue of decision making in cases where the welfare of humans and the environment appear to be in conflict. Most of the literature in environmental ethics is concerned with making the case for placing moral value in the environment; few ethicists have taken on the practical aspect of how to make it work in the real world.

Environmental ethics is a hopeful resource out of which more non-conflictual decision making paradigms might be constructed because it is grounded in a vision of ecological harmony which emphasizes an interactive, interdependent relationship between humans and the environment. Humans and non-human life forms are all seen as belonging to Earth's community of life–sharing a "web of life." This vision overlaps in many ways with, and indeed is influenced by, a feminist vision of mutuality and caring in human relationships. Thus, one might expect that decision making paradigms growing out of such philosophies would embody an ecological principle that would distinguish them. For example, such paradigms might be distinguished by a sensitivity to the welfare of all parties involved, the weak as well as the strong, the non-human and the human alike. They might also be distinguished by an ecological vision of how interested parties interact within the decision making process, emphasizing non-adversarial mechanisms.

THE FREDONIA SAWMILL CLOSURE CASE

The setting of the story is spectacular. The North Kaibab plateau, located about 25 miles south of Fredonia, is a 60 by 35 mile stretch of high (avg. elevation 8,000 feet) forested land in the Arizona Strip. Bounded on the south by the Grand Canyon and on the north by the

Vermillion Cliffs of Southern Utah, it is probably one of the most beautiful spots on earth. A visitor described the forests of the Kaibab Plateau in the 1880s:

> The trees are large and noble in aspect and stand widely apart...
> Instead of dense foliage (referring to the dense forests of the east),
> we can look far beyond and see the tree trunks vanishing away
> like an infinite colonnade. The ground is unobstructed and inviting.
> (Freeman, 1983)

Though geographically in Arizona, and under that state's political aegis, the North Kaibab is separated from most of Arizona by the Grand Canyon. Traditionally it has been more closely linked to the lives of people living in Southern Utah. In the latter half of the 19th century the early Mormon pioneers were sustained by the abundant deer herds of the Kaibab (they named it "Buckskin Mountain") and the rich foraging opportunities available for their cattle, sheep, goats, and horses. In the late 1800s, it is believed that up to 20,000 cattle and 200,000 sheep grazed the Kaibab Plateau. The plateau became an integral part of the lives of the early settlers, a tradition of reliance that has continued to the present day.

In 1909, Teddy Roosevelt, who was a frequent visitor to the Kaibab Plateau hunting mountain lion and deer, designated the North Kaibab both a game preserve and a forest reserve. This dual title presaged future conflicts over wildlife and timber.

The government started selling timber from the North Kaibab on a large scale in 1944 to help produce wood for military use during World War II. Since 1948, Kaibab Industries, which built the Fredonia mill, has been the only purchaser of timber on the North Kaibab plateau. The timber harvest volume grew from 1.5 MBF (million board feet) in 1944 to a high of almost 72 MBF in 1983. As shown in Figure 1, a large increase in harvest volume occurred in 1983, and this was more or less maintained for seven years. This increase was the result of a shift from selective to even-aged timber management by the USFS.[1]

The increased volume resulted in a second shift being added at the Fredonia mill, which began operating 24 hours a day. A number of factors, some of them unrelated to environmental issues, contributed to a slow decline prior to 1990. However, beginning in 1990, when controversy over timber harvesting on the North Kaibab came to a head, the volume of timber harvested dramatically declined.

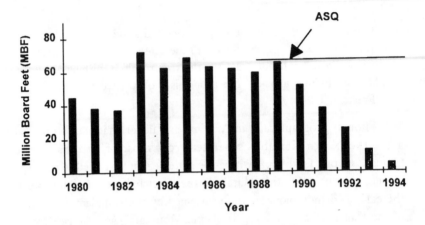

Figure 1. North Kaibab: Actual Harvest Volumes. ASQ = Allowable Sale Quantity. The ASQ indicated is as specified in the Kaibab Forest Plan, as signed in 1988 (USFS, 1987b). Data for all years except 1994 were provided by the North Kaibab Ranger District. 1994 data were provided by Kaibab Industries (TimberDataCo., 1994).

In 1991, one shift of workers was laid off at the mill, and in February of 1995 the mill formally closed, laying off the remaining 216 workers. The mill equipment was sold at auction two months later, on April 24th.

"What happened?" is obviously a complex question. A clue is contained in data assembled by the U.S. Forest Service (USFS) (see Figure 2) which compares diameter classes of trees on the Kaibab National Forest to a 1909 survey which reported that the forest was an "unbroken body of mature timber" (Burnett, 1991). As shown, more trees per acre were found in 1989 than in 1909 in all but one small diameter class (three inch trees).

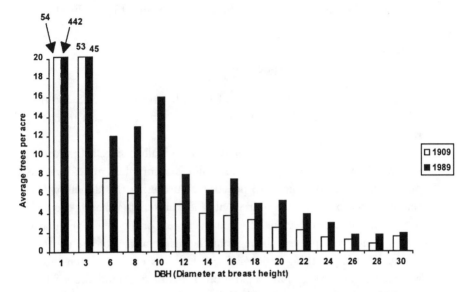

Figure 2. 1909 Comparison to 1989 Forest Survey Data (USFS): Ponderosa Pine Type-North Kaibab (North Kaibab Ranger District, personal communication). 1909 data were mathematically converted from information originally provided by Lang and Stewart in 1910 (Lang and Stewart, 1910). 1989 data were from the most recent forest inventory.

From one point of view these data suggest that the North Kaibab Forest has not been over-logged and indeed is thriving. On the other hand they suggest that the character of the forest has changed. As shown in Figure 2, the relative increases in trees per acre are lowest for the largest trees, suggesting a decline in the percentage of the forest occupied by old growth ponderosa. Indeed, the crux of the Kaibab controversy was a perceived decline in old growth due to over-logging, with accompanying adverse effects on wildlife habitat.

The story can perhaps best be summarized by reviewing the positions of the key players.[2] The major players aside from the USFS were: The Arizona Game and Fish Department (AGFD); the timber harvesting industry, Kaibab Forest Products, Inc. (a division of Kaibab Industries); the environmental groups (most consistently represented by the Plateau Group of the Sierra Club, the Northern Arizona Chapter of the Audubon Society, and the Arizona Wildlife Federation); a variety of experts, including University and USFS scientists and private consultants; and the local communities (primarily Kanab, UT and Fredonia, AZ).[3]

THE GOVERNMENT AGENCIES

A key element in this case was friction between the USFS and the AGFD over the establishment and implementation of forest management practices.

The USFS has been managing the North Kaibab since it first came under federal control in 1909. The USFS is a complex, multi-layered bureaucracy that is difficult to penetrate. Furthering this difficulty are the many turnovers due to retirements and transfers that have occurred in the Southwestern Region. There are very few of the key USFS players left who were present throughout the major phases of the controversy. Decision making process in the USFS is rendered even more complex by the geographic separation of major decisionmakers from each other and from the North Kaibab. The Kaibab National Forest Supervisor's office is in Williams, Arizona, on the other side of the Grand Canyon some 350 miles south of Fredonia where the North Kaibab District Ranger Station is located. The Williams office manages both the South and the North Kaibab which together make up the Kaibab National Forest. These two parts of the forest are separated by the Grand Canyon and are quite different in character. The Southwestern Regional Forester's office is in Albuquerque, New Mexico. Management decisions affecting the North Kaibab were often given as regional directives from Albuquerque.

Though there are indications that there was controversy within the USFS itself over timber management direction, the predominant view was that concerns of AGFD and environmental groups were overblown and misguided. It is probably fair to say that the Forest Service resented what it saw as excessive interference by AGFD and environmental groups in their mandate to manage the forest.

The AGFD was established in 1928 (ArizonaState, 1928). In contrast to the USFS, the AGFD has a relatively simple administrative structure which affords a great deal of independence to regional offices and to individuals. For example, over the years one AGFD Wildlife Manager has been assigned to the North Kaibab. He is stationed in Fredonia, and operates out of his house. The major AGFD players in this case were at the regional office in Flagstaff. The AGFD Commission in Phoenix oversees the activities of the regional offices, and must approve all official actions such as administrative appeals. Commissioners are appointed by the Governor, and thus the political leanings of the Commission usually reflect those of the current administration. A major activity of AGFD is to sell hunting and fishing licenses, and income from this activity is an important budgetary resource. AGFD views itself as mandated to vigorously advocate for wildlife in the State.

The official relationship between AGFD and the USFS is spelled out in a series of memoranda of understanding between the two agencies that have been revised and updated over the years. Under these agreements, AGFD is given advocacy powers, and the USFS is required to consult with AGFD. Though the USFS must listen to the views of AGFD, they are not required to accept them. It is the USFS that is charged with making the final decisions about what happens in the forest.

From the perspective of the AGFD, USFS management decisions were driven primarily by the need to meet timber harvest objectives, which AGFD thought were unrealistically high. AGFD also believed that the USFS gave short shrift to wildlife constraints in planning timber sales. For example, in a 1982 inter-office memo to the AGFD Director, the Regional Habitat Specialist outlined problems on the North Kaibab, and compared the forest management situation to "an automobile being owned and driven by timber with other forest users as passengers all advising on where and how to drive (AGFD, 1982)." From the perspective of AGFD, the forest had hit a wall. The forest had over-allocated what they had—they had promised everybody something and those people finally came to the table and said: "We want it." And when they started dividing it up there wasn't enough to go around.

Though the two agencies consider that over the years their interactions have been positive overall, by the late 1980s differences of opinion had grown to open conflict. AGFD was an intervenor in appeals to the Kaibab Forest Plan, itself initiated an administrative appeal of a timber sale, and strongly and publicly objected to subsequent timber management decisions by the USFS (For example, see (AGFD, 1990; AGFD, 1993)). Currently, there is concern at AGFD that some of those involved may lose their jobs as a result of political backlash resulting from the mill closures.[4] There is also concern that the Arizona legislature is considering gutting the agency.

THE INDUSTRY

Kaibab Forest Products, Inc. is the timber harvesting division of Kaibab Industries, Inc. (KI), a privately owned company founded in the early part of the century by the Whiting family. KI is still wholly owned and operated by the Whitings. The annual income of the company is about 300 million dollars. In addition to operating several small sawmills (until recently), KI owns about a dozen service stations in the Phoenix and Tucson areas, and some real estate and metal bending companies. Since the Fredonia mill closed, one mill has remained, in Panguitch, Utah. The small amount of timber that is still being harvested from the North Kaibab has been processed at the Panguitch mill since the Fredonia mill closed. However, KI recently decided to close the Panguitch mill as well.

From the industry perspective, the closure of the Fredonia mill was a direct consequence of a campaign by the Arizona Game and Fish Department, supported by environmental groups, to end timber harvesting on the North Kaibab. The industry feels they were caught in the middle of a power struggle between the AGFD and the USFS. One industry representative made the following comparison:

> It's like the analogy of the neighbor showing up at a family dispute; they're fighting next door and you ring the door bell and ask them what's going on and the husband and wife attack you.....

Wildlife preservation issues involving the Kaibab squirrel, the Northern goshawk, and the Mexican spotted owl are believed to have been based on incomplete, and in some cases even bogus data. The industry believes that wildlife became the major focus, not because of any real threat to wildlife by continued logging, but because, by focusing on wildlife, the power of existing laws such as the Endangered Species Act (ESA) could most effectively be brought to bear against continued timber harvesting. Thus, the industry believes that the motivation of AGFD and environmental groups was not out of any real concern that wildlife were being harmed by timber management practices, but that these groups used wildlife preservation as an effective wedge to halt timber harvesting—a convenient means to an end.

The industry also believes that more than adequate protection for old growth was assured in the Forest Plan,[5] and that this was largely ignored by the AGFD and the environmental groups in the ensuing debate and rhetoric. The industry feels that this helped these groups marshall support for their positions because it allowed them to claim that the forest was being destroyed, which played on the fears of the less informed public.

The industry cites two major causes that led directly to drastic reductions in timber harvesting, and hence to the decision to close the mill:

> • First, environmental groups persistently relied on the administrative appeal process as a delaying tactic. On one occasion, the AGFD also appealed a sale. These appeals were nicknamed "29 cent appeals" because anyone could initiate them just by responding to public notice of a proposed timber sale with a letter. The appeals focused on technical or legal issues relative to the sale and not on whether or not timber harvesting should take place. All appeals were eventually disallowed by the USFS. However, the time taken for the appeal process drastically slowed timber sales. The USFS could not proceed with a sale under appeal, and further, was reluctant to offer other timber sales while one sale was under appeal. Figure 1 illustrates the dramatic effect of this tactic on timber harvest volumes.
> • Second, unreasonable wildlife constraints were placed on the attributes and configuration of forest areas suitable for timber harvest. These constraints effectively "locked up" the forest.

In attempts to make their point of view count, Kaibab Industries offered educational programs to the community, sat on commissions, lobbied at the State and Federal levels, testified at hearings, instituted legal proceedings, and hired consultants to conduct independent studies of forest conditions. However, the industry believes that because their economic interests were so closely tied to timber harvesting, whatever they did or said was not perceived as credible. Ultimately they had to rely on the USFS. From the industry's point of view, the USFS caved in to a variety of pressures, and ended up making a decision that many in the USFS did not support.

THE ENVIRONMENTAL GROUPS

Environmental groups began to get involved in the late 70's and early 80's, partly as a result of complaints about poor visual quality from members who were hiking or birding in the forest, and partly because of the involvement of these groups in the passage of the Arizona Wilderness Act of 1984. Though a number of environmental groups were active at various times during the controversy on the North Kaibab, two groups were most consistently involved—the Plateau Group of the Sierra Club and the Northern Arizona Audubon Society. These groups perceive that the North Kaibab has been over-cut, and they see this as the direct result of greed on the part of Kaibab Industries and an "old-boy" network in the USFS tied to a period when forest management was driven more by timber harvesting than ecological sustainability. They believe that industry attempted to keep up with the market's demand for timber by capitalizing on its historically close relationship with the USFS on local and regional levels, and also by skillful lobbying in Washington. On more than one occasion, they maintain, if the industry did not think they could get what they wanted on the local or regional level, they would go directly to Washington.

A Sierra Club memo (SierraClub, 1995) distributed to members cites two major reasons for the closure of the mill:

> • First, overcutting of the North Kaibab, which was caused in part by a USFS computer model which grossly overestimated the amount of available saw timber. These over-optimistic projections led to timber sales which produced as little as 50% of the projected wood volume. Rather than lower targets, the USFS attempted to maintain the high projected sale quantities by advancing timber sales. This meant that the schedule for reentry into already logged areas was speeded up. From the perspective of the environmental groups the forest was literally being used up faster than it could maintain itself.
>
> • Second, Kaibab Industries failed to re-tool the Fredonia mill for smaller trees even though the average diameter of harvested trees was steadily decreasing, and even though other mills in the region were retooling for smaller diameter logs. In fact, the company knew in 1989 that the mill would have to either re-tool or close in a few years and they failed to take action either to re-tool the mill or to inform the local communities that were dependent on the mill until much later in the process.

THE EXPERTS

Many debates involved empirical data and scientific theories, which were addressed by various committees and in scientific studies. Some of the questions debated are quite complex, involving ecological, biological, and population issues that are either difficult to factually determine, or that are subject to differences of opinion among experts. Examples are: Inventory and modeling data relating to whether or not the forest was being over-cut; population studies relating to possible effects of logging on the Kaibab squirrel and the goshawk, and scientific studies aimed at determining what the forest looked like in the 19th century or what kind of forest best supports the goshawk.

THE COMMUNITY

The local communities most affected by the controversy were Fredonia and Kanab. (Kanab is in southern Utah six miles north of Fredonia).[6] As a community, Kanab did not become aware of the controversy until it was quite far along, in 1991. By then the Forest Plan had long since been finalized and, as noted above, it was already probably too late. In retrospect, one resident of Kanab likened the situation to a cancer victim who waits too long to go to the doctor. When he finally goes, it's too late:

> What we've done is finally woke up to the fact—we've got a case of cancer—and can we survive?

When they finally became aware of the situation, Kanab and Fredonia residents made considerable effort to voice their concerns. They formed a group called CORE (Committee of Responsible Environmentalists), attended meetings, testified at hearings, and wrote hundreds of letters. For a small, rural community with limited economic resources, and citizens fully occupied with jobs and family responsibilities, mustering the time and resources to make their voices heard alongside the other better-funded and more experienced players was a huge effort. And, indeed, it was too late. Today, the community feels that their concerns were not seriously taken into account in the ultimate decision-making process. Basically, they feel used and cannot understand the logic of a process that has resulted in such serious negative consequences for their community.

In fact, the failure of the public process to acknowledge likely impacts to the community from decisions under consideration is evident both in the final 1987 Forest Plan and in the Environmental Impact Statement (EIS) supporting it. In the final version of the Forest Plan, the affected small communities are not mentioned once, despite the fact that an entire section in the Plan is devoted to "Public Issues and Management Concerns" (USFS, 1987b), pp 3–9. Furthermore, in the EIS ((USFS, 1987a: 97–98) supporting the Forest Plan there are only two sentences that even mention Kanab and Fredonia, and these present contradictory conclusions:

- "The Fredonia-Kanab-Page area is similar to the situation at Williams where the local economy is heavily dependent on retail sales and services to tourists."
- "(Timber industry) employment is significant to local communities such as Fredonia where over 75 percent of employment is connected directly with the timber industry."

CONSEQUENCES FOR THE RURAL COMMUNITIES

It is too soon to determine the consequences of the mill closure and the curtailment of timber harvesting on the health of the forest and its wildlife. In the best of circumstances this determination would be complex, involving wildlife population and tree density and growth studies that would take years to accomplish, and would be certain to be controversial. Such studies will probably never be undertaken in any systematic way. However, the consequences of the mill closure for the surrounding small communities are neither difficult to determine nor are they controversial.

For Kanab and Fredonia, Kaibab Industries was their largest employer. In 1994, KI's annual payroll comprised about 18 percent of the area's non-farm wages. As a result of the mill closure, unemployment rates in the Kanab-Fredonia area rose from 8% in 1994 to close to 14% in the Spring of 1995 (Carroll et al., 1995). Among the displaced workers and their families there are many stories of emotional pain, economic hardship, and effects on family relationships.

For example, one individual had worked for KI for 29 years when he was laid off at the age of 57. The second day on a new job (with no health benefits) he had a heart attack and is now disabled and unable to work at all. Another employee, who had been with KI for 32 years, at 60 years of age and with dependents still at home, enrolled in the Dislocated Worker Program at the local Job Service office. Six months later he was still looking for work when his house burned down. Because he lived in an outlying area he had no fire insurance. A number of workers also had such serious back problems from years of lifting heavy lumber that they were unfit for most new job opportunities. Some of these men are receiving disability payments, but most have families and cannot subsist without additional income.

Statistical summaries only hint at the hardship underneath, but they help to give an overview of the disruption that has been caused in the life situations of these 216 workers and their families.[7] The average age of the workers was 43 (the younger ones had been already laid off in 1991), and two thirds of them had worked for KI for 20 years or more.

Even though most workers were older,[8] a third had three or more dependents still living at home, and over 20 workers had five or more dependents. Thus, it was not just the workers, but whole families, some of them quite large, that were affected.

The KI dislocated workers were eligible, just as any dislocated workers in the U.S., to apply for job training and relocation assistance which is guaranteed through the U.S. Job Training Partnership Act (JTPA). Because the Fredonia mill was in Arizona, most JTPA funds came from that state, with a smaller contribution of JTPA funds from Utah. Because of the relative isolation of the Fredonia/Kanab area from Arizona's JTPA administrative offices, it was decided to contract with the Utah Job Service Center in Kanab, which became the principle contact point for the workers. The dedicated people at the Job Service Center provided material help such as making workers aware of training and counseling programs and assisting with job search efforts, and also provided moral support. As of June 30, 1994, 127 workers had taken advantage of the dislocated worker program.[9]

Six months into the layoff, 44% of the 216 workers had found jobs. However, this figure needs qualification. Many new jobs were temporary, or did not carry health benefits. Most of the workers who found employment (62%, 59 workers) either were forced to move to find work, taking their families with them, or began commuting to distant locations. This meant that they spent the week at the distant job site and then drove home on the weekends, with obvious repercussions on family relationships. Some workers attempted to drive 100–200 mile commute distances daily in order to stay with their families.

Additionally, the proximate result, dislocation of 216 workers, is only part of a net of negative consequences that is broadly cast, and will affect the future as well as the present. The suffering will be projected into the future, not only because of continuing economic hardship for the workers, their families, and the communities, but also because of a severe negative impact on the willingness of the community to cooperate with government agencies or environmentalists on many other environmental issues that are pressing in this rural area.

The arguments that have been offered to justify the job dislocation which occurred in the North Kaibab case share an apparent lack of serious concern or responsibility for the suffering that has been caused. All of these arguments define the issue as one of separate interests in conflict, and define the solution as necessarily furthering the interests of one party at the expense of the other. Thus, the issue is viewed as one of competing values—values associated with preserving the forest for future generations on the one hand and preserving logging jobs for the small rural communities on the other.[10] Here are some examples:[11]

1)   Job dislocation is an unfortunate, but necessary byproduct of choosing the greater value. "It may be hard to look someone in the eye and say: 'I'm going to do away with your job', but it is not as hard as saying: 'I'm going to destroy the resource that we have so (you) can keep your job.'

2)   It has always been true that workers have been temporarily displaced as free markets grow and change. Other factors unrelated to environmental challenges are contributing to job loss in the timber industry, such as recent declines in demand for timber ((Booth, 1994): 237–238) or reduction in work force due to automation. If workers had not been laid off now, they would no doubt have been laid off in the future for other reasons.

3)   The overall economic effect of the loss of a few hundred timber-related jobs, when calculated on a per capita basis, is small (Booth, 1994: 125–172). A tragedy is when IBM lays off 20,000 people, not when 300 mill workers in Arizona lose their jobs.

4)   Logging corporations have severely damaged old growth

forests over many years of exploitation, and current job loss is simply an unfortunate byproduct of long overdue restitution.

All of these arguments seek to justify why, even though it may have been unfortunate, it was on some level all right for the community to suffer, given the circumstances of the case. In other words, there are plenty of reasons to justify the suffering but there is no accountability for the suffering.

In fact, if we ask who is responsible for the suffering of the community, we will find that in the current process no one is. Responsibility certainly does not reside in the public laws governing the process. Nor do any of the major players – the USFS, environmental groups, AGFD, or the industry—see that they share responsibility for the suffering of the community. In effect, these small communities are considered by all parties to be pretty much on their own. As one of the environmentalists said:

> They (the communities of Kanab and Fredonia) had years to antic- ipate this problem, and years to try to do something about it.... If they want to keep their community together, they have to do something to try to improve themselves.

There may be some truth to this, but there is also a kind of cold-heartedness that I find distressing. It may well be true that the communities need to become more involved in shaping their own future. Yet, must that involvement take place in isolation – as just another disembodied "interest" vying for success among other competing "interests"?

It is the conflictual nature of the process, the rhetoric that supports it, and the lack of accountability that is disturbing. This is a kind of "war games" approach to public process which assumes that outcomes must involve winners and losers. Furthermore, it is political process played out as a power struggle that, in large part, does not include the most impacted group.

The Environmental Ethics of Paul Taylor

Paul Taylor, in *Respect for Nature*, has constructed an environmental ethical system that is impressive for its intricacy and philosophical rigor. He seeks to embody in his philosophy an "ethical ideal of harmony between human civilization and nature (Taylor, 1986: 307ff)." Briefly, his model consists of a belief system (a biocentric outlook), an attitude (respect for nature), and a system of rules and standards. The **biocentric outlook** recognizes: (1) that we are in community with nature, part of an "interdependent web of life"; (2) that each individual organism is an independent teleological center having its own inherent worth and "pursuing its own good in its own unique way"; and (3) that no species, including the human species, is superior to any other (species impartiality). The attitude of **respect for nature** means that one believes that all animals and plants have a good of their own (i.e., have inherent worth independent of whatever value or use they may have to humans), and that humans have a *prima facie* moral duty to promote that good. Taylor's system of **rules and standards** includes three categories. First, four "Rules of Duty" (nonmaleficence, noninterference, fidelity, and restitutive justice) which specify moral considerations relevant to actions involving the environment. Second, "Standards of Virtue," including such character traits as conscientiousness, integrity, patience, courage, and temperance. And, third, five "Priority Principles" (discussed below) which serve to guide decision making where Rules of Duty or human and environmental interests appear to conflict. The biocentric outlook, the attitude, and the system of rules and standards work together in that the belief system supports and makes intelligible the attitude of respect; the attitude, in turn, predisposes one to follow rules and standards which embody respect for nature.

Taylor's decision making framework involves five "priority principles" which guide decision-making, and a classification of interests as "basic" or "nonbasic."

Basic interests for humans are the "necessary conditions for the maintenance and development of our personhood," such as subsistence, security, autonomy, and liberty. Taylor is less clear about what constitutes basic interests for nonhumans. However, he suggests that certainly included is the right to life, and whatever else that "once we become factually enlightened about what protects or promotes their good, (and)... can *take their standpoint*...(we can) judge... is, from their point of view, an important or unimportant event in their lives...." Nonbasic human interests may be incompatible or compatible with the ethical ideal. For example, hunting for pleasure is considered to be inherently incompatible, whereas "replacing a native forest with a timber plantation" (perhaps surprisingly) is considered to be compatible.

The five priority principles are:

• Self defense—that we have the right to protect ourselves against harmful or dangerous organisms. Thus basic interests of humans override the basic interests of nature provided harmful or dangerous organisms are involved. This principle, for example, legitimates the use of antibiotics.

• Proportionality—that in cases where the natural systems in question are harmless to humans, greater weight in decision making is to be given to "basic" versus "nonbasic" interests, preserving the concept of species impartiality. The principle of proportionality applies when basic interests of nature are in conflict with nonbasic interests of humans that are intrinsically incompatible with the ethical ideal. Thus, for example, deer hunting solely for pleasure would not be allowed.

• Minimum Wrong and Restitutive Justice—that in cases where human interests are nonbasic and intrinsically compatible with respect for nature, these interests may be pursued at the expense of the basic interests of the environment provided that the method of pursuing the non-basic human interest is the least harmful to living beings (human or non-human) of any alternative method available, and provided that compensation is provided for harm done. Taylor emphasizes that he is not suggesting a consequentialist, or utilitarian "balancing" exercise to determine the course which produces the least harm for the greatest benefit (Taylor, 1986: 284). Rather, his method is deontological in that the harm done to every individual is considered to be wrong regardless of the net value that might be gained in the world by the action. The principle of minimum wrong entails that we choose the course of action that harms the smallest number of individual living things. Importantly, however, choosing such a course of action does not excuse us from adequately compensating those who are harmed. The duty to compensate is governed by the Principle of Restitutive Justice.

• Distributive Justice—This principle provides for a just distribution to all parties when all interests involved are basic. It specifies that such interests must be given equal weight in the decision making process. Like the Principle of Minimum Harm, it is also governed by the Principle of Restitutive Justice.

Nowhere in the laws or guidance governing the decision making processes that occurred on the North Kaibab does one see principles such as these.[12] The Principles of Minimum Wrong, Distributive Justice, and Restitutive Justice are clearly applicable to the North Kaibab example. This is true regardless of what action one decided was most justified based on the facts of the case. Thus, on the one hand, the facts could[13] demonstrate that the forest was being overcut and that wildlife were being harmed. The least harmful action to take might then be to curtail timber harvesting to the point where Kaibab Industries would be forced to close the Fredonia mill, resulting in the dislocation of 216 workers. In this case, since in Taylor's ethical system *both* humans and non-humans have intrinsic value, the Principle of Minimum Wrong would identify such dislocation as harm requiring compensation according to the Principle of Restitutive Justice.[14] If, on the other hand, the facts of the case did not clearly demonstrate that the forest was being overcut or that significant harm to wildlife was occurring, it would still be true that timber harvesting was killing trees and interfering with the well being of at least some individual wildlife. Thus, the Principles of Minimum Wrong and of Restitutive Justice would still apply. But, in this case they would apply to the forest rather than to the workers. Perhaps the Principle of Minimum Wrong would be satisfied by choice of a timber harvesting management strategy that protected the healthiest and oldest trees and that was the least disruptive to wildlife. The Principle of Restitutive Justice might be satisfied by, for example, allocating increased acreage to wilderness, or protecting parts of the forest from disturbance for a number of years on a rotating basis.

Taylor's scheme makes an important contribution toward a more humane decision making process. Yet, there is incongruity in the model resulting from what appears to be an attempt to fit an ecological, essentially communitarian, vision, into an individualistic ethical framework. Thus, in *Respect for Nature* Taylor opens with a discussion of human ethics that is clearly grounded in a Kantian tradition of individualism. He emphasizes autonomy in his definition of personhood, and gives a central place to respect for autonomy and individual choice in moral rules governing human interactions (Taylor, 1986: 37ff). This view is then carried over into his proposal for an environmental ethic. Consider for example, the definition of a biocentric outlook discussed above. The first (and possibly the third) facets of this central concept embody an ecological view, whereas the second aspect reflects an individualistic view. The former suggests the centrality of caring, mutual support, cooperation, compassion, trust, responsibility for others, sharing, and nurturing, whereas the latter suggests autonomy, freedom, noninterference, and separateness.

In the principles and rules that Taylor goes on to develop, individualism appears to dominate. Thus, the "rules of duty" (nonmaleficence, noninterference, fidelity, and restitutive justice), and the "priority principles" (self-defense, proportionality, minimum wrong, distributive justice, and restitutive justice) reflect the vision of a world of separate individuals, each pursuing separate interests, coming together only when interests conflict. Most of these priority principles, particularly "self-defense," "proportionality," and "minimum harm" are reminiscent of just war principles, serving only to reinforce the conflictual nature of the construction. Even though Taylor consistently softens this model by reminding us of the ethical ideal that transcends conflict, the model remains a basically conflictual paradigm. Nevertheless, the model offers important assistance in the North Kaibab case by suggesting that, through the Principle of Restitutive Justice, accountability for the dislocation of workers should be a part of the decision making process.

However, I would suggest that this is not enough. It is not enough because Taylor's individualistic model cannot accommodate the kind of qualitative change in "view" that is needed if an adequate compensatory system is to be constructed. In order for the decision making process to be accountable to the workers and their small communities, it must first "see" them in a way that meaningfully includes them. It is possible that a philosophy grounded in religious values will support such a wider view that includes both the forest, its creatures, and the small human communities as all part of a larger Community. Perhaps if one begins with such a view one will seek solutions that benefit *both* the environment and local communities. With this question in mind, I would now like to examine the Christian-based environmental ethics of James Nash.

The Environmental Ethics of James Nash

In his thoughtful book *Loving Nature*, James Nash searches for Christian foundations for an environmental ethic. He begins with a discussion of "the environmental problem", and suggests nine "ecological virtues" (such as sustainability, frugality, solidarity, and humility) that are needed if humans are to take up a truly ecological attitude toward the environment. He then offers an optimistic view of Christian theology as a foundational resource for these virtues. He is cognizant of the need to "ecologically and ethically reform" Christianity in this context in view of the serious criticism of environmental ethicists who have taken exception to such Scriptural passages as:

> Be fruitful and multiply, and replenish the Earth and subdue it: and have dominion over the fish of the sea and over the fowl of the air and over every living thing that moveth upon the earth.

He examines a number of doctrinal topics such as creation, covenant, divine image, incarnation, sin, judgment, and redemption, and explores the meanings within them that support a Christian environmental ethic. He concludes that "the whole creation and all its creatures are valued and loved by God," and that "all creatures and things are to be treated as sacred"; that Christianity affirms "ecological relationality; and, that "humans have 'natural' rights to use biophysical goods as resources to satisfy human needs and fulfill our cultural potential, but we also have moral responsibilities to use these resources frugally, fairly, and prudently in respect for our coevolving kin." He also interprets the scriptural term "dominion" as "responsible representation, reflecting the divine love, including justice, in all relationships with humanity and the rest of the biophysical world." "Ecological negligence" is considered to be an "expression of sin," and a "human violation of the ecological covenant" (primarily the Noachic), and God is viewed as "exercising ecological judgments against ecological sins to call the human community to ecological repentance." Finally, Nash sees ecological responsibility as "an inherent part of the ministry of the church."

Following Taylor's three-fold formulation of the components of an ethical theory, if the **outlook** upon which Nash builds his environmental ethic is Christian doctrine, the defining **attitude** is love—the call to be "the ecological equivalent of the good Samaritan." Nash emphasizes that the Christian understanding of love does not apply in all of its facets to "ecological love"—human love for the environment. For example, loving non-human creatures and the environment does not suggest they are our equals "because of the unique capacities of humans to experience and create moral, spiritual, intellectual, and aesthetic goods." This inequality justifies "preferential treatment (to humans) in conflict situations." Further, though ecological love is less dominated by self-sacrifice than love toward humans, it does involve "giving up at least some of our own interest and benefits for the sake of the well-being of.... ecological communities" (Nash, 1991: 149–150). Indeed, the demands of Christian ecological love are great. In this regard Nash discusses six "ecological aspects" of Christian love: beneficence, other-esteem, receptivity, humility, understanding, and communion.

It is out of this basic understanding of love in an ecological context, and of the Christian imperative to focus on the needs of the weak and suffering that Nash sees a model for "justice in an ecological context" emerging. Again, following the threefold format of Taylor, the third component of an environmental ethic, **rules and standards**, is found in the chapter entitled "Christian Love as Justice." Nash seeks a justice that is circumscribed by love, and finds this in a Christian statement of distributive justice:

> ...distributive justice can be defined as love calculating, ordering, differentiating, adjudicating, and balancing dues or interests in the midst of conflicts of claims or interests, in order to provide a proper share of all scarce and essential values and resources for all parties with stakes in the outcome (Nash, 1991: 168).

And, further, he sees injustice as "the social form of sin – that self-centered human inclination to defy God's covenant by grasping more than our due and thereby depriving others of their due." Justice then becomes "love overcoming sin (Nash, 1991: 168)."

While it is not Nash's goal to develop a systematic decision making scheme as did Paul Taylor, he does discuss some elements of such a framework:

- A set of Human Environmental Rights (Nash, 1991: 171), which are basically anthropocentric, such as the right to a sustainable environment, and a set of eight prima facie Biotic Rights (Nash, 1991: 173) that apply to the non-human environment independent of its value to humans. These are: (1) The right to satisfy basic needs and to perform individual and/or ecosystemic functions; (2) the right to healthy and whole habitats; (3) the right to reproduce; (4) the right to fulfill their evolutionary potential; (5) the right to freedom from human cruelty; (6) the right to redress through human interventions in order to restore a semblance of the natural conditions disrupted by human actions; and (7) the right to a fair share of the goods necessary to sustainability of one's species.

• A set of two "over-ride principles" drawn from just war theory. These are, first, the principle of proportionality (permitting an over-ride of rights only as a "last resort" and with "minimum harm" (Nash, 1991: 190); and second, the principle of discrimination (requiring that collateral damage to the action be minimized, i.e., that innocent bystanders not be harmed).

• Following the suggestion of Herman Daly and John B. Cobb (Daly and John B. Cobb, 1989), some type of rights hierarchy that affirms the non-egalitarian relationship between humans and nature on the one hand, and among creatures in nature on the other. Nash is not specific about what such a ranking would entail, but he sees it as essential to any workable decision making apparatus. The degree of justification for an over-ride of basic biotic rights would be determined by where in the rights hierarchy the particular species or environmental elements in question resided.

• Finally, the whole process would be infused with love in an ecological context, the "spirit of the law." With this requirement, Nash reaffirms the centrality of love in this Christian-based ethic.

There are formal similarities between the ethics of Taylor and Nash. For example, Taylor's Priority Principle of Restitutive Justice is basically the same as Nash's sixth Biotic Right, and principles derived from just war theory have an important place in both systems. Both authors also base their ethics on relational models, Taylor's secular and Nash's Christian. There are also formal differences, notably opposite opinions about the reasonableness of species impartiality. However, the essential difference between the two relative to this discussion is that, by bringing Christian love into a justice framework, Nash warms up— humanizes—Paul Taylor's "respect-based," individualistic model. This is because the concept of love, particularly as formulated in a religious context, is more consonant with such attributes as communion and mutuality than is the concept of respect in Taylor's model, which, while quite adequately accommodating other-regard, has difficulty with these additional facets of relationality. By grounding his environmental ethic in love Nash is thus able to keep relationality more prominently present than Paul Taylor was able to do in his ethic. Nash bears this out when he emphasizes that Christian love is the more general category, and that "justice is nothing more, but also nothing less, than one indispensable dimension of Christian love (Nash, 1991: 167)."

It appears clear that in Nash's holistic system, as in Taylor's, the Kaibab workers and the small communities would neither be left out of the decision making process nor would they be inadequately compensated if decisions resulting in job dislocation were considered necessary. If avoidance of damage to the forest and its creatures could be shown to justify the over-ride of the basic human rights of the workers, the suffering of the workers, their families and their communities would clearly represent collateral damage in Nash's system, and would presumably be subject to the same redress as would the environment in the reciprocal case. In fact, Nash speaks of such a situation in his discussion of the "economics-ecology dilemma (Nash, 1991: 197–199)." He acknowledges that "protecting old-growth forests may force some loggers to search for alternative jobs," and suggests "imaginative and sensitive" intervention strategies including "not only the standardized unemployment insurance, but also counseling, job retraining, employment assistance, economic incentives to attract new enterprises, and regulations to ensure fairness to workers in unavoidable plant closures (Nash, 1991: 199)." This is consistent with his repeated concern for "the moral mandate to respond holistically and relationally," but not to "act in ways... (that) cause or aggravate other social or ecological problems, and if possible, contribute to the resolution of them" (Nash, 1991: 220).

Though Taylor's individualism has been softened in Nash's Christian-based ethic, dualism, hierarchy, and conflict are still present. Christianity is naturally dualistic, and this is not surprisingly embodied in Nash's system. For example, the favored status of human beings over other living things is asserted in a graduated system of value, which is "indisputably hierarchical." In fact, Nash asserts: "that is its strength." Also, though justice is "grounded in neighbor-love," it involves the oppressed and the oppressor and operates as "love overcoming sin" in a "redistributive" process that Nash sees as paying the penalty for past sins (Nash, 1991: 221). It seems likely that suffering will inevitably be a part of this retributive process. And, indeed Nash's use of just war principles seems to underline a war-like atmosphere, and to be inconsistent with his sensitive development of the ecological aspects of Christian doctrinal principles. Thus, in spite of the overall sensitivity in Nash's presentation to a holistic view of human beings in community with the environment, I am still concerned that an underlying conflictual paradigm may too readily accommodate suffering as a normal outcome when "rights conflict and moral claims compete (Nash, 1991: 189)."

A BUDDHIST PERSPECTIVE

The relevance of Buddhism to environmental ethics has been widely discussed.[15] Most of this discussion focuses on two aspects of Buddhist thought. First, on the ethical implications of the concept of sunyata (or "emptiness") which, as developed particularly in later schools of Buddhism, easily accommodates the assignment of value to existants beyond anthropomorphic concerns, such as natural objects. And, second, on the interrelated concept of pratitya sammutpada (dependent origination), which emphasizes the interdependence of all existence.[16] The value of these two components of Buddhist theory to environmental ethics is illustrated here by the work of Jay B. McDaniel in *Of God and Pelicans: A Theology of Reverence for Life* (McDaniel, 1989). This work is the first attempt of which I am aware to provide a comprehensive environmental ethic founded in Buddhist principles. In addition to Buddhist philosophy, McDaniel draws on an eclectic philosophical base including Christianity, process theology, and feminism.

Using Taylor's three-fold classification scheme[17] McDaniel's ethic might be construed as: (1) A Christian/Buddhist **biocentric outlook**, consisting of two major elements: A view of a "life-centered God" drawn primarily from process theology; and a view of reality drawn from the Buddhist concept of Emptiness; (2) **Attitudes** of reverence and active goodwill towards nature; and (3) **Rules and standards** including "biocentric practices" toward individual animals and ecological communities drawn from the literature of animal rights and land ethics, three basic moral virtues (reverence for life, noninjury, and active goodwill), and guidelines drawn from process thought for distinguishing "degrees of intrinsic value (McDaniel, 1989: 76)."

McDaniel develops his understanding of a life-centered God, and hence the model for human activity in the image of God, in light of an inclusive, ecological world view. In this world view, human life is an expression of nature, not separate from it, and nature is neither mechanical nor static, but dynamic, evolutionary, and intrinsically creative. In this context, McDaniel explores the nature of the divine love of a "life-centered" God. He takes on the task of explaining how God can love all of nature when, from the perspective of individual animals in nature (e.g., prey) suffering seems to be programmed into the world God created. McDaniel develops an essentially pantheistic understanding of divine love in this context, in which God suffers along with sufferers, non-human as well as human, and in which suffering is a natural part of an instability-redemption cycle built into the ecological whole. Such a cycle, McDaniel's process analysis suggests, is necessary to achieve the richness of experience life offers as well as its promise of freedom, creativity and positive change.

McDaniel uses the Buddhist concept of Emptiness to inform a view of reality that process theologians see as complementing the concept of God. In this view, "God" represents the "actuality" of the ultimate, or Absolute, and Emptiness represents the "reality" of the Absolute.[18] McDaniel discusses three aspects of Emptiness–Suchness, *pratitya sammutpada*, and impermanence.

First, he quotes Masao Abe in defining Suchness as "the as-it-is-ness of an entity, the sheer occurrence of an entity as uncategorized, spontaneous happening in its own right." He suggests, following Suzuki, that an appreciation of the meaning of Suchness helps us to "have a feeling for" individual organisms in that we are reminded that "we share a common identity with all other actualities" (in that we are all spontaneous happenings). And, further, that "our own categories of thought are limited, that there is something about beings in nature—humans included—that cannot be framed in words and names" (in that the suchness of entities is independent of one's ability to perceive or know them).

Second, as discussed by McDaniel, *pratitya sammutpada*, or dependent origination, means both that entities are causally influenced externally by other entities, and that they are internally influenced by the immanence of entities. Thus, *pratitya sammutpada* is a radical, non-hierarchic model of relationality in that we are not only interactively in relationship with others and the environment, but we are actually *constituted* through this relationship. For McDaniel, the concept of *pratitya sammutpada* contributes to an environmental ethic in that it reminds us that "we cannot exist apart from matrices" (the natural community) because "we ourselves are compound individuals... (who) dependently originate in relation to other beings, and... the natural world is immanent within us (McDaniel, 1989: 103)."[19]

Third, the Buddhist concept of impermanence applies not only to every entity, from insects to mountains, but to every moment of experience. Process thinkers even apply impermanence to the Christian concept of God, to which they attribute adjectives such as "fluid" and "adaptive." For McDaniel, a biocentric spirituality embraces transience to the point that one even lets go of God "as the one exception to change." The result is "acceptance of impermanence... (as) an aspect of that wholeness, that shalom, toward which we are called by God (McDaniel, 1989: 109)."

McDaniel sees an appreciation for the truth of these three aspects of Emptiness as an "inward disposition" supporting a Christian biocentric "feeling for" nature both at the level of individual organisms and at the ecological, or community level. This feeling, or outlook, also includes appreciation for, and celebration of, a dynamic, inevitably changing world.

It is useful to compare the biocentric **outlook** of McDaniel to those of Taylor and Nash in order to approach the question of whether McDaniel's ethic might suggest less conflictual paradigms of public decision making than the two other proposals. One sees a progressively more relational vision beginning with the individualistic model of Taylor, to the Christian relational-dominion model of Nash, and finally to the Buddhist organic-relational model of McDaniel. In Taylor, the focus is on individual organisms as "independent teleological center(s)," each separately pursuing their interests. In Nash, it is on a loving God and humans "in community" with nature. In McDaniel, relationality has taken on new meaning. We are not only in community with nature (and each other), "we are actually *constituted* through this relationship." God not only loves nature and is in community with it, God suffers and changes along with nature.

Appreciating the full meaning of relationality changes how one views the decision process that resulted in so much suffering in the small communities in Northern Arizona. Appreciating the interdependence and connectedness of everyone involved, one no longer sees the process as a kind of war game producing "winners" and "losers." No longer can the suffering of these small communities be justified as unfortunate but necessary collateral damage in the "just war" of environmental preservation. Instead, appreciating the full meaning of relationality, one sees that all parties, both "winners" and "losers," are inextricably bound together in an atmosphere of suffering and negativity. Hopefully, one also sees that the potential exists to reform the process so that it becomes more humane, creative, and positive.

One way to approach this goal may be to consider possibilities for less conflictual decision making paradigms. The "organic-relational model" may offer a helpful resource. Though McDaniel does not directly address cases where human and environmental interests are in conflict, he does offer six characteristics of a lifestyle compatible with the organic-relational model. Two of these characteristics are particularly pertinent to this discussion: "value pluralistic thinking" and "relational power" (McDaniel, 1989: 126–130).

Value-pluralistic thinking emphasizes appreciation and validation of difference rather than its denial or denigration. McDaniel quotes John Cobb when he describes value-pluralistic thinking as "a way that excludes no ways." It offers a non-exclusionist, non-elitist alternative to value-hierarchic thinking. As McDaniel says: "(Value pluralistic) thinking is a way that hierarchicalizes as a last, not a first, resort (McDaniel, 1989: 127)." I take McDaniel's meaning to imply that value pluralistic thinking does not preclude discriminating judgment or decision making. Rather, I interpret it to be more dispositional in that one might imagine that a decision-making process seeking to embody value pluralistic thinking and the actions of individuals involved in such a process would be characterized by virtues such as caring, openness, and humility. In contrast, a decision process embodying value-hierarchic thinking would be associated with qualities such as opinionatedness, competition, and bias.

How a principle such as value pluralistic thinking could be carried into the arena of public process is a topic much larger than this paper, but various possibilities suggest themselves. For example, one might imagine that a process seeking to embody this principle would be constructed so that all parties were "seen" equally, regardless of their relative political power, economic clout, or otherwise advantaged position. Just what this might mean from a public policy perspective is by no means a simple question, but here is an example from the Kaibab case:

U.S. Job Training Protection Act (JTPA) funds are allocated to all areas of the U.S. using a formula based primarily on population density. In all areas of the country the funds are available for two activities—job training and job relocation. On the one hand, such a procedure might be said to be fair because it results in equal treatment for all. However, from a value pluralistic point of view, it might be concluded that the program is unfair because it is blind to the special needs of particular areas. Thus, with reference to the Kaibab case, it may be sufficient for dislocated workers in a big city to receive job training because in a big metropolitan area there are diverse job opportunities available. However, in a rural area such as the Arizona Strip, where entire communities are heavily dependent on one industry, job training, though obviously helpful, is not sufficient. Furthermore, such a blanket policy ignores the cultural traditions of this rural, largely Mormon area in that there is not the same mobility that there tends to be in big cities. Thus, many of the dislocated workers and their families were second and even third or fourth generation families in the area. Thus, to assume that all that is needed is a program that "picks up the pieces" so to speak by providing money to learn new job skills and to relocate is not really to "see" the needs of these small communities. "Seeing" involves not only understanding that these small rural areas are not just "little cities," but are qualitatively different from large urban centers. It also involves valuing that difference. For those who do not have direct, lived experience of rural life, such as the vast majority of lawmakers, this second facet of "seeing" requires value pluralistic thinking.

Relational power is defined in contrast to unilateral power:

> Unilateral power has as its aim the control of others in a way that subverts their own creativity and minimizes their opportunities for reciprocal influence. By contrast, relational power has as its aim the influencing of others in a way that appreciates and inspires their creativity and invites reciprocal influence (McDaniel, 1989: 129).

Relational power involves "the strength to be creatively vulnerable." It acknowledges that we are both influenced by others and influence others in every human interaction. But more than this, it suggests that it is in this reciprocal influencing that creative power lies. From a public process perspective it suggests that it is not ultimately productive to "win" by forcing our views on others, who then become the "losers." It suggests that such limited outcomes will only result in polarization, and in the longer term, new and bigger battles. The principle of relational power suggests that a successful process will change all participants, and forge a solution that transcends former interest-laden views.

Many examples of the failure to utilize the principle of relational power could be cited from the Kaibab case. Two examples are illustrative:

- In a discussion with environmentalists which revealed that they had never visited Kanab or Fredonia, it was nevertheless explained how important getting "out in the field" was in general "in order to get our views across." Thus, the attitude is not one of wanting to interact with the communities in order to get to know them better and possibly learn from their experience, but rather it is to influence them.[20]
- Particularly in the later stages of the controversy the USFS presented numerous workshops for the communities to explain what was at issue. Some in the community attended these workshops and made a valiant effort to understand the issues presented, some of which were highly technical. There is generally a positive feeling toward the USFS as to their intent in presenting these workshops and as to the content. However, from the perspective of the principle of relational power, the workshops were rather paternalistic and unilateral. This was not so much the fault of the USFS as of the process itself as conceived under NEPA. The primary subject matter was predetermined by the process, which focused primarily on technical issues relating to timber and wildlife management. Thus, the community, whose issues were social, cultural, and economic, had no meaningful forum in which to develop their ideas. They were relegated to students rather than full participants.

The principle of relational power suggests a more proactive, inclusive process. For example, a series of workshops aimed at creating a situation conducive to relational power might have included sessions run by representatives of the community; or community representatives might have been included in drawing up the agenda for the workshop; or entire workshops organized by the community might have been included in an overall workshop agenda for all players (USFS, AGFD, and environmental groups).

There are many aspects of the North Kaibab case that were characterized by value-hierarchic thinking and unilateral power. From critical decisions by the USFS that were made from afar with little or no input from people who actually worked in the forest, to non-negotiable demands of environmentalists and their abuse of the appeals process, to unrelenting advocacy on the part of the AGFD, and to the demonization of environmentalism by the industry and the small rural communities, there was consistent failure on the part of all or nearly all parties to incorporate the qualities of value-pluralistic thinking and relational power. Unfortunately there is nothing unique in this regard about the Kaibab case. Value hierarchic thinking and unilateral power are standard operating procedure in most examples of public decision making on environmental issues.

This is not to say that there were not some efforts made in more positive directions on the part of some individuals in some circumstances. And, it is not to deny that at least some aspects of the NEPA process are intended to be sensitive to a value-pluralistic vision. But, it is fair to say that, overall, the process was dominated by qualities associated with value-hierarchic thinking and unilateral power. Had the process embodied more elements of value pluralistic thinking and relational power, the suffering of the communities might not have occurred, the forest and its creatures might have been protected and preserved as well, and the current polarized, negative atmosphere might not exist.

In this paper I have looked to principles of environmental ethics as a way to think about fairness in environmental decision making. I chose the North Kaibab example because it involved both human and environmental suffering. It thus required a more inclusive application of the relational biocentric vision embraced by environmental ethics than in most examples in the literature.[21] Also, I have emphasized a religious perspective because I believe it has something to offer to philosophical environmental ethics in that it helps to focus reflection on how to actualize moral thought in public process. Religious values remind us of the importance of personal virtue, regardless of the formal structure of public process; religion locates value outside of self-interest; and a truly religious perspective also challenges us to acknowledge our lack of ultimate understanding, and to question our own firmly held positions with open eyes and humility. Environmental decision making paradigms could only be benefited by paying more attention to such qualities.

REFERENCES

AGFD. (1982). Analysis of current timber harvest situation on the Kaibab and Coconino National Forests. Internal memo to the Director of the AGFD from the Region II Habitat Specialist.

AGFD. (1990). Governor's Office Timber Issues Briefing, Arizona Game and Fish Department.

AGFD. (1993). Review of U.S. Forest Service Strategy for Managing Northern Goshawk Habitat in the Southwestern United States, Arizona Game and Fish Department.

Arizona State. (1928). Arizona Revised Statute. Title 17.

Badiner, Allan Hunt. (1990). *Dharmagaia: A Harvest of Essays in Buddhism and Ecology.* Parallax Press, Berkeley, CA.

Booth, Douglas E. (1994). *Valuing Nature: The Decline and Preservation of Old-Growth Forests.* Rowman & Littlefield Publishers, Inc., Lanham, MD.

Burnett, Howard. (1991). Green Island in the Sky. *American Forests,* May/June.

Carroll, Norman, Steve Crosby, Joe Judd, Scot Goulding, Roger Holland, Glen Martin, Karen Alvey, Peter Solie, Ray Clark, Dixie Brunner, Jim Matson, Roger Carter, and Cindy Roundy. (1995). Kane County Delegation Visit with Governor Michael Leavitt., St. George, UT.

Daly, Herman E. and Jr. John B. Cobb. (1989). *For the Common Good: Redirecting the Economy Toward Community, the Environment, and a Sustainable Future.* Beacon Press, Boston, MA.

Freeman, Duane R. (1983). The North Kaibab Revisited: A Look at Policies and Management. Master of Science, Colorado State University.

Haney, Elly. (1993). Towards a White Feminist Ecological Ethic. *J. Feminist Studies in Religion* 9 (1–2): 75–93.

Lang, D.M. and S.S. Stewart. (1910). Reconnaissance of the Kaibab National Forest. Unpublished report, 58 p., USFS.

Macy, Joanna. (1991). *Mutual Causality in Buddhism and General Systems Theory: The Dharma of Natural Systems.* State University of New York Press, Albany, NY.

McDaniel, Jay B. (1989). *Of God and Pelicans: A Theology of Reverence for Life.* Westminister/John Knox Press, Louisville, KY.

Murti, T.R.V. (1955). *The Central Philosophy of Buddhism: A Study of the Madhyamika System.* George Allen and Unwin Ltd., London.

Nash, James A. (1991). *Loving Nature: Ecological Integrity and Christian Responsibility.* Abingdon Press, Nashville.

Nash, Roderick Frazier. (1989). *The Rights of Nature: A History of Environmental Ethics.* The University of Wisconsin Press, Madison, WI.

Scoville, Judith N. (1995). Value Theory and Ecology in Environmental Ethics: A Comparison of Rolston and Niebuhr. *Environmental Ethics* 17: 115–133.

SierraClub. (1995). Memo to chapters: "Double Time into Oblivion: The Real

Story of the Fredonia, AZ, Saw Mill and the Kaibab National Forest",
Sierra Club.

Taylor, Paul W. (1986). *Respect for Nature: A Theory of Environmental Ethics.*
Princeton University Press, Princeton.

Tenzin Gyatso, His Holiness the Dalai Lama. (1992). A Tibetan Buddhist
Perspective on Spirit in Nature. In *Spirit and Nature: Why the Environment
is a Religious Issue*, ed. Steven C. Rockefeller and John C. Elder: pp. 109–123.
Boston, MA: Beacon Press.

TimberDataCo. (1994). Contract Activity Report. Volume Harvested, Sold and
Remaining. USDA Forest Service Region 3, Southwestern Region, Timber
Data Company, Eugene, OR.

USFS, Southwestern Region. (1987a). Environmental Impact Statement for the
Kaibab National Forest Plan, USDA Forest Service, Southwestern Region,
Williams, AZ.

USFS, Southwestern Region. (1987b). Kaibab National Forest Plan, USDA
Forest Service, Southwestern Region.

NOTES

1. Selective harvest, sometimes called "pick and pluck," involves harvesting
    individual trees; "even-aged" management can take different forms, but it
    involves cutting stands of trees. Even-aged management can vary from
    clear-cutting large tracts of land to shelterwood harvests on small acreages
    that have the appearance of small clear-cuts but which leave seed trees
    uncut so that replanting is not required. On the North Kaibab, even-aged
    management was applied as shelterwood harvests, at first on larger tracts of
    land, and later on small acreages.

2. Portions of the material included in this section are based on interviews
    with the USFS, AGFD, Sierra Club and Audubon Society, Kaibab
    Industries, and community people.

3. Though both the North and South Kaibab forests were involved in the
    debate, I have restricted this discussion to the North Kaibab forest and
    adjacent communities.

4. The mill in Fredonia was not the only mill in the Southwestern Region to
    close in the last few years.

5. The Forest Plan designated 15% of the forested area as functioning old
    growth and prohibited cutting trees 36 inches and greater in diameter.

6. The discussion in this paper is limited to the town of Kanab.

7. I am grateful to the Utah Job Service office in Kanab for supplying me
    with demographic information on the dislocated workers.

8. Workers were covered by the Western Conference of Teamsters Pension
    plan, the specifics of which were negotiated through the union employment

contract with KI. The plan included a 5-year vesting requirement for eligibility. All vested workers 55 years of age or older at lay-off were eligible to apply for a pension benefit, which was pro-rated for workers under age 65. Of the thirty-four workers who were 55 years of age or older at lay-off, only nine applied for pension benefits. Those who did not apply did so either because they were not vested, or because they elected to wait until they were older to apply rather than to take a pro-rated benefit Workers who were under age 55 at lay-off will also be eligible to apply for pension benefits when they reach 55 years of age.

9. Of the workers who did not apply for assistance, 16 were rehired or retained by KI, 6 retired with pension or SSI, 10 moved, and 27 live in outlying areas.

10. For discussion of this kind of balancing argument in other cases see Booth, 1994: 237–238.

11. Taken from interviews conducted for this project.

12. If decisions were guided by any ethical philosophy it was utilitarian. For example, in the Record of Decision for the Kaibab Forest Plan the Regional Forester states that his goal was to "maximize net public benefits" USFS Kaibab Forest Plan, Record of Decision, April 15, 1988.

13. I use the conditional tense here because it is not my intention to address the question of which perspective on the condition of the forest was correct.

14. Since Taylor's concern is to adequately specify the conditions of an environmental ethic, he does not discuss application of the Principle of Restitutive Justice to humans. However, it is entirely consistent with his overall discussion, and I suspect he would support this inclusive interpretation.

15. See the historical summary and citations in Nash, 1989: 51, 112–117. More recent examples include Tenzin Gyatso, 1992 and the collected essays in Badiner, 1990.

16. For an excellent discussion of the ethical implications of pratitya sammutpada, see Joanna Macy's "Mutual Causality in Buddhism and General Systems Theory: The Dharma of Natural Systems (Macy, 1991).

17. I have, hopefully, not damaged McDaniel's presentation by taking it somewhat out of context in order to fit it into Taylor's classification scheme.

18. It should be noted that McDaniel presents only a partial representation of "ultimacy" in Buddhism. In the Madhyamika, *Tathata* (or Suchness) is only one aspect of the Absolute. The other is *Tathagata*. Whereas *Tathata* is the Real, or the Truth, itself, and impersonal, *Tathagata* is "who knows the truth". *Tathagata* is associated with the Buddha, a being freed of limitations (see discussion in (Murti, 1955), pp276–289). Thus, in Buddhism, "actuality" is not absent from the concept of the Absolute, as some might interpret McDaniel's text to suggest.

19. Also see McDaniel's discussion of *pratitya sammutpada* in (McDaniel, 1990), p238.

20. For helpful discussion addressing issues of elitism in environmentalism see (Haney, 1993).

21. The need for an environmental ethic that "takes the human community seriously as a center of value" has also been discussed recently by Judith N. Scoville (Scoville, 1995).

Learning from the Earth:
Key to Sustainable Development

Paula González, SC

It has taken until very late in the 20th Century for human society to begin to realize that the planet cannot afford 'development' for the "other two-thirds" of the world's people—*if* it is to be achieved using current development models. Industrialization causes severe damage to our very 'life support systems'through: 1) destructive practices such as mining, drilling, deforestation and mechanized agriculture; 2) polluting of water, air and soil through use of the thousands of chemicals that have come into common use since World War II; and 3) the ever-increasing use of fossil fuel and nuclear energy. The other critical factor is the rate of population growth, which cannot continue at its present rate—(over 90 million annually!)—without exceeding the food production capacity of the potentially arable land, perhaps within the next 50 years. The number of births and deaths must become equal—and this will happen, either by human choice or by ever-increasing human misery.

It is clear that for continuation of human life on *this* finite planet beyond the next century, the global population must be stabilized within the carrying capacity of the planet and its life support systems must be restored. These goals can be achieved only through a transformation of human economic, political, social and religious institutions modeled on "nature."

There are hopeful signs that movement in that direction has begun to move to the forefront of human consciousness. *Our Common Future*, the 1987 report of the Brundtland Commission, was aptly titled, as it established the global context within which current problems must be addressed.[1] It warned of the growing threat to our planet from environmental degradation, global poverty, pollution and disease. Five years later, the United Nations Conference on Environment and Development (UNCED) brought together an unprecedented number of world political leaders at Rio de Janeiro to discuss the challenge of sustainable development. Simultaneously, tens of thousands of ordinary people were involved in the Global Forum or "People's Summit." Out of the Rio Conference emerged *Agenda* 21, the blueprint which outlines the actions necessary to implement the 27 principles agreed upon in the

Rio Declaration on Environment and Development.[2] As seen in Figure 1, these principles flow from the recognition of the interdependent nature of the Earth and define the rights of peoples to development and their responsibility for safeguarding the common environment.

Many of the human activities called for in Agenda 21 will require significant involvement of the scientific community. However, recent "development" approaches—facilitated by advances in science-based technology and engineering—have been integrally destructive of soils, atmosphere and water. Thus, science itself may have to change radically (and quickly!) in order to play an appropriate role in designing adequate approaches for addressing today's unprecedented environmental challenges.

It is obvious from the Rio principles that scientists must broaden their knowledge and learn new skills if they are to interact with social, political, religious and cultural leaders to achieve "sustainable development"—economic improvement for all peoples that is not ecologically destructive, Clearly, it is essential that all citizens, especially those in decisioh-making roles, become quickly aware of the growing threat-to the continued existence of *Homo sapiens* beyond the 21st century. Thus learning becomes the primary societal need and personal imperative for every human alive today.

The deep wisdom required to engage the giant challenges we face necessitates an understanding of the most basic principles of the phenomenon of "life" on the planet. Nearly four billion years ago, the first living cells evolved 'simple' unicellular creatures (similar to today's bacteria) which were able to nourish themselves from the rich variety of chemicals characteristic of the early Earth's turbulence. These prokaryotic organisms multiplied exponentially and as temperature dropped and Earth stabilized chemically, they faced a serious environmental crisis. Either their numbers would be reduced to the carrying capacity of their surroundings or they would become extinct. However, simultaneous with these large increases in populations, another phenomenon had been at work genetic mutation. Many different prokaryotes had developed, some of which could feast on dead prokaryotes and others on compounds produced by their metabolism. These new micro-organisms formed the first ecological 'communities' and the growing web of inter-relationships became the first aquatic proto-ecosystem.

After about 100 million years, a mutation appeared that made the 'surrounding environment' include directly the energy from the sun. Some of the prokaryotes developed chlorophyll-containing plastids which could convert radiant energy into.glucose. Living cells could now 'munch sunshine.' The byproduct of this photosynthetic activity precipitated several dramatic events. As oxygen was released it reacted with the rocks, changing the chemical nature of the land. Also, the carbon monoxide, ammonia and hydrogen sulfide in the atmosphere were transformed and the concentration of oxygen increased rapidly. By two billion years ago, the transformation of lithosphere, hydrosphere and atmosphere was significant and the prokarygtic communities began to be destroyed by the very oxygen they had produced.

This could have been the "end of life on Earth" as a result of a massive die-down—but other mutations had produced cyanobacteria, the blue-green algae. These amazing organisms had learned how to use oxygen in what is now the near-universal process of respiration -and with a ten-fold increase in energy for life functions. Atmospheric oxygen now rose even more rapidly and the outer layer of atmospheric oxygen—the ozone layer—thickened to the point of no longer permitting the passage of the most energetic solar photons. When oxygen levels rose above 21%, many of the cyanobacteria were threatened. But just below 21% oxygen (20.79%, as we all learned in high school science), the 'combustion' involved in respiration reached maximum efficiency and Earth's complex interacting web of biosphere, hydrosphere, lithosphere and atmosphere stabilized in a dynamic equilibrium.

The second great era of life began with the emergence of eukaryotic cells about two billion years ago and has blossomed into a variety of forms which would have been unimaginable during the long period when bacteriawere the dominant life forms. Colonial forms began to develop—some parasitic, some symbiotic. After-about one billion years, heterotrophic organisms emerged on the evolutionary stage—creatures which could nourish themselves by engulfing other living creatures. Now predator and prey began to co-evolve into the patterned ecosystems of the Proterozoic seas.

But the greatest "surprise"—the mutation responsible for the enormous explosion of biological variety during the last billion years—was yet to come. The development of sexual reproduction opened the door to greater and greater specialization of cell structure and function. About 700 million years ago, multicellular organisms appeared and developed for over 100 million years—until during the most severe Ice Age in Earth's history, 80-90% of species became extinct!

Many of the primal 'biological inventions" weathered the cold 20 million years, after which followed the now-familiar Paleozoic, Mesozoic and Cenozoic eras. Only in the last 2.1 million years of this long drama has the genus Homo been present modern *Homo sapiens* only 40,000 years! Recent human history has occurred in what will probably be known as the terminal phase of the Cenozoic era. During the past century, humans have come to control many Earth processes, plundering the planet's resources in a devastating manner. The present mode of human presence is not sustainable. Thus, from the perspective of continued human existence, we live in an evolutionary moment perhaps as crucial as those which saw the emergence of early life, of photosynthesis, of heterotrophy and of sexual reproduction the major milestones in the history of life on Earth!

According to Thomas Berry, we have entered the Ecozoic era and are called to view the universe as a communion of subjects rather than as a collection of objects.[3] A cultural historian, he has joined Brian Swimme, a mathematical cosmologist, to produce *The Universe Story*, a volume whose subtitle hints of the new.way in which we might look at the 15-billion-year history of the universe: "From the Primordial Flaring Forth to the-Ecozoic Era: A Celebration of the Unfolding of the Cosmos."[4]

Perhaps, as James Lovelock suggests through the Gaia Theory, the Earth may be a single living system in which the conditions necessary for 'life' have been produced and are maintained in a homeostatic state by the living creatures as they have evolved.[5] (It is important to note that even the manner in which I describe this hypothesis is currently a matter of debate in the scientific community.[6])

Understanding such an Earth would necessitate interdisciplinary approaches to its study, including not only the physical and biological sciences but social and political science as well (the latter to deal with the appearance of a single species, *Homo sapiens*). Many other holistic approaches are beginning to-suggest that we are in the midst of what Thomas Kuhn calls the growth of a new paradigm—a synthesis of scientific, technological and cultural change to a planetary worldview.[7] The same type of comprehensive Vision is evident in Peter Russell's works, *The Global Brain* and *The White Hole in Time*, which focus on the role evolving human consciousness plays in the movement toward an advanced global civilization in a biosphere restored to health.[8, 9]

Duane Elgin compares the development of the human species to that of an individual in *Awakening Earth: Exploring the Evolution of Human Culture and Consciousness.*[10] He suggests that industrial societies must turn away from materialism and commercialism as organizing values in order to move from adolescence into the maturity of a planetary-scale "species-civilization" that can *live* harmoniously within the web of life. He notes that a Gallup poll taken before the 1992 'Earth Summit' found that among a substantial majority of people, in 18 of 22 very diverse nations and representing a wide range of income levels, the well-being of the Earth was placed ahead of personal economic concerns.

Thus, there seems to be an intuitive understanding growing among many people that we must make some radical changes in our manner of relating to our Earth. What is lacking is a shared vision of how to move toward a co-evolutionary approach which integrates Western and Eastern views, scientific and humanistic views-into an organic whole. Integrating the material and consciousness (spiritual?) aspects of life can be synergistic in releasing the human evergy and creativity needed to develop a civilization that is sustainable and humanly satisfying.

Agenda 21 is a 'first draft' of one step in that direction, but at present only a tiny fraction of Earth's peoples realize the urgency of the times. As we edge closer to the new millenium, the social and political climates throughout the planet evidence that the adolescent stage of the human family is far from over.

Clearly, bringing together the accumulated human wisdom and scientific approaches of East and West can move humanity toward maturity, but the "unlearning" of old habits and ways of thinking may take more time than we have. Another approach is that of "relearning" the wisdom of the Earth. It has become increasingly clear to me that environmental degradation is the result of ignorance of the most basic— 'facts of life.' Virtually everyone is vaguely aware that pollution of air, water and soil is undesirable. However, because of our "objectification" of the material universe very few persons—especially those in urban industrial centers—realize that the "global environmental crisis" is inside their homes inside their very bodies! These are lessons Earth.can teach—a wisdom which many indigenous peoples still possess!

ECOSYSTEMS AS TEACHERS

The ecosystem—not the individual organism—is the structural and functional unit of 'life' on Earth. Thus, careful (meditative?) observation of any ecosystem can reveal three important lessons about sustainability: interdependence, balance and wholeness. (A look at the Rio principles in Figure 1 will show that these are lessons which underlie the action steps necessary to move toward sustainable development).

I. Interdependence

Three major types of organisms comprise an ecological community, the basis of any ecosystem: 1) Producers, which capture radiant energy and store it in the bonds of chemical molecules; 2) Consumers, which obtain energy for life processes by eating producers or other consumers which have eaten producers; and 3) Decomposers, which obtain their energy for life by breaking down producers to chemical forms which then return to the environment.

II. Balance

The biotic drama includes two primary processes which are universal from bacteria to elephants. Expressed simply, photosynthesis might be thought of as "air, earth and water dancing in the sunlight." In every green cell, the following occurs:

$$6\ CO_2\ +\ 6\ H_2O\ \xrightarrow[\text{radiant engery}]{\text{chlorophyll}}\ C_6H_{12}O_6\ +\ 6\ O_2$$

  (air)   (mineral-containing water)   ("food")   (air)

This reaction, which occurs exclusively in the cells of green plants (producers), is the source of the vast majority of the energy responsible for "life."

Animals (consumers) take in various "foods" (stored solar energy) and through various enzyme-mediated steps these are broken down—releasing the energy stored in the chemical bonds for use in life processes. In every plant and animal cell, the following process of respiration occurs:

$$C_6H_{12}O_6 + 6\ O_2 \xrightarrow{\text{enzymes}} 6\ CO_2 + 6\ H_2O + \text{Energy}$$

A careful look at these two simplified equations illustrates dramatically the balance characteristic of the living world. They are the reverse of each other!

But the story is not yet complete. The dynamic equilibrium characteristic of a mature ecosystem cannot be achieved or maintained without the contribution of the Decomposers. These microbial alchemists receive their energy for life by releasing the chemical bond energy still stored in fallen leaves, animal moltings, etc., and in the enormous array of dead Producers and Consumers.

III. *Wholeness*

The universe is a single whole made up of perhaps trillions of galaxies—the macrocosm. Yet, study of the interrelationships of stars within a galaxy, or of planets around one star, or of interacting communities of life-forms within specific environments, or of the harmonious interaction of organs within the body of an organism, or of the elegant micro-ecological activities within a single cell, or of the fascinating behavior of atoms within molecules, or of subatomic particles, reveals that each of these assemblages is itself a "whole." Each is a microcosm—a hologram reflecting the universe!

Thus, the biosphere as we know it cannot exist except embedded in perfect balance and interdependence witli what for so long we have called the 'non-living' world—the lithosphere, hydrosphere and atmosphere. It is clear from the processes of photosynthesis and respiration that the biota are made of air, earth and water energized by the sun! It seems logical that if humans *truly understood* that "you are what you eat," these life support systems would not be taken for granted—nor would they be polluted! It is likely also that a true 'realization of these exquisite interrelationships would restore to our industrial-model psyches a badly-needed sense of awe and reverence. In primal peoples, such attitudes often arose from fear of the unknown and unpredictable. A 21st century sense of awe can be nourished through technological discoveries made possible by using space exploration, satellites, electron microscopes computers, bubble chambers and the host of other clever ways we humans have invented to expand the reach of the human senses.

The industrial model has been very "successful" (from the perspective of present values) for over a century, but the problems currently posed by its continuation derive from a primary design error—(which probably can be corrected!). A simple diagram will illustrate why it is not sustainable on a finite planet:

NATURE'S 'ECONOMICS'   (See p. 15 for a larger.version of this figure).

Industrial 'Economics'

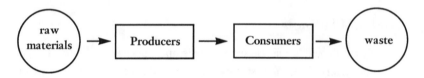

The major economic and environmental problems of diminishing resources and pollution (with their enormous potential for spawning inequitable distribution, war, famine, disease, etc.) do *not* occur in Nature. The reason can be made quite clear through a simple illustration. (see "Nature's 'Economics'" below)

In summary, for *Homo sapiens* to continue as a long-term participant in the story of life on Earth, the transformation of all our human systems from static, linear patterns to self-regenerating, interconnected, cyclic patterns must occur within the relatively near future.

Already such ideas as those mentioned earlier and such initiatives as Agenda 21 indicate that "mutations" leading away from "doomsday" are accumulating in the minds and hearts of a growing number of humans. Increasing among many people is the recognition of the basic error of the "scientific endeavor" since the 17th century—perceiving the natural world as a machine rather than as an organic living reality.

Whether or not the Gaia Hypothesis proves to be "scientifically valid"—(and this will depend on how "science" evolves)—is *not* nearly as important as its value as a new way of perceiving the reality of Earth's interrelationships—and thus the proper "role" of humans in the "uni-

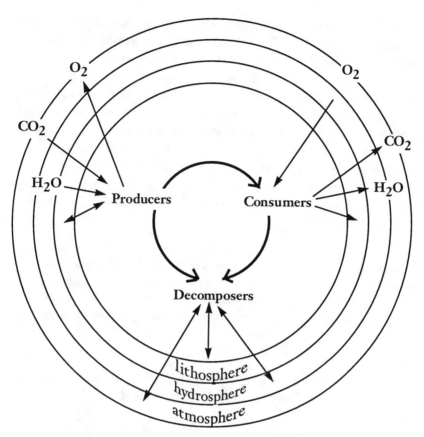

Nature's 'Economics'

verse story." Obviously, it necessitates completely new ways of "doing science." This new (ancient?) metaphor calls those of us who have been educated as "scientists"—whether or not we are engaged in the "scientific endeavor"—to realize how singularly prepared we are to probe deeply the new ideas which are emerging like so many "mutations." Because of the enormous impact the 'scientific world's' attitudes, values and proclamations have on society, it is imperative also that we realize both the responsibility and the opportunity which is ours at this critical moment in human history!

Our 300-year worldview of the universe as a machine has-been responsible for producing many scientists who instead of being "natural philosophers" have become "technocratic tinkerers." Our times call for philosophers!

This mechanistic paradigm is responsible also for science becoming the most secularized of human pursuits. This is tragic both *for* society and for individual scientists. With their insights into the workings of Nature, they are in the best possible position to understand that "communing with Nature" can lead to deep contemplation of the Eternal Mystery from which all the wonders of the universe come forth. Such a vision could motivate billions of people to become actively involved in furthering such initiatives as Agenda 21 and the many similar 'mutations' of human attitudes and values which are arising all around us. We scientists could be powerful catalysts in transforming the current destructive paradigm if we were to explore deeply the implications of the following for the 'scientific enterprise':

> In relation to the earth, we have been autistic for centuries. Only now have we begun to listen with some attention and with a willingness to respond to the earth's demand that we cease our industrial assault, that we abandon our inner rage against the conditions of our earthly existence, that we renew participation in the grand liturgy of the universe.[11]

MAJOR IDEAS IN THE RIO DECLARATION ON ENVIRONMENT AND DEVELOPMENT

1. People are entitled to a healthy life in harmony with nature.
2. Development today must not compromise the development and environment needs of present and future generations.
3. Nations must assess the environmental impact of proposed activities and develop laws to provide compensation for environmental damage caused beyond their borders.
4. The polluter should bear the cost of pollution.
5. Scientific uncertainty shall not be used to postpone cost effective measures to prevent environmental degradation.
6. To achieve sustainable development, environmental protection shall constitute an integral part of the development process.
7. Eradicating poverty and reducing disparities in living standards are essential for sustainable development.
8. Nations must eliminate unsustainable production and con-

sumption patterns, and promote appropriate demographic policies.

9. Sustainable development requires better scientific understanding of the problems; nations should share knowledge and innovative technologies which promote sustainability.

10. The full participation of women is essential to achieve sustainable development, as are the creativity of youth and the knowledge of indigenous peoples.

11. Peace, development and environmental protection are interdependent and indivisible; warfare is inherently destructive of sustainable development.

NOTES

1. Brundtland, Gro Harlem (chair), *Our Common Future*, New York: Oxford University Press, 1987.

2. Keating, Michael, *The Earth Summit's Agenda for Change: A Plain Language Version of Agenda 21 and the Other Rio Agreements*, Geneva: Centre for Our Common Future, 1993. (Note: The full text of *Agenda 21: The United Nations Programme of Action from Rio*, can be obtained from: UN Publications, Sales Section, Room DC2-0853, United Nations, New York, NY 10017.)

3. Berry, Thomas, *The Dream of the Earth*, San Francisco: Sierra Club Books, 1988.

4. Swimme, Brian and Thomas Berry, *The Universe Story*, San Francisco, Harper Collins, 1992.

5. Lovelock, James, *Gaia: A New Look at Life on Earth*, London: Oxford University Press, 1979.

6. Schneider, Stephen H. and Penelope J. Boston (eds.), *Scientists on Gaia*, Cambridge, MA: The MIT Press, 1991.

7. Kuhn, Thomas S., *The Structure of Scientific Revolutions*, Chicago: University of Chicago Press, 1970.

8. Russell, Peter, *The Global Brain: Speculations on the Evolutionary Leap to Planetary Consciousness*, Los Angeles: J.P. Tarcher, Inc., 1983.

9. Russell, Peter, *The White Hole in Time*, San Francisco: Harper, San Francisco, 1992.

10. Elgin, Duane, *Awakening Earth: Exploring the Evolution of Human Culture and Consciousness*, New York: Wm. Morrow & Co., 1993.

11. Berry, Thomas, *op. cit.*, p. 215.

PART THREE

The Religious
Experience
in an
Ecological Context

Theology of Ecology

Gene Wilhelm

One of the penalties of an ecological education is that one lives alone in a world of words. Much of the damage inflicted on land is quite invisible to laymen. An ecologist must either harden his shell and make believe that the consequences of science are none of his business, or he must be a doctor who sees the marks of death in a community that believes itself well and does not want to be told otherwise.

— Aldo Leopold

Little did I realize that my four-months experience north of the Arctic Circle as a University of Missouri student assistant ecologist would change my life forever. Chosen for my ornithological expertise, I was invited to help a zoology professor complete research on the ecology of the brown lemming. This hamster-size arctic rodent is noted for its extreme population cycles: literally exploding in numbers every four and one-half years, then abruptly crashing to a few individuals in a matter of weeks. By coincidence, several avian species were major predators of the brown lemming, and thus my opportunity to work in the high arctic.

I will never forget flying northwest of Fairbanks, Alaska, through a deeply eroded pass in the Brooks Range at the end of May and seeing the vast arctic slope for the first time. Tundra, blanketed in snow, stretched from horizon to horizon. The relatively flat plain was interrupted now and then by polygonal earth, stark geological evidence of the power and control of semi-permanent ice masses beneath the land's surface. No trees were visible after leaving the Brooks Range, for the tundra realm harbors mostly lowly plants like mosses, lichens, grasses, and sedges. Permafrost, scant precipitation, nearly continuous strong winds and a short growing season prevent trees from growing. The tundra is truly a frigid desert. After flying several hours, our plane finally landed at Barrow on the Arctic Ocean, 500 air miles south of the North Pole. Nicknamed "land of the midnight sun," Barrow was, until 1990, the largest Inupiat (coastal Eskimo) community in Alaska and home of the

255

Arctic Research Laboratory, Office of Naval Research, United States Navy, since World War II.

The Inupiat (the name means "people of the icy coast") are a fitting example of human adaptation to one of the harshest environments on earth. For millennia, caribou skin clothing worn in layers, parka hoods lined with wolverine fur and seal skin boots and mittens protected them against the long and bitter cold arctic winter. They travelled on sea-ice when they had to in winter using dogteams and sleds. Summer travel on land meant that both dogs and people carried the family's belongings. The umiak, a large open boat using driftwood frame and walrus skin covering, was used primarily for whale hunting, while the one-man kayak was used to hunt seal, walrus, polar bear, and swimming caribou. Seals also were hunted at the sea-ice edge in spring or at their breathing holes in the sea-ice in winter. In spring and autumn, brief seasons though they be, abundant arctic char were trapped in stone weirs or speared in freshwater streams. Spears also were used, along with bows and clubs, to kill small game such as snowshoe hare, kit fox and wolverine.

For centuries the people used the huge bones of whales as frames for their winter sod houses but switched to open skin tents in summer. They rendered whale blubber and seal fat into oil for heating and cooking. The people wisely stayed indoors most of the long, cold, and dark winter celebrating their good fortunes with dancing, singing, eating, drinking, performing skits, and elders telling long stories about their origin, their homeland, their sacred place of earth straddling the tundra and the sea, and about the spirits that kept them safe. Slowly, over many generations, a symbiosis developed among sea-land-people so that all three elements fused into one functional unity that was inseparable until the arrival of the Europeans.

A local Inupiat guide, with the English first name of Pete, was assigned to help me get settled. Pete was an unusually tall (for an Eskimo), husky middle-aged man who moved many years ago from the interior to the coast seeking government employment. His keen mechanical abilities were known throughout the native community, a trait that was quickly noticed by the Navy. Pete was hired as a full-time assistant mechanic by the ONR.

Pete taught me so many things about the sea, tundra, and his people. He showed me how to identify migrating whales along the coast by their backs, flukes, and spouts. He took me to Barrow Spit, four miles north of the village, which was a traditional waterbird hunting ground. For many generations Inupiat hunters stretched long sinew nets between high driftwood poles to snare migrating loons, swans, geese, ducks, and shorebirds by the thousands. After bleeding the birds, the hunters would place the game in pits chiseled deep into the permafrost for long-term refrigeration. Each family in the village had such a pit, and once filled, hunting ceased for another year. Pete also taught me to always wear my parka because even on the calmest day of the short summer fierce, cold winds and fog can occur unexpectedly and make you sick or even crazy.

Over the weeks Pete and I became close friends but I sensed something was bothering him. Our three-man research team was kept busy eighteen hours a day, seven days a week, because the height of the lemming population cycle started a few weeks after our arrival. Scores of live lemmings were collected on the tundra and transferred to the laboratory for weighing, aging, measuring, sexing, and describing pelage colors and patterns. Many lemmings were tested for swimming ability, terrestrial mobility, and social interactions. Some lemmings were killed, dissected, internally examined and then prepared as study skin specimens for future laboratory or museum research.

Finally, on July 25, my nineteenth birthday, Pete asked me two questions which eventually changed my life. "Tell me, dear friend Gene," he said, "why do you kill my little brother lemmings? You do not eat them or make parkas from their tiny skins. And why do other scientists (there were sixty from thirteen universities) kill my winged brothers: the snowy owl, jaeger, and raven? Each one of those winged brothers is wise in its own way and teaches our people how to live. The snowy owl is our constant companion on the vast open tundra, even in the long, dark, and bitter cold winter, and warns my people of danger. The jaeger, who lives mostly at sea, tells my people that when he returns to the tundra in great numbers, many little brother lemmings will soon follow. And brother raven is noted for his intelligence and cunningness and for those reasons is our messenger between sea and land spirits and our people. The other scientists do not eat my winged brothers either, nor do they save their feathers where the power of flying resides."

Then Pete continued: "My people only kill what they must for survival, especially during the long, dark, and bitter cold winter. I hunt brother seal when there is enough light on the ice next to the sea.

There I hunch motionless, sometimes for hours, over his breathing hole in the ice, watching carefully a downy feather of brother loon that is suspended over the hole. Brother seal and I talk with each other *in silence*. I plead with brother seal that he sacrifice his own life so that the lives of my wife, two daughters, and me will survive the remainder of the harsh winter. Brother seal asks me in return, what will I do for him and his family? I tell him that I promise to spare the lives of his other family members and I will return his bladder to the Sea Spirit, mother of all sea brothers and sisters, large and small, who lives in the deep waters, so that she will be pleased and release more seal brothers in the future. When the least bit of air stirs the feather, I know that brother seal finally has decided to help me and surfaces just as I plunge my harpoon into the hole. Every part of brother seal is used by my family; nothing is wasted and thrown away. I do not return to brother seal's breathing hole ever again, nor do my people. But I do return brother seal's bladder to the Sea Spirit, as promised. My family is thankful to brother seal for sacrificing himself so that we may live through the remainder of winter and we celebrate our thankfulness with eating, singing, dancing, and telling the story of all our sea brothers and sisters."

I was dumbfounded by Pete's questions and awed by his vivid story. After reflecting and pausing for a minute in silence, I could only mutter: "I don't know, Pete, why I do it." Being utterly dependent for one's existence on taking the life of other beings, the Inupiat is necessarily related to the game he seeks in a particular ecospiritual way. As hunter he has a kin relationship with all wildlife, his brothers and sisters. He recognizes the uniqueness in intelligence, sensibility, socialization, and roles each animal plays in the ecoscheme of things. He truly exercises respect, reverence, responsibility, reciprocity, gratitude, and wit for brother seal, otherwise the extremely alert animal would not willingly present himself as sacrifice. Pete utilized every part of brother seal, not because he believes in the intrinsic virtue of thrift, but because the marine animal had died for him. By graciously accepting the warm energy- and nutrient-laden carcass as a supreme gift, and by honoring its willing sacrifice by respectfully handling its physical remains, Pete, the Inupiat hunter, confirms and revitalizes the traditional sacred contract between human beings and kindred animals of all kinds. His empathy for the elegant creatures of tundra and sea and his keen sense of place in arctic Alaska and in the universe compels him to communicate with all creatures, all kindred, with the same reverence with which he addresses his own family members and ancestors. The relationship between hunter and game, between human being and beast, is thus *horizontal*. It is an ancient and familiar negotiation, punctuated by moments of joy and grief between equals.

Pete's questions and story made me reexamine what I was doing. Did it make personal sense, ecospiritual sense, to collect and kill brown lemmings? Was the scientific worldview set in motion by Descartes and Newton so long ago still relevant? By embracing reductionism (the belief that by stripping nature to its most elementary components allows us to gain insights that can be fitted together again to reveal the deepest secrets of the universe), was I learning anything valid about the arctic ecosystem?

By early September I knew that I could no longer kill wild creatures of any kind for the sake of science. Instead, I was determined to find the answers to my own questions and to learn more about *primal peoples* (the term implies "original" or "first" human occupants of a local landscape), especially about their ecospiritual worldview.

Over the next several years, I learned that the scientific paradigm so devoutly adhered to by the Western World, and the power and utility of reductionism, were seriously flawed. Werner Heisenberg discovered that "we can never really know what nature is because in order to observe it, we have to control it and thus change it." Neils Bohr found that "the properties of subatomic particles can be described only by probability, never with absolute certainty." Finally, parts of nature were shown to interact *synergistically* so that the actions and properties of a system as a whole cannot be predicted on the basis of what is known about its individual components. "Thus, while science yields powerful insights into isolated fragments of the world," states Suzuki, "their sum total is a disconnected, inadequate description of the whole."[1] In sum, the Cartesian-Newtonian worldview with its scientific reductionism is inadequate in solving the current global ecocrisis because it fails to comprehend the complexity of life on earth.

At various times I have been privileged to live, work, and learn from many primal peoples in Africa, Australia, and Latin America. From these intimate experiences I have come to believe that primal peoples' worldviews contain something profound, relevant, and powerful for our own contemporary scientific and technologically addicted Western society. Such personal enlightenment also forced me to investigate why Judeo-Christianity lacked interest in the current ecocrisis and whether there is some common ground in the primal peoples', Judeo-Christian and postmodern scientific worldviews to suggest hope for the future of humanity.

Each of us has a worldview which determines how one "sees" the world and each of us "assumes" that one's worldview is the correct and only view. Worldviews are neither right nor wrong, only different, and are determined by one's culture which consists of a value system and technological capacity. Note that it is the values held by a culture that guide the development, type, and amount of technology.

CONTEXT: THE ECOCRISIS

Our current ecocrisis is difficult to fathom because of its global dimension and its insidious nature. It is subtle and gradual, like a cancerous cell, involving the seemingly innocuous activities of everybody on earth. It creeps up on us daily so that we become used to environmental decay and ecological diminishment, so much so that many people even deny that it is occurring. Like true addicts, we find every available avenue to deny what a few others (primal peoples, for example) can clearly see: that global warming, ozone depletion, species extinction, and worldwide toxic pollution stem from the ecoimpact of industrial civilization and the sheer weight of human numbers. The end result is that life on earth is diminishing both in quantity and quality.

In fact, what is happening at the end of the twentieth century is not just another historical transition or another cultural change in human activity. Instead, the devastation of the planet that humans are bringing about is negating billions of years of earth development. Although the human species is incapable of extinguishing everything, we are wreaking ecohavoc on earth processes and functions by setting in motion dynamic forces that are obliterating all life-support systems.

Life on earth is indeed a chancy situation. At least at five different times in the geologic past glaciers, volcanoes, and perhaps even meteors and comets have razed the earth, contributing to the obliteration of many species. Paleontologists tell us that mass extinctions occurred at the end of the Paleozoic Era, some 220 million years ago, and again at the end of the Mesozoic Era, some 65 million years ago. However, in both these cases new earthen developments gradually (between 10 and 100 million years) took place that were remarkably successful in the expansion of living forms. It is doubtful that humans now have enough time to await such new developments.[2]

Yet something unprecedented is going on now. We are at this moment in space-time facing an eco-catastrophe unequaled in the history of the earth. For the first time in its four and one-half billion years' existence, a single biological species, *Homo sapiens*, has simultaneous control of earth processes as primary geomorphological agent, ecological dominant, and major decision maker over life and death. It is the human who now makes chasms in the earth as deep as the Grand Canyon or mountains as high as the Alleghenies; it is the human who not only dominates all plant and animal life but also plays god in making new life-forms; and it is the human major decision maker who chooses what waters, soils, plants, animals, and whole ecosystems live or die. Never in the history of earth has there been a biological organism with so much power and control over the ecosphere. In less than a century, *Homo sapiens* will have destroyed what evolution took millions of years to establish, jeopardizing its own existence in the process.

The eco-crisis, therefore, is in reality one of origin, a distorted worldview rooted in the sins of human pride, exaggerated self-importance, and greed plus broken relationships to earth, creation, and its Creator. Today, most humans have forgotten that they are earthlings, born of earth, reared and nurtured by its life-support systems and henceforth to return to it. Humankind has so divorced itself from this earthly bond that few ever ask the critical questions surrounding true identity and genesis. Who am I? Where did I come from? How did I get here? Why am I here? What should I do? Where am I going and when?[3]

These questions and their answers not only concern genesis but also relate to attitudes of behavior and to values or the lack of same. They are universal to all cultures and predate everything else in them. Thus, postmodern scientifically advanced and technologically addicted late twentieth-century Western society has severed its ties with earth, nature, and creation. In so doing, it has lost all cognizance and perception of space-time and the numinous presence in the universe. Sallie McFague indicates that we are dealing with a wily, crafty enemy—*ourselves*—as the perpetrators of the ecocrisis. She emphasizes that the moral issue of our day—and the vocation to which we are called—is whether we and other species will live and, if so, how well. For it is not enough to change our lifestyle; we must change what we value.[4]

What do we need to know then to make sense of our lives as individuals and as a human society? What can we do amidst so much earth-human turmoil to solve the ecocrisis?

AT THE BEGINNING

On a calm but bitter cold night, in the dead of winter, I hiked to the top of a grassy knoll overlooking a frozen lake in rural central Minnesota to get an unobstructed view of the heavens. The dark moon period of early January helped me focus on the brilliant starlight above which daintily filtered through millions of light years of space to illuminate the surrounding snowy lowlands.

Suddenly, in the upper corner of my right eye, I caught a glimpse of a long flash of purple-blue light with a bright yellow head streaming through the low atmosphere at a forty-five degree angle of descent. Then, as quickly as it appeared, it vanished in mid-air above the frozen lake.

It was, of course, an infinitesimal part of a meteor that had silently entered the earth's atmosphere from outer space at tremendous speed. Friction caused the particle to burn up and disintegrate.

Such an encounter was a vivid reminder that although earth too is an infinitesimal speck in the vast universe, it and its inhabitants are still interconnected, in fact, part and parcel of the cosmos. Some primal peoples believe that meteor showers and falling stars are direct empowering bolts of cosmic energy recharging the mind, body, and spirit of earth and its many beings. Of course, such outer-space bombardments of physical contact are constantly happening night and day everywhere in the earth's atmosphere. If we need visual proof of such connections, they are all around us to see.

Everything that exists in the universe came from a common origin, even our human ancestry stretches back through all life-forms to the stars, galaxies, and the primeval fireball itself. And because of postmodern (twentieth century) science and technology, we are the first generation of humans to look into the night sky and see the birth of stars, galaxies, even the afterglow of the primordial fireball.[5] We now know empirically that the universe is so vast that it contains billions of galaxies, each containing hundreds of billions of stars. Our galaxy, the Milky Way that you can see on a clear night, is just one among billions in the cosmos.

The universe is truly *unique*, a singularity in itself, only one of a kind. We cannot compare it with anything else because there is no second universe, nothing to compare it with. It is the ultimate *holos*, the entire, complete, one whole. Basic to such a whole is the simultaneous interrelatedness, interconnectedness, interdependentness, interpenetratedness, and interbondedness of all phenomena within it and the clear assumption of unity—*oneness*—as opposed to fragmentation, isolation, and separateness. This trait of many within one is important to stress because the same is true for earth.

The basic dynamism of the universe, including earth, is the *attraction* that each part within it has for every other part. Our galaxy, the Milky Way, is attracted by every other galaxy and the Milky Way attracts every other galaxy. The same is true for stars, planets, even humans as we well know. In fact, this primal alluring cosmic activity is the basic reality of the universe, permeating the cosmos on all levels of being from galaxies to subatomical particles. We cannot explain scientifically these allurements infusing everything and everybody. We can only become aware of them and reflect upon their meaning. They are indeed a great mystery of various forces: gravitation, electromagnetism, weak and strong nuclear reactions, chemical attractions, biological and human allurements. In fact, without cosmic allurement there would be only chaos; with it comes the fecundity of life, the ultimate expression of creation.

The universe is coded to become more and more different through the process of creativity or creation. Each new *difference* is an expression of the unlimited potential that is constantly unfolding in the universe. Nothing in the cosmos is exactly alike. Every blade of grass, insect, fish, bird, mammal, human, community, continent, constellation, or galaxy is different. In other words, everything at all levels of material is *one of a kind*. This principle can be illustrated at both the macro and micro levels. Although our planet earth is one of nine planets in our solar system, no two are alike. Only earth can support life which came about after billions of years of delicate and precise preparation. And at the micro level, although millions of bacteria may occupy one square foot of topsoil, scientists have yet to find two bacteria exactly alike. In fact, for years biologists thought that 1.5 million species presently occupy earth, but recent field research now points to at least 10 million to 30 million life-forms on earth and some scientists estimate as high as 100+ million. Ninety percent or more of all these life-forms are minute to microscopic. In fact, if it wasn't for the basic foundation of such tiny life-forms, no higher species—including the human—could survive.

Another principle of the universe is that of increased subjectivity or *interiority* which keeps each being grounded intimately to the source of the vast universe. This capacity for interiority involves increased unity of function through ever more complex organic structures. Increase in subjectivity is associated with increased complexity of a central nervous system and a brain; in the human this principle is remarkably expressed in the deep atomic structure of our genes where we carry the "memory" of the whole of the creation story. By "listening" inwardly we can truly experience directly the initiating power and bonding force of the universe. This principle links the psyche of individual living human beings to the spaceless-timeless force of reality.

The principle of *communion* assures all things, all beings, that each has a place and a role to play in the community of life. Nothing is ever created in isolation from the rest of reality. There are no islands in the universe. Every fragile individual of every species at every level of existence has significance for the whole. The power to imbue meaning into the seemingly least of beings is coded directly into the process of creation. This principle bonds together all parts of the puzzle of existence into one whole, one "*unity*."

The last principle of *change* is true of everything, everywhere in the universe. The whole universe and all of its parts are dynamic, not static as suggested by Medieval thinkers. Natural selection, natural variation, and mutation are processes of change that serve to describe organic evolution. Change is inevitable and universal. All of these principles interact and are interconnected and interdependent upon each other.

Thus, postmodern science has shattered the view of reality that had prevailed in the western mind since the seventeenth century. In place of the static, mechanical, linear worldview that was hypothesized by Descartes and Newton, twentieth-century scientists have discovered a universe that is dynamically alive, fluid, interconnecting, and continuously emerging. In fact, one of the most surprising revelations from postmodern science is the continuum between matter and energy or, more precisely, the "unified matter/energy field" which overturns traditional hierarchical dualisms such as nonliving/living, flesh/spirit, and nature/human being.[6] Another revelation is that earth with its multiple levels of life, each with a rich array of life-forms and individuals, is an *inverse hierarchical system* from earth-up instead of sky-down. This particular kind of "diversity within unity" is a critical point for it radicalizes interrelationships and interdependencies commencing at the microscopic level. The "unseen" is responsible for all that is visible.

The implications of such discoveries are truly profound. For one, the universe story, and earth's part in it, is longer and more diversified than formerly believed. Astrophysicists tell us that the universe is at least fifteen billion years old and that it is continuously unfolding and expanding. Earth itself is nearly five billion years old and is recognized by ecologists as a complex community of communities of interconnected life-forms at different life-levels that together function like a single organism.

Another implication stemming from recent universe discoveries is that each of us is part of the sum total of fifteen billion years of unbroken evolution. Each of us is unique in kind and space-time: there is no other person here and now, or ever will be, who is consciously thinking, reflecting, knowing, understanding, deciding, and doing as you or I. Each of us is truly an "earthling" in body-spirit. Eistein said that "Science's most important role is to communicate cosmic consciousness to those who are receptive to it." This is our ultimate goal as human beings.

A final implication is that the insights of astrophysics are beginning to resonate through other branches of postmodern science. Of these, ecology, the science that studies the nature of nonliving-living systems of earth, is the new multidisciplinary focus that demands far more knowledge, understanding, reflection, and application of sustainable interrelationships among organisms (including the human) within natural ecosystems.

THE REALM OF ECOLOGY*

There are some truths, even fundamental ones, that are apt to elude us. The most basic truth regarding our earthhome is that all living

---

* Portions of this section have appeared in *Appalachian Highlands: A Field Guide to Ecology* by Gene Wilhelm, Ph.D., published by Appalachian Science in the Public Interest, Livingston, Lentucky, 1997. Used here by permission.

beings, from the minute to the gigantic, are related in some manner to each other and to their environment. In fact, we are all earthlings. This fact, while mainly important as a physical principle, carries implications even of a spiritual dimension.

Humans from the dawn of their existence have been curious about their environment, about differences between plants and animals from place to place (Fig. 1). For nearly 100,000 years people lived in small, somewhat mobile bands gathering, scavenging, fishing, and hunting for food. These primal peoples depended completely on their local natural environment for survival. Population size was limited directly and quickly by the availability of food and water. In time, with the use of fire, advanced weapons such as the atlatl or spear thrower, and more sophisticated tools, these small groups made some imbalances in their environment, as do all life-forms at all times everywhere, but these disruptions in the long run limited and controlled the number of people and established a new dynamic equilibrium with the local natural environment. So our early ancestors responded and worked *with* earth rather than controlling and manipulating it. Primal peoples were *equal* members with other creatures and learned to survive by understanding and cooperating with earth processes. Indeed, such peoples were the *first true ecologists*, gaining knowledge and wisdom about interrelatedness and unity in their home community and its surroundings.

One of the most significant changes in human history developed between 10,000-12,000 years ago. People began the long process of learning how to domesticate plants and animals. Over several thousand years the importance of gathering, scavenging, fishing, and hunting declined as more people became farmers and shepherds. And as the number of agriculturalists increased and spread over the earth, they created an ecoimpact far exceeding that of the primal peoples. Forests and grasslands were replaced with large areas typically planted with a single crop such as wheat. Poor management of such cleared areas allowed vital topsoil to wash away and pollute streams and lakes with silt. Land clearing destroyed and altered the habitats of plant and animal species, endangering their existence and in some cases causing or hastening their extinction. Irrigation without proper drainage led to the accumulation of salts in topsoil, diminishing soil fertility. Pests that were controlled naturally by the diverse array of species in forests spread much more rapidly in areas planted with a single crop. So the development of agriculture brought about a fundamental modification in human relationship with earth as more people began shifting from gathering and hunting to agricultural production and urban dwelling.

What eventually emerged among some of the agricultural societies in the Old and New Worlds just a few thousand years ago is a so-called "advancement" in human culture—*civilization*—with its complex features: development of a state and a ruling elite, cities, monumental constructions, slave labor, a class system, advances in knowledge (especially mathematics, medicine, and science), art, a division of labor (including the development of a peasantry as food producers), and strong religious beliefs. The latter emphasized a hierarchial system which legitimized and fostered control over people and earth. This earth-dominating theology established a hierarchy with gods at the top, followed by priests, urban dwellers, farmers, slaves, animals, and plants in that order. But even more fundamental changes were soon to follow.

Humans have learned how to find and use more energy in their attempts to change and control the environment. Early humans had to rely on their own muscle power to survive. Agricultural societies eventually learned to use draft animals and later wind and water power to help them exert more control over the land and their food supplies. During the eighteenth century, however, industrial societies made a gigantic leap by discovering how to unlock on a larger scale the chemical energy stored in fossil fuels: coal, oil, and natural gas. The Industrial Revolution had arrived and earth would never be the same again. Mining and logging to provide industries with raw materials have disrupted more of earth's surface and have threatened and endangered more plant and animal species in the last 200 years than were afflicted in all previous human history. By decreasing the need for most people to engage in agriculture, industrialization has caused massive shifts of human population from rural to urban areas, creating a new array of social, political, economic, and environmental issues. Currently this "leaving the land" process continues unabated. Increasingly more of our time, energy, funding, and new forms of technology must be used to correct the ill effects of earlier so-called "advances" or "progress." But finally we are waking to the dangers of clinging to a faith that science and technology can forever resolve the problems they created in the first place. "The power of science and technology is undeniable, but their consequences are far wider than we ever foresee."[7]

Perhaps it should not be any surprise that in the late 1960's the general public was unaware of the term ecology, a word coined by the German zoologist Ernst Haeckel to mean "the relationship of the animal to its organic and inorganic environment." Of course, the origin of the word is the Greek *oikos*, meaning "home," "household," or "place to live." As a topic of public discussion, ecology stirred little attention, even among most biologists. But by 1972 ecology had become a household term, thanks in large measure to Earth Day I on April 22, 1970. Still ecology was misused and misunderstood. Too many people failed to comprehend that ecology studies the interrelationships of all organisms and their environment and that "human beings must be included among the species so studied." They only vaguely realized that the relationship is two-way, that just as the environment has an impact on the organism, so an organism has an impact on its environment. Finally, the shattering view of earth from outer space forced on us the realization that *earth is finite* and that what it is and what it contains are all that we have.

Because it deals with life, ecology has been considered a part of biology. In the early part of the twentieth century the major introductory path to biology was "nature study" or "field science" (Fig. 1). This was a time when people were just awakening to the world around them. Earth had ceased to be an enemy; in fact, it had been conquered. Fields were cleared, great forests subdued, and wildlife was no longer a threat. The conservation movement was budding and nature study was a part of nearly every school curriculum. Out of this background of close encounter with earth and an interest in life, the science of biology emerged. But as the country experienced World Wars I and II, it became more urbanized and industrialized and people lost contact with earth. Interest in biology from a field approach also declined.

Part of the reason for the swing away from natural history lies in biology itself. For a long time traditional biology started and ended with the naming of organisms. It was largely descriptive taxonomy, weak in quantitative data, and lacking the strong conceptual foundation that marked physics, chemistry, and mathematics. As a result, natural history, once a rigorous subject, lost its position among the sciences and became equated with emotionalism and superficiality.

With the environmental awakening in the early 1970's, however, interest in natural science began to revive. Books on natural history and ecology have become popular sellers and environmental studies and education have returned to many classrooms. More people are seeking a closer contact with earth and a lifestyle more sustainable for this and future generations.

So natural history evolved into ecology and ecology into a science that has at least entered the public consciousness. Where the old focal point was kinds of species or taxonomy, the new focus is the essence of living—nonliving systems at the ecosystem, ecoregion, and ecosphere levels (Fig. 1). As this trend in ecoawareness intensifies, at least three results are occurring: 1) At the autecology level more emphasis is being given to the "how and why" the individual human is interrelated and interconnected to family, neighborhood, community, ecosystem, ecoregion, and ecosphere. What is emerging is a "deep personal ecology," an ecology of inner-self or self-consciousness, a perception of reality that each of us is earth conscious. 2) Simultaneously, at the synecology level more attention is being placed on how the all-encompassing earth community—the ecosphere—interrelates to the ultimate source of everything: the universe (Fig. 1). Such a raising of human consciousness at the micro and macro levels simultaneously is an ecospiritual venture that not only answers the questions of who we are, why we are here, and where we are going, but also prepares us for entering a new ecocentric geological era, what Berry calls the "Ecozoic."[8] 3) Finally, although young as a science, ecology already has identified powers, strands, principles, and laws that reflect the discoveries of postmodern science and the principles of the universe. Such fundamental truths will be used to analyze the worldviews of primal peoples and Judeo-Christianity and are briefly listed here.

Although there are many powers in the universe, several "cardinal powers" are critical for interrelating earth and its inhabitants to the cosmos. Primal peoples have known about these powers for thousands of years, but only recently have we discovered them. For example, *air* moves as wind which represents the expansion of being, the dynamic of celebration. *Water*, on the other hand, is a liquid that readily absorbs, assimilates, and represents awareness and sensitivity in general. *Soil* is the nurturing power of life, of fecundity of being from the microscopic to the gigantic. The dynamic of *memory* is expressed in the way earth "remembers" four and one-half billion years of evolutionary history. Plant and animal life-forms represent ultimate imagination, exploration, discovery, and freedom of expression and activity. By looking at the night sky on a clear night one cannot help but reflect upon *allurement.* The night sky is something special because it is the space-time when most of us can feel and see this cosmic attraction. Finally, the *light* of our day-star, the sun, is the greatest power of all because it forces us to probe the meaning of self in direct relationship with everything else. All life is dependent upon the day-star, the sun. Thus by making physical and psychic contact with these elements of earth, we permit these powers to enter our consciousness.

There are six strands in the web of nonlife-life, each interrelated, interconnected, interdependent, and interbonded to each other and to the whole: variety-similarity, patterns, interactions-interdependencies, continuity-change, cycles-rhythms, and evolution-adaptation. Each strand listed in pairs is on a continuum, again reflecting the continuum of all the principles of the universe.

Finally, the principles and laws of postmodern ecology are:[9]

* Each species and each organism can tolerate only a certain range of environmental conditions (principle of tolerance range).
* No population can keep growing indefinitely (principle of carrying capacity).
* Earth is not only more complex than we think, but more complex than we can ever think (principle of complexity).
* We can never do just one thing on earth, for everything we do creates effects that are often unpredictable (first law).
* Everything is interconnected and intermingled with everything else (second law).
* Any chemical that we produce should not interfere with any of earth's natural biogeochemical cycles in ways that degrade earth's life-support systems (third law).
* Earth's life-support systems can take a lot of stress and abuse, but there are limits (law of limits).

CURRENT WORLDVIEWS

Although rarely found today, the living exemplifications of primal peoples have a different worldview than contemporary Western society. Humanity is not the center of the universe nor the measure of all things. Humans are the weakest and most uncertain element of the cosmos, but they are nevertheless conscious of its order and their role of responsibility in it. Human thought has no other objective than to discover how they are placed in the world (not why) and how to adjust to it, lest cosmic orderliness and human existence be compromised. The feeling of belonging to a whole is expressed at first by submission of the individual to the band, clan, or tribe. In fact, the individual exists solely as a member of a group or people. In defining this group ethic, the band not only includes living and dead people but also plants, animals, all physical elements, and the entire cosmos.[10]

> Each individual is an organic member of the group, which is itself an organ of the All. The sum of these solidarities weaves a web that includes the known world. This universe is perceived as a great living body in which the behavior of each group and of each individual favors or compromises the existence of totality. Ordinary actions become rituals, and these are the symbolic and real responses of the cosmogony in which are expressed the participation in the relationship of the human to the All. Each attitude reproduces a universal model, and the ensemble of models constitutes the order of the universe.

Nearly everywhere one searches in the "tribal-based" cultures of the world, there is evidence of a striving for a harmonious equilibrium with earth. Since most of the cultures of this consciousness had their origins in gathering, scavenging, fishing, and hunting as opposed to agriculture, a higher continuity to principles of harmonious equilibrium persists through space-time. Even when many of these cultures moved to low-technology horticulture, the bond with earth systems was central to the many institutions that they created. Unity with earth was paramount for the primal peoples and thus separation became an expression of deviance. Bonding to earth and all its forms represented far less an expression of "primitive belief and superstition" than it was a true expression of the most poignant spirituality. Native cosmology is unconcerned with making distinctions among a supreme being, humanity, and other elements of reality. Instead, a divine spirit is in everything, everywhere. Humans are agents of a spiritual process that stems from the universe and permeates all levels of being.

Suzuki and Knudston list some fundamental qualities of Native ecological perspectives and contrast them with conventional scientific ones:[11] Natives view the earth as sacred, science as profane or mere property; Natives have a sense of reverence for earth vs. human domain over it; A spirit is dispersed throughout the cosmos vs. a spirit concentrated in a single monotheistic Supreme Being; Humans are assigned enormous responsibility for sustaining harmonious relationships with earth vs. unbridled license to follow personal or economic whims; Humans have an obligation to maintain the balance and health of earth as a solemn daily spiritual duty vs. abstract ethical imperatives that can be ignored as one chooses; Natives emphasize the need for reciprocity (routine gratitude and sacrifice) to earth in return for benefits derived from it vs. unilateral extractions; Nature's bounty is considered to be precious gifts embedded in its living web vs. "natural resources" passively awaiting exploitation; Natives honor earth through daily personal prayer vs. only intermittently, if at all; Wisdom and ecoethics are discernible in the structure and functioning of earth vs. a lofty product of human reason far removed from earth; The universe is a dynamic interplay of elusive and ever-changing natural forces vs. an array of static physical objects; The universe is alive and animated by a single, unifying life-force vs. reducing the universe to progressively smaller conceptual bits and pieces; Natives accept that the universe will always possess unfathomable mysteries vs. the cosmos is completely decipherable to the rational human mind; finally that the proper human relationship with earth is a continuous dialogue (that is, a two-way, horizontally equal communication between humans and other elements) vs. a monologue (a one-way, vertical imperative) between unequals.

As Suzuki and Knudtson conclude:[12]

> Thus, this ancient, culturally diverse aboriginal consensus on the ecological order and the integrity of nature might justifiably be described as a "sacred ecology" in the most expansive, rather than in the scientifically restrictive, sense of the word "ecology." For it looks upon the totality of patterns and relationships at play in the universe as utterly precious, irreplaceable, and worthy of the most profound human veneration.

This inherent spiritual dimension of primal peoples does not imply that their "nature-wisdom" is somehow naively romantic, ethereal, or disconnected from ordinary life. Their knowledge about earth and the cosmos is firmly rooted in reality, in keen long-term personal observation, interaction, thought, and sharpened by the daily rigors of uncertain survival. Its validity rests largely upon the authority of hard-won personal experience. The junction between knowledge and experience is tight, continuous, and dynamic, giving rise to "truths" that are likely to be correspondingly intelligent, fluid, and vibrantly "alive."

Today with little notice more vast archives of knowledge and expertise of earth-human processes are slipping into oblivion, leaving humanity in danger of losing its past and jeopardizing its future. Stored in the memories of elders, healers, midwives, farmers, fishermen, and hunters in the estimated 15,000 cultures of primal peoples remaining on earth is an enormous trove of wisdom.

This largely undocumented knowledge base is humanity's lifeline to a time when people accepted nature's authority and learned through trial, error, and observation. The secrets of primal peoples' success in long-term survival have been living in harmony and balance with nature, attaining synchrony between natural and human systems, and achieving a transcendence of the separateness between human and planet/cosmic systems. But earth's original peoples are dying out because of world development or being absorbed into modern civilization. As these primal peoples vanish so does their rich irreplaceable knowledge of earth-human processes. How can we as fellow human beings, as religious people, let these special peoples' generations of accumulated wisdom slip into oblivion? Because Western society's worldview is opposed to that of primal peoples', reinforced by an attitude and value system that states the human is the center of the universe. More specifically, we believe that humans are the source of all value and nature (separate from us) exists solely for our use. Human success is based on material wealth which implies that production and consumption must rise endlessly because we have a right to an ever-increasing material way of living. Furthermore, minerals and energy resources are unlimited since all we need is better technology to discover and exploit such resources. We need not adapt ourselves to the natural world (again separate from us) since we can remake it or substitute for it to suit our own needs through science and technology. The most important nation, therefore, is the one that can command and use the largest share of the world's resources and the ideal person is the self-made individualist who does her/his own thing, hurting supposedly no one in the process.

Although most of us would disagree with these values, we act individually and collectively as if we did, and that is what counts. Further, shockingly in this period of eco-awakening, American Christians are still little concerned about the eco-threats to earth and its life-support systems. Christians generally have little awareness of the larger consequences of the mass destruction that is taking place on earth.

Why isn't Christianity dealing with the eco-crisis in a priority way? Why hasn't theology shown any effective responsibility for the state and fate of earth? Shouldn't those of us who are Christians be truly moved by the beauty, splendor, and magnificent biological diversity of earth? And if we are so moved, shouldn't we honor earth in a profound way and stop its destruction now? That we haven't done so reveals that a disturbance exists at a more basic level of consciousness and on a greater order of magnitude than we dare admit to ourselves or even think about. It seemingly is deeply imbedded in our Christian theological tradition, in our very language, in our Christian worldview of reality.

In general, there has been a lack of interest in ecology on the part of America's theologians, Protestant and Roman Catholic. A bibliographic study by Sheldon in 1986 revealed a paucity of titles on nature, creation, and the environment in theological journals prior to 1967 and surprisingly few books.[13] Most of the works were anthropocentric in outlook, although some had clear statements of what presently is referred to as "environmental stewardship." Only eight works were located with publication dates before 1950, the most significant book being *The Holy Earth* by Bailey in 1915 which mentioned stewardship and caring for creation. Joseph Sittler's books, *A Theology of Earth* in 1954 and *Nature and Grace* in 1964, were considered major luminaries in the theology of nature and Baer's *Land Misuse: A Theological Concern* in 1966 was among the first theological books to see the need for church involvement in land use issues. So some environmental awareness was present in American Christianity.

But note what happened in 1967 when Lynn White published his article "The Historical Roots of Our Ecological Crisis" in *Science*. From 1969 on numerous papers were direct responses to White's accusation that environmental attitudes of the Judeo-Christian tradition stemming from the book of Genesis in the Bible were responsible for our current ecocrisis. There is no question that White's paper, perhaps more than any other single factor, was responsible for raising environmental consciousness in the American Christian press. Unfortunately, American Christian theology, as a discipline, only responded when it was "hit where it hurt" and failed to react to earlier environmental alarms going back to the nineteenth century. Although Earth Day 1970 did raise the ecoconscience of the nation as a whole, few papers by Christian authors cite it directly. In fact, the theology of nature, creation, or ecology as a subject still remains ill defined on this side of the Atlantic. And although there has been more written in Europe, no synthesis has occurred and few contributors are aware of the literature waiting to be tapped. Thus a distinct theology of earth, nature, or creation does not presently exist. Until there is a formulated theology, how can pastors be informed? Until pastors are trained in the theology of ecology or the theology of nature, who will instruct the laity? American Christian seminaries and schools of theology should accept this intellectual challenge with haste and stay clear of tunnel vision by incorporating an interdisciplinary approach to the tasks of having ecologists and theologians working together. It is long past the time when theologians should be talking only to other theologians.

Theology must pay serious attention to the view of reality operative in its culture. If it does not, it becomes irrelevant. The problem with Christianity today is that it has not kept abreast with the current view of reality, the worldview of postmodern science. Yet what postmodern science is telling us—that the universe is a whole with all things interrelated—has been common eco-spiritual knowledge for most of human history and prehistory. Christians are among the last to recognize this truth because its theological tradition has been shaped within the worldview of a static universe. As Edwards says:[14]

> The great theological synthesis of St. Thomas Aquinas, for example, was formed within a culture which took for granted that the world was fixed and static, that the Sun and the Moon and the five known planet stars revolved around the Earth in seven celestial spheres, moved by angels, that beyond these seven spheres there were the three heavens, the firmament (the starry heaven), the crystalline heaven and the empyrean, and that there was a place in the heavenly spheres for paradise. It was assumed that human beings were the center of the universe, that Europe was the center of the world and that the Earth and its resources were immense and without any obvious limits.

The theological shift between the mindset of Aquinas' day and postmodern science's today is enormous but the gap has been narrowing since 1967. American theologians have reinterpreted traditional doctrine in light of the idea of stewardship which has remained a consistent theological theme to the present.[15] The "dominion" granted in Genesis 1:28 did not connote despotism, they said, but trusteeship. For Biblical support the stewardship contingent goes to Genesis 2:15 in which God placed the first man in the Garden of Eden "to till it and keep it." This, they contend, constitutes a directive for humanity to take care of or serve the rest of creation. Still, a large part of the Christian stewardship argument is anthropocentric in character: take care of earth or you will either perish or be punished by an angry God. Guilt figured as a mainstay of the appeal. But latent in modern stewardship is the idea that earth is God's, not the human's, and thus it is morally wrong to abuse it regardless of the consequences for humanity. Earth or nature has its own intrinsic, as well as utilitarian, value and rights.[16]

> While it is important to attempt to reassert the stewardship motif in its pristine form, it is also necessary to strike at the heart of the problem, to confront impoverished and impoverishing individualism with the relational anthropology of the Jewish and Christian traditions. The crisis of the environment is directly linked to the problem of humanization. For unless nonhuman beings are treated as "thou," human beings will be treated as "it". . . . Far more adequate and far more faithful to the Christian tradition is the reappropriation of the companionship motif of the biblical creation stories.

Human responsibility toward creation must move beyond stewardship for the sake of both theology and ecology. Theologically, stewardship has been open to a deist interpretation whereby the Creator is seen as having begun creation and then handed over care for it to humanity. When the image of stewardship dominates our imagination, the Creator can be removed from the scene as humans are given oversight of earth and move center stage in the drama of creation. Too easily the duty of caring for creation becomes the task of "shaping and controlling our world." Just as a steward is unanxious for the master's presence lurking over his shoulder, so humanity is content to keep the Creator in a distant heaven. Companionship, on the other hand, evokes an ecological attitude toward creation. And the difference in attitude will be reflected in an environmental ethnic grounded on a relational anthropology, according to Himes and Himes.[17]

Although stronger, the companionship motif is still inadequate to alter the Christian cosmology so prevalent today. However divine, God is seen as fundamentally a transcendent being, existing apart from or outside the universe. In fact, God created and has power or dominion over the universe. Humans are connected with the divine but they also have to transcend the world of material reality to reach the divine realm. Hence, there is a sense of detachment from earth, for human destiny lies beyond earth in a heavenly realm. True, earth and its various elements are a reflection of the divine and thus are sacred, but the earth itself and its manifestations are not spiritual, only material. Therefore, if earth is detached from God and us, we humans are free to probe it through science, use, control, and change it through technology to suit our whims.

This worldview is a fallback to the tradition of the "descent metaphor" and "spiritual motif" of the biblical tradition as interpreted by Origen, Aquinas, and other early fathers of the church as well as more recent theologians.[18] But there is another way of reading the Scriptures, such as through the eyes of Ireneaus, Augustine, St. Francis of Assisi, Luther, and Calvin, who stressed the ecological motif.[19]

> Standing in this theological tradition with one's thought shaped primarily not by the metaphor of ascent but primarily by the metaphor of migration to a good land and the metaphor of fecundity, one will as a matter of course look to the dynamics of Hebraic faith, to the proclamation of Jesus, and to the theology of Paul and the Pauline authors of Colossians and Ephesians as the normative biblical tradition. For this way of thinking, when all has been said, the divine economy is, at once, the divine ecology. Creation and redemption, redemption and creation, are symmetrical, held in unity by the overarching and undergirding power and wisdom of God's gracious lordship.

In the 1990's theologians have no choice but to face up to the ecocrisis and its meaning for Christianity. Geologian Thomas Berry, in searching for a new synthesis of science and faith, has proposed a new cosmology, a new story—*The Universe Story*—which is in sync with postmodern science and creation spirituality. Denis Edwards has focused more directly than Berry on what the Christian tradition itself can offer by reexamining Karl Rahner's contributions to theology in the book *Jesus and the Cosmos*. Sallie McFague has developed the idea of the universe as *The Body of God*, the title of her 1994 book. These and other current explorations are challenging attempts to close the theological gap between traditional and postmodern Christianity.

There are two sides to theology-ecology. The religious side, theo-ecology, presents us with an accurate object lesson in correlationship. If we have any doubt that we are bonded to nature and its life-support systems, and to one another, members of a single family living in one common home—the earth—a long explanatory examination would suggest more than a few second thoughts. Every living creature on earth depends upon, and is shaped by, the DNA molecule which had its origin with the start of life itself. Biochemistry has demonstrated that there are fundamental similarities at the molecular level among all living creatures from bacteria to human beings. Molecular biology has demonstrated "not only that the prime carriers of hereditary information in all living organisms are the nucleic acids (DNA and RNA) but also that the code that translated the information from base sequence in proteins (and thence to their structure and function) was the same in all living organisms."[20]

All living creatures are interconnected with each other and with the atmosphere, hydrosphere, and lithosphere in such a way that each part of the system depends upon the other. Together they form the ecosphere (Fig. 1) which makes life possible and which has the possibility of sustaining life. Recall the symbiotic relationship, the unity that was established, among land-sea-Inupiat. Or take the Aborigines of Australia, who, after fifty-thousand years of occupying the same land, have not destroyed forests, nor polluted water, nor endangered wildlife, nor caused toxic contamination of land-sea-air, and all the while have received abundant food and shelter. To this day they live long, productive, healthy lives and leave spiritually confident.[21] As Carmody stated:[22]

> Cosmic history may seem slow to us tiny onlookers who only witness a millisecond of the universal day. In itself cosmic history is constant change, as continents shift, stars recede, mountains thrust to the skies. . . . But nature or the cosmos is not something outside us. We are something inside it, parts of the cosmic whole. Consequently, we must make religious, ultimate sense of nature, working out its place in our scheme of things. Like our friends, our family members, our enemies, our bodies, our selves, nature begs correlation with the love at the center of our faith.

Eco-theology, on the other hand, is concerned with the whole cosmos as fundamental unity in the one Creator who creates it, sustains and empowers it, and brings the whole to completion. Matter-life-consciousness form one single history of evolution. In this special theological scheme of things, the human is understood as the cosmos come to self-consciousness, "for it is the nature of matter to develop toward consciousness, and the material universe achieves its own self-awareness in humans and in human communities. The history of the universe continues in the human community, in culture, and in human interactions with the Earth."[23] Evolutionary change is empowered and sustained through the dynamic impulse of the divine being operating from within creation. The purpose of creation, therefore, is the fecundity, richness, and diversity of all that is from the Creator and sustained by the Spirit. God is the breath of each and every creature (divine immanence) and God is the energy empowering the entire universe (divine transcendence). By its very nature, however, Christian eco-theology focuses on the incarnation process of Jesus' birth, death on the cross, resurrection, redemption, and salvation as the universe reaching the climax of its history. Jesus is truly part of the history of the cosmos, of the earth, the most critical moment in the biological evolution of the universe. Creation is the unification of all life, the whole universe, in Christ. This is the mystery of God's will, the salvation, unification, and gathering of the cosmos in Christ. As Edwards states:[24]

> In the resurrection, Jesus of Nazareth becomes the Cosmic Christ. The risen Christ is the power of the divine at the heart of the creation, but this divine power is not mediated through the humanity of Jesus, the first fruits of the new creation.

Resurrection of the body puts the emphasis where it should be in eco-theology, on the physical basis of all life, all creation. Creation and redemption are understood as two moments in the one process of God's self-communication with the world. "In Jesus of Nazareth, God accepts the cosmos, and the cosmos accepts God, and these two acceptances constitute a unity."[25]

ONE STORY

The world views of postmodern science, ecology, primal peoples, and Christianity are in the process of converging on one truth, one reality, One Story. The overall powerful theme of interrelated matter and energy within a singular, whole universe is evident in all these world-views. This ecological context is expressed vividly in the interrelated, interconnected, interdependent, interpenetrated, and interbonded principles of the universe that permeate everything, everywhere; in the vibrant eco-spiritual continuity of the primal peoples over 100 millennia and in the rich traditional roots of Judeo-Christianity. There is a fundamental division between "Native" and Western ecological perspectives, perhaps best described as "sacred ecology" vs. "secular ecology." Despite this difference, both worldviews are parallel modes of acquiring knowledge about the universe, both a distinct, positive science. Also, spokespersons of both perspectives are issuing similar messages about the underlying interrelationship of all nonlife-life to the whole cosmos and warning about the deteriorating state of natural systems on earth.

Christianity's roots are rich and deep. Thus it is the responsibility of its current theologians to interconnect such troves of traditional wisdom with postmodern science's and primal peoples' views of reality. To help in this mission, Christianity always has had two great books of revelation: Sacred Scripture and creation itself. It must be emphasized, however, that any biblical theology of creation has to embrace the whole Bible from Genesis to Revelation in order to achieve a holistic perspective. The creation story is a powerful proclamation that creation is understood in terms of *interrelationship* between a Creator and all creation. In light of primal peoples' wisdom, Christians should consider themselves not merely companions but earthly kin, sisters and brothers, to all other creatures. Humans are made in the image of God, not because we are above the rest of creation, but so we can be in interpersonal relationship with the Creator's self, who takes delight in all creation, who is continuously engaged with creation, sustaining and empowering all things through eternal love. Thus the Creator is simultaneously immanently transcendent-transcendently immanent.

But the Bible is only the first of the two great volumes of divine revelation. Creation itself is all around us and needs our immediate attention. We are profoundly responsible for the rest of creation because we now have the full picture, the One Story. That story suggests a decentering of the human as superior being to recentering the human as creation come to self-consciousness at this given point in space-time. Matter has come to consciousness in humankind, in conscious thought, self-reflection, community, culture, science, art, and love. We have the knowledge and the power to help the process of the ongoing creation continue or destroy ourselves and many other species. We have the freedom to choose life or death for our species, but regardless, earth will continue with or without us. Our function at this crucial turning point in the creation process is to choose. The questions are: Will we accept our proper place in the eco-scheme of things of belonging to the whole? When, where, and how do we start rethinking and redoing just about everything in our lives?

A sense of oneness with earth, our only true home, and all of its life-forms is a necessary first step. An informed sensibility is the prerequisite second step. We must start with placed self at home within the family unit first, then the neighborhood, congregation, and community. We must redefine what it means to be human in the One Story so that we can reinhabit earth in a sustainable-livable way, that is, abide by the "home rules" of ecology. We must literally reconnect with earth through our senses by giving full attention to one other being than self. If we were to give other beings, even those who are indifferent to us, full attention, we would most probably act differently than we do presently toward them; for from this kind of knowing follows a doing most appropriate to what and who that being is. We must commence raising ecological self-consciousness in stages from initial meeting one other being, to full commitment, to changing one's values, attitudes, and perceptions of reality. Stages in that process start with an inner feeling and/or an outward curiosity, to initial discovery, to awareness, to a sensitivity, to a formal or informal education, to understanding, to appreciation, to perception, to a change of values and attitudes, to responsibility, to a commitment, to a personal ecoethic (credo and action), to personal fulfillment by practicing daily respect, responsibility, reciprocity, and reverence to earth. All of these stages are on a continuum and all individuals in any society are situated in one of these stages. One can see by examining these various stages how difficult it is to promote eco-ethics, for there is no shortcut in attaining that goal. Most citizens of earth are stuck at one of the early stages of the process. However, if we possess awe for creation by showing humility, thanksgiving, and love for earth through daily acts of preserving, restoring, healing, caring, sharing, and celebrating, the result will be a balance and harmony, a dynamic equilibrium of sustainability-livability between earth and humans.

If there is hope for a rediscovery of earth and spirit, it will not be found in looking back to an innocence once lost, a simplistic return to the paradise of Eden. Instead it will demand a reaching through and beyond the harshest criticism leveled by the whole of the Western spiritual tradition. Talk of a paradigm shift won't do. Such talk allows us to think we are still in control. It implies that we can fix our thinking. We can rearrange our assumptions. We can retain our species' position as primary decision-maker. We can treat other species as though they were here to serve our purposes only. The paradigm shift illusion is thinking that we can think ourselves out of our present dilemma. The illusion is the belief that what is called for now is some great, new intellectual effort. What is really called for is simple honesty: that the human has met its match in earth and that our species is ignorant in earthly matters. It will require a *metanoia*, a profound spiritual transformation and a turning away from all efforts to manage the divine eternal mystery. Only then may it be possible to encounter a second naivete, a renewed sense of wonder glimpsed within the myriad sites and life of sacred earth.

Metanoia can be a fleeting experience unless reinforced by action. And action not based on a fundamental change in thinking can be easily misdirected. Christians need to achieve balance between changed thinking and changed lifestyle, between spiritual deepening and worldly action.

One of the recent discoveries of postmodern science is that all matter and energy everywhere in the cosmos have a tendency to seek out higher and higher levels of organization and complexity. Human beings, as the cosmos come to self-consciousness, emerge as part of this self-organizing movement of the universe. They share a common heritage with the whole cosmos, from their origin in the primordial fireball to their evolutionary relationship as kin with all life on earth. For in the end, there is only One Story, the sacred story of the Divine-Holy-Nameless-One.

Fig. 1. Traditional Levels of the science of ecology by Gene Wilhelm, Ph. D. 1993.

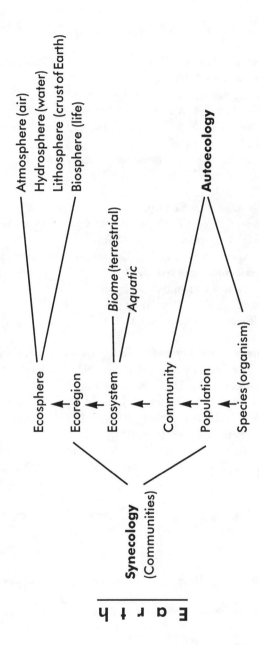

Ecosystem: A life community and abiotic environment plus system of complex coordinated unities. Can be at the micro to the macro level. Ecosystem is the normal unit of space used by the ecologist and it is *the newest emphasis in biodiversity preservation.*

Ecology: The science that studies the interactions, interrelationship, interconnections, and interdependencies of organisms to their environment and the processes involved in such exchanges. The science of the essence (nature) of living/non-living systems of Earth: *the new scientific focal point*

Natural History: The study and description of different plant and animal organisms and minerals of Earth: emphasis on taxonomic classification: *the old focal point.*

Human Curiosity: The human species always has noticed differences in biota (native plants and animals) in time and place on Earth. Human curiosity was the beginning of science.

NOTES

1. David Suzuki and Peter Knudtson, *Wisdom of the Elders* (New York: Bantam Books, 1992), p. xxix.
2. Gene Wilhelm, "Extinction is Forever," *The Egg: An Eco-Justice Quarterly*, Vol. 13, No. 3 (Summer 1993), pp. 4–5 & 18.
3. Gene Wilhelm, "Attaining Eco-Ethics through the Senses," *The Egg: An Eco-Justice Quarterly*, Vol. 10, No. 4 (Winter 1990–1991), pp. 4–9.
4. Sallie McFague, *The Body of God: An Ecological Theology* (Minneapolis: Fortress Press, 1993), p. 17.
5. Denis Edwards, *Made from Stardust: Exploring the Place of Human Beings within Creation* (Victoria, Australia: Collins Dove, 1992), p. 38.
6. McFague, *The Body of God*, p. 16.
7. Suzuki and Knudtson, *Wisdom of the Elders*, p. xxx.
8. Brian Swimme and Thomas Berry, "The Ecozoic Era," Chapter 13 in *The Universe Story* (San Francisco: Harper, 1992), pp. 241–261.
9. G. Tyler Miller, Jr., *Living in the Environment* (Belmont, CA: Wadsworth Publishing Co., 1990), inside front cover and pp. 150–151.
10. Joseph Goetz, S.J., "Man in Primitive Religions," in *A Christian Anthropology* (St. Meinard, IN: Abbey Press, 1974), p. 8.
11. Suzuki and Knudtson, *Wisdom of the Elders*, pp. 16–18.
12. *Ibid.*, pp. 18–19.
13. Joseph K. Sheldon, *Rediscovery of Creation: A Bibliographical Study of the Church's Response to the Environmental Crisis* (Metuchen, NJ: The American Theological Library Association and The Scarecrow Press, 1992).
14. Denis Edwards, *Jesus and the Cosmos* (Mahwah, NJ: Paulist Press, 1991), p.3.
15. Roderick Frazier Nash, *The Rights of Nature: A History of Environmental Ethics* (Madison: University of Wisconsin Press, 1988), pp. 96–110.
16. Michael J. Himes and Kenneth R. Himes, "The Sacrement of Creation: Toward an Environmental Theology," *Commonweal*, Vol. CXVII, No. 2 (Jan. 26, 1990), p. 46.
17. *Ibid.*, p. 46.
18. H. Paul Santmire, *The Travail of Nature: The Ambigious Ecological Promise of Christian Theology* (Philadelphia: Fortress Press, 1985), p. 217.
19. *Ibid.*, p. 217.
20. Denis Edwards, *Made from Stardust*, p. 44.
21. Marlo Morgan, *Mutant Message Down Under* (New York: Harper Collins Publishers, 1994), p. 111.
22. John Carmody, *Holistic Spirituality* (New York: Paulist Press, 1983), pp. 17–18.
23. Edwards, *Jesus and the Cosmos*, p. 107.
24. *Ibid.*, p. 111.
25. *Ibid.*, p. 111.

Fig. 1. Traditional Levels of the Science of Ecology. Modified from Eugene P. Odum, *Ecology and Our Endangered Life Support Systems* (Sunderland, MA: Sinauer Associates, Inc., Publishers, 1993), p. 26.

How to Love a Worm?
Biodiversity:
Franciscan Sprituality and Praxis

James F. Edmiston, OFM

Casual observation and common sense indicate that numerous and unique creatures live on the earth. Not only is there such diversity, but no two living organisms have ever been exactly alike or experienced the universe in exactly the same way. Individuality is normative!

The diversity of living organisms overwhelms the human senses and peeks the imagination. Scientists attempt to describe and categorize the living diversity. Theologians and philosophers attempt to explain the implications of such a creation. Diversity and individuality influence our personal are corporate behaviors. To observe, explore, and attempt some understanding of this diversity and individuality as expressed through living creatures can enrich our lives.

The purpose of this work is to acknowledge our experiences of biodiversity, and look into the Franciscan tradition for some theological underpinnings to support the preservation of biodiversity. Ideas only take us so far, practical suggestions for actually experiencing and teaching others about biodiversity will be made.

BIODIVERSITY

Humans live on a planet containing at least 1 million and possibly as many as 10 to 100 million different, distinct life forms—species.[1] Scientists and philosophers struggle with the process of separating, categorizing, and identifying the "types" of life and how to distinguish between the distinctly different species. Regardless of how the taxonomists proceed to describe the differences in life forms, from molecular to organismal, through population and community levels of organization, the diversity of life on planet earth is rich. From the perspective of an individual human person—awareness of biodiversity is wonderfully overwhelming!

People of the twentieth-century who dedicate themselves to studying the diversity and distribution of life tell us the number of different species is drastically declining.[2] Much of the decline is related to activities of our human species. As our population grows, we occupy more space, and our activities destroy and consume resources other species need to survive.

Accepting that the diversity of earth's life forms is declining, why is this a concern and what is our response? Just asking the question implies that we have some interest, and that we are interconnected with other life forms. These interconnections influence what we eat, what we wear, what medicines we can develop, and even how we come to aesthetically appreciate the living earth.

Commercial and medical implications of declining biodiversity have been clearly established. The realization that many new human medicines come from endangered tropical plants has caused grave concern.[3] But, the question of declining biodiversity transcends our anthropocentric focus, as people begin to realize that personal human life decisions have implications for other life forms.

Books have recently been written that explore the large scale and subtle implications for finding answers to declining biodiversity. E. O. Wilson particularly addresses the interrelationship between biological processes, sociological systems and the reduction of biodiversity. Recommendations presented in Wilson's book involve soliciting support for national and international programs to inventory and preserve the remaining biodiversity.[4]

Beyond these sophisticated and succinctly written popular materials with their wide-ranging proposals for programs, the question remains to be experienced and understood from a personal context. To focus on people in the United States with Western philosophical and spiritual backgrounds who are engaging in a process of formulating responses to the issue of declining biodiversity, I would like to consider: How do people in the U.S. generally view their relationship to creation? How does the Franciscan tradition within Western spirituality inform us about biodiversity? What practical methodologies are available to us that can assist our understanding, and help us to build appropriate relationships with other species? While the effects of reducing biodiversity are seen globally, these questions face each human person, right now.

PERSONAL RELATIONSHIPS WITH CREATION

To appreciate someone or something, we must know them. We must enter into relationship with the person or creature, with the painting or the sunset. In some way, a person, event, creature, or concept must be experienced, our brains must be neurologically stimulated, if we are to develop a relationship that includes our effective and affective dimensions. To know is the first step to appreciation and love.

The air we breathe and the chemical components of our bodies are continuously cycled through the bodies of almost all living creatures. Such intimate connections often go unnoticed. Yet, even people whose lives are centered on industrial and technological pursuits seem to have an inner-longing for experiences of other living organisms. Notice how people pack up the hiking, camping, and fishing equipment, and clog the urban highways for weekend and vacation returns to nature. Even with these extensive personal, and often highly commercialized "return to nature" adventures—the typical lifestyle within the twentieth-century U.S. society is structured to continuously avoid a person's connections with creation.

Think about a typical day in urban America—most of our time is spent going from one temperature and humidity controlled space to another, rarely do our feet touch the soil, and the extent of our interaction with other living species is at best the recognition of trees in rows along the streets. Daily encounters with other living animals is limited to a glimpse of an urban squirrel or sparrow.

People living in the rural U.S. have similar encounters with other species. U.S. agriculture has become big business. Agricultural fields have become food factories. Natural landscapes have become backdrops for commercial enterprises, rather than integrated components of daily rural life.

Even when we are interacting with other species, our anthropocentric bias shows. The animals we like are "cute as a puppy" or "cuddly as a bear," demonstrating our vertebrate bias. Even the invertebrates which we respect reflect human qualities—"busy as a bee." Colorful butterflies and moths receive some attention, but only as they stimulate our emotions through the visual spectrum. Even colorful creatures are being commercially exploited as components of jewelry and other ornaments. From the perspective of our domesticated anthropocentric lifestyles, rain forests, ecological cycles, invertebrates, and biodiversity remain abstract concepts for most people.

Some efforts to construct artificial rain forests in special buildings, to present a sanitized version of nature through the television media, or to enhance ecological components of educational curriculum indicate that twentieth-century people of the U.S. have not totally ignored our

relationships to other organisms. Every school age child has some exposure to concepts of animals and plants, or photosynthesis and respiration. However, environmental concepts often remain within the abstract
realm of academic training and entertainment. Relationships with other
organisms rarely become integrated conceptual components of daily life.

If our concern for other life forms is genuine, the need exists to create opportunities for each person to enter into relationships with other
creatures, enabling us to experience the earth from another creatures
perspective. To personally know other creatures that are not like us
can enable us to appreciate how our life interconnects with millions of
other life forms.

BIODIVERSITY AND FRANCISCAN SPIRITUALITY

Looking for people from our Western spiritual traditions who
have modeled relationships with other creatures, the most frequently
cited exemplar is Francis of Assisi. He was a thirteenth-century nature
mystic, officially designated as patron of ecology by the Roman Catholic
Church, and presented in Lynn White's publication on the relationship
between culture and the environment as a source for such a model.[5]
Unfortunately, the typical representation of Francis in the U.S. is as a
plaster statue in the middle of a bird bath!

A recent collection of essays emphasizes the wide-ranging influence
of the humble man from Assisi relating that, "As an enormously free
and spontaneous person, he nevertheless adhered faithfully to the institutional church; a fully alive human being, he embraced suffering; a true
lover, he chose celibacy; born into relative affluence, he chose
poverty."[6] Such paradoxes have inspired people to look at the values
behind religious communities, economics, and politics. Francis' life is an
inspirational model of love and simplicity enshrined in an ultimate
respect for each person, each relationship.

Millions of people throughout the last 800 years have resonated
with his approach to life, to creation, and to the divine. A recent *Time*
magazine article presents him as one of the ten most influential people
in history.[7] Francis and his followers have quite possibly inspired more
publications than any other spiritual traditions. Francis' spirituality has
permeated the world.

With the late twentieth-century focus on environmental concerns,

Francis has become an important source of inspiration about creation. Particularly, Francis' "Canticle of the Creatures" has been the source for personal reflections, and critical analysis.[8] Richard Rohr explores Francis' relationship with creation.[9] Keith Warner articulates a connection between Francis' and the philosophical movement of deep ecology.[10]

Declining biodiversity was not a concern for medieval people, but the significance of creatures is a continual theme in many of the early Franciscan writings. Nature themes in the medieval Franciscan sources are systematically explored by Edward Armstrong and Roger Sorrell. Their works clearly present the impression of Francis' contemporaries about his intimate relationships with many different creatures.[11]

Events in Francis' life indicate he not only aesthetically appreciated creation, but he entered into significant relationships with other life forms. Francis attempted to empathically know creation. A summary statement about Francis and his attitude toward creatures is found in the *Legend of Perugia* as,

> "He had so much love and sympathy for them [fire and creatures] that he was disturbed when they were treated without respect. He spoke to them with a great inner and exterior joy, as if they had been endowed by God with feeling, intelligence, and speech."[12]

A key example of Francis disposition is seen when Thomas of Celano tells that as Francis was walking, whenever he noticed a worm crawling across the road, he would gently lift the worm from harms way. The biographer attributes Francis' action to the allegorical representation between Jesus Christ and the worm through an interpretation of Psalm 21:7, "I am a worm, not a man."[13]

Creatures stimulated Francis to reflect upon aspects of God's incarnation. This led Francis to a high level of regard for each creature. For Francis, each creature, regardless of status, commands respect, and elicits a spiritual relationship with people. Through the simple, yet profound act of lifting a worm from the road, Francis experienced incarnation, and became intimately involved with creation.

BIODIVERSITY AND THE FRANCISCAN INTELLECTUAL
TRADITION

From Francis' spirituality, an intellectual tradition emerged through the medieval universities. Bonaventure (1221–1274) and John Duns Scotus (1266–1308) were Francsican Friars and scholars who in their writings represent the philosophical and theological essence of the tradition.[14] The continuing development of the Franciscan intellectual tradition has been characterized by Philotheus Boehner, O.F.M. and reviewed by Zachary Hayes, O.F.M. as critical, scientific, progressive, and practical.[15] Philibert Hoebing, O.F.M. recently showed how the thought of Bonaventure and Scotus were rooted in Francis' intuitions and nature mysticism.[16]

John Duns Scotus developed his concept of "haecceity" which means "thisness" or individuation. "Haecceity" expresses what we already know through experience about the diversity of organisms and the individuality of each living organism. From the concept of individuation comes a further realization that due to complexity, historical progression, and diversity, each individual organism has a unique perspective in history that has never been, and never will be, like the perspective of any other living organism. Kenan Osborne, O.F.M. summarizes this when he wrote, "Scotus makes the claim that individuation must be based in the very substance of a thing or person, not in some accidental aspect of a thing or person."[17] Individuation is how the universe is constructed! And according to Hoebing, "it is this *haecceity* that gives each creature its special value and real worth in the eyes of God."[18] Hoebing quotes Wolter and O'Neill,

> "If we reflect on this Scotistic conception of individuality in the context of what he believes God to be, we discover that it means that God's creative love wanted just this person or this creature to exist, rather than its twin or perfect copy."[19]

Hoebing clearly summarized the Franciscan perspective of creation as

> "Scotus offers a theology and a cosmology according to which the very nature of beauty and order in the universe requires not only a multiplicity of species, but also a number of individuals within a species."[20]

While our experience and aesthetic appreciation of biodiversity provides ample reason for protecting and preserving the multitudinous expressions of life, Scotus and his Franciscan successors offer something more. Their concept of "thisness" would suggest that preserving many different life forms is a way to cooperate with the fundamental substance from which life expressed in the form of individual creatures operates. Here is a *Theology of Biodiversity* that needs to be individually and corporately realized, then we can draw each other into experiences of individuation, and allow this perspective to move us toward biodiversity preservation.

EXPERIENCING INVERTEBRATES

To begin the process of retrieving individuation from our spiritual heritage, each person needs to feel as though they have received a personal invitation to encounter the "thisness" represented in creatures that are not of our species. A role of scientists, and especially scientists who stand with professional feet in both the humanities and biological science disciplines, is to teach and preach about creatures.

A particular focus could be the most numerous creatures that share our world—the invertebrates. Enabling others to teach and to preach through the eyes of a worm or a fly brings us back to Francis' respect for creation melded with our zoological science. Such an "invertebrate" perspective on the world can provide an intriguing view that heightens sensitivity to creation.

A personal sensitivity to biodiversity reduction can emerge if scientists, teachers, and ministers enable people to build relationships with organisms that do not reflect our anthropocentric bias. Over the last 20 years, I have been engaged in those activities, and I offer you a personal perspective, and a few simple exercises that can change, indeed have already changed, the world views of students and parishioners.

HERBERT ZIM, PORCH LIGHTS, AND *NOSTIMA*

As a 5 year old boy, I knew already my life would somehow involve working with or studying insects. Introduced to the insect world through Herbert Zim's Golden Guide Series, I would spend my preschool days filling jars and bottles with many creatures.[21] I fondly remember the thousands of creatures that would fly to our porch lights. I also came to sadly realize that in my lifetime the populations of these common North American species have been reduced because of habitat destruction.

I have been privileged to spend many hours with a group of species humans only know through their taxonomic names as members of the genus *Nostima*. The name *Nostima* being derived from the Greek word meaning "beautiful, elegant"! These minute shore flies have probably only been consciously known by several scores of humans throughout history. Few people have seen their small bodies (1 to 3 mm long) bespectacled with golden and silver patches. They fly on their gossamer wings along the shores of streams and lakes feeding upon patches of blue-green algae. I entered their world, and had to build an intellectual, and even spiritual relationship with these organisms.

Entering their lives, I became personally aware that the entire universe for an individual *Nostima* fly larva is a several square centimeter patch of algae. It has been not only an intellectual curiosity, but a moment of grace and a privilege to see the world from another creatures viewpoint. Similar experiences have recently been published in a series of essays by prominent biologists who began their careers as children in their encounters with invertebrate creatures.[22]

After realizing the perspective of a fly, I was able to acknowledge that the smallest environmental disturbances effect individual living creatures. Such sensitivity led me to change the context from which I view my world. Providing opportunities for such experiences change the way people think of their world, and other forms of life. To begin entering into a relationship with a creature, a person usually must know something about the creature, ideally through a direct and positive encounter.

NETS AND FUNNELS

I often ask groups of people to tell me some animals they know about, and the typical cat, dog, horse, cow examples come to mind. Then, I ask them to tell me some invertebrate animals they know. After a pause, people will begin to think of different insects, and then their favorite seafood will usually come to mind as the remember crabs, shrimp, and clams are invertebrates. Probably most groups of people could only list several hundred, at most a thousand species they have encountered in their lives. Of the 10 million or more different species, daily life in the U.S. would bring us into contact with very few different organisms.

In the most respectful, and least invasive way, people need to have the opportunity to experience the undetected creatures surrounding them. Three uncomplicated, yet effective methods of experiencing biodiversity that can be elaborated in many ways for the pre-school child and adult are (1) yard sweeps, (2) soil extractions, and (3) stream walks.[23]

YARD SWEEPS

Obtain a net. If you don't have access to an educational institution, almost every toy store and department store in the U.S. sells them for less than $5. Go to a domestic "backyard" environment. If you're doing this with a group, ask them to identify any animals that are around them. Most groups will look for squirrels and birds. Take your net, lower the net to the ground in front of you, and begin a back and forth sweeping motion touching the tops of the grass plants with your net. Continue this sweeping motion, move forward through the yard about 10 steps, capture any "invisible" things that may be in the grass.

When people begin this activity for the first time, the usual response is, "He really has lost his marbles, let's get out of here!" But, those who don't run away after experiencing a grown person sweeping through the grass with a net are usually overwhelmed with the quantity and diversity of creatures that have been obtained. Even on the poorest days, the summer North American yard catch includes many (typically several hundred) organisms, including quite a few species of flies, leafhoppers, froghoppers, spiders, gnats, beetles, moths, caterpillars, and many more. The best part of the activity is to see the look on the faces of people, as many for the first time in their lives, experience biodiversity, and it's in their own back yard.

Depending on the reason for doing this activity, the catch can be released or taken back to the lab or kitchen table for further examination. The discussion of insect consciousness and trauma is beyond the scope to this essay. Killing the creatures or confining them for extended periods could defeat the purpose of exposing people to biodiversity. Likewise, be sensitive that many people have learned to fear insects and other small organisms. A discussion of why these harmless animals live in our backyards is a necessary component of exposing people to a new part of their world.

SOIL EXTRACTIONS

The soil under our feet, even in cities, is densely teeming with thousands of different macroscopic, and microscopic organisms. Similar to the yard sweep, an appreciation for the richness and quantity of soil organisms can change how people see their world.

Anyone can easily set up a device called a Berlese Funnel to extract and observe these organisms. Obtain a funnel (any size), a small piece of screen (about 1 square inch) that will fit inside the funnel, a 60 watt desk lamp, and a jar with some rubbing alcohol. Obtain enough soil from the yard to fit inside the funnel, and after putting the piece of screen inside the funnel, place the soil on top of the screen. Place the funnel over the jar with the alcohol, leaving a space between the spout of the funnel and the top of the alcohol. Place this jar and funnel with soil under the lamp. The heat from the lamp will dry the soil, and the organisms will move away from the drying area and eventually fall into the alcohol. Depending on the quantity and wetness of the soil, organisms such as springtails, centipedes, millipedes, diplurans, proturans, and many more will begin to appear in the alcohol, usually within hours after setting up the sampler.

As with the sweep activity, the quantity and quality of life found in the backyard can be overwhelming to people who have never considered that biodiversity is not just on television or in a rain forest.

STREAM WALK

Almost every person I ever met likes to play in water! Taking groups to a stream or pond in search of biodiversity is another overwhelmingly positive experience for those who have never been exposed to this part of their world. The setting will depend on the availability of access to a water body, but usually local park service personnel or environmental groups can help.

Aided with jars and bottles, and ideally white enamel pans, looking for organisms under stones and rocks and among the vegetation in a stream or a pond can produce a richly rewarding experience. Carefully done, the disturbance of the creatures and area can be even less than that caused by a heavy rainstorm. To see stoneflies, mayflies, dragonflies, damselflies, beetles, and worms face-to-face as they live in a stream can effect human thinking and behavior patterns.

Real-life experiences of biodiversity can part the veil of culture, and connect people with other life forms. To begin a relationship with the animals and plants that live with us is a first step to awareness of problems caused when habitats such as streams are destroyed. These few simple exercises if engaged by those who care—parents, ministers, and teachers—can be an important first step in helping people to understand the need for building relationships with other creatures.

CONNECTIONS: SPIRITUALITY AND SCIENCE

Science and spirituality are mostly considered to be distinct and separate approaches used to construct meaning from our experiences of the world. However, these distinct approaches rarely come together in the lives of most twentieth-century U.S. people. Each day we are confronted with the systematic empirical observations collected through scientific methodology that describe the effects we have on the world and upon its life. Our biological sciences clearly inform us that many species are becoming extinct. Even as we are informed that biodiversity is declining, our actions to stop the destruction seem to be paralyzed.

Human action based solely upon response to information is empty, and does not engage the emotions. Even though our science has done a good job in providing the data, our hearts need to be moved toward acting on the data. Our science needs to connect with our spirit.

People of the U.S. culture are gradually moving from positions of reacting to information toward integrating our science with the human spirit. Responding to the decline in biodiversity is a situation where we can turn to our spiritual resources in order to engage with our science in an integrated way. We don't need to save species; we need to build relationships with other species. A rich resource for modeling the integration of our science with our spirit is found within the Franciscan spiritual and intellectual traditions.

The integration of our scientific method with our experiences of spirituality begins to be realized not at the level of institutional religion, but within the individual person. The voices of contemporary women and men who are involved with science, and who also have a deep sense of the underlying mystery expressed through the individuation of creation need to be heard. In my own case, the systematic and personal exploration of the lives of invertebrates has revealed to me a new perspective on creation that lifts up the important roles individual creatures play.

After I saw the world from the perspective of a fly larvae, the world never looked the same. Each living creature becomes an instrument of creation that cries out to be respected for its role and for its individuality. Species no longer become abstractions, but realities to be lived through each unique life in each unique moment of time. Connecting with as many of these life forms as possible has changed me into a person who not only continues to explore the diversity of life, but also is able to reverence the creator through appreciation of the individuals who constitute the diversity.

Building relationships with other species can help rejoin information with the soul. Building relationships with other species can promote connecting our spirituality with our science. Building relationships with other species will promote receptivity to national and international policies that can reduce the reduction of biodiversity. And the people most important in this rejoining are the parents, teachers, and ministers who can skillfully articulate the connection between science and spirituality, and are able to preach from an "invertebrate" perspective. These facilitators will provide opportunities to help us begin making connections that will determine what life forms will survive!

NOTES

1. Wilson, E. O., *The Diversity of Life* (New York: Penguin Books, 1992), p. 124.
2. Ibid, pp. 242–247.
3. Ibid, pp. 271–276.
4. Ibid, pp. 297–326.
5. White, Jr., L., "The Historic Roots of Our Ecological Crisis," *Science* (1967) 155: 1203–1207.
6. Dennis, M., J. Nagle, C. Moe-Lobeda, and S. Taylor, *St. Francis and the Foolishness of God* (Maryknoll, NY: Orbis Books, 1993), pp. 8.
7. List of the ten greatest people of the millennium in "Beyond the Year 2000," *Time* 140 Special Issue, Fall 1992.

8. Dennis, pp. 104–120.

9. Rohr, R., "Christianity and Creation A Franciscan Speaks," In *Embracing Earth Catholic Approaches to Ecology*, ed. A. J. La Chance and J. E. Carroll (Maryknoll, NY: Orbis Books, 1994), pp. 129–155.

10. Warner, K., "Was St. Francis a Deep Ecologist?" In *Embracing Earth Catholic Approaches to Ecology*, ed. A. J. La Chance and J. E. Carroll (Maryknoll, NY: Orbis Books, 1994), pp. 225–240.

11. Armstrong, E. A., *St. Francis: Nature Mystic the Derivation and Significance of the Nature Stories in the Franciscan Legend*, (Berkeley, CA: University of California Press, 1973); Sorrell, R. D., *St. Francis of Assisi and Nature Tradition and Innovation in Western christian Attitudes toward the Environment*, (New York: Oxford University Press, 1988).

12. "Legend of Perugia," In *St. Francis of Assisi, Writings and Early Biographies*, ed. M. A. Habig, (Chicago: Franciscan Herald Press, 1972), p. 1027.

13. Thomas of Celano, "First Life of St. Francis," In *St. Francis of Assisi, Writings and Early Biographies*, ed. M. A. Habig, (Chicago: Franciscan Herald Press, 1972), p. 296.

14. Biographical dates for Bonaventure and Duns Scotus from the *New Catholic Encyclopedia*, (New York: McGraw Hill, 1967).

15. Hayes, Z., "In Search of an Identity: Franciscan Schools in a Changing World," In *Franciscan Charism and Higher Education*, Symposium Celebrating the 25th Anniversary of Neumann College, Aston, PA.

16. Hoebing, P., "St. Francis and the Environment," In *Divine Representation Post-modernism and Spirituality*, ed. A. W. Astelle, (Purdue Univeristy: Paulist Press, 1994), pp. 210–15.

17. Osborne, K. B., "Incarnation, Individuality, and Diversity," *The Cord* (1995) 45.3:25.

18. Hoebing, p. 209.

19. Wolter, A. B. and B. O'Neill, *John Duns Scotus: Mary's Architect* (Quincy, IL: Franciscan Press, 1993), p. 37.

20. Hoebing, p. 210.

21. Zim, H. S. and C. Cottam, *Insects: A Guide to Familiar American Insects*, revised edition (New York: Golden Press, 1961).

22. Wilson, E. O., "A Grassroots Jungle in a Vacant Lot;" Rothschild, M., "Ages Five to Fifteen: Wildflowers, Butterflies, Frogs;" Eisner, T., "The End of Superstition;" Pyle, R. M., "Butterflies in Winter," In *Wings* (1995) 18:3–21.

23. A clearly written popular source tht includes technical methods and information about the invertebrates mentioned is the original or revised edition within the Peterson Field Guide Series by Borror, D. and R. E. White, *Insects of America North of Mexico* (Boston: Houghton Mifflin, 1970).

The Big Questions:
Birth and Death

Elliott A. Norse

When the editors first asked me to write about relationships of ecology and religion, I felt both honored and hesitant. This interface is rich with topics worth examining, and examining two bodies of thought that have so often seemed in opposition seemed most intriguing. However, I am not an expert in religion—even my own religion (Judaism)—and was concerned that I would, therefore, have to offer a personal perspective. That poses a problem: Personal perspectives are very personal. And what could be more personal for a scientist—a person whose objectivity and rationality about *what is* is one of two defining characteristics (the other being curiosity about what is)—than to reveal thoughts and feelings about religion, much of which lies in the realm of faith beyond the outermost reaches of rationality?

I accepted because the gulf between science and religion underlies nearly all of the crises that threaten the Earth and its inhabitants, including the biggest crisis: stopping the loss of the Earth's biological diversity and integrity. Throughout my life I have met people who believe that humans are the only species that counts, that the Earth and all other species exist for us to use as we wish. This viewpoint is so prevalent that it cannot simply be dismissed. Increasingly in recent years, however, I have met people who believe that humans are stewards who must protect and tend nature. These two contrasting views are both based on values that stem from religious beliefs about humans' place in the universe, not from science. As the crush of human population enters the last redoubts of nature, the fate of the Earth's species and ecosystems—a subject of increasing concern to scientists—is likely to hinge on which of these two views prevails. Hence, anything that might inspire people to start bridging the gap between religion and science could lessen the plagues that (choose one or both) God or our human nature visits upon us.

First, a clarifying definition: Among the biological sciences, which focus the diverse processes of life, ecology is the study of interactions among species and their environment. Most ecologists study interactions in microorganisms, plants or nonhuman animal species. But because humans are the species that most profoundly affects the millions of other species and the environment we share—the Earth—human ecology is central to most any discussion about the environment.

In addition to its fascinating ramifications, there is a powerful political reason to explore the possibilities for reconciliation between ecology and religion. The USA was torn over civil rights for black people and the Vietnam War in the 1960s and '70s. In both cases, pressure built steadily for fundamental change but society's inertia was insurmountable until religious congregations became committed and actively involved. When tens, hundreds, then thousands of congregations and religious leaders demanded change, things changed.

Now our planet is facing the most devastating biological catastrophe in its last 65 million years: the massive worldwide loss of biological diversity and integrity. American society is again politically torn. On one side are those who believe that consumption of the resources in public lands and waters and private ownership of land take precedence over all other values, that God wants humankind to dominate and subdue the Earth. On the other side, those who believe that we have responsibility to be stewards of our environment, to care for Creation and for the interests of future generations even if it means that some people must curtail their appetites and delay financial gains for the short term.

I write at a time when the so-called "Wise Use" Movement (an alliance of right wing property-rights anti-environmentalists fueled by shrimping, ranching, logging, mining, real estate and agribusiness interests) and its followers in the 105th Congress are pressing for weakening of the Endangered Species Act after having succeeded in overriding environmental protection provisions of the ESA, the National Environmental Policy Act and the National Forest Management Act during the 104th. While a seemingly secular desire to maximize short-term profit is a clear theme in this anti-environmental coalition, there is an unmistakable religious undercurrent to justify it; in some instances, religious justification comes to the surface. For example, James G. Watt, the former Secretary of Department of the Interior under President Ronald Reagan who is revered by anti-environmentalists, stated that consuming resources only hastens the coming Apocalypse and hence, the Kingdom of Heaven. The blatant anti-environmentalism of his reign in the early 1980s was blunted by leaders of both major parties in Congress, but his philosophical followers in Congress made major gains in the 1994 elections that continue to influence US policy to this day.

Modern religious belief affects our environment both for better and worse. As a scientist, two things are clear to me:

1) that humankind is absolutely dependent on biological diversity, that the millions of other species and the ecosystems they constitute provide the products and services on which our well-being and survival depend; and
2) that the accelerating impact of 5.8 billion humans profoundly threatens the diversity and integrity of life on Earth.

As an observer and participant in the making of public policy for nearly 20 years and as a citizen concerned about the well-being of my country and planet, I am convinced that humankind will not succeed in slowing and stopping environmental disaster of scarcely imaginable proportions unless organized religions of all kinds mobilize and act decisively on behalf of our environment. Science is essential—we need objective information on the status of species and ecosystems and the processes that sustain life—but it is not sufficient. Too few people are able or willing to trust science. Rapprochement between science and religion seems to be the only hope.

Although there is no lack of topics worth exploring, limitations of space in this book and the scarcity of similar opportunities led me to conclude that I should have a go at The Big Questions: where we come from and where we go, birth and death, generation and degeneration. These (along with what we do while we are here) are central questions for people of both science and faith, and have profound implications for the environmental crisis and the strife among nations, within nations and within individuals that, in combination, make us feel that we are ever farther from the Eden whence we came.

Be forewarned: my explorations might seem strange, presumptuous or even offensive to some people. Birth and death are such big topics to contemplate that for many they are too awesome or awful, terrific or terrible (these pairs of words, now used as opposites, really mean the same thing) to speak or even think about. In polite conversation, people customarily avoid mention of processes such as egestion, mating, birth, disease and death, or allude to them by using euphemisms. (For example, I remember vividly how my mother and her friends always said "CA" as a way to avoid pronouncing the dreaded name cancer, as if speaking its name gave it power) But such processes are the subjects that biologists study, the very stuff of our science, so I hereby request "special dispensation" from the reader to examine The Big Questions. It is my intention to provide food for thought and even comfort to religious people who have grappled with big questions and have not always been satisfied with the answers. And by doing so, I hope to help, at least in the minds of some, to help reconcile ecology and religion. So, having put some Gregorian chants on the CD player and closed my eyes for a moment, I'm ready to take the plunge.

BIRTH: NULLIPARITY AND IMMORTALITY

I have three stepsons, but like clerics in some religions and many environmentally conscious people, I chose not to have my own children. By the most basic biological criterion, stepchildren don't count and nulliparity (not having biological children) makes me a failure. Yet I have an inherent love for children, and I often wonder what it would have been like to have a child who bears my genes, a child I could have nurtured since birth and taught about trees and insects and why the wind blows. Yet something that arose from my Jewishness has ameliorated the sadness that I have often felt about being childless.

Evolution is the central concept in biology. An understanding of how living things change through time and how their inherited features affect their persistence in our always-changing world is integral to the study of life at all levels of biological organization, from molecules to ecosystems. I cannot imagine a real biologist who does not understand that, just as I cannot see why understanding evolution must be irreconcilable with believing in God or being devoutly religious. It is deeply troubling that some religious traditions and many of their adherents have rejected a body of understanding that is demonstrable to anyone open to the overwhelming weight of evidence and reason. It is hardly less troubling that many of my colleagues in biology, having come from religious traditions whose teachings reject biologists' vast and growing understanding about evolution, have, as a result, felt compelled to loosen or even cast off the cloak of religion. Both science and religion—the two most powerful founts of concern about the fate of life on our world—and our living planet have all lost as a result.

What drives evolution is an imperative inherent in the DNA molecule, the imperative to reproduce itself. This recalls a saying I first heard from my wonderful high school zoology teacher, Norman Scovronick, that evoked howls of laughter from his students: "A chicken is an egg's way of making another egg." The notion seems delightfully absurd. Eggs can't think or act. And besides, that's not the way people usually look at things.

But let's examine this. An Atlantic cod in a fish market (assuming, after overfishing on Canada's Grand Banks and Georges Bank between Canada and the USA, that we can still find one) seems like a substantial fish in its own right, weighing several pounds and possessing eyes, a barbel on its chin, jaws, fins, scales and internal organs that outfit it for life in the cool waters above the seabed. But from the perspective of its genes, it is nothing more than a nicely equipped package for proliferating its unique combination of the genetic information coded in its DNA. Not only is its distinctive anatomy a manifestation of this genetic imperative; so are its distinctive behaviors, internal physiological processes and the interactions with myriad other species where it lived. The same is true of the teeming *Escherichia coli* bacteria in our large intestines, the trees that (if we're lucky) line the horizon and, not least, us.

The general statement of this principle is: What we are and what we do is our genes' way of getting us to maximize our "Darwinian fitness," the term evolutionary biologists use to measure genetic contribution to future generations. Darwinian fitness doesn't necessarily mean large muscles, sharp teeth, high speed or brilliance. It means success— generation after generation—in perpetuating an organism's DNA.

Reproducing the carrier of those genes is how nature does this. And reproduction means not only the actual production of offspring, but the investment in them that affects the probability that they will pass on their genes.

Species can be arrayed along a continuum in parental investment per offspring. Each sexually reproducing plant or animal gathers energy that it uses to maintain itself and to reproduce. Some individuals are more successful than others at gaining energy and nutrients (just as some people manage to get higher incomes than others), but each individual of each species has only so much energy to invest in reproduction. Some species, such as most octopuses, Pacific salmon and century plants, mobilize all the energy they devote to reproduction and spend it at once, reproducing in a "big bang," then dying. Others, such as mussels, rhinoceroses and Douglas-fir trees produce young repeatedly after they are mature. But whether they reproduce just once or repeatedly, because the energy that can go to reproduction is finite, there is a crucial trade-off that species have been forced into over evolutionary time. Some species (for example, Atlantic cod) have developed reproductive strategies that include making huge numbers of young but invest little in each of them, and others (for example, great white sharks) make few young but invest a great deal in each.

Evolutionary biologists have long known that parents in many species take care of their young in many ways. Some pack more food into their eggs or seeds, others watch over their young. But it is revealing that a number of species also invest in individuals that are not their own young, for example, their siblings. There is a strong evolutionary reason for this: The individuals they help bear more of their genes than others do.

Allow me to explain from my individual perspective: Any of the kids I might have fathered would have had half of the genes in the nuclei of my cells and half of those in my wife's. My mother and father each had half of my genes, but they are no longer alive. My sister has about half of my genes (it could be more or less than half by chance alone), but her reproducing days are over. Her son, my nephew, is my closest relative who can still reproduce; he shares roughly a quarter of my genes. That is why, in an evolutionary sense, it pays me to invest in improving his Darwinian fitness; doing so improves my fitness as well. Indeed, nothing I do for myself will improve my fitness because I decided to have no children, but whatever I do to improve his fitness is evolutionarily advantageous for me, in that they help me pass on at least some of my genes. Possibilities might include introducing him to (presumably fertile) women, teaching him the intricacies of growing tomatoes or giving him money for his unborn children's college tuition. Such acts are my best prospects for getting my genes perpetuated. My next closest relatives who could still reproduce share only about one sixty-fourth of my genes, so my nephew, with one-fourth, is clearly a far better bet.

In an evolutionary sense, I share fewer genes and am progressively less close to people outside my particular family who are members of the interbreeding population of which I am a member (which could be

Jews, Americans or whatever), to humankind as a whole, then to other hominoids (humans share about 98% of our genes with chimpanzees), other primates, other mammals, other chordates, other animals, other eukaryotic organisms (those with a nucleus clearly bounded by a membrane, including plants and fungi), and other living things (we can call the others bacteria for simplicity's sake, although they are fundamentally far more diverse than our eukaryotic kin). The mice hunted by spotted owls in the ancient forests of Douglas-fir trees and the bacteria that live on and in them are all my relatives—we share the same evolutionary origins some tens of millions (mice), hundreds of millions (owls) or billions (bacteria) of years back—but they are all much more distant kin than my species, my population and my family.

There are many variations on the theme of organisms passing on their genes. From evidence including the spread of antibiotic resistance, biologists learned that some bacteria can pass genes to other species of bacteria. Many animals, plants and fungi undergo the more familiar kind of sexual reproduction, which involves halving a parent's genetic legacy and combining with that of another parent, but some have some kind of asexual reproduction, which creates genetically identical copies of a parent. Of course, life is a gamble, and many individual organisms never pass on their genes. But it is clear that the driving force that compels pines to produce copious pollen, salmon to swim hundreds of miles to suitable spawning beds and people to spend so much time thinking about money and sex (and buying "sexy" cars, clothes and make-up) is genetic.

This evolutionary perspective sheds an evolutionary light on God's biblical command to the ancient Hebrews to "be fruitful and multiply" and God's promise that they will become exceedingly numerous. It also explains features of Judaism that are still practiced to varying degrees, including the centrality of marriage and the family (now under assault by secular society, but still central in Judaism), the requirement that a man whose brother dies must marry and care for his brother's widow and children (no longer practiced), and the prohibition against sexual intercourse when a wife is menstruating and hence, unable to conceive (still practiced by many observant Orthodox Jews). All of these are pronatalist practices; whether they became religious rules by accident or design, they have been instrumental in the survival of a people that has long been surrounded by other peoples, some of them enemies. Our individual behavioral drives (again, human sexual desire is an evolutionary means contrived by our genes to ensure their perpetuation) and the elaborate and strict codes of behavior embodied in the rules in Judaism and other religions have the mutually reenforcing effect of pushing us to increase our fitness relative to that of other individuals and groups.

Unfortunately, our sex drives, which were so essential to our survival when our populations were small and vulnerable and which are a source of great pleasure for many, also have some very negative consequences in today's world. On an individual level, they are a component in behaviors that harm other people emotionally (for example, rape, incest and child molestation) and cause death (for example, by passing on the AIDS virus). Even more important, they propel the births of huge numbers of children into families ill-equipped to care for them, creating what seem to be endless cycles of misery and social pathology, and increasing pressure on the other species of living things.

On a population level, the desire to pass on our genes is almost universally accompanied by a disdain or hatred for other populations whose genes differ even slightly from our own, leading to discrimination, competition and even genocide against other populations of people. To justify killing our fellow humans, even our very close relatives (e.g., Serbs and Croats), we need only to dehumanize them, that is, to distance them from us genetically in our minds. This "us versus them" distinction underlies the inter-religious, inter-ethnic and inter-national conflicts that cause so many deaths and divert such vast amounts of resources to weapons that could end our existence suddenly or kill us over a slightly longer time span by diverting resources from other essential endeavors.

Newspapers and TV shows focus disproportionate attention to acquiring resources, to sex and to people killing one another. But as horrific as it is when someone blows up a building to make a political point or takes the life of a spouse in a jealous rage, people killing people is not nearly so great a threat to us as another that most people think about far less. What threatens humankind more is the damage we do to other species that are more distantly related to us, the devastation of biological diversity, the living things that (choose one or both) God or evolution shaped and nurtured. Why? Because humankind is utterly dependent on biological diversity: everything we eat, every drop of water we drink, every breath of air we breathe comes to us courtesy of myriad living things serving their own interests. The perfumed air, sweet water and delicious fruits of Eden were and are gifts from living things, certainly no less the creations of God than we are ourselves. Yet most religions and laws extend far less protection to other species than they do to humans. It is ironic and revealing that people who fervently proclaim themselves "pro-life" for opposing abortion are seldom outspoken in opposing the rampant destruction of life in our forests, lakes and seas.

In focusing so much on even trivial aspects of humankind (who was caught stealing what, who is wearing what this year, who won what game, how much is someone willing to pay for what stock, etc.) we are missing a much, much larger story whose outcome will determine our survival and our prospects of finding oneness with what made us. The news (one has to look carefully for it, for news media devote very little attention to it) is worrisome. The Earth is rapidly losing species. They are being eliminated by overexploitation, physical destruction and chemical pollution of their habitats and the introduction of alien species to places where they had never before occurred. Ecosystems (tropical rainforests, ancient temperate forests, coral reefs, tallgrass prairies, the entire Aral Sea) are disappearing. The biogeochemical processes that maintain the habitability of our planet have been pushed so far out of whack that the carbon dioxide content of the atmosphere is rising steadily, far more dangerous ultraviolet radiation is scourging the land and sea, less and less water is fit to drink and the topsoils that feed us are being eroded and washed into the sea.

What is causing these enormous changes? The human population, which is already severely stressing the Earth's life support systems, is doubling every 40 years. Nearly everybody is struggling to raise his or her standard of living by increasing the consumption of resources; everyone wants to live as they see Americans living on syndicated broadcasts of *Dallas* and *Dynasty*. But the Earth's living systems cannot handle even current assaults without breaking down. As 90 million more people join us annually and we urge them to emulate our patterns of consumption, we are undoing the integrity of our planet, which, for those who believe in God, is destroying God's Creation.

These causes, in turn, are being driven by psychological, spiritual and genetic forces within us. Processes at both the individual and population levels underlie our rapidly increasing destruction of our environment. We fill our own needs so that we can reproduce and cover the Earth with our progeny. And we seek to eliminate anything unlike us that competes with us and inadvertently eliminate those that don't serve our purpose. Once we killed lions and wolves because we feared that they might eat us. The species we are eliminating now are those whose bodies or homes we covet, or simply disregard.

Whether we are willing to recognize it or not, we are kin to all other life on this planet, and our fate is inextricably intertwined with the diversity of life. If the living things that generate our medicines disappear, we will sicken. If the living things that regulate our climate are killed, we will suffer ever-increasing occurrence of "unusual" weather. The fishes in our waters whose livers are consumed by tumors, the lichens that can no longer survive the polluted air of our cities, the dolphins succumbing to new kinds of epidemics and the mounting numbers of endangered species are all sending us a message, one as clear as the messages of the Biblical prophets: we are doing something very wrong, and we must change our ways. If we ignore them, we will pay dearly, just as the ancient Hebrews did when they ignored God's biblical commands.

Humans have enormous power. Unlike any other species in the Earth's history, we have taken on the God-like power of changing the entire planet, thereby threatening all of its inhabitants, including ourselves. Whether we have God-like wisdom and compassion to curtail the destructive use of our power is an open question.

What most distinguishes humankind from all other species is something that I first realized by contemplating my religion. The persistence of the Jews as a more or less identifiable entity for more than three millennia has been a product of our distinctive culture. The commandments and traditions about what we can and cannot eat, how we must treat our families, other people, beasts, trees (yes, there is strict prohibition, even during the siege of an enemy town, against destroying its fruit trees) and the land, and how goodness is rewarded and wrongdoing is punished, have all been detailed and passed between succeeding generations in the Torah, the Talmud and other religious writings. This is culture, the non-genetic information passed among contemporaries and, through myths, principles, songs, stories, writings, films, art and artifacts, among generations. Some came to modern Jews from crowded European ghettos of the 1940s, some from impoverished Ukrainian shtetls of the 1880s, some from Egypt's flourishing Jewish communities in the 1200s, some from the scholarly debates in Babylonia in the 400s, some from the time of David, Moses and Abraham 1,400, 1,800 and 2,500 years earlier.

Realizing that this ancient set of accumulated ideas and principles is my legacy led me to see that for myself and for all people, there is an alternative to Darwinian fitness.

In essence, passing on genes—the most basic function of life—maintains information, temporarily defying entropy, the disordered state described in the Second Law of Thermodynamics that ultimately prevails in any system. While entropy will eventually prevail and the passing of genes will end (because the Universe is finite, there is no chance of immortality), the story of life is and will be a very, very long one. While continents drifted apart, asteroids crashed into the Earth and the Wise Use Movement arose and prepared its assault, living things have maintained and modified the fragile genetic thread of continuous information since the dawn of life, more than 3,500 million years ago. The vast majority of bearers of that information have disappeared. But because some succeeded in passing on their genes before they died, there are today 10, 30, perhaps even 100 million different species of guardians of their variants of the DNA that miraculously assembled when the Earth was young. This remarkable diversity of life, each individual singlemindedly devoted to perpetuating its version of that information, is the greatest of (choose one or both) God's or evolution's inventions.

What makes humans different from all other forms of life about which we know is the degree to which we employ culture as a second means of passing information from generation to generation. Certainly other species have culture: Many years ago a small English bird called a blue tit learned to pull the tops off milk bottles, allowing it to drink the cream, and passed this information on to others far faster than a genetic mutation could spread through the population. And some years ago a Japanese macaque monkey invented washing grain on a beach before eating it, apparently as a way to avoid ingesting sand, thereby passing it on to others via "monkey see, monkey do." It is even hypothesized that Atlantic cod learn migration routes from other cod. But the amount of nongenetic information passed along in other species (with the possible exception of dolphins and great whales) is a mere trickle relative to the great flowing river of human culture. Through our myths, tales, aphorisms and books, we maintain the nongenetic stream of information flowing through the days, years and millennia. Whether or not my genes came from Moses, Hillel, Maimonides, Einstein, Michael SoulJ or Mel Brooks, important parts of my culture certainly did. My identity is shaped by their ideas, along with those of Lao Tsu, Aristotle, Hildegard von Bingen, Darwin, Robert MacArthur and many others who do not appear to have been members of my Jewish gene pool. I have many cultural parents.

Genetically I am a dead-end, a failure. I may love my tall, strong stepsons, but they are not my spawn. Yet I do not feel like a failure, because I have made many a contribution to posteriority, my bid for immortality. I whispered a joke to a girl in my third grade class that might have changed her thinking. I played a recording of Carl Nielsen's Symphony #3 for my sister and thereby changed the mix of music to which she listens. I wrote a chapter and some books on biological diversity that have changed the minds of some decision makers about the way we treat life on Earth. Very soon, in a few minutes or decades, I will die, but I have strewn humankind and this planet with my cultural legacy. The fate of my genes is already determined, but what my brain has thought and shared, and the actions that have resulted, might, just might, have irreversibly changed the future of life on God's Green Earth, at least in small ways. For that, I feel satisfaction.

Our genes compel us to reproduce. Since long before biblical times, our cultures have reenforced that message (the Cro-Magnons of Europe carved robustly curvy female fetishes tens of thousands of years before the Canaanites' strikingly similar ones). But culture—including religion—also provides us an alternative means of attempting immortality by sending our concepts and recipes, jokes and rituals, beliefs and ethics into the future. Individuals' cultural contributions are no more equal than their genetic contributions, but most everyone has something to contribute, and some have contributions of such enduring value that vast numbers of people will adopt them (often without knowing the source) and share them with others.

In the Torah and teachings of some other religions, the miracle of life is symbolized by a tree. If we are to avoid killing millions of twigs and branches in the Tree of Life and then the trunk and roots themselves, it will be because we embraced this alternative way to seeking immortality. Our evolving culture will replace our evolving genome as the focus of our generative energy. To save the Earth and ourselves, we must employ the ancient, uniquely human way of transmitting who we are to satisfy our deeply imbedded drive for immortality.

DEATH: WE *ARE* IMMORTAL

Gary Fields, my oldest friend, lives on the other side of the continent, but we are closer than most brothers. Not long ago he sent me a note that caused me to cry. He told me that the mother of his closest pre-Elliott childhood friend had died. Her own son—Gary's childhood friend—had died in his early 20s, and she thought of Gary as a special link to the son she had lost. Now she, too, was gone.

My heart went out to him. I asked myself "What is a friend?" and an answer immediately leapt into my head: a friend is someone for whom you cry. Death had cut the thread of her life, he grieved, and I grieved for him. And for the loved ones I have lost. And for the people I have never met who die in filthy refugee camps, angry inner cities and lonely apartments. I cried and cried. Then I started thinking about why we die.

This must be one of the most puzzling, painful questions we can ask, and one of the greatest benefits of religions is the comforting answers they provide. Some religions hold out the promise of a perfect Heaven for good people or martyrs; others opt for reincarnation, another go-around here on Earth, albeit in a different package. One way or another, religions give us hope for transformation and immortality.

It seems so illogical: we are brilliant painters or loving friends or special saleswomen or cheery babies or insightful scholars and death takes us. We go quietly or we go fighting for every last breath, suddenly or with lots of warning, but death still wins. Always.

How can we live knowing this? Seeing our friends and family members go? Knowing that we will precede or follow them? Death must be the biggest of all mysteries.

I don't want to die. It has taken me all this time to start understanding myself enough to heal the inevitable damage of upbringing, to have found the woman I love, to cherish in fullness my closest friends and my family, to make my contribution to my species and my world, to savor so many things. I don't want to die and I don't want anyone I love to die. But it's going to happen, and with all my friends and skills and scientific knowledge, I'm absolutely powerless to stop it.

But while there is no antidote to death, there is amelioration. I can live every minute of my life as if it counts, savor the good things of this world, fight to protect them, laugh, sing, celebrate, see, feel, taste, learn, give, love and... die.

If only we had assurance that we and our loved ones will somehow survive, that we will again be reunited and all will be right. Religions ask us to accept this on faith, and great numbers of people do, at least sometimes. But as experienced clergy know all too well, faith is difficult to accept and maintain. If only we had some demonstrable indication that we will be here forever....

We do. And I will be the first to admit that it is not all that we would like, it is not the universal talisman that will comfort all people whenever faith falls short. But I suspect that it would be of some comfort to some people sometime, and on a question notably short of satisfying answers, that is not nothing.

You see, we are made of chemical elements: carbon, hydrogen, oxygen, nitrogen, sulfur, phosphorous, calcium, iron and many others. When our mothers are pregnant, they nurture us with these elements as we grow *in utero*, then provide precisely what we need through their milk and, with our fathers (those who are lucky enough to have fathers who do this), feed us until we can feed ourselves. Eating and breathing provide our cells the chemical energy we need to do work—walking, lifting, digesting and thinking—and the chemicals from which we make our bodies. We cannot absorb all the chemicals we ingest, so we egest the remainder. And we cannot forever hold on to all that we have absorbed, so we excrete or exhale them. Ingest, inhale, egest, excrete, exhale, on and on and on. In maintaining this flow of chemical elements, we transform ourselves and our environment.

The availability of the chemicals of life depends on living things. The Earth's atmosphere, at first, was a witches' brew of chemicals that you and I could not breathe. It was fine for various early marine bacteria, however, which prospered in these conditions for aeons. The air became breathable for us (and poisonous for most of them) because, starting more than a billion years ago, blue-green bacteria in the sea produced enough oxygen as a waste product of their photosynthesis that the atmosphere started accumulating free oxygen. This was a disaster for many of the early bacteria, which took refuge in places where oxygen couldn't reach, but spurred the evolution of ones that could tolerate and use oxygen. Life created our modern, breathable (except in Los Angeles, Beijing and a growing list of similar places) atmosphere.

Similarly, phosphorous is a vitally important nutrient for plants (when people buy bags of garden fertilizer marked with three numbers, such as 20-5-10, the middle number indicates the percentage of phosphorous). Usable forms of phosphorous are generally in scarce supply on the Earth's surface because plants suck it up so quickly. But there are places where plants are scarce and phosphorous concentrations are very high. One of the best-known is on small islands and cliffs where seabirds have roosted for thousands of years. The phosphorous compounds from the fishes they have eaten and egested accumulate on the rocks, forming thick guano deposits. People mine these deposits for use as fertilizer.

There are also places where calcium compounds accumulate because animals and plants with calcium skeletons have lived and died in vast numbers. The most famous of these where this process is still ongoing is Australia's Great Barrier Reef, where countless corals, clams, snails and calcium-absorbing algae have harvested calcium from the water that flows across them and incorporated it into their bodies, only to die and be overgrown by still other organisms doing the same thing until a thick layer of calcium carbonate, or coral rock (a kind of limestone) accumulates. The young stages of seaweeds, corals, snails and many other organisms settle on coral rock and, by growing, contribute to the growth of the reef. From the bodies of the dead come the substrate for new lives.

Most of the heavier elements of which we are made were born in the stars, spread throughout the galaxy when stars exploded and accumulated when the infant Earth coalesced some 4.5 billion years ago, so, in a very real sense, each of us is made of stardust. Living things acquire the elements they need, package them in different ways and eventually release them, where they are taken up and transformed, recycled by biological, geological and chemical (biogeochemical) processes countless times. Some things are reused quickly, some are stored for long periods, but nothing is wasted and nothing really disappears. The very atoms that were part of Moses, Lao Tsu, Gautama Siddhartha, Jesus, Mohammed and Bahaullah are still with us and part of us. Every person in the world, every mushroom, leaf and bird, has carbon from King David, sulfur from Confucius and oxygen from Joan of Arc. And when enough time has passed for our elements to be redistributed, everyone in the future will carry elements from us. So, each of us is a new assemblage of atoms that were part of those we most revere. And for as long as the Earth survives, something in each of us will be in everyone else.

In this sense, we are all immortal, and we are all one.

Is this the stuff of science or religion? The miracles of being are no more or less miraculous either way. But by rethinking our religions and lovingly reshaping them to reflect what we have learned about the world we inhabit and the forces that created us, each and every one of us can revere, protect and sustain Creation. Our religions gave us the direction we needed to sustain ourselves for millennia when the voice of science was quiet, indeed. Knowing what science now teaches, people are faced with the choice of holding on to beliefs that will bring a sorry end to Creation as we know it, or of renewing our faiths to sustain life on God's Green Earth. My fondest hope is that we will make the right choice.

Becoming a Spiritual Witness in a Scientific Profession

Robert J. Kent

As a science educator, and one involved in the management of our coastal resources, I find myself thinking about prayer and its relationship to guiding and motivating people.

Accept, O Lord, our thanks and praise for all that you have done for us. We thank you for the splendor of the whole creation, for the beauty of this world, for the wonder of life, and for the mystery of love.[1]

It wasn't too many years ago when I received in the mail an invitation to attend an Earth Day event that involved people praying and chanting, and ringing bells, in celebration of the day. I scoffed at the idea, thinking it some kind of New Age event at which I would feel very uncomfortable. What could such an event possibly accomplish in helping with the problems threatening to destroy the quality of our coastal environment, I asked myself. Now I think I may have learned.

My line of work is science-based. I work for the National Sea Grant College Program, modeled on our agricultural land grant college system, in which university faculty conduct research and extension staff convey the results of university-based research to communities, businesses, and the public. Our mission in Sea Grant is the wise use and protection of our coastal resources. With so many people living along the coast, this portion of our environment is suffering from a wide variety of abuses, ranging from exploitation of resources to dumping of toxic materials into coastal waters.

One of our major goals in Sea Grant is to try to get people from all walks of life passionately interested in the coastal environment, and to take action to improve coastal environmental quality. We call this environmental stewardship. We strive to empower the best scientific minds to address coastal issues by providing funding opportunities for research, and then extending this information from the university to where it can be applied. For example, we have helped people better understand the water quality issues in the Long Island Sound, identifying the key environmental problems and their causes. This science-based information is offered to a wide variety of local and state government units to help them in preparing a management plan for the Sound. However, a management plan will never be funded and implemented unless there is strong public support.

A new Sea Grant initiative is in the area of sustainable communities. Sustainable development means finding ways to live and employ people over the long haul, without causing environmental degradation. This allows a community to survive in an area for many generations. Too often in the past, commercial exploitation has so damaged the natural environment that communities become "unlivable," with polluted air and water, and natural resources wasted. Sea Grant is working to introduce the concept of sustainable living, and to help communities protect their environment while providing economic opportunity. Can people learn to worry about future generations and their welfare? Will they be willing to change their lifestyle if needed? What will motivate them to change? Can communities find new indicators of prosperity to replace consumption and accumulation of more and more material goods?

How does one build support for such programs in the first place? How do we get busy people who hardly ever get down to the water anyway to care about the life in the sea, and the health of the ecosystem? It is no easy task, as my years of work in this field have shown me. As a further challenge, one of the chief aquatic environmental problems of the 1990s is what we call nonpoint source pollution. Unlike a highly visible factory that causes "point source" pollution, nonpoint source pollution results from everyone's daily activities. The toxic materials used around our houses, the oil dripping from our cars, the fertilizers and pesticides misapplied around our homes, the litter we leave on the streets are all forms of nonpoint source pollution. When it rains, rainwater washes over the land, carrying these pollutants into the ground water, or down roadways and pipes to coastal waters.

Stopping nonpoint source pollution means people must care about the problem enough to change their life styles to minimize their contribution to the problem. Building support for government programs is hard enough; asking people to actually change the way they live is even harder.

O merciful Creator, whose hand is open wide to satisfy the needs of every living creature: Make us, we beseech thee, ever thankful for thy loving providence; and grant that we, remembering the

account that we must one day give, may be faithful stewards of
thy bounty...

I suppose I am a lot like many other Americans. As a young boy
growing up, I attended church, sang in the youth choir, and served as an
acolyte. During my high school days, I drifted away from church, and
although I remained interested in spiritual things, I never prayed.
Becoming trained in science and natural resource management, I began
to think more and more like a resource manager, one who uses scientific
information to manage our natural resources. I saw no connection
between spirituality and resource management, which is strange, since
most people in my field are in it because of a childhood reverence for
nature. Many natural scientists and resource managers I know entered
the profession because of a driving, motivating force to save nature. As
children, we spent many pleasurable years enjoying nature, observing
the natural world around us. We grew up fond of turtles, snakes, birds,
salamanders, frogs, squirrels, insects, wild flowers, trees, whatever we
found. We instinctively knew these creatures were wonderful, and
innately worthy. We enjoyed hiking, camping, boating, fishing or hunting.

Training in natural resources taught us to see nature as a resource.
After taking classes in forestry, I viewed a forest in terms of its timber
production capability. Wildlife became a resource to be managed for
annual yields to harvest. Having been trained to think like a scientist,
and, I suppose because of certain professional peer pressures, emotions
and feelings became further and further removed from my resource
management responsibilities.

After years of not attending church, one day I felt compelled to go
back. Compelled really is not a strong enough word, I felt I received a
message from above to go back! I had a void in my life, a spiritual void,
a lost connection with my past and my heritage, which I wanted to fill.
This got me back into praying again, at least on Sundays. Looking
through the Book of Common Prayer I happened across the Lectionary
(the daily guide for Bible readings), and asked my priest how to use it.
Soon, I was saying morning and evening prayer, and doing other daily
devotions, on a regular basis. I always felt better when I did, and missed
the experience when busy days kept me from my routine.

I felt better, but what did all this praying accomplish? In the *Prayers
of the People* I prayed for peace, for unity of people, for the aged and

infirm, for the poor and the oppressed, for those who have died. Did the world around me change? Not that I could detect. Yet I changed, it dawned on me, and that was the real purpose of prayer, not to change the world, but to change me. Of course, if I changed enough, so would others that prayed, and so the world could change.

> For the good earth which God has given us, and for the wisdom
> and will to conserve it, let us pray to the Lord.

Science may help us to better understand the natural world around us, and to give us the information we need to correct past damages and to change our behavior, but science alone will probably not motivate large numbers of people to change. Unfortunately, a lot of the scientific information about our natural world today is discouraging, and people are tiring of hearing about environmental problems. If I were to be effective in motivating and changing people, it became clear to me, I needed a tool in addition to science. I needed something that would make people feel good, that would give them the moral grounding to want to change, and that would make them feel personally responsible for what was happening to their coastal environment.

When we think of the natural world as God's creation, when we give thanks to God for creating it, when we take seriously our responsibility to God to protect his creation, we will be much more likely to strive to lead the kind of life that protects rather than harms. Prayer, on a regular basis, regularly reminds us of our duty, and regularly gets us thinking about the sacredness of life.

The fact that almost nothing in our country is seen as sacred anymore strikes me as one of the root causes of our environmental problems. I remember so vividly exploring the natural world as a child, and feeling so connected to frogs, turtles, and the other creatures I found. I feel they were indeed sacred. I loved to lay under our silver maple tree and to contemplate it. Those experiences of connection with the natural world made me a steward, someone who cared for and protected the world around me. If the natural world is thought of as merely a stockroom full of resources for our pleasure, well, we will treat it very non-reverently, won't we?

How can we get ourselves and others outside of the consumerism culture in which we find ourselves? Advertising is all around us, all the time. It creates needs in us for the latest products people want to sell us.

It takes a strong person to resist the urge to buy the newest and latest fashionable item. Unless we are steadfastly grounded in another value system, supported by a community of people with similar values, we probably can't resist or find happiness outside of consumer culture.

Could I, as a science-based person, working for a government-funded research and education institution, begin to talk about the role of spirituality and religion in relation to the environmental issues of the day? At first, the obvious answer seemed to be, "No way!" Science and religion are supposed to be separate, aren't they? Render unto Caesar what is Caesar's. But, as time passed, I began to think differently. I began to combine the scientific and religious aspects of my life by beginning an Earth Day Service at my parish church. It is for me a perfect match, a love of nature, a love of sacred tradition, a love of science, and a love of God. It was very well received. I spoke about our water quality issues, and about caring for God's creation. Many people came up to me after the service to talk more about their similar feelings.

A friend of mine cared so much about our coast, he wanted to do something special to attract interest to coastal resource problems. Having been a rower in college, his plan was to "*R*ow *A*round the *I*sland in *S*upport of the *E*nvironment," a program he called RAISE. Long Island, New York, as the names implies, is a very big island, some 110 miles long, with New York City located on the western end. I helped my friend organize his row with his son, so that coastal consciousness events were set up at nineteen different communities along the route. The RAISE program was a great success. George and I knew this was a spiritual voyage for him, his family, and for me. We just could not let him begin his trip without a prayer. As host of the press event for George's send-off on his two-week row, I decided I would lead a prayer for George and his journey. We used an 1872 edition of the *Book of Common Prayer*, saying the Prayer for Those Going off to Sea. It was a wonderful way to launch George on his journey, and again, people commented to me how nice the saying of a prayer was.

> O eternal God, who alone spreadest out the heavens, and rulest the raging of the sea; we commend to thy Almighty protection, thy servants George and Jeremy, for whose preservation on the great deep our prayers are desired. Guard them, we beseech thee, from the dangers of the sea, from sickness, from the violence of enemies, and from every evil to which they may be exposed.

Conduct them in safety to the haven where they would be, with a grateful sense of they mercies.

I find that all around me people are yearning for meaningful rituals that can help them focus on the wonder of life on our planet. The renewed interest in Native American thanksgiving ceremonies is one example. Those of us who are science trained, yet believe in living a spiritual life, have a special responsibility to share our beliefs. It gives credence to the notion that science and spirituality are not mutually exclusive. The interesting thing that happens when we speak out, when we have the courage to lead a prayer or ritual, is that many similar-minded people come out of the woodwork. We find others that feel as we do, and we find there are a surprising number of them. By speaking out, by setting examples, we provide a setting in which others can come forward with their feelings. This can lead to the formation of cohesive groups and networks of people with shared values that can work together for common environmental goals.

In the 1960s, when I was a college student, alienation was a major topic of discussion in and out of the classroom. People felt alienated from the culture around them. It was not providing the moral framework and values people felt they needed. Back then, we talked about forming small communities to live in, where each person had meaningful work. Today, although we don't use the term alienation much anymore, we do speak of dysfunctional families and communities. The cause is the same, a lack of shared, meaningful values to guide life. I have spent most of my life trying to feel a part of something meaningful, to be rooted in a community that makes sense to me.

Most children in America receive religious training as I did when a child. Many forget or abandoned religious or spiritual life as adults. Perhaps our teachers weren't good enough, for if we re-examine our roots, we may find much of value. Not long ago, I attended a conference called "God, The Environment and the Good Life" at the University of New Hampshire. Speakers from many religious backgrounds were on hand. The message I remember most was from a rabbi who said we really can't just shop around and jump from one religion to another looking for something better. That approach denies who we are, our heritage, our roots, our grounding in the world. All religious traditions have beauty and just purpose, but all have committed sins too. I took his message to heart and re-examined by our Christian faith, which has been charged by some as responsible for many of the environmental problems we see today. Yet, the over-riding theme of the New Testament is the superiority of the spiritual life to the material, the life of the world.

St. Augustine can be our "role model." He said the world is really two worlds, the "city of man," and the "city of God." A true Christian lives in the corrupt city of man, but his task is to minister to it the best he can while trying to remain uncontaminated by it and grounded in the city of God. I like that image. It means we don't retreat into some little protective oasis for ourselves. We work in the world, with the problems of the world, yet striving to bring good and meaning to it. I may call this bringing God's light to the world; you may call it something else. But it is a special way of treating our fellow humans and our fellow non-humans, and a way of leading our personal, spiritual life.

A professor friend of mine who worked in the field of floriculture once told me, back when I was a 4-H agent, to make sure that I had flowers at all my 4-H events. This would make the events seem special. Should we not have some sense of sacredness and beauty in our environmental programs and all we do as well?

Science will help us better understand the natural world and human impacts on it. Science can help us restore some of the damage we have done. Science can help us develop new technologies that will help us live more gently on the Earth. Spiritual living can motivate and guide us to take the actions we need to get the job done of restoring planetary health, and lead us to sustainable living. The two realms are compatible and complementary.

I leave you with a prayer.

Almighty God, giver of all good things:
We thank you for the natural majesty and beauty of this land.
They restore us, though we often destroy them.
Heal us.

NOTES

1. All prayers in this essay are from The Book of Common Prayer, 1979 edition, of the Episcopal Church.

Back to Eden:
The Sacredness of Wilderness
Landscape in
Christian Thought

Keith Warner, OFM

"The sense of religion pervades the wildest places and most
of the wildest hearts."

— the Dali Lama

The accelerating rate of extinction is the greatest environmental
and moral issue of our generation. Our unravelling of the web of interconnected life is an affront to the creativity of God and ranks as our ultimate human folly. The rate of extinction we humans are precipitating is
unlike anything in the history of life on our planet, and through our
destruction of other species we threaten the continuation of our own
existence as well. The species *Homo Sapiens* is using the diversity of
Creation as a proverbial canary as it further explores the coal mine of
human-caused damage to our planet. Sadly, we fail to heed its gasps.

In this essay I am not going to address this issue directly. I am a geographer, not a conservation biologist, and I recommend the pursuit of
this in a work by someone better qualified, such as Edward Wilson in
his *The Diversity of Life* or *How to Love a Worm* by my confrere, Jim
Edmiston OFM (in this volume). I do want to address directly the question of wilderness, because this is the most critical element needing
preservation for the continued existence of other life forms. Loss of
habitat is by far the most significant factor in the current wave of extinction, so preserving wilderness and wild areas is essential if we are to
check the tide of species loss. Because so few Christians presently value
wilderness preservation for the purpose of preserving biological diversity, I wish to present something of a "back door" strategy, describing
how God has used wilderness as the stage for encountering the divine. I
would prefer that humans learn to value all other forms of life for their
own intrinsic value, but will have to content myself in this essay with de-
bunking the misconception that Christianity is inherently anti-wilder-
ness. In this era of environmental crisis I am a pragmatist; it matters not
to me what motivates people to preserve wilderness.

I am here going to argue for the preservation of wilderness on a
merely anthropocentric basis.[1] Wild lands have been the locus for

335

encounter between the human and the divine in many religious traditions, and certainly in the Judeo-Christian religions with which I am
most familiar. The explosion of consumption, population and technology over the past two centuries has severely eroded the quantity and
quality of wilderness, and it is now quite difficult to find pristine places
that have not been degraded, altered, or at least littered by other human
beings, thus damaging habitat and threatening wildlife and species diversity. We are now making choices that will decide whether our grandchildren inherit any large scale tracts of untrammelled lands. In an ideal
world, Christians, indeed all people of faith, would unite to preserve the
diversity of Creation, but it is clear this is not yet happening. I hope,
therefore, to address the conservation of wild areas from a different perspective, a perspective that will "inspire" (i.e., inject the spirit into!)
those who cannot see the value of protecting wilderness for the sake of
species diversity. Wilderness is critical to the future diversity of species
on this planet, but I also believe it is essential for the future of spiritual
values in our world. God has historically chosen wilderness as the primary stage of the divine encounter. Now threatened on all sides, it calls
us to advocate its protection. If we do not, our religious traditions will
suffer a profound spiritual loss.

The discipline of geography, specifically in the investigation of landscape, offers us many ways to address the human experience in wild
landscape, so after introducing some tools of geography, I will turn to
some examples of mystics and ascetics in the Christian tradition who
have very much valued wilderness landscape, demonstrating that there
has always been a concern for wild places as a privileged place of
encountering God. By arguing for the defense of wilderness on the basis
of their critical role in the development of Christian spirituality, I hope
to present one more reason for people of faith to engage in the struggle
for conserving wild lands and wild habitat, and to thus contribute to the
preservation of our planet's biological diversity.

THE EXPERIENCE OF WILD LANDSCAPE

I am writing from the perspective of a Franciscan Friar, a geographer, and a student of spirituality. I am convinced that "an experience of
nature" is critical to engage people in support of conservation. Neither
reading about nature nor watching it on television have sufficient power

to transform our attitudes and lifestyles. My own experiences of nature have been so powerful as to profoundly re-direct my life's course. I was raised in an affluent suburb and throughout my childhood I couldn't figure out why anyone would "want to go out and get dirty" camping or hiking. Yet God's grace led me into work which put me in direct contact with creation daily. For five years I was a member of a Christian reforestation co-op in the Pacific Northwest, and the experience of making myself vulnerable to nature in that way left a profound mark on me.

Reforestation in the Pacific Northwest is exhausting work done under harsh conditions. It is considered among the most demanding manual labor still done, similar in difficulty to working an Alaskan fishing boat or an offshore oil rig. Our co-op reforested tracts that had been clear cut a year or a decade previously on slopes at times so steep that most people wouldn't even try to hike on them. Planting is done during the winter, and the ideal weather conditions for the seedling are in a cold rain, which seemed endless during the winters in the Cascade Range. There were many days when we planted just a few hundred feet below the snow level. We had to put a tree in every ten feet or so, which meant we had to clamber through all manner of brush, vines, sticks, and logging debris to find a planting spot. Trees had to go in regardless of the surface conditions, so we had to scrape away bark, duff, and vegetation to put in seedlings. I typically left the staging area with 30–45 pounds of seedlings, which took an hour or two to plant.

Five seasons of tree planting in the Pacific Northwest gave me the chance to see a lot of forest landscape, or more accurately, ex-forest landscape now reduced to the monotony of industrial tree farms. The forests' complexity, resilience and beautiful diversity brought about by millennia of evolution are being displaced for industrial convenience and profit. My own awakening as an environmentalist was rooted in the growing sense of alarm with which I observed the destruction of America's ancient forest ecosystems. Weyerhauerser, Champion International, Georgia Pacific and the U.S. Forest Service, to name a few, were stripping trees out of the forest as fast as they could, and in the process, soils were compacted, thousands of square miles of habitat were being destroyed, and streams were damaged to the point of being unusable for fish. In my first season I was proud of being able to put trees back into nature. Five years later I had begun to seriously question the morality of working for an industry that was only concerned with extracting profits from nature. I experienced the (uncut) forest as a wilderness of beauty, but it was clear that decisions made about the woods were made by people who saw it very differently. My concern for wilderness, and how people perceived and experienced wilderness landscape, eventually led me to the academic discipline of geography and more formal study of landscape.

When an average person says "I love the environment and I think it should be better protected," what do they really mean? If the speaker has taken some college courses in sciences or environmental studies, they would probably define this to mean some form of ecological system, generally terrestrial. Yet for the majority of people, when they use the term "environment" they are really referring to what a geographer would call landscape. When asked what their experience with "the environment" has been, they will most likely describe a camping trip, or hiking, or taking a boat ride, and they will talk about the trees, meadows, rocky peaks and beautiful bodies of water. Whereas most scientists are able to interpret, describe and perhaps quantify the various components they observe in a landscape, for most lay people an "experience in nature" consists of a non-verbal sensory experience of landscape punctuated at times by the excitement of seeing a wild animal.

As simplistic as this might seem to someone with a scientific background, those of us who are interested in promoting environmental awareness and a greater concern for nature and natural systems need to take these kinds of experiences into account when trying to encourage people to act in a way that is more environmentally friendly. I care passionately about nature, natural landscapes and natural systems, but I acknowledge that very few people are going to devote the time and energy necessary to understanding them well. Nevertheless, I am convinced that unless human beings are able to interact with nature in a direct, experiential way, they will not change their behavior or voting patterns which impact the environment. The United States has reached something of a political impasse in protecting wild areas. Much of wilderness we have left does not have political protection (for what that is worth) while increasing demands by real estate development and resource extraction industries are applying relentless pressure on them. The American public will not modify its behavior for an abstract concept. I believe the best hope for influencing more concerned behavior is in the context of a *relationship*, and that this relationship is primarily experienced by a majority of people through natural landscape. In other words, natural landscape can serve as a liaison between humans of this technological age and "the environment."

WHAT IS LANDSCAPE?

The concept of landscape, however, is a bit difficult to define, and as such, it has generally not been seen as a useful concept by scientists. Until recently it has only been used in geography, which has itself been something of a Rodney Dangerfield of the sciences: it can't get no respect. Ironically, geography mothered the study of what are now Biology and the Earth Sciences. Before the scientific revolution, everything in the natural world that could be described spatially fell under the study of geography. With the explosion of specialization in the sciences, the subjects now studied by biologists, geologists and climatologists were given their own departments, leaving geography to concentrate on a more interdisciplinary approach.[2]

The study of geography can be divided in the following ways: spatial patterns of human behavior, or cultural geography; spatial patterns of the natural world, or physical geography; cartography (currently being revolutionized by computerization, which has developed into an integrated tool of geographic analysis known as G.I.S., or Geographic Information Systems); and the human-land relationship, which includes the study of landscape. Landscape geographers have concentrated their studies on how human beings have expressed their values through their behavior in a landscape, on how humans express their values by manipulating or altering a particular piece of land. But using the term "landscape" has its own problems.

"*Landscape* is an attractive, important and ambiguous term," according to D.W. Meinig. It is attractive because it suggests to most people an idealized scene or outdoor setting, usually involving some component of nature. Most folks would use the term as a verb, as a synonym for 'prettify.' It is important because it can be used in a technical setting by geographers, artists, historians, and land use planners, although each would define the term differently. Meinig insists that *landscape* cannot help but be an ambiguous term because it is used by such a wide range of people.[3]

Nevertheless, I agree with Meinig that it is important; it belongs in the discipline of geography because it deals with a sense of a concrete place. Most people associate geography with maps, and rightly so, for they are symbolic abstractions of spatial relationships. If maps represent spatial relationships in the abstract, then the study of landscape concerns itself with spatial relationships in the specific. Studying the human-landscape interaction investigates how humans interact with a specific space.

Almost all study of landscape concerns itself exclusively with how humans express their values through their manipulation of their cultural landscape. Meinig regards

> "...all landscapes as symbolic, as expressions of cultural values, social behavior, and individual actions worked upon particular localities over a span of time....And every landscape is a code, and its study may be undertaken as deciphering of meaning of the cultural and social significance of ordinary but diagnostic features...."[4]

Meinig is describing the study of places to understand what human beings value. He is primarily concerned with the expression of values made manifest by how humans alter or create landscapes, and there is no shortage of landscapes that qualify for this. Meinig, like most landscape geographers, concerns himself with how humans have modified landscape for their own social use and aesthetic pleasure. Most landscape geographers investigate how things like roads, homes, urban design and commercial development express cultural values; in other words, how people express values through their interaction with culturally created landscape.

I am interested in the human experience of the opposite kind of landscape, wilderness. Geographers speak of three kinds of landscapes which reflect the long-term human occupancy of our planet: city, countryside and wilderness. These three exist on a continuum which marks both the density of human occupation and the extent of human-caused disturbance of the landscape. But a more precise definition proves to be elusive, because wilderness is essentially a cultural construction. It is something which does not exist in pre-agricultural societies, where there is no sense of distinction between cultivated and uncultivated land.

Roderick Nash, in *Wilderness and the American Mind*, tells a story which best describes this:

> "I had the opportunity to talk, through an interpreter, with a man who hunted and gathered in the jungles of Malaysia. I tried with-

out success to discuss wilderness. When I asked for an equivalent word I heard things like 'green places,' 'outdoors,' or 'nature.' Finally, in desperation, I asked the interpreter to ask the hunter how he said 'I am lost in the jungle.' An exchange occurred at the conclusion of which the interpreter turned to me and said with a smile that the man had indicated he did not get lost in the jungle. The question made as little sense to him as would asking an American city dweller how he said 'I am lost in my apartment.' Lacking a concept of controlled and uncontrolled nature, the Malaysian had no conception of wilderness."[5]

In other words, wilderness is a term which originates only in a culture where hunting and gathering have been replaced by an agricultural society, where a people needs a word to express "not-cultivated" land. In a like manner, the term "countryside" evolves from the need to describe a place where humans dwell in a landscape distinct from the city or town.

How do we in late 20th Century North America define wilderness? The Wilderness Act of 1964 is helpful for a legal definition, but since wilderness is a cultural construct, a social definition might be more helpful. The best way to address this question is by dividing it in two. William Kirk, an Irish geographer, maintains that there are two types of environment: the *phenomenal environment*, the one of empirical facts, and the *behavioral environment*, the environment as subjectively perceived.[6] In looking at a wilderness environment phenomenally, one can quantify the level of disturbance, such as trail or road density, vegetative disturbance through logging, grazing or introduced exotic plants, or pollution from upstream and upwind sources. These are among the most important factors in degrading habitat for wildlife. They often mark the first step in the process of bringing wilderness lands under cultivation or human settlement. Arresting these processes is critical to preservation of the wilderness necessary for the ongoing survival of so many species.

But in my experience, wilderness has great value as a behavioral environment as well. After I finished my career in tree planting, I worked in a highly stressful job as a social worker, and I longed for the beauty of the forests. Through a series of unlikely events, I had landed in inner-city Cincinnati, Ohio, and there I was bombarded by the harshness of the landscape on the street and the ugly consequences of people living on top of each other. Instead of the silence and space of a natural forest, my senses were jarred by the concrete jungle: the rude noises of cars filled the air, belching bus fumes stifled the narrow canyons between high buildings, summer's heat was re-radiated all night by big blocks of brick buildings, and throngs of people seemingly swallowed up any sense of self. I discovered that in moving into the city I really missed the "feel" of the woods.

I sought solace in the Kentucky woods. I found an area that had been preserved from logging and began to visit it frequently that I might recover a sense of self and solicitude that I felt robbed of me by my inner-city lifestyle. Even as I appreciated and explored this area well, I began to realize how small, crowded and over-used it was. Every small clearing suitable for setting up my tent seemed to have human trash in it. Unless I was visiting during inclement weather, I always ran into other people. This frustrated me as I sought a solitary place in which to pray to my God. I began to set a goal of trying to camp for two days without seeing anyone. I was fatigued from working with people during the week; couldn't I have a few precious hours of solitude? Even though I tried to hide from other campers, I could not escape from them. The population explosion hit me in a personal way. Soon afterward I moved back to attend school in my native California, but discovered that even though there was less trash in the campgrounds there, the wilderness areas were still crowded. I began to realize how rare the privilege to escape the crowds for true wilderness solitude.[7]

I went to the wilderness to renew my spirit. How can I describe my experience of the divine in nature? What did I feel, hear, touch, smell, that provoked me to love and contemplate Creator-God? Although I am reluctant to use the term "mysticism," I am afraid that few other words come close to describing the feelings of transcendence and spiritual unity I experience in wilderness. I feel like I have crept back into a place where all is in harmonious right relationship, like I have escaped from the insanity of industrial civilization to grasp for a short while an elusive peace and tranquility. Flower-covered meadows and cathedral groves suggested to me the experience of our mythic ancestors, Adam and Eve, in the Garden. Out of many deep experiences of prayer and spiritual refreshment, I decided to confirm my commitment to working for a healthy relationship with God and Creation by becoming a Franciscan Friar. And I began to investigate whether I was the only one who had these kinds of experiences in the wild.

WILDERNESS IN THE ASCETIC TRADITION

Of course, I quickly realized that I was not the only one to seek out solitary, wild places for prayer and spiritual nourishment. I discovered how rich yet complex is my Christian tradition of viewing nature.

I confess freely and do not deny that part of the reason I want to present these perspectives is to correct a prevailing erroneous assumption: Christianity (with its roots in Judaism) has always been fundamentally an anti-nature religion. I do not wish to quote and disprove those who have raised this accusation in its various forms; I will leave that task for others.[8] I prefer simply to broaden the perspective of the reader by presenting some lesser known Christian thinking about wilderness. But I wish to underscore in the strongest possible terms that Christianity in its essence is not anti-nature. Contemporary critics rightfully identify certain movements in Christianity that are indifferent or hostile to nature, but these are rooted more in the values of their contemporary culture. Christianity may be guilty of complicity with broader anti-nature currents in society, but this is different from being inherently anti-nature.

Most critics of Christian attitudes toward nature fail to discuss the complexity and diversity of attitudes in the Bible and Christian history. This complexity is well described by Roger Sorrell who calls it "creative ambiguity."[9] George H. Williams, in a little-known book *Wilderness and Paradise in Christian Thought*, provides us with a very helpful sketch of the various interpretations of the wilderness and the garden from the Christian perspective. Williams, in presenting his study, does not deny the contradictions present in the Scriptures.

> "We shall find that in the positive sense the wilderness or desert will be interpreted variously as a place of protection, a place of contemplative retreat, again as one's inner nature or ground of being, and at length as the ground itself of the divine being. We shall find that in its negative sense the wilderness will be interpreted as the world of the unredeemed, as the wasteland, and as the realm or phase of punitive or purgative preparation for salvation....It is in fact a survey of the persistence of the ambiguity of the Hebraic experience of the wilderness and the equally distinctive prophetic understanding of the precariousness of the garden. ....The whole of biblical history has, in fact, been interpreted in terms of the wilderness motif; of the struggle between the religion

of the desert and the religion of the city; or again, of the fall from the garden (paradise) devastated by sin, the wandering in the wilderness and the vision of a second Eden."[10]

The Revised Standard Version of the Bible uses the term "wilderness" 281 times. A lot of spiritual drama took place on this stage. Williams identifies three themes of spiritual encounter in wilderness: wasteland as the realm of demons and death, the desert as the Place of the Covenant, and the wilderness as the place of refuge, purgation, and consecration. The first has received far too much attention, in my opinion, and I recommend Williams' treatment of the second. I wish to elaborate here a bit more on the third.

To support my thesis that the experience of wilderness landscape, of negotiating a wild perceptual geography, was essential to the development of Christianity, I offer the reader several examples from two eras of Christian Spirituality that are famous for their flowering: Desert Monasticism of the Christian Patristic Era and the surge of spirituality of the High Middle Ages.

The call of the desert to Christians during the first few centuries of Christianity gave birth to the first ascetic movement in Christianity. *The Life of St. Antony* of Egypt (d. 356) was the first hagiography (biography of a saint) which was the most influential piece of early literature treating early Desert Monasticism. Although not the first Christian Monk, his hagiography was the first to use this term. Antony spent much of his life escaping from the city and people, fleeing to nature so that he could find precious solitude. He eventually found a refuge of prayer on a mountain in the inner Egyptian desert. *The Life* describes not only Antony's home but also how he felt about it: "Antony, as though inspired by God, fell in love with the place."[11] His satisfaction with living in the desert wilderness is also demonstrated by his response to a philosopher who asked him how he could endure his solitude without books: "My book, philosopher, is the nature of created things, and as often as I have a mind to read the words of God, it is at my hand."[12] He also is reported to have compared a monk outside the desert with a fish out of water.[13] The desert landscape and wilderness solitude it provided are of great value to Antony. He was not able to fulfill his vocation as an ascetic in the city; he was called to the desert wilds and found answers there he could not find among the social world.

St. Jerome (d. 420) described Antony's "Inner Mountain" with obvious appreciation for the solitude offered by the cells there and the beauty of the location.

"There was a high rock mountain about a mile in length. Water sprang forth from the crevices and flowed down to its base, where some of it was absorbed by the sand and the rest, falling deeper, gradually formed a river shaded by numerous palm trees overhanging from both shores, making the location very pleasant and comfortable...Here Antony had sought refuge from the multitudes who came to him and from the companionship of his disciples."[14]

Jerome obviously appreciates the landscape and the beauty it provides. The desert fathers and mothers went to the desert for a variety of reasons: to flee the corruption of cities, to wage war with demons, and to escape taxation. More important than these, however, is that they wanted to encounter the holy, and this they did in the solitude of the desert. Jerome wrote: "to me the town is a prison, and solitude is paradise."[15] For these ascetics, the experience of the desert landscape was essential for their encounter with the divine.

St. Basil was a contemporary of Jerome and he wrote a remarkable praise of wilderness retreat and the tranquility its landscape brought. I quote at length because it is the first extensive Christian written praise of a natural landscape:

"It is a lofty mountain overshadowed with a deep wood, irrigated on the north by cold and transparent streams. At its foot is spread a low plain, enriched perpetually with the streams from the mountains. The wood, a virgin forest of trees of various kinds and foliage which grows around it, almost serves as a rampart;...My hut is built on another point, which uplifts lofty pinnacles on the summit, so that the plain is outspread before the gaze, and from the height I can catch a glimpse of the river flowing around...flowing with a swifter course than any river I know, for a short space billows along the adjacent rock, and then, plunging over it, rolls into a deep whirlpool, affording a most delightful view to me and to every spectator, and abundantly supplying the needs of the inhabitants, for it nurtures an incredible number of fishes in its eddies. Why need I tell you the sweet exhalations from the earth or the breezes of the river? Other persons might admire the multitude of the flowers, or the lyric birds, but I have no time to attend to them. But my highest eulogy of the spot is, that, prolific as it is of all kinds of fruits from its happy situation, it bears for me the sweetest of all fruits, tranquility."[16]

Basil has found a wilderness that delights him. Even though he claims he has no time to attend to river's breezes, the birds and the flowers, only praise for tranquil solitude, Basil, like Antony, has fallen in love with a place. This description captures the essential qualities of the wilderness hermit's relationship with his landscape: the place is valued for its beauty, it is a refuge from contact with other human beings, and the peace and solitude offered clears the stage for encountering the divine. Elsewhere Basil describes the benefits of a wilderness setting: "the contemplation of nature abates the fever of the soul, and banishes all insincerity and presumption."[17]

The Cistercians of the twelfth century marked a new chapter in attitudes toward nature. They were a reform movement within the Benedictine monasticism which sought to return to the simplicity of following Christ. They established abbeys in remote locations far from other human settlements, seeking a return to a sort of Eden-like paradise, undisturbed by contact with the rest of the world. Although they sought raw wilderness in order to transform it to "productive" land, they took delight in the wild landscape they encountered. An English monk described the coming of the French Cistercians to a beautiful wilderness site in England and setting up simple, rude huts where they would later build the abbey of Rievaulx:

"The spot was by a powerful stream called the Rie in a broad valley stretching on either side. The name of their little settlement and of the place where it lies was derived from the name of the stream and the valley, Rievaulx. High hills surround the valley, encircling it like a crown. These are clothed by trees of various sorts and maintain in pleasant retreats the privacy of the vale, providing for the monks a kind of second paradise of wooded delight. From the loftiest rocks the waters wind and tumble down to the valley below, and as they make their hasty way through the lesser passages and narrower beds and spread themselves in wider rills, they give out a gentle murmur of soft sound and join together in the sweet notes of a delicious melody. And when the branches of lovely trees rustle and sing together and the leaves flutter gently to the earth, the happy listener is filled increasingly with a glad jubilee of harmonious sound, as so many things conspire together in sweet consent in music whose every diverse note is equal to the rest. 'His ears drink in the feast prepared for them, and are satisfied.' Such was the story—the true story—which Aeldred was told by his friend. At this point he exclaimed, 'And where, oh where, is the way to those angelic men, to these heavenly places?'"[18]

This description of the founding of the Abbey of Rievaulx describes a landscape in a similar fashion as did Basil his wilderness hermitage. The monks came as a group, but they nevertheless sought to practice the discipline of solitude and prayer in this remote location. The Cistercians certainly did not preserve the landscape in the same condition they found it, but neither did they see it as a barren or evil wasteland. Aeldred saw the site and its inhabitants as a sample of heaven. There was a profoundly affective component in their relating to these wild lands.

The most celebrated ascetic experience in Christianity during the Middle Ages occurred when Francis of Assisi was stigmatized on Mt. Alverno. Francis had started his brotherhood some fifteen years previously, but it grew so quickly that he was unable to steer it or keep it faithful to his own vision. He responded to this by intensifying his own life of prayer in the wilderness. During the last few years of his life, he spent the majority of his time in wilderness hermitages. He and a companion or two would venture for weeks at a time to remote places for prayer, taking little more than a blanket and few pieces of bread and constructing little brush arbors for shelter. In September of 1224, Francis and three companions were in the middle of a forty day retreat on the remote hilltop of Mt. Alverno. Francis had a vision of an angel bearing the marks of the Crucified One, and his identification with Christ was so strong that on his own body the nails and wounds of his Savior appeared.

Was it accidental or incidental that Francis was in the wilderness when this happened? I believe not. Francis was enthralled with the beauty and diversity of nature because he saw God's creativity and fecundity in it. He preached to nature, sang of it and loved it. Not surprisingly, hunger for a deeper relationship with God led him to the wild. The experience of solitude and beauty in a wilderness landscape set the stage for Francis to be conformed profoundly into the likeness of his savior.[19]

In all four of these examples, these ascetics sought to retreat from "the world." Their understanding of "the world" was not our modern idea of planet, but rather the human culture in which they were raised.

They sought to encounter God in a place *outside* of human culture. Most people feared to leave their familiar landscape, their perceptual world. To encounter the divine, these saints had to leave behind the geography of safety of their social world. But the descriptions presented here demonstrate that it was not just a choice *against* human interactions, but a choice *for* interaction with God and nature through landscape.

RECOVERING A TRADITION

Roderick Nash is probably the best known environmental historian who has researched perceptions of wilderness in North America, most notably through his *Wilderness and the American Mind*. He did groundbreaking research on the origin of the concept and how it was applied in North America. I do fault him, however, for failing to identify and describe the range of responses to wild nature. In the opening chapters, he describes in broad strokes the responses of several cultures over several centuries to wilderness. This kind of over-simplification is an oversight on his part. A fuller description of the kinds of responses is required of us today.

John Rennie Short does a fine job of describing two archetypal responses to wilderness: the classical and romantic. The classical finds value in all places that have been made habitable by human beings. Human use is that which confers meaning on a place. Outside of human settlements, wilderness is an area of waste, chaos and desolation. It is, in the classical viewpoint, something to be feared. The romantic response take the opposite tack: rather than seeing human settlement as progress, they believe the present is a shadow of the spiritually richer and deeper life of the past. For the romantics, untouched spaces have the greatest significance because they have not been contaminated by human contact. "Wilderness for the romantics is a place to be revered, a place of deep spiritual significance and a symbol of an earthly paradise." He proposes that in the Western world the classical position was dominant until the last two centuries when the romantic conception began to gain more ground. Short's model is helpful, but it is incomplete.[20]

Since the industrial and technological revolution, the classical view has been largely supplanted by what I term the *materialist* view of nature. With machines as our intermediaries, we do not fear nature so much as see it as a commodity, as something to be harnessed for our economic profit. Nature is not something to be feared or respected, but rather extracted. Seen through the lens of a materialist culture, wilderness is a natural storehouse of economic goods awaiting our access. Nature is objectified, quantified, and slipped into economic equations without regard for the right of its constituent parts to continued existence. In the materialist view of nature, wilderness has no value because economic activity is prohibited there, and this is a profoundly rationalistic, profane view of nature. The most important things in life are not economic. Commercial activity does not give our spirits life.

Nash and other critics are correct in their criticism of the way Christianity has tended to view nature negatively. They are wrong, however, in their assumption that Christianity has always had a singular, fully coherent response. Given the creative ambiguity of Biblical attitudes toward nature, one can only expect the religion rooted in these scriptures to hold somewhat ambivalent attitudes. Christianity is, in part, guilty. Not of providing the basis of exploiting nature, but of complicity, of "going along with" the changes in European cultures. As the four examples above demonstrate, however, there is a tradition, albeit a clearly minority tradition, that sees nature, wild places, and wilderness as a sacred.

Above all I wish to promote among Christians, and to the extent it is helpful, other persons of faith, a return to the roots of our spiritual tradition. I do not believe any religious tradition in its origin was inherently anti-nature. People have, however, mixed fear in with religious beliefs, and this can be a very dangerous thing. By returning to our roots, Christians can recover the authentic power of the religious experience in natural landscape. I believe this kind of experience can provide the impetus to fight for the changes in lifestyle essential to the preservation of wild places.

In their thinking about the wilderness they enjoyed, Christian ascetics understood their flight to the wilds as a return of sorts to the garden of Eden. Eden represented a paradisiacal wilderness garden, where human beings existed in a state of harmony and unmitigated grace. For them, the wilderness was a glimpse of heaven. It has been likewise for me, and I pray that our children have the opportunity to experience this as well.

NOTES

1. As a Franciscan, I am deeply committed to promoting what is today called a "biocentric" view of nature. I am convinced that, short of describing it as a theocentric or Christocentric view, this view best represents Francis' perspective. By arguing, in this essay, for wilderness on anthropocentric grounds, I in no way wish to distract from the need to adopt a biocentric view. See my essay "Was St. Francis a Deep Ecologist?" in Albert La Chance and John Carroll *Embracing Earth: Catholic Approaches to Ecology* (Maryknoll NY: Orbis, 1994).

2. Geography is so interdisciplinary that universities do not agree on whether it belongs among the sciences or the social sciences. At Columbia, geography is even found in the Business School!

3. D.W. Meinig, editor, *The Interpretation of Ordinary Landscapes* (New York: Oxford University Press, 1979), 1-2. J. B. Jackson, one of the deans of the study of American landscape, admits that after 25 years of study, he still finds the concept of landscape as fairly elusive. This may go a long way toward explaining why the study of landscape is short on respect.

4. *Ibid.*, 6.

5. Roderick Nash, *Wilderness and the American Mind*, (New Haven: Yale University Press, 1982) xiv.

6. In John Rennie Short, *Imagined Country: Society, Culture and Environment* (New York: Routledge, 1991) 1-2.

7. Consider, if you will, where one might find wild "pristine" landscape. Certainly not in the Boston-Washington DC Megalopolis, home to a quarter of our nation's residents. All but a few scattered, small patches of the Appalachian Mountains have been logged and disturbed. Travelling west, the Ohio and Mississippi River valleys have been converted to farmland and the riverine systems have been re-plumbed. With the establishment of huge farms, the slaughter of the bison and the suppression of fire on the Great American Plains, the natural biological systems have been completely disrupted. Most, if not all, of the forests in the American West have been extensively grazed, and with that grazing many native grasses have been extirpated. Most grasses in central and southern California are European exotic species which have competitive advantage in disturbed (grazed) landscapes. All but the last 5% of native forests have been cut, and those not cut are frequently modified by human fire suppression efforts. In the Sierra Nevada of my native state, Yosemite National Park's landscape was grazed before and after its establishment as a park. I have gone hiking in numerous legally designated wilderness areas only to encounter man-made dams, grazing induced erosion, and landscape disturbed by mining activities. A landscape undisturbed by human activity may not exist in California, or for that matter, in the contiguous 48 states. See Dave Foreman and Howie Wolke

The Big Outside (Tucson AZ: Big Outside Books, 1991).

8. For criticisms of Christianity, see the classic Lynn White Jr., "The Historic Roots of Our Ecologic Crisis," in *Science*, March 10 1967, 1203-12. While helpful to Christians for being provocative, White's essay is really more the expression of opinions than historical scholarship. For a discussion of this, see: Hargove, Eugene C., "Religion and Environmental Ethics: Beyond the Lynn White Debate," in Eugene C. Hargrove, ed., *Religion and Environmental Crisis* (Athens: University of Georgia Press, 1986), and Callicott, J. Baird, "Genesis and John Muir," in Carol S. Robb and Carl J. Casebolt, eds., *Covenant for a New Creation* (Maryknoll NY: Orbis, 1991).

9. Roger Sorrell, *St. Francis of Assisi and Nature* (New York: Oxford University Press, 1988).

10. George H. Williams, *Wilderness and Paradise in Christian Thought* (New York: Harper and Brothers, 1962) 5-7, 10.

11. Athanasius *Life of St. Antony*, Robert T. Meyer tr. (New York: Newman Press, 1950), Paragraph 49-50.

12. Pelagius the Deacon and John the Subdeacon, "The Sayings of the Fathers," in Helen Waddell, *The Desert Fathers* (Ann Arbor: University of Michigan Press, 1957), p. 129.

13. Derwas J. Chitty, *The Desert a City* (Oxford: Basil Blackwell and Mott, Ltd, 1966), p. 6.

14. St. Jerome, "The Life of St. Hilarion," tr. Marie Liguori Ewald, in *The Fathers of the Church: Early Christian Biographies*, ed. Roy J. Defarrai (Washington D.C.:The Catholic University of America Press, 1951), p. 271.

15. H. B. Workman *The Evolution of the Monastic Ideal* (London, 1913) p. 31.

16. Quoted in A. Biese, *The Development of the Feeling for Nature in the Middle Ages and Modern Times* (NY: Blackwell, 1905) 32-3.

17. D. B. Wallace-Hadrill, *The Greek Patristic View of Nature* (Manchester, 1968) p. 33.

18. Daniel Walter *The Life of Aeldred of Rievaulx* (Kalamazoo MI: Cistercian Publications, 1994), 98 (Chapter 6 of MS).

19. The best discussion of Francis' relationship with nature can be found in Roger Sorrell, *St. Francis of Assisi and Nature* (New York: Oxford University Press, 1988), and chapter 6 of H. Paul Santmire *The Travail of Nature* (Minneapolis: Fortress Press), 1992.

20. Short, *op cit.*, 5-24.

Epilogue

Keith Warner, OFM

The quality and diversity of the contributions to this volume testify that the dialogue between religion and ecology has been going on for some time and continues to take shape. Despite the historic suspicion of scientists by religious leaders and the reluctance of some scientists to acknowledge the role of religion in shaping authentic human values, these contributors have made peace between their religious and scientific vocations. I believe we have progressed to a new level of maturity in the relationship between the ecological science and our spiritual traditions, a maturity marked by humility and mutual respect. We have had to acknowledge that more scientific knowledge without moral values will not necessarily improve the health and integrity of our bioshpere. And we are all too aware of the silence among most religious leaders about the ongoing destruction of our environment.

Where do we go from here? How can we promote an integrated response to our ecological crises? What actions can we take to encourage the religious and scientific community to work together? The discussion between religious traditions and ecology that we have witnessed in this volume has the core characteristics of any dialogue: both sides must both speak and listen.

Ecologists know that scientific knowledge, by itself, cannot save. The contributors to this volume realize that the ecologists have a pressing social responsibility beyond their field and lab work: they must communicate the message of the impact our species is having on our planet's biosphere and they must help raise the social value of the natural world. As the work of Edward O. Wilson, Al Fritsch, Cal DeWitt, and Stephanie Kaza (to name just a few) has shown, speaking to the religious community in America and using spiritual and moral terms can have an impact. More scientists should be encouraged to make their religious faith public; this will only increase the credibility of ecologists among religious communities. For example, Cal DeWitt and Paula Gonzalez have a tremendous influence because they speak from their religious and ecological traditions. Religious leaders and members of churches, synagogues, temples, and congregations are listening, and they are beginning to respond.

Sadly, many religious leaders have yet to acknowledge that the scientists in their congregations are playing the role of prophets. Ecological scientists are bringing news to religious communities and society at large that is not popular. Painful as their message may be, we must welcome them, hear their message and respond. To deepen the dialogue, we must move to help our culture heed those with scientific data, to help more people pay attention. Armed with solid information about the ecological impact of current environmental behavior, religious groups can increase the way that society values nature. Religious groups are now facing the challenge of addressing the need to shape public policy, corporate behavior, and the individual choices we make which shape our relationship to the environment. How can they do so? Priests, pastors, rabbis, and religious leaders have a moral pulpit from which they speak. They can critique the societal values which have fostered the ecologically destructive behavior of North American culture. As they listen to the need to respond with compassion to environmental problems, they can challenge us to find more equitable and compassionate solutions, and, as McCann pointed out, such solutions require some imagination, but they are possible. To pass on the gift of Creation to future generations, we will have to learn to live in a sustainable manner, and, as Gonzalez points out, this will require us to learn from the earth, a task at which ecologists are most skilled.

Environmental ethics have only emerged as a sub-discipline in this generation, but unless they can take root in the behavior of individuals and social groups, they will be a dead letter. With so many religions emerging from a relationship with nature, religious movements can strengthen their original roots and contemporary relevance by stressing environmental ethics. The practice of ethics is built on a foundation of virtues. Churches and religious groups must, formed by the information of those with ecological expertise, update the practice of the classic virtues for our age. Humility, simplicity, love, and compassion, for example, are needed now more than ever as we face the environmental consequences of our actions. Those of us who are religious leaders, whether at the local, regional or national level, have the responsibility to preach these virtues, addressing individuals, households and economic institutions.

To fulfill their role in our society, our religious institutions must commit themselves to helping everyone value nature more. Ecological sustainability and environmental balance need to be taught from pulpit and in religious education settings. Increased scientific data by itself will not change our treatment of ecosystems. Religious leaders must help our society learn to re-value nature, to care for it and treasure it again. Buddhism, Bahai, Christianity and Judaism all have traditions of caring for nature, and we need leaders to show us how to do this. Incorporating sacred elements into our rituals, praying for those creatures—human and nonhuman—suffering from environmental abuse, encouraging simplicity and mindfulness: these are just a few examples of how we can re-sacralize nature, make it sacred again. The Jewish tradition has many celebrations related to human dependence on the land, and Roman Catholicism has many feast days which allow its members to re-connect with nature. Religious education can incorporate concern for the earth in many aspects. Preaching about our responsibility for nature's well-being and our dependence upon it can play a role.

The religious community can make a vital contribution to addressing our environmental problems by continuing to call scientists to focus their efforts on addressing human and ecological problems. Science profits from ethical dialogue. All scientific investigation is in service of someone or some thing. Who makes the decisions about where funding for scientific investigation leads? How can religious leaders challenge political and educational leaders to direct funding for sciences toward our pressing environmental problems? How can science and industry assist our society to move away from short-sighted consumption toward sustainability? Religion's concern with questions of ultimate value should offer guidance toward our social choices. Moral voices from our religious communities can help bring science into dialogue with social and environmental needs.

Religion and Ecology both address the nature of interdependent relationships, and ultimately points of convergence between them is long past, and my prayer is that the work and testimony of the contributors in this volume have helped you, the readers, recognize the relationship between religion and ecology in your professional, vocational and personal lives. Our world is now too small and our environmental problems are too great for these two dimensions of our lives to work in opposition to or in isolation from each other. May the dialogue of the book enhance this relationship.

Contributors Biographies

Susan P. Bratton holds the Lindaman Chair of Science, Technology and Society at Whitworth College and is the author of two books on Christianity and environmental ethics, *Six Billion and More: Human Population Regulation and Christian Ethics* and *Christianity, Wilderness and Wildlife: The Original Desert Solitaire.* She has worked for the U.S. National Park Service as director of a field laboratory in Great Smoky Mountains National Park and as coordinator of a research cooperative at the Institute of Ecology of the University of Georgia.

John E. Carroll is Professor of Environmental Conservation at the University of New Hampshire. He has authored and edited a number of books on international environmental diplomacy and policy, including *Environmental Diplomacy* (University of Michigan Press) and *International Environmental Diplomacy* (Cambridge University Press), and books on ecology and religion, including *Embracing Earth* (Orbis) and *The Greening of Faith* (University Press of New England).

Calvin B. DeWitt is Professor of Environmental Studies at the University of Wisconsin-Madison, Madison, Wisconsin and Director of Au Sable Institute near Mancelona, Michigan. He is a member of the University of Wisconsin graduate faculties of Land Resources, Conservation Biology and Sustainable Development, Water Resources Management, and Oceanography and Limnology and is a Fellow of the University of Wisconsin Teaching Academy.

Mary Louise Dolan, CSJ, is a sister of St. Joseph, a cell biologist, and Director of the MA in Earth Literacy Program at Saint Mary-of-the-Woods College in Terra Haute, Indiana. Previously, she taught biology for over twenty years at the College of St. Rose in Albany, NY, and has been a staff member of Spiritearth, a Center for Ecological Spirituality located first in Boston, MA and then Saugerties, NY.

James Edmiston, OFM, is a Franciscan friar, educator, and entomologist. He is Assistant Professor of Biology at Quincy University in Quincy, Illinois. He has been teaching value-based environmental science courses at the secondary and undergraduate levels in Ohio and Illinois for fourteen years. As a research entomologist, he investigates the biology and systematics of shore flies.

Albert J. Fritsch, S.J., is the Director of Appalachia—Science in the Public Interest, in Mt. Vernon, Kentucky. He is an author and a chemist by training and has worked for three decades with environmental organizations in both Washington, DC and in his native Kentucky. He directs regional appropriate technology projects as well as a more extensive environmental Resource Assessment Service.

Paula Gonzalez, futurist, educator and environmentalist, is a Sister of Charity in Cincinnati, Ohio. Since 1970 she has offered numerous seminars and retreats on various aspects of planetary awareness. She is also an energy-conservation consultant with expertise in passive solar design and superinsulation and is a founder of EarthConnection, a center for learning and reflection about living lightly on the Earth located on the Sisters of Charity grounds in Cincinnati.

William Gregg holds degrees in biology, botany and ecology and has worked for the Department of the Interior since 1971, as an ecologist for the National Park Service, the National Biological Service, and the U.S. Geological Survey. He is currently the International Activities Officer for the U.S.G.S.'s Biological Research Devision. He became a Baha'i in 1979.

Wes Jackson, author and editor of numerous publications, is President of The Land Institute near Salina, Kansas. After completing his education in biology, botany and genetics, Dr. Jackson taught biology at Kansas Wesleyan University and established the Environmental Studies program at California State University in Sacramento, where he became a full professor. He resigned that position to found The Land Institute in 1976.

Carl F. Jordan is a Senior Ecologist and Adjunct Professor of Botany at the University of Georgia. Dr. Jordan began his professional career working for the Atomic Energy Commission studying the effects of radiation and reactor effluents on the environment. He has done extensive research in the Amazon rain forest in both Venezuela and Brazil and is the author of numerous articles and six books, the most recent of which is the textbook entitled *Conservation* (Wiley).

Stephanie Kaza is Associate Professor of Environmental Studies at the University of Vermont where she teaches religion and ecology, nature philosophy, radical environmentalism and ecofeminism. Dr. Kaza is a long-time student of Zen Buddhism, practicing at Green Gulch Zen Center, California. She is the author of *The Attentive Heart: Conversations with Trees* and is currently writing *Green Buddha Walking*, an environmental interpretation of Buddhist philosophy and practice.

Robert J. Kent is Marine Program Coordinator for New York Sea Grant, a university-based marine science research porgram and part of the National Sea Grant College Program. He has an MA in environmental studies and is a member of St. Anselm's Episcopal Parish on Long Island, New York.

Joyce McCann is currently completing an MA degree in environmental ethics at the Graduate Theological Union, studying at the San Francisco Theological Seminary; her essay in the present collection is an outgrowth of her work at GTU. After receiving her PhD in Biology from the University of Colorado, Dr. McCann helped develop the "Ames Test" microbial mutagenesis assay for environmental carcinogens at U. C. Berkeley. Dr. McCann is also interested in the biological effects of electromagnetic fields and in Buddhism.

Elliot A. Norse, President of Marine Conservation Biology Institute in Redmond, WA, is a marine and forest conservation biologist. He received his PhD. in marine ecology from the University of Southern California (1975) and subsequently worked for the U.S. Environmental Protection Agency, the President's Council on Environmental Quality, the Ecological Society of America, The Wilderness Society and the Center for Marine Conservation before founding Marine Conservation Biology Institute in 1996.

Robert Patterson is a Professor in the Crop Science Department at North Carolina State University, where he has been engaged in teaching and research in Agronomy since 1968. His research has taken him to Africa, Asia, South and Central America, and Europe; he is the author of numerous scientific papers in the fields of soil science and agronomy.

Keith Warner, O.F.M., is a Franciscan Friar, geographer, writer and educator living in San Francisco, California. After completing an MA in Spirituality at the Franciscan School of Theology in Berkeley, California, he began working at St. Anthony Foundation, a large Franciscan social service center in San Francisco, where he teaches about homelessness, poverty and environmental concerns from the perspective of Franciscan values.

Gene Wilhelm received a BS from St. Louis University, an MA from Louisiana State University, and a PhD from Texas A. & M. He has taught biogeography, ecology, ornithology, environmental problems, human ecology and conservation biology at St. Louis University, McGill University, the University of Virginia and Slippery Rock University in Pennsylvania, where he was Professor of Environmental Studies from 1972–1982. He has done research in east and west Africa and South America and was Vice President of Education at the National Audubon Society in New York from 1982–1985. He lives in Slippery Rock, Pennsylvania and conducts awareness sensitivity to nature workshops around the world.

Edward O. Wilson is Frank B. Baird, Jr. Professor of Science and Curator of Entomology at Harvard. He received the National Medal of Science in 1977 and has twice received the Pulitzer Prize in nonfiction, for *On Human Nature* (1979) and *The Ants* (with Bert Holldobler, 1990).